Statistics for People Who (Think They) Hate Statistics Using R

In honor and memory of Neil J. Salkind and thanks to Leni Salkind

Sara Miller McCune founded SAGE Publishing in 1965 to support the dissemination of usable knowledge and educate a global community. SAGE publishes more than 1000 journals and over 600 new books each year, spanning a wide range of subject areas. Our growing selection of library products includes archives, data, case studies and video. SAGE remains majority owned by our founder and after her lifetime will become owned by a charitable trust that secures the company's continued independence.

Los Angeles | London | New Delhi | Singapore | Washington DC | Melbourne

Statistics for People Who (Think They) Hate Statistics Using R

Neil J. Salkind

Leslie A. Shaw

Cornell University

Los Angeles | London | New Delhi
Singapore | Washington DC | Melbourne

FOR INFORMATION:

SAGE Publications, Inc.
2455 Teller Road
Thousand Oaks, California 91320
E-mail: order@sagepub.com

SAGE Publications Ltd.
1 Oliver's Yard
55 City Road
London EC1Y 1SP
United Kingdom

SAGE Publications India Pvt. Ltd.
B 1/I 1 Mohan Cooperative Industrial Area
Mathura Road, New Delhi 110 044
India

SAGE Publications Asia-Pacific Pte. Ltd.
18 Cross Street #10-10/11/12
China Square Central
Singapore 048423

Printed in the United States of America

ISBN: 978-1-5443-2457-9

This book is printed on acid-free paper.

SFI label applies to text stock

19 20 21 22 23 10 9 8 7 6 5 4 3 2 1

Acquisitions Editor: Helen Salmon
Content Development Editor: Chelsea Neve
Editorial Assistant: Megan O'Heffernan
Production Editor: Jane Martinez
Copy Editor: Gillian Dickens
Typesetter: C&M Digitals (P) Ltd.
Proofreader: Liann Lech
Indexer: Jeanne R. Busemeyer
Cover Designer: Karine Hovsepian
Marketing Manager: Shari Countryman

BRIEF CONTENTS

DETAILED CONTENTS

PREFACE

Any book is always a work in progress, and this new addition to the family of *Statistics for People Who (Think They) Hate Statistics* is no exception. Over the past 17 years or so, many people have told us how helpful this series is, and others have told us how they would like it to change and why. In working on this R edition, we were trying to keep the informal tone, easy-to-follow examples, and useful figures and tables for learning statistics while introducing R as a useful, free tool to support that endeavor. So, the things you loved about other books in the series you will continue to love about this book. We also realize that moving to R can be intimidating, so most of the heavy lifting to learning R occurs in the early chapters when the statistical ideas are simpler. After hypothesis testing is introduced, R plays more of a support role.

This book was written for the introductory statistics course offered to undergraduates, but it can also be used at the graduate level for students enrolled in their first statistics course. After a great deal of trial and error, some successful and many unsuccessful attempts, and a ton of feedback from students and teachers at all levels of education, we have attempted to teach statistics in a way that we (and many students) think is unintimidating and informative. We have tried our absolute best to incorporate all of that experience into this book.

For students, what you will learn from this book is the information you need to understand what the field and study of basic statistics is all about. You'll learn about the fundamental ideas and the most commonly used techniques to organize and make sense out of data. There's very little theory (but some), and there are few mathematical proofs or discussions of the rationale for certain mathematical routines. Why isn't this theory stuff and more in *Statistics for People Who (Think They) Hate Statistics Using R*? Simple. Right now, you don't need it. It's not that we don't think it's important. Rather, at this point and time in your studies, we want to offer you material at a level we think you can understand and learn with some reasonable amount of effort, while at the same time not be scared off from taking additional courses in the future. We (and your professor) want you to succeed.

So, if you are looking for a detailed unraveling of the derivation of the analysis of variance F ratio, go find another good book from Sage (we'll be glad to refer you to one). But if you want to learn why and how statistics can work for you, you're in the right place. This book will help you understand the material you read in journal articles, explain what the results of many statistical analyses mean, and teach you how to perform basic statistical tasks.

There are always new things worth consideration and different ways to present old themes and ideas. Here's a list of what you'll find that's different in this R edition of *Statistics for People Who (Think They) Hate Statistics Using R.*

- Two chapters early in the book devoted to first installing R (necessary) and RStudio* (helpful) and then introducing some basics that will be useful in mastering the R portion of the activities
- A decision tree chart showing when it is appropriate to select regression in Chapter 18
- Corrected effect size formulas to accompany *t* test results in Chapters 13 and 14
- Update to some examples in the book to include more recent examples from a wider variety of disciplines
- Chapter 20, which describes statistical methods beyond this course, has been updated to include some more commonly used methods; R examples were added for most methods
- Additional tips, cool websites, and useful R information in Appendices A and G.

In addition to the videos helping you to master R, the website contains all of the example syntax and data sets, organized by chapter. All of these media resources are available on the open-access SAGE edge site: **edge.sagepub.com/salkindshaw**.

Any typos and such that appear in this edition of the book are entirely our fault, and we apologize to the professors and students who are inconvenienced by their appearance. We have all made every effort in this edition to correct previous errors and hope we did a reasonably good job. Let us hear from you with suggestions, criticisms, nice notes, and so on. Good luck.

Leslie A. Shaw

Cornell University

salkindshaw@gmail.com

*RStudio and Shiny are trademarks of RStudio, Inc.

ACKNOWLEDGMENTS

Neil Salkind deserves the biggest thanks for making this book possible. In early 2017, Neil decided he wanted to write an R edition in the series of *Statistics for People Who (Think They) Hate Statistics*. So what did that mean? That meant Neil needed to learn R; you can never really take a professor completely out of the classroom, either as a student or as a teacher. He reached out to a friend who reached out to me (Leslie Shaw) as someone who could teach him the basics of R and work on some of the R material for the book. In early summer, Neil started working on the book and made headway with the early chapters. Unfortunately, less than 6 months later, Neil's health took a turn for the worse and he passed away in November.

With the support of Sage and Leni Salkind, I stepped in to take over the writing of this book, leaning heavily on all of the work that Neil had put into the series. In turn, I also leaned on Karrie Shogren from the University of Kansas, the friend who introduced me to Neil and who had worked on other books with Helen Salmon at Sage. Karrie connected me with Helen and shared what she had learned from her own authorship experiences. Helen Salmon, Senior Acquisitions Editor—Research Methods and Statistics, was supportive throughout the process, providing the vision for this coauthorship and book. Editorial Assistant Megan O'Heffernan walked me, a newbie, through the many details required to bring the book to life. One last thanks specific to this series goes to Bruce Frey, the person who picked up the other books in the series. Bruce generously shared his thoughts on the writing process and provided background on the series. He also responded to my random e-mails about examples, data sets, and screenshot software, just to name a few topics.

Lastly, many thanks to my community both near and far who supported me during this journey.

We would like to thank the following reviewers for their feedback on the manuscript:

Patrick Bolger, Texas A&M University

Candace Forbes Bright, East Tennessee State University

Perry Carter, Texas Tech University

Scott Comparato, Southern Illinois University

James Cortright, University of Wisconsin, River Falls

Jacqueline Craven, Delta State University

George Harrison, University of Hawaii at Manoa

Michael J. Kalsher, Rensselaer Polytechnic Institute

Matthew Phillips, University of North Carolina, Charlotte

Jeff Savage, Cornerstone University

Shlomo Sawilowsky, Wayne State University

Daniel Scheller, University of Texas at El Paso

Maggie Stone, Marshall University

Mary Beth Zeni, Ursuline College

ABOUT THE AUTHORS

Neil J. Salkind received his PhD in human development from the University of Maryland, and after teaching for 35 years at the University of Kansas, he was Professor Emeritus in the Department of Psychology and Research in Education, where he collaborated with colleagues and worked with students. His early interests were in the area of children's cognitive development, and after research in the areas of cognitive style and (what was then known as) hyperactivity, he was a postdoctoral fellow at the University of North Carolina's Bush Center for Child and Family Policy. His work then changed direction to focus on child and family policy, specifically the impact of alternative forms of public support on various child and family outcomes. He delivered more than 150 professional papers and presentations, wrote more than 100 trade and textbooks, and is the author of *Statistics for People Who (Think They) Hate Statistics, Theories of Human Development,* and *Exploring Research.* He edited several encyclopedias, including the *Encyclopedia of Human Development,* the *Encyclopedia of Measurement and Statistics,* and the *Encyclopedia of Research Design.* He was editor of *Child Development Abstracts and Bibliography* for 13 years. He lived in Lawrence, Kansas, where he liked to read, swim with the River City Sharks, work as the proprietor and sole employee of big boy press, bake brownies (see Appendix I for the recipe), and poke around old Volvos and old houses.

Leslie A. Shaw received her PhD in psychology from the University of Kansas, specifically in quantitative psychology. Before returning to school for this graduate degree, Leslie worked first in systems integration, took a break to get a master's degree in counseling from North Carolina Central University, and then returned to work in the nonprofit arena, all in Durham, North Carolina. The nonprofit work at the Center for Child and Family Health focused on child abuse prevention and early intervention. Her academic interests were in mathematics and psychology, leading to the natural choice of quantitative psychology for further graduate work. During graduate school, she worked on a variety of projects from university class enrollment, alumni donations, community policing, and self-determination. She also taught statistical computing labs and introductory statistics in a team-teaching format. The self-determination research led to more opportunities at the Beach Center on Disabilities and Kansas University Center on Developmental Disabilities to contribute to research on the Supports Intensity Scale, both adult and child versions, and the Self-Determination Inventory: Self Report. After graduation, she held a postdoctoral position at the Kansas University Center on Developmental Disabilities, where she also taught a class each semester in the quantitative psychology program. This opportunity led to a research associate position at the Yang-Tan Institute on Employment and Disability in the ILR School at Cornell University. She has coauthored more than 20 articles to date, and she serves as a statistical consultant for the journal *Intellectual and Developmental Disabilities.* She now lives in Ithaca, New York, where she likes to read, cook dishes for Ecovillage community potlucks, take hikes to view waterfalls in the area, hang out with friends, and travel.

DIGITAL RESOURCES

SAGE edge™

Visit **edge.sagepub.com/salkindshaw** for additional resources

SAGE edge for instructors supports your teaching by making it easy to integrate quality content and create a rich learning environment for students with:

- **R syntax and data files** available for download and use with exercises in the book
- **Screencast tutorial videos** that demonstrate setting up the data and running selected problems from the book in R
- Chapter-specific **test banks in Word®** for a diverse range of multiple choice, T/F, and short answer questions, all tied to learning objectives
- Editable, chapter-specific **PowerPoint®** slides that offer complete flexibility for creating a multimedia presentation for your course

SAGE edge for students enhances learning, it's easy to use, and offers:

- **R syntax and data files** available for download and use with exercises in the book
- **Screencast tutorial videos** that demonstrate setting up the data and running selected problems in R
- **eFlashcards** that strengthen understanding of key terms and concepts
- **eQuizzes** that allow students to practice and assess how much they've learned and where they need to focus their attention

PART I

YIPPEE! I'M IN STATISTICS

"Well, if it isn't a significant subset of our study group!"

Not much to shout about, you might say? Let me take a minute and show you how some very accomplished scientists use this widely used set of tools we call *statistics.*

- Fake news has been a hot topic since the 2016 U.S. election. One venue for fake news was Twitter. Some researchers at Northeastern University, Harvard University, and University at Buffalo SUNY examined fake news exposures and sharing from August to December 2016. They found that only 1% of Twitter users were exposed to 80% of the fake news, and only 0.1%, that is one tenth of 1%, were responsible for sharing fake news. The people most likely to engage with fake news were more conservative, older, and very focused on political news. So, have the media made a mountain out of a molehill?

  Want to know more? Why not read the original work? You can find more about this in Grinberg, N., Joseph, K., Friedland, L., Swire-Thompson, B., & Lazer, L. (2019). Fake news on Twitter during the 2016 U.S. presidential election. *Science, 363,* 374–378.

- Sue Kemper is the Roberts Distinguished Professor of Psychology at the University of Kansas and has worked on the most interesting of projects. She and several other researchers studied a group of nuns and examined how their early experiences, activities, personality characteristics, and other information related to their health during their late adult years. Most notably, this diverse group of scientists (including psychologists, linguists, neurologists, and others) wanted to know how well all this information predicts the occurrence of Alzheimer's disease. Kemper and her colleagues found that the complexity of the nuns' writing during their early 20s was related to the nuns' risk for Alzheimer's 50, 60, and 70 years later.

  Want to know more? Why not read the original work? You can find more about this in Snowdon, D. A., Kemper, S. J., Mortimer, J. A., Greiner, L. H., Wekstein, D. R., & Markesbery, W. R. (1996). Linguistic ability in early life and cognitive function and Alzheimer's disease in late life: Findings from the nun study. *Journal of the American Medical Association, 275,* 528–532.

- Aletha Huston (a very distinguished professor emerita) from the University of Texas at Austin devoted a good deal of her professional work to understanding what effects television watching has on young children's psychological development. Among other things, she and her late husband, John C. Wright, investigated the impact that the amount of educational television programs watched during the early preschool years might have on outcomes in the later school years. They found convincing evidence that children who watch educational programs such as *Mr. Rogers* and *Sesame Street* do better in school than those who do not.

  Want to know more? Why not read the original work? You can find more about this in Collins, P. A., Wright, J. C., Anderson, R., Huston, A. C., Schmitt, K., & McElroy, E. (1997, April). *Effects of early childhood media use on adolescent achievement.* Paper presented at the biennial meeting of the Society for Research in Child Development, Washington, DC.

All of these researchers had a specific question they found interesting and used their intuition, curiosity, and excellent training to answer it. As part of their investigations, they used this set of tools we call *statistics* to make sense out of all the information they collected. Without these tools, all this information would have been just a collection of unrelated outcomes. The outcomes would be nothing that Grinburg and colleagues could have used to reach a conclusion about fake news, or Kemper could have used to better understand aging and cognition (and perhaps Alzheimer's disease), or Huston and Wright could have used to better understand the impact of watching television on young children's achievement and social development.

Statistics—the science of organizing and analyzing information to make it more easily understood—made these tasks doable. The reason that any of the results from such studies are useful is that we can use statistics to make sense out of them. And that's exactly the goal of this book—to provide you with an understanding of these basic tools and how researchers use them and, of course, how to use them yourself.

In this first part of *Statistics for People Who (Think They) Hate Statistics Using R,* you will be introduced to what the study of statistics is about and why it's well worth your efforts to master the basics—the important terminology and ideas that are central to the field. This part gives you a solid preparation for the rest of the book.

STATISTICS OR SADISTICS? IT'S UP TO YOU

Difficulty Scale ☺ ☺ ☺ ☺ ☺
(really easy)

WHAT YOU WILL LEARN IN THIS CHAPTER

- ✦ What statistics is all about
- ✦ Why you should take statistics
- ✦ How to succeed in this course

WHY STATISTICS?

You've heard it all before, right?

> "Statistics is difficult."
>
> "The math involved is impossible."
>
> "I don't know how to use a computer."
>
> "What do I need this stuff for?"
>
> "What do I do next?"
>
> And the famous cry of the introductory statistics student: "I don't get it!"

Well, relax. Students who study introductory statistics find themselves, at one time or another, thinking at least one of the above and quite possibly sharing the thought with another student, their spouse, a colleague, or a friend.

And all kidding aside, some statistics courses can easily be described as *sadistics*. That's because the books are repetitiously boring and the authors have no imagination.

That's not the case for you. The fact that you or your instructor has selected *Statistics for People Who (Think They) Hate Statistics Using R* shows that you're ready to take the right approach—one that is unintimidating, informative, and applied (and even a little fun) and that tries to teach you what you need to know about using statistics as the valuable tool that it is.

If you're using this book in a class, it also means that your instructor is clearly on your side. He or she knows that statistics can be intimidating but has taken steps to see that it is not intimidating for you. As a matter of fact, we'll bet there's a good chance (as hard as it may be to believe) that you'll be enjoying this class in just a few short weeks.

And Why R?

Throughout this book, you'll be shown how to use R, a statistical analysis tool, for the analysis of data. No worries; you'll also be shown how to do the same analysis by hand to assure you of an understanding of both.

Why R? Simple. **R** is both free and very powerful. No more renting software for the semester or trying to connect to your school's site for shared software. Just open your computer, launch RStudio (or your editor of choice—more about that in the next chapter), and start working. Throughout this book, we will use R for simple calculations and all statistical examples. We will explore the power of graphics to show us our data. And, we will close early chapters with a few other ways to do the same statistical analysis. In the second half of the book, when the statistics get a little more complicated, we will shift to using built-in functions, assuming that you have learned the basics of R. By the time you finish this book and your class, our hope is that you will feel comfortable with R and, through the use of R, start to understand the power of statistics.

A 5-MINUTE HISTORY OF STATISTICS

Before you read any further, it would be useful to have some historical perspective about this topic called statistics. After all, almost every undergraduate in the social, behavioral, and biological sciences and every graduate student in education, nursing, psychology, social welfare and social services, anthropology, and . . . (you get the picture) is required to take this course. Wouldn't it be nice to have some idea from whence the topic it covers came? Of course it would.

Way, way back, as soon as humans realized that counting was a good idea (as in "How many of these do you need to trade for one of those?"), collecting information became a useful skill.

If counting counted, then one would know how many times the sun would rise in one season, how much food was needed to last the winter, and what amount of resources belonged to whom.

That was just the beginning. Once numbers became part of language, it seemed like the next step was to attach these numbers to outcomes. That started in earnest during the 17th century, when the first set of data pertaining to populations was collected.

From that point on, scientists (mostly mathematicians, but then physical and biological scientists) needed to develop specific tools to answer specific questions. For example, Francis Galton (a half-cousin of Charles Darwin, by the way), who lived from 1822 to 1911, was very interested in the nature of human intelligence. He also speculated that hair loss was due to the intense energy that went into thinking. No, really. But back to statistics.

To explore one of his primary questions regarding the similarity of intelligence among family members, he used a specific statistical tool called the correlation coefficient (first developed by mathematicians), and then he popularized its use in the behavioral and social sciences. You'll learn all about this tool in Chapter 7. In fact, most of the basic statistical procedures that you will learn about were first developed and used in the fields of agriculture, astronomy, and even politics. Their application to human behavior came much later.

The past 100 years have seen great strides in the invention of new ways to use old ideas. The simplest test for examining the differences between the averages of two groups was first advanced during the early 20th century by William Sealy Gosset, who we will talk about in Chapter 14. Techniques that build on this idea were offered decades later and have been greatly refined. And the introduction of personal computers and such programs as Excel has opened up the use of sophisticated techniques to anyone who wants to explore these fascinating topics.

The introduction of these powerful personal computers has been both good and bad. It's good because most statistical analyses no longer require hours of hand calculations or access to a huge and expensive mainframe computer. Instead, a simple personal computer costing less than $250 or a cloud account can do 95% of what 95% of the people need. On the other hand, less than adequately educated students (such as your fellow students who passed on taking this course!) will take any old data they have and think that by running them through some sophisticated analysis, they will have reliable, trustworthy, and meaningful outcomes—not true. What your professor would say is "Garbage in, garbage out"; if you don't start with reliable and trustworthy data, what you'll have after your data are analyzed is unreliable and untrustworthy results.

Today, statisticians in all different areas, from criminal justice to geophysics to psychology to determining whether the "hot" hand really exists in the NBA (no kidding—see the 2014 *Wall Street Journal* article at http://www.wsj.com/articles/SB10001424052702304071004579409071015745370), find themselves using basically the same techniques to answer different questions. There are, of course, important differences in how data are collected, but for the most part, the analyses (the plural of *analysis*) that are done following the collection of data (the plural of *datum*) tend to be very similar, even if called something different. The moral here? This class will provide you with the tools to understand how statistics are used in almost any discipline. Pretty neat, and all for just three or four credits.

If you want to learn more about the history of statistics and see a historical time line, a great place to start is the University of Southampton in the United Kingdom (http://www.economics.soton.ac.uk/staff/aldrich/Figures.htm).

Okay. Five minutes are up, and you know as much as you need to know about the history of statistics. Let's move on to what it is (and isn't).

STATISTICS: WHAT IT IS (AND ISN'T)

Statistics for People Who (Think They) Hate Statistics Using R is a book about basic statistics and how to apply them to a variety of different situations, including the analysis and understanding of information.

In the most general sense, **statistics** describes a set of tools and techniques that are used for describing, organizing, and interpreting information or data. Those data might be the scores on a test taken by students participating in a special math curriculum, the speed with which problems are solved, the number of side effects when patients use one type of drug rather than another, the number of errors in each inning of a World Series game, or the average price of a dinner in an upscale restaurant in Santa Fe, New Mexico (not cheap).

In all of these examples, and the million more we could think of, data are collected, organized, summarized, and then interpreted. In this book, you'll learn about collecting, organizing, and summarizing data as part of descriptive statistics. And then you'll learn about interpreting data when you learn about the usefulness of inferential statistics.

What Are Descriptive Statistics?

Descriptive statistics are used to organize and describe the characteristics of a collection of data. The collection is sometimes called a **data set** or just **data**.

For example, the following list shows you the names of 22 college students, their major areas of study, and their ages. If you needed to describe what the most popular college major is, you could use a descriptive statistic that summarizes their most frequent choice (called the mode). In this case, the most common major is psychology. And if you wanted to know the average age, you could easily compute another descriptive statistic that identifies this number (that one's called the mean). Both of these simple descriptive statistics are used to describe data. They do a fine job allowing us to represent the characteristics of a large collection of data such as the 22 cases in our example.

Name	Major	Age	Name	Major	Age
Richard	Education	19	Elizabeth	English	21
Sara	Psychology	18	Bill	Psychology	22
Andrea	Education	19	Aaliyah	Psychology	23
Steven	Psychology	21	Maya	Education	21
Jayden	Education	20	Carlos	Education	19
Pam	Education	24	Dipak	Psychology	18
Manuel	Psychology	21	Makayla	English	22
Liz	Psychology	19	Courtney	Psychology	24
Nicole	Chemistry	19	Jose	Psychology	21
Mike	Nursing	20	Dominic	Chemistry	18
Isabella	History	18	Emily	Spanish	19

So watch how simple this is. To find the most frequently selected major, just find the one that occurs most often. And to find the average age, just add up all the age values and divide by 22. You're right—the most often occurring major is psychology (nine times), and the average age is 20.3 (actually 20.27). Look, Ma! No hands—you're a statistician.

What Are Inferential Statistics?

Inferential statistics are often (but not always) the next step after you have collected and summarized data. Inferential statistics are used to make inferences based on a smaller group of data (such as our group of 22 students) about a possibly larger one (such as all the undergraduate students in the College of Arts and Sciences).

A smaller group of data is often called a **sample**, which is a portion, or a subset, of a **population**. For example, all the fifth graders in Newark (one author's fair city of origin), New Jersey, would be a population (the population is all the occurrences with certain characteristics, in this case, being in fifth grade and attending school in Newark), whereas a selection of 150 of these students would be a sample.

Let's look at another example. Your marketing agency asks you (a newly hired researcher) to determine which of several names is most appealing for a new brand of potato chip. Will it be Chipsters? FunChips? Crunchies? As a statistics pro (we know we're moving a bit ahead of ourselves, but keep the faith), you need to find a small group of potato chip eaters who are representative of all potato chip fans and ask these people to tell you which one of the three names they like the most. Then, if you do things right, you can easily extrapolate the findings to the huge group of potato chip eaters.

Or let's say you're interested in the best treatment for a particular type of disease. Perhaps you'll try a new drug as one alternative, a placebo (a substance that is known not to have any effect) as another alternative, and nothing as the third alternative to see what happens. Well, you find out that more patients get better when no action is taken and nature (and we assume that's the only factor or set of factors that differentiates the groups) just takes its course! The drug does not have any effect. Then, with that information, you can extrapolate to the larger group of patients who suffer from the disease, given the results of your experiment.

In Other Words . . .

Statistics is a tool that helps us understand the world around us. It does so by organizing information we've collected and then letting us make certain statements about how characteristics of those data are applicable to new settings. Descriptive and inferential statistics work hand in hand, and which statistic you use and when depends on the question you want answered.

And today, a knowledge of statistics is more important than ever because it provides us with the tools to make decisions that are based on empirical (observed) evidence and not our own biases or beliefs. Want to know whether early intervention programs work? Then test whether they work and provide that evidence to the court that will make a ruling on the viability of a new school bond issue that could pay for those programs.

WHAT AM I DOING IN A STATISTICS CLASS?

You might find yourself using this book for many reasons. You might be enrolled in an introductory statistics class. Or you might be reviewing for your comprehensive exams. Or you might even be reading this on summer vacation (horrors!) in preparation for a more advanced class.

In any case, you are a statistics student, whether you have to take a final exam at the end of a formal course or you're just in it of your own accord. But there are plenty of good reasons to be studying this material—some fun, some serious, and some both.

Here's the list of some of the things that our students hear at the beginning of our introductory statistics course:

1. Statistics 101 or Statistics 1 or whatever it's called at your school looks great listed on your transcript. All kidding aside, this may be a required course for you to complete your major. But even if it is not, having these skills is definitely a big plus when it comes time to apply for a job or for further schooling. And with more advanced courses, your résumé will be even more impressive.
2. If this is not a required course, taking basic statistics sets you apart from those who do not. It shows that you are willing to undertake a course that is above average with regard to difficulty and commitment. And, as the political and economic (and sports!) worlds become more "accountable," more emphasis is being placed on analytic skills. Who knows, this course may be your ticket to a job!
3. Basic statistics is an intellectual challenge of a kind that you might not be used to. There's a good deal of thinking that's required, a bit of math, and some integration of ideas and application. The bottom line is that all this activity adds up to what can be an invigorating intellectual experience because you learn about a whole new area or discipline.
4. There's no question that having some background in statistics makes you a better student in the social or behavioral sciences, because you will have a better understanding not only of what you read in journals but also of what your professors and colleagues may be discussing and doing in and out of class. You will be amazed the first time you say to yourself, "Wow, I actually understand what they're talking about." And it will happen over and over again, because you will have the basic tools necessary to understand exactly how scientists reach the conclusions they do.
5. If you plan to pursue a graduate degree in education, anthropology, psychology, nursing, sociology, or any one of many other social, behavioral, and biological pursuits, this course will give you the foundation you need to move further.
6. There are many different ways of thinking about, and approaching, different types of problems. The set of tools you learn about in this book (and this

course) will help you look at interesting problems from a new perspective. And, while the possibilities may not be apparent now, this new way of thinking can be brought to new situations.

7. Finally, you can brag that you completed a course that everyone thinks is the equivalent of building and running a nuclear reactor.

TEN WAYS TO USE THIS BOOK (AND LEARN STATISTICS AT THE SAME TIME!)

Yep. Just what the world needs—another statistics book. But this one is different. It is directed at the student, is not condescending, is informative, and is as basic as possible in its presentation. It makes no presumptions about what you should know before you start and proceeds in slow, small steps, which lets you pace yourself.

However, there has always been a general aura surrounding the study of statistics that it's a difficult subject to master. And we don't say otherwise, because parts of it are challenging. On the other hand, millions and millions of students have mastered this topic, and you can, too. Here are 10 hints to close this introductory chapter before we move on to our first topic.

1. You're not dumb. That's true. If you were, you would not have gotten this far in school. So, treat statistics as you would any other new course. Attend the lectures, study the material, duplicate the examples, do the exercises in the book and from class, and you'll do fine. Rocket scientists know statistics, but you don't have to be a rocket scientist to succeed in statistics.

2. How do you know statistics is hard? Is statistics difficult? Yes and no. If you listen to friends who have taken the course and didn't work hard and didn't do well, they'll surely volunteer to tell you how hard it was and how much of a disaster it made of their entire semester, if not their lives. And let's not forget—we always tend to hear from complainers. So, we'd suggest that you start this course with the attitude that you'll wait and see how it is and judge the experience for yourself. Better yet, talk to several people who have had the class and get a good idea of what they think. Don't base your expectations on just one spoilsport's experience.

3. Don't skip lessons—work through the chapters in sequence. *Statistics for People Who (Think They) Hate Statistics Using R* is written so that each chapter provides a foundation for the next one in the book. When you are all done with the course, you will (I hope) continue to use this book as a reference. So if you need a particular value from a table, you might consult Appendix B. Or if you need to remember how to compute the standard deviation, you might turn to Chapter 5. But for now, read each chapter in the sequence that it appears. It's okay to skip around and see what's offered down the road. Just don't study later chapters before you master earlier ones.

4. Form a study group. This is a big hint and one of the most basic ways to ensure some success in this course. Early in the semester, arrange to study with friends or classmates. If you don't have any friends who are in the same class as you, then make some new ones or offer to study with someone who looks as happy to be there as you are. Studying with others allows you to help them if you know the material better or to benefit from those who know some material better than you. Set a specific time each week to get together for an hour and go over the exercises at the end of the chapter or ask questions of one another. Take as much time as you need. Studying with others is an invaluable way to help you understand and master the material in this course.

5. **Ask your teacher questions, and then ask a friend.** If you do not understand what you are being taught in class, ask your professor to clarify it. Have no doubt—if you don't understand the material, then you can be sure that others do not as well. More often than not, instructors welcome questions. And especially because you've read the material before class, your questions should be well informed and help everyone in class to better understand the material.

6. **Do the exercises at the end of a chapter.** The exercises are based on the material and the examples in the chapter they follow. They are there to help you apply the concepts that were taught in the chapter and build your confidence at the same time. If you can answer these end-of-chapter exercises, then you are well on your way to mastering the content of the chapter. Correct answers to each exercise are provided in Appendix D.

7. **Practice, practice, practice.** Yes, it's a very old joke:

Q. How do you get to Carnegie Hall?

A. Practice, practice, practice.

Well, it's no different with basic statistics. And R. You have to use what you learn and use it frequently to master the different ideas and techniques. This means following and repeating the examples, doing the exercises at the end of most chapters, and taking advantage of any other opportunities you have to understand what you have learned.

8. **Look for applications to make it more real.** In your other classes, you probably have occasion to read journal articles, talk about the results of research, and generally discuss the importance of the scientific method in your own area of study. These are all opportunities to see how your study of statistics can help you better understand the topics under class discussion as well as the area of beginning statistics. The more you apply these new ideas, the fuller your understanding will be.

9. **Browse.** Read over the assigned chapter first; then go back and read it with more intention. Take a nice leisurely tour of *Statistics for People Who (Think They) Hate Statistics Using R* to see what's contained in the various chapters. Don't rush yourself. It's always good to know what topics lie ahead as well as to familiarize yourself with the content that will be covered in your current statistics class.

10. **Have fun.** This might seem like a strange thing to say, but it all boils down to you mastering this topic rather than letting the course and its demands master you. Set up a study schedule and follow it, ask questions in class, and consider this intellectual exercise to be one of growth. Mastering new material is always exciting and satisfying—it's part of the human spirit. You can experience the same satisfaction here—just keep your eye on the ball and make the necessary commitment to stay current with the assignments and work hard.

About Those Icons

Throughout this book, you'll find a small-steps icon like the one you see here. This indicates that a set of steps is coming up that will direct you through a particular process. Sometimes you will use R to do these steps. These steps have been tested and approved by whatever federal agency approves these things.

The R icon lets you know that the information focuses on R or RStudio. These tips will be used to highlight a new detail or explain something that we skipped explaining earlier in the book.

WHAT ELSE DOES THIS BOOK CONTAIN?

R is introduced in Chapter 2, where you will learn some basics and install R and RStudio. Chapter 3 invites you to start making friends with R. Working through these chapters is all you really need to do to be ready to use R with the exception of minor differences covered in Appendix A, where we talk about R on the Mac.

Appendix B contains important tables you will learn about and need throughout the book.

And, in working through the exercises in this book, you will use the data sets in Appendix C. In the exercises, you'll find references to data sets with names like "Chapter 2 Data Set 1," and each of these sets is shown in Appendix C. You can either enter the data manually or download them from the publisher's site at **edge.sagepub.com/salkindshaw**.

Appendix D contains answers to end-of-chapter questions.

Appendix E contains a primer on math for those who could use a refresher.

Appendix F provides a list of useful Internet sites for statistics and R.

Appendix G introduces the 10 commandments of data collection.

Appendix H is the glossary for the book.

And Appendix I offers the long-sought-after brownie recipe (yes, you finally found it).

Key to Difficulty Icons

To help you along a bit, we placed a difficulty index at the beginning of each chapter. This adds some fun to the start of each chapter, but it's also a useful tip to let you know what's coming and how difficult chapters are in relation to one another.

- ☺ (very hard)
- ☺ ☺ (hard)
- ☺ ☺ ☺ (not too hard, but not easy either)
- ☺ ☺ ☺ ☺ (easy)
- ☺ ☺ ☺ ☺ ☺ (very easy)

Glossary

Bolded terms in the text are included in the glossary at the back of the book in Appendix H.

Real-World Stats

Real-World Stats will appear at the end of every chapter as appropriate and, hopefully, will provide you with a demonstration of how a particular method, test, idea, or some aspect of statistics is used in the everyday workplace of scientists, physicians, policy makers, government folks, and others. In this first such exploration, we look at a very short paper where the author recalls and shares the argument that the National Academy of Sciences (first chartered in 1863, by the way!) "shall, whenever called upon by any department of the Government, investigate, examine, experiment, and report upon any subject of science or art." This charter, some 50 years later in 1916, led to the formation of the National Research Council, another federal body that helped provide information that policy makers need to make informed decisions. And often this "information" takes the form of quantitative data—also referred to as statistics—that assist people in evaluating alternative approaches to problems that have a wide-ranging impact on the public. So, this article, as does your book and the class you are taking, points out how important it is to think clearly and use data to support your arguments.

Want to know more? Go online or go to the library and find . . .

Cicerone, R. (2010). The importance of federal statistics for advancing science and identifying policy options. *The Annals of the American Academy of Political and Social Science, 631*, 25–27.

Summary

That couldn't have been that bad, right? We want to encourage you to continue reading and not worry about what's difficult or time-consuming or too complex for you to understand and apply. Just take one chapter at a time, as you did this one.

Time to Practice

Because there's no substitute for the real thing, most chapters will end with a set of exercises that will help you review the material that was covered in the chapter. As noted above, the answers to these exercises can be found near the end of the book in Appendix D.

For example, here is the first set of exercises (but don't look for any answers for these because these are kind of "on your own" answers—each question and answer are highly tied to your own experiences and interest).

1. Interview someone who uses statistics in his or her everyday work. It might be your adviser, an instructor, a researcher who lives on your block, a health care analyst, a marketer for a

company, a city planner, or. . . . Ask the person what his or her first statistics course was like. Find out what the person liked and didn't like. See if this individual has any suggestions to help you succeed. And most important, ask the person about how he or she uses these new-to-you tools at work.

2. We hope that you are part of a study group or, if that is not possible, that you have a telephone, e-mail, instant messaging, or webcam study buddy (or even more than one). And, of course, plenty of texting and Facebook friends. Talk to your group or a fellow student in your class about similar likes, dislikes, fears, and so on about the statistics course. What do you have in common? Not in common? Discuss with your fellow student strategies to overcome your fears.

3. Search through your local newspaper (or any other publication) and find the results of a survey or interview about any topic. Summarize the results and do the best job you can describing how the researchers who were involved, or the authors of the survey, came to the conclusions they did. Their methods and reasoning may or may not be apparent. Once you have some idea of what they did, try to speculate as to what other ways the same information might be collected, organized, and summarized.

4. Go to the library (either in person or online) and find a copy of a journal article in your own discipline. Then, go through the article and highlight the section (usually the "Results" section) where statistical procedures were used to organize and analyze the data. You don't know much about the specifics of this yet, but how many different statistical procedures (such as *t* test, mean, and calculation of the standard deviation) can you identify? Can you take the next step and tell your instructor how the results relate to the research question or the primary topic of the research study?

5. Find five websites that contain data on any topic and write a brief description of what type of information is offered and how it is organized. For example, if you go to the mother of all data sites, the U.S. Census (http://www.census.gov), you'll find links to hundreds of databases, tables, and other informative tools. Try to find data and information that fit in your own discipline.

6. And the big extra-credit assignment is to find someone who actually uses R for daily data analysis needs. Ask if there is anything specific about R that makes it stand out as a tool for their type of data analysis. You may very well find these good folks in everything from political science to nursing, so search widely!

7. Finally, as your last in this first set of exercises, come up with five of the most interesting questions you can about your own area of study or interest. Do your best to come up with questions for which you would want real, existing information or data to answer. Be a scientist!

Student Study Site

Get the tools you need to sharpen your study skills! Visit **edge.sagepub.com/salkindshaw** to access practice quizzes and eFlashcards, watch R tutorial videos, and download data sets!

PART II

WELCOME TO THE INTERESTING, USEFUL, FLEXIBLE, FUN, AND (VERY) DEEP WORLDS OF R AND RSTUDIO

You surely know that things are always changing, and it is no different with the study of basic statistics, which is the focus of the book you are holding in your hands: *Statistics for People Who (Think They) Hate Statistics Using R*.

What's changing?

In previous years, and for thousands and thousands of students, statistics was taught using software programs that were very expensive and constantly needing upgrades (which you are charged for), and often, these upgrades were not easily available.

After the creation of R, these restrictions no longer held sway. Not only is R free and readily available, but it is also very flexible with easy-to-learn basics.

Our goal in Part II of *Statistics for People Who (Think They) Hate Statistics Using R* is to introduce you to two major tools to help you in your learning the basics of statistical analysis and the ideas behind those analyses.

First, in Chapter 2, we will introduce you to the R programming language or programming environment and step you through the install of R on your own computer. You'll learn some vocabulary specific to R and how to ask for help. We will finish the chapter talking about working in R through editors and walking you through the installation of RStudio.

Then, in Chapter 3, we'll show you how **RStudio** can be used as a convenient *graphic user interface,* or as a fancy calculator. We will also show you how R can work for you in taking your first steps to mastering basic statistics by using built-in functions that will tell you what you need to know about your statistic.

Why use R and not Excel or SPSS? Read on and we think you'll become convinced that this relatively new tool will prove to be your favorite of them all.

HERE'S WHY WE LOVE R AND HOW TO GET STARTED

Difficulty Scale ☺ ☺
(takes a bit of practice, but after a while a new way to look at things!)

WHAT YOU WILL LEARN IN THIS CHAPTER

- ✦ Understanding what R is and a short history of where R came from
- ✦ Understanding the pluses and minuses of using R
- ✦ Defining *open source*
- ✦ Downloading and installing R
- ✦ Learning a new language, R
- ✦ Using R Help
- ✦ Learning some important lingo
- ✦ Downloading and installing RStudio
- ✦ Understanding RStudio

A VERY SHORT HISTORY OF R

Way back in the olden days (1996), Ross Ihaka and Robert Gentleman published a paper titled "R: A Language for Data Analysis and Graphics" in the *Journal of Computational and Graphical Statistics.* That paper was the formal beginning of this adventure they called a "statistical computing language." They actually started work around 1992. And, yes, it's called R because of the first letter in each of the first names of the original authors.

Many statistical and programming packages existed before then (such as SPSS, Stata, Minitab, and S that R is based on), and many were very popular and (still are) successful. It's difficult to judge what the motivation was for Ihaka and Gentleman to make this significant contribution, but at least part of it was to deliver a set of very powerful and flexible tools to the community at large and one that would be free for the using and open to change.

Currently, R (often referred to as **R base**) is maintained and kept very alive through the R Development Core Team and the R Foundation.

THE PLUSES OF USING R

There are several reasons why R has become so popular over the past few years.

First, it is absolutely, no questions asked *free,* meaning you never need to spend a penny for new software every time there's a new version or rent it from some company.

It is *open source,* meaning that the underlying code in which the R environment is constructed is available to anyone (and that means anyone) who wants to tinker with it, improve it, try out new ideas, and so forth. No more proprietary warnings or licenses for you to agree to, no more subscriptions or monthly payments. More about this in a note to you later in this chapter.

Instant Startup!

Want to jump right in and find out who has contributed to the creation and maintenance of R? If you've already installed R (perhaps you did before this class started or it's on the school's server you are working from), type

```
> contributors()
```

exactly as you see it here at the prompt in the R Console window, which is a "greater than" symbol that looks like this:

```
>
```

and press the Enter or Return key and take a look. If you have yet to install R, be patient—that's to come and you can then try the `contributors()` function.

Enter or Return or Nothing!

And remember this, R will just sit there and look at you unless you press the Enter or the Return key. R has no idea what you want it to do unless you press one of those keys that tells R to go ahead and get busy.

UPPERCASE Is Uppercase and lowercase is lowercase

There are all kinds of differences between computer programs based on different programming languages. R, which is based on a programming language called S, follows very strict rules about using uppercase (such as TRUE) and lowercase (such as true). For example, `contributors()` will get you a list of contributors, but `Contributors()` will get you an error message. We promise.

THE MINUSES OF USING R

But even with all those advantages above (and there are plenty more), R can be complicated and a bit intimidating. Some people just don't want to mess with anything that resembles a programming experience and that's okay. The help text can also seem cryptic at times until you become comfortable reading it (hint: check out the examples to see how the function works with real-life data). And while there are other minuses of R, most of those minuses are beyond the scope of this book.

R has developed some interfaces that make some R tasks close to a point-and-click experience like so many of the other programs that you use every day. In Chapter 3, we'll show you how to use RStudio, an interface that makes R easier to understand and to use.

OTHER REASONS TO USE R?

- R *can be installed on almost any computer* with any operating system, including Windows, Mac, Linux, and others as well.
- R *produces great graphics!* The quality is superior to those in commercial software such as SPSS, SAS, and Stata.
- R has *very few system requirements,* meaning that it will work on almost any computer that has enough memory to operate a word processor or a spreadsheet.
- Finally, R is *incredibly flexible,* which is a large part of the reason why R has become so popular. If you want to, you can dive deep into the very basis of the programming part of R and tweak your commands and results as you see fit. For nerds (especially) and non-nerds, this is a very big plus. But if you're a beginner, then no worries—R can take you as far as you want to go, and you will still see impressive results.

A SHORT NOTE TO YOU (AND TO YOUR INSTRUCTOR) ABOUT OPEN SOURCE (AGAIN!)

R is a particularly interesting tool for a whole variety of reasons, but there are a few more things that are important to know.

First, it is an open source programming environment, which means that it is open to ideas for how it might be changed for future users, and it is open to change by anyone who wants to do such. That's the really good thing about any open source product. And, most open source products are free.

Second, the nature of open source endeavors means that the programs change on a regular basis, so it is important for you to always check to see if the version of R that you have installed on your computer (which you will learn about in this chapter) is the most current.

Third, because it is open source, this means that R nerds and non-nerds alike are always making contributions that make the product better, easier to use, more convenient, and more powerful. So, at times, what you see on your computer screen may not match exactly what you see in the illustrations in the pages that follow—things change. But, relax. Nothing will be so different that you will not be able to follow and learn.

Fourth, the flexibility and open source nature of R also means that there are many different ways to do the same thing. And there will be more ways to do the same thing in the future. Our goal in this book is to show you what we think is one of several simple ways to reach a specific outcome. You may find other ways to accomplish a task and that would be great. We're here to show you how to use R, in one of many different ways, as an analytic tool.

And finally, R has many different uses and functions. Because it is undergoing an unending revision where there is always something new, you can take what you read here and do fine throughout the rest of the pages of *Statistics for People Who (Think They) Hate Statistics Using R*. Or, you can delve further and further, as far as you want to go, and explore the many facets of R on your own—and we encourage you to do so.

If you master the material in this chapter (getting R installed, picking an editor, and learning some new lingo) and the next, you will have a sufficient set of tools to master the chapters on specific statistical analysis techniques that follow.

WHERE TO FIND AND DOWNLOAD R

The first step in using R is, of course, to download it to your computer. Here you go:

1. Go to https://cran.r-project.org/, and as you can see in Figure 2.1, there is a link to install R on one of the many platforms that is supported.

FIGURE 2.1 ● The opening screen for installing R.

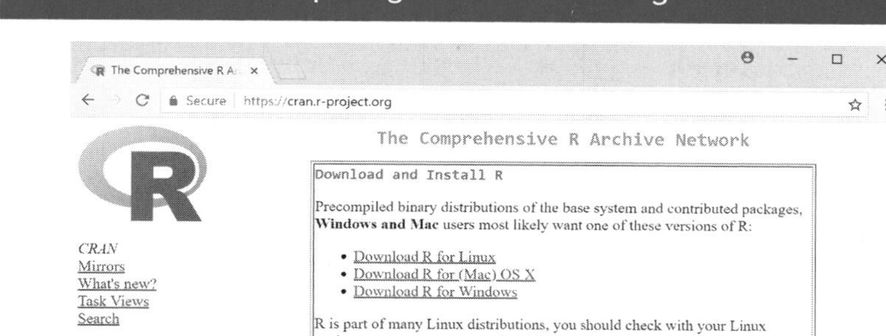

Visit **edge.sagepub.com/salkindshaw** to watch an R tutorial video on this topic.

We'll be installing the Windows version, but as you can see, the Linux and Macintosh versions are readily available. Click on the version you want to install. As you can see in Figure 2.2, you can click on the "install R for the first time" link and R will start the download process of the R base (the most basic version and all you need).

FIGURE 2.2 ● Installing R for Windows.

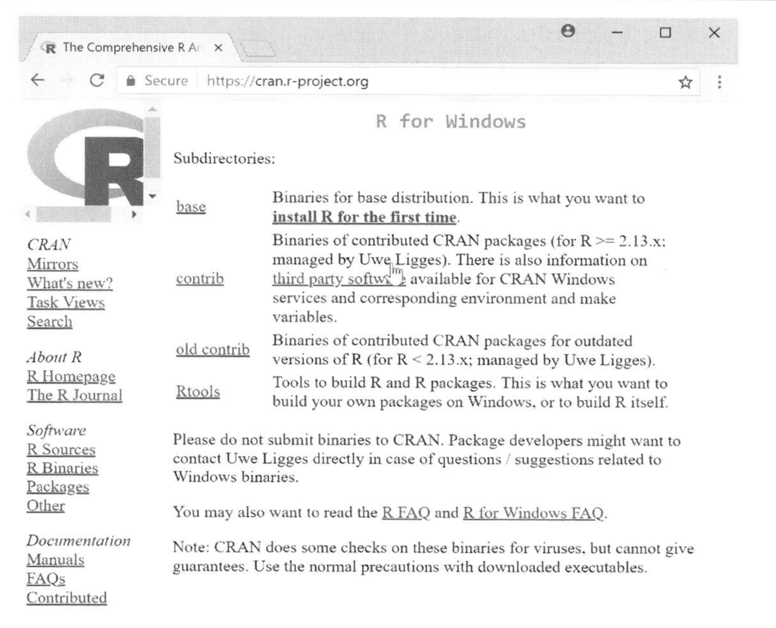

From this point on, the installation is just like the installation of any Windows program (or whatever other platform or operating system you are using such as Linux or Macintosh). We installed R Version 3.5.1 because that was the most recent version when we were writing this book. You can install that version or a newer version. The examples, practice, and problems use functions that should work regardless of which version of R you install on your computer.

Finding R

You can get most of what you need at https://cran.r-project.org/ with the *cran* part of this web address representing Comprehensive R Archive Network (or CRAN), but there are many other places as well. Take a look at http://www.r-project.org/ to reach the R Project for Statistical Computing site that will also provide the latest news about R, new versions that are available, information about the R Foundation, and more. You can also find resources and help here.

Staying Current

You can go to https://www.r-project.org/ and find out what the most current version of R is by looking at the contents headed "Under News." You can always check how current your version is by looking at the RGui opening screen, the R Console, as shown in Figure 2.3 (which in this case was R Version 3.5.1). If your version is out of date, then a simple reinstall of R will fix that.

2. Once the file is downloaded, open it up and follow your computer's operating system instructions to install R. Once this is complete, an R icon (which looks like this R) should appear on your desktop. When the time comes to use R, you can double-click that icon and the RGui opening screen as you see in Figure 2.3 will appear. Go ahead and try it!

The Opening R Screen

This opening screen is called the **R Console** (look in the upper left-hand corner of the window). It's where you enter all the R command lines you want to execute as well as read in data and much more. In fact, it's R central, and as you will see in the next chapter, it's where you'll find results from your commands. At the top are menus, which are described in Appendix A. We are now going to spend a little time in the R Console to make sure R installed properly and introduce you to some new lingo. Later in this chapter, we will install RStudio and use RStudio throughout the rest of the book.

Let's first check to see if R is working properly on your computer. If you have launched R on your computer and can see the R Console window, then you have successfully installed R, the first step required for the chapters that follow. If R was

FIGURE 2.3 ● The opening R screen.

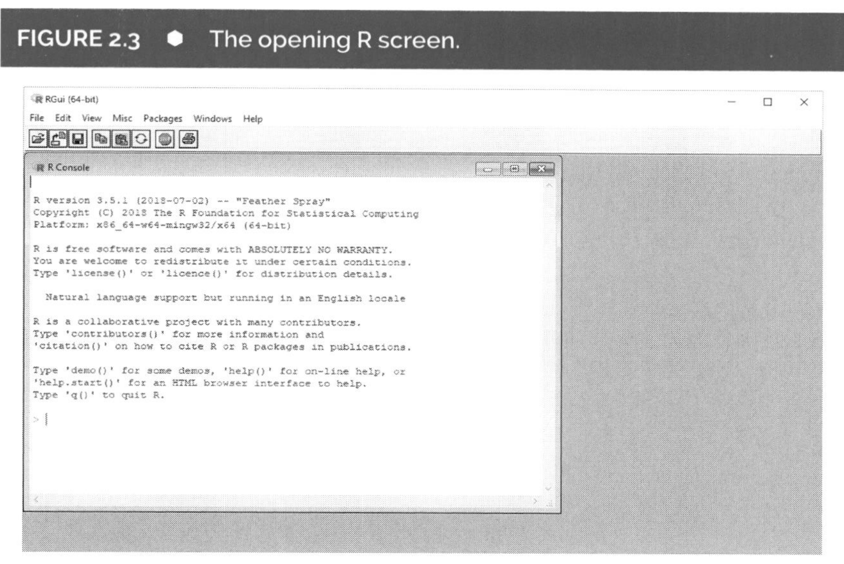

installed correctly, you should be able to easily add some numbers together in the R Console window. At the >, type in the following and hit the Enter or Return key:

```
> 2 + 3
```

R should have added those two numbers together for you, printing the result in the next line like this:

```
[1] 5
```

The "[1]" at the start of the line refers to one line of output. The 5 is the total of the two numbers you asked R to add. If you did that successfully, then R was successfully installed. For now, you can follow along with the next few examples as we learn some new terms and how to get help, or you can close the RGui and wait until we talk about RStudio later in this chapter. All commands we will show work in both RGui and RStudio as they both use R installed on your computer.

What Is a GUI?

Ever since modern programming came on the scene (actually around the mid-19th century with Ada Lovelace and her work on Charles Babbage's difference engine—whew), how information was "input" into computers has resulted in many different programming languages.

(Continued)

(Continued)

At one point, it was all *assembly language*, represented by the binary state of 1s or 0s. Then came a multitude of programs such as Basic, Unix, Fortran, Python, C++, and more and more. And, then came input devices such as the mouse and the stylus.

But still, we humans (and especially those of us who are not programmers) need as simple a way as possible to tell a computer what to do with the information we want manipulated, analyzed, transformed, and so on.

Enter the *graphical user interface* or *GUI* (yes, pronounced "gooey") that allows users to more easily understand what needs to be done and how. Windows is GUI based, as is the Macintosh user interface. And, now we bring you the RGui once you install R—two for the price of one! You could use R at the command prompt, but there are few reasons to use R that way. The RGui enables you to run commands and get answers. More user-friendly is RStudio, software that we will install later in this chapter. RGui is what you launch when you double-click on the R icon on your desktop.

When R loads up (R base is what's loaded) and appears on your computer, R is ready to use. The folks behind R believe that analyses you can do with R base are such convenient tools that to make them immediately available is the best bet to get you started using R as quickly as possible.

PACKAGES AND FUNCTIONS IN R

Earlier in this chapter, we talked about contributions that can make R better. You can use these programs by installing what are called **packages**. Packages (available in the thousands and thousands—no kidding) were written to perform certain types of tasks and allow you to easily locate, use, and update them when necessary. For example, the *stats* package, which we will use in every chapter, is automatically part of the R base and automatically available when you start R. Each package has a collection of functions and often some data you can use to practice, and the stats package alone has 37 functions that start with the letter *a*. But, what are functions?

Functions are, simply, a collection of commands that do some work for you. For example, if you use the sort function on a set of numbers, R will reorganize the numbers from smallest to largest. What if you wanted the numbers to start with the largest value and work down to the smallest? R can do that for you! We just need to learn how to tell R what we want.

How do you know what packages are available and what they do? The CRAN website stores all of the packages and maintains a list of all packages currently available for your use. If you go to any web browser and search for "R packages list," one of the top links should take you to this website: https://cran.r-project.org/web/packages/available_packages_by_name.html. The left side of the page is an alphabetized list of package names. The right side shows a short description for each package. The top of that webpage should look similar to Figure 2.4. And remember, new packages are always being added (even by the hour). In the next chapter, we will walk through finding out what packages you have on your computer.

FIGURE 2.4 ● The start of the list of currently available packages in R.

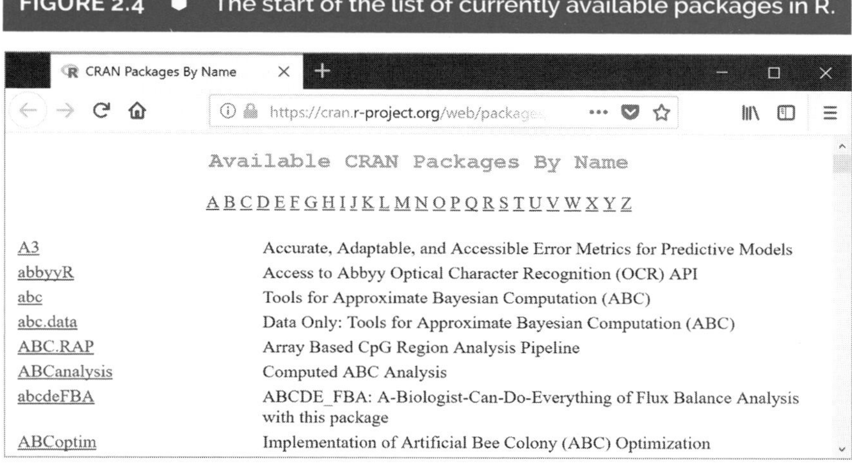

Want to find out what's contained in a package and what that package might allow you to do? Easy. If you are looking at the webpage above, find the package in the list you want to know more about and click on the name. From R we can use the help function. For help on the stats package, we would type the following in the Console at the > prompt:

```
> library(help = "stats")
starting httpd help server . . . done
>
```

and hit Enter. RGui should launch a web browser with some basic information about the stats package. Click on the Index link in the center bottom of the browser. You will see a window as shown in Figure 2.5 that explains what the package contains and a brief description of what each function does (and the version, which in this case is 3.5.1).

Almost any R function begins with a directive (such as data or help) followed by open and closed parentheses like this (), but within those parentheses is what you want the R function to operate on. So, for example, `help()` will give you a general window on help, and as you have seen earlier, `data()` will give you a general window on data sets available in R. The stuff that goes between the parentheses is called an **argument**.

FIGURE 2.5 ● Finding out what a package can do.

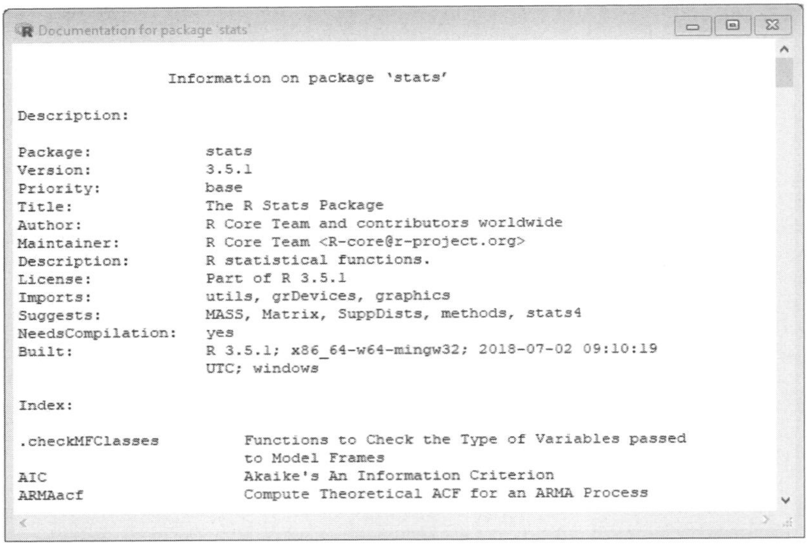

```
Documentation for package 'stats'

                Information on package 'stats'

Description:

Package:            stats
Version:            3.5.1
Priority:           base
Title:              The R Stats Package
Author:             R Core Team and contributors worldwide
Maintainer:         R Core Team <R-core@r-project.org>
Description:        R statistical functions.
License:            Part of R 3.5.1
Imports:            utils, grDevices, graphics
Suggests:           MASS, Matrix, SuppDists, methods, stats4
NeedsCompilation:   yes
Built:              R 3.5.1; x86_64-w64-mingw32; 2018-07-02 09:10:19
                    UTC; windows

Index:

.checkMFClasses         Functions to Check the Type of Variables passed
                        to Model Frames
AIC                     Akaike's An Information Criterion
ARMAacf                 Compute Theoretical ACF for an ARMA Process
```

A NOTE ABOUT FORMATTING

Throughout the rest of the book, R syntax and output will be presented like in the section above where we asked R for some help. Specifically,

- The ">" at the start of the R Console line where syntax is entered
- `Blue, monospaced font` mimicking what you type in R—the syntax
- **`Black, monospaced font`** mimicking what R returns—the output

When we instruct you to enter some syntax at the prompt, we are telling you to place your cursor after the ">" in the R Console and start entering the syntax from the example. Once each command is complete, just hit Enter or Return (depends on your keyboard—most of the time we will tell you to hit Enter), and in most cases, R will tell you what it thinks. Easy? Great!

BUNCHES OF DATA—FREE!

Just one of the very cool things about R base is that it comes with a ton of free data sets that you are welcome to explore. So, when you first install R, you will find that there are hundreds of data sets ready to read into R.

If you want to see them, enter

```
> data()
```

in the R Console. Look at Figure 2.6, which shows a subset of all the data sets that come with the downloaded version of R base. For example, you can see the data sets named *state.abb* and *women* (see women at the bottom of Figure 2.13).

FIGURE 2.6 ● A list of R data sets—free for the using.

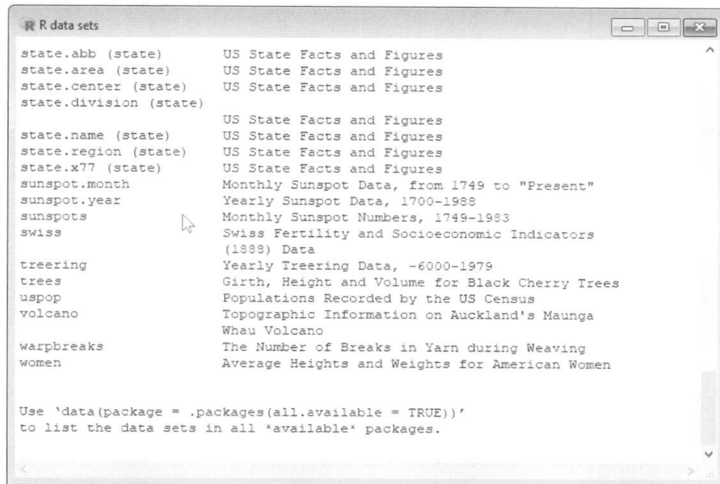

GETTING R HELP

Everyone, especially those starting out on such an ambitious endeavor as learning R, can use help once in a while. R offers a myriad of help, including menu options on the Help menu.

If you are a brand-new user, the best place to start is the FAQ on R (https://cran.r-project.org/doc/FAQ/R-FAQ.html). The FAQ lists question after question, starting with an Introduction through "What Is R," as well as add-on packages (same as the packages we mentioned earlier) and lots more.

This is the place to start and an even better place to become familiar with R just by spending some time browsing, paying attention to examples of how other people have used R to do what you want to do.

GETTING HELP ON HELP

To get help on help, you just type

```
> help()
```

in the R Console.

And, when you type `help(help)`, you will see a window as shown in Figure 2.7, which provides you with information on what type of help R offers.

FIGURE 2.7 ● Help on help!

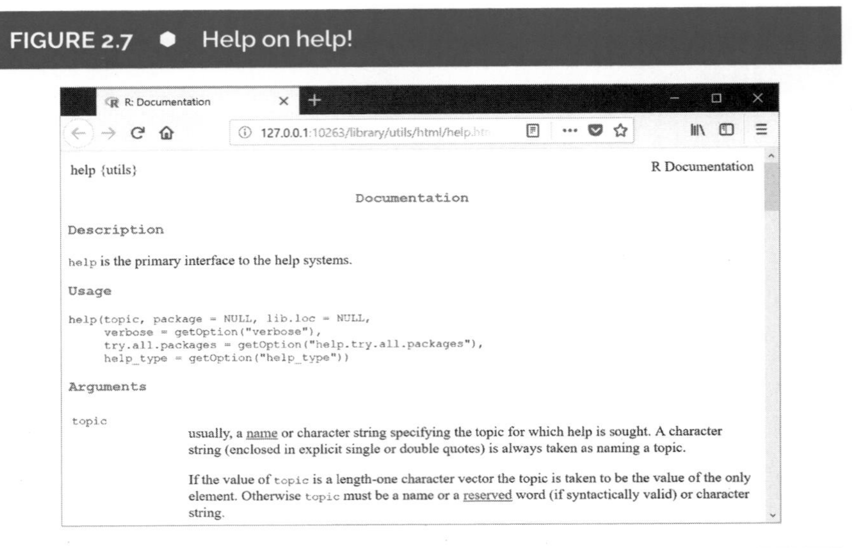

Have a Question? Use ?

Another very easy way to get help is just to type a question mark and the function you need help on, such as `?mean` or `?plot`. If there's no help on whatever function you enter, R will tell you so. Use two question marks for searching keywords, like `??mean`. This will return a list of help pages that contain the word *mean*, including the mean function.

Once you start to use R, you can search for keywords, packages, or even functions. Now, sometimes these help windows can provide lots of information that is very concise without much explanation as to how to accomplish a particular task. But, it's a good beginning. As you use R more, this level of help will become more and more informative.

Finally, it may be overwhelming, but hundreds of sites on the Internet can help you, and here are just a few. There are also many other users who were also new to R, and they might have asked the exact same question you want to ask. Try typing your question into any search engine to see how it was answered. Sometimes seeing an example is all you need to get going again on your statistics adventure with R.

If no one has asked your question, you might want to ask your question to get help. Most R websites are community based, so whatever question you ask will often be answered by several experts who can guide you along the way. Remember, there are no stupid questions—just ones from folks who are not as experienced as others. Take advantage!

Getting Help with R (at https://www.r-project.org/help.html) is the R Foundation's help desk, maybe your first and last stop because it provides so much clear information about getting help with R. It's a treasure.

Stack Overflow (at https://stackoverflow.com/) is a site where developers (or coders or programmers or whatever you want to call them) can be asked questions. If the question is a repeat, they will tell you and usually provide a link to the original post, which will also contain an answer to your question.

Help for R (at http://search.r-project.org/) offers a ton of topics devoted to R. You may also want to start with R Wiki, which offers you a very good basic understanding of what R is and how it works.

RStudio, the next application you will install, has its own community website (at https://community.rstudio.com/). In fact, the RStudio community is one of the more welcoming sites to new R users. Check out the Welcome to the RStudio Community topic to get the most use out of this website and start giving back to others new to R.

How About an Example?

Okay, you've tried help and you have some good information to start with but you really crave an example of how a function might be used. In the R Console, type `example(mean)` and hit Enter. You'll see examples that will probably prove to be very useful.

SOME IMPORTANT LINGO

Every programming language has its own way of framing concepts and ideas, and some of the most important are listed and defined here.

An **object** is anything that is created in R. For example, if you create a data set that consists of 20 scores for one variable named *time,* that set of scores is called an object. Or if you run an analysis and save the results, the results are an object. If you compute the product of 4 times 3 and store the result, then the product, 12, is an object.

A **vector** is a collection of data that are the same type (in this case all numeric), such as 1, 2, 3 or 4564, 6545, 34356. A single number could be stored, and it would still be called a vector. You could also store a collection of words in a vector, such as months of the year like May, December, August, and February. If you try to put both numbers and text in a vector, R will treat the whole vector like text. Vectors are the most basic objects in R. Throughout *Statistics for People Who (Think They) Hate Statistics Using R,* we will create vectors from the various data sets that will be used for practice.

ATOMIC Vectors

There are six types of information that you can store in a vector in R. But what does *atomic* mean? Vectors can store information, and how it is stored depends on its type, or atom, the smallest unit that you as an R user will enter and manipulate.

(Continued)

(Continued)

- Logical: TRUE or FALSE
- Integer: a whole number
- Double: a number that can contain a decimal point
- Complex: a number that contains an imaginary part (yes, this is a real thing!)
- Character: text that is also referred to as a string
- Raw: bytes of information expressed as hexadecimals

A **function** is a tool that R uses to complete some kind of operation. For example, the `mean()` function provides an average of a set of values by adding up the values and dividing by the number of observations, and `plot()` uses data to create a graph.

An **argument** is what a function acts on. So, if you see the function `mean(x)`, and the argument is `x`, R will produce an average for whatever you defined as the object named x.

And a package is a collection of functions such as the *stats* package (which we will use often), but some others are named such things as *survival* (which does survival analysis), *class* (which helps classify information), and *graf* (a graphics package). Want to see (in a way different than we did before) all the packages that have been installed in the version of R that you downloaded? In the Console after >, type

```
> library()
```

and then press Enter. You will see a listing of R packages that are currently available on your computer with this download of R.

A **data frame** is collection of information (vectors) that is arranged in rows and columns (and can just be a single row or a single column) and can contain different types of variables such as you see (both text and numeric).

Weight	Items Completed	Age
154	65	24
210	72	35
156	77	41
151	81	34
98	60	12

Data Frame or Matrix?

Another rows-and-columns organizational tool in R is called a matrix, which is a combination of rows and columns that contains values all of the same type. You can have all numbers, all text fields, or even a collection of true/false values.

A **list** is an object that contains many different types of objects within it. For example, you could create a list that would hold a data frame as one element, a vector of means for your data frame variables in the second element, and a vector of standard deviations for your third element. To make things even more confusing, if you look up the definition of a list on r-project.org, the definition for list will tell you that it is a vector. What? The official R language distinguishes between atomic vectors and list vectors. We won't spend time on lists in this book, but if you stick with R, you may find you like using them to store your objects.

Here are some of the major statistical functions we'll use throughout *Statistics for People Who (Think They) Hate Statistics Using R* and the chapters in which they will appear. Some of them have already been downloaded along with R.

Chapter	Function	What It Does
2	`help()`	Find information on a package or function so you know how to use it
3	`read.csv()`	Import a data set into R for use
4	`mean()`	Calculate the arithmetic mean of a vector of numbers
5	`sd()`	Compute the standard deviation of a vector of numbers
6	`plot()`	Draw a picture of your data
7	`cor()`	Calculate the correlation between two variables
8	`alpha()`	Calculate a statistic of reliability for a measure
10	`scale()`	Change the mean and possibly standard deviation of your vector
12	`pnorm()`	Determine the probability for a z statistic
13	`t.test()`	Compute the t test statistic for independent samples
14	`t.test()`	Compute the t test statistic for paired samples
15	`aov()`	Calculate analysis of variance
16	`Anova()`	Obtain Type III sum of squares results
17	`cor.test()`	Calculate the correlation and get the probability of the statistic
18	`lm()`	Estimate a linear model for regression
19	`chisq.test()`	Calculate a chi-square statistic

OK. Let's review what you have learned so far.

1. R is a programming environment often used to assist in the analysis of data.
2. It is an open source package that is incredibly flexible but also requires lots of attention to detail.
3. When you download R, you get a ton of additional resources including data sets, packages, and extensive help.
4. Case (upper and lower) counts, so be sure and enter a function correctly and exactly.
5. R is a treasure chest of tools. The more you use it, the more you will be able to maximize its power.

RStudio

With the install of R, you also received RGui, the default graphical user interface that comes with R. On Windows, RGui can be challenging to use, even for experienced R users. Instead, we are going to use RStudio from the company RStudio (https://www.rstudio.com/). The RStudio interface is actually called an *IDE* or an *integrated development environment*. It accesses R on your computer like RGui does, but RStudio contains some features that will make life easier as you learn.

RGui or RStudio?

RStudio uses the same commands we used in the sections above when we introduced you to `help()`, `data()`, and `library()`. RStudio is just another (and easier) way to use R. So, all the R commands you will ever learn will work in RStudio. RStudio uses R that you installed on your computer, only dressed up.

Have You Already Installed R?

RStudio uses R that is already on your computer. If you decided to wait until later to install R, you have come to later! Go back to "Where to Find and Download R" and follow the steps to install R on your computer. Then, come back here to follow the steps to install RStudio.

WHERE TO FIND RSTUDIO AND HOW TO INSTALL IT

Here are the steps to follow to install RStudio:

1. Go to https://www.rstudio.com/products/rstudio/download.

2. As you can see in Figure 2.8, you have several choices as to the version of RStudio you want to install, including a free version for the individual computer, referred to as RStudio Desktop. Click the DOWNLOAD button for the RStudio Desktop for either the Open Source or Commercial License.

Visit **edge.sagepub.com/salkindshaw** to watch an R tutorial video on this topic.

FIGURE 2.8 ● The RStudio installation site.

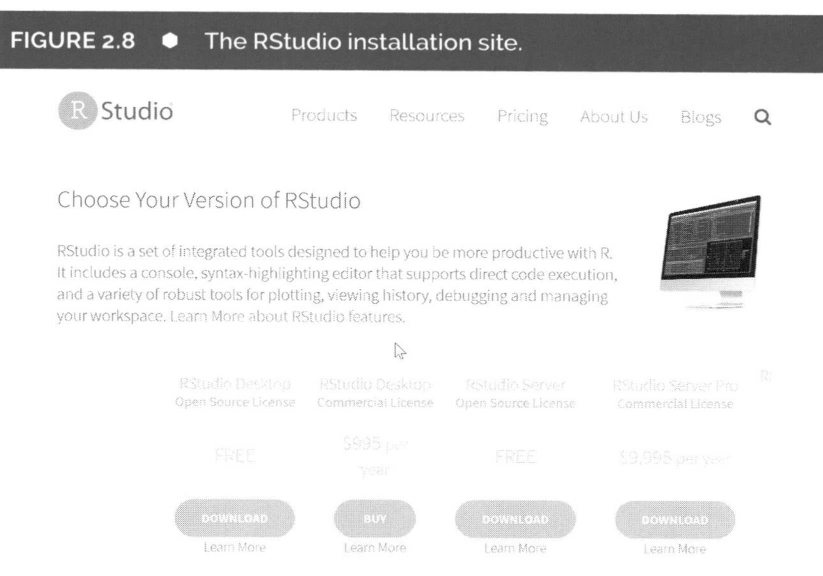

3. As you see in Figure 2.9, you will be given several options regarding which operating system or platform you are using. Double-click the one that fits your platform (such as RStudio Windows or RStudio Mac OSX).

FIGURE 2.9 ● Selecting a version of RStudio to install.

Installers for Supported Platforms

Installers	Size	Date	MD5
RStudio 1.1.456 - Windows Vista/7/8/10	85.8 MB	2018-07-19	24ca3fe0dad8187aabd4bfbb9dc2b5ad
RStudio 1.1.456 - Mac OS X 10.6+ (64-bit)	74.5 MB	2018-07-19	4fc4f4f70845b142bf96dc1a5b1dc556
RStudio 1.1.456 - Ubuntu 12.04-15.10/Debian 8 (32-bit)	89.3 MB	2018-07-19	3493f9d5839e3a3d697f40b7bb1ce961
RStudio 1.1.456 - Ubuntu 12.04-15.10/Debian 8 (64-bit)	97.4 MB	2018-07-19	863ae806120358fa0146e4d14cd75be4
RStudio 1.1.456 - Ubuntu 16.04+/Debian 9+ (64-bit)	64.9 MB	2018-07-19	d96e63548c2add890bac633bdb883f32
RStudio 1.1.456 - Fedora 19+/RedHat 7+/openSUSE 13.1+ (32-bit)	88.1 MB	2018-07-19	1df56c7cd80e2634f8a9fdd11ca1fb2d
RStudio 1.1.456 - Fedora 19+/RedHat 7+/openSUSE 13.1+ (64-bit)	90.6 MB	2018-07-19	5e77094a88fdbddddb0d35708752462

4. Proceed as you install any new application for your operating system and you will shortly see the RStudio icon on your desktop, which looks like this **R**. In this case, a shortcut was placed on the Windows desktop.

5. Double-click the RStudio icon and you're ready to go with the RStudio opening screen as shown in Figure 2.10.

FIGURE 2.10 ● The RStudio opening screen.

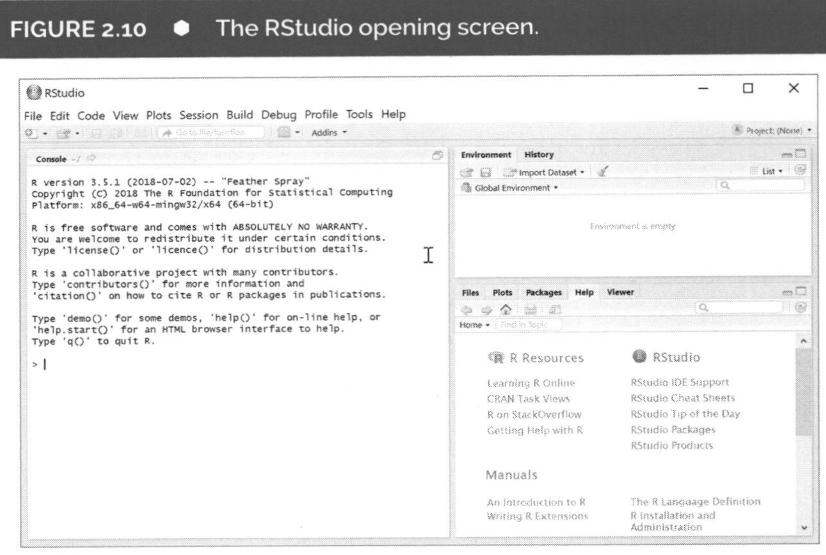

TAKE RSTUDIO FOR A TEST RIDE

Recall, after installing R, we tested adding 2 and 3 in the R Console window of the RGui. Let's do the same thing with RStudio. In the R Console window, type

```
> 2 + 3
```

and hit the Enter or Return key. Like before, you should see

```
[1] 5
```

to indicate one line of output and the result of your addition is "5."

If you have gotten this far, you have installed both R and RStudio and tried some simple commands in the R Console. You have also started to learn some R lingo. You probably saw some words that you know but now know their definitions in R.

We are now going to spend a little more time with RStudio, introducing you to the menus. Pay attention to the big ideas. You will see more new terms and phrases on the menus, like "Workspace" and "Set Working Directory." By the end of Chapter 3, you will know what these mean along with a dozen other words and phrases, so don't worry about it. Right now, you are trying to learn how things are organized, so if you need to find something in the coming chapters, you will have an idea of where to look.

Windows or Mac

What if you have an older Mac OS and could not install RStudio? Don't worry. Students using the Mac OS have told us that RGui on Mac is nice to use. And in Chapter 3 and the rest of the book, where possible, tasks that can be done by clicking on a menu or entering a command in the R Console will be demonstrated both ways, so you will be able to follow along using the commands.

ORDERING FROM RSTUDIO

As with any GUI, RStudio comes with a series of menus that contain a variety of options, kind of like any menu in a restaurant. Here's a summary of RStudio's 11 menus and what you can find on each one.

File

By using options on the File menu, you can do such things as start a new project, save the data you are working with (very important), access recent projects, close a project you are working on, and quit RStudio altogether. The File menu shown in Figure 2.11 is where you will spend a considerable amount of time as you develop sets of RStudio commands (called *scripts*) and want to continue working on them.

FIGURE 2.11 ● The File menu.

Edit

Our first try at creating a set of commands or a script often will need some touchups, and that's where the options on the Edit menu (shown in Figure 2.12) come in. Here you can do the usual Cut, Copy, and Paste but also clear the entire Console with one menu item click, Redo and Undo what you have just entered, and search for specific commands.

FIGURE 2.12 ● The Edit menu.

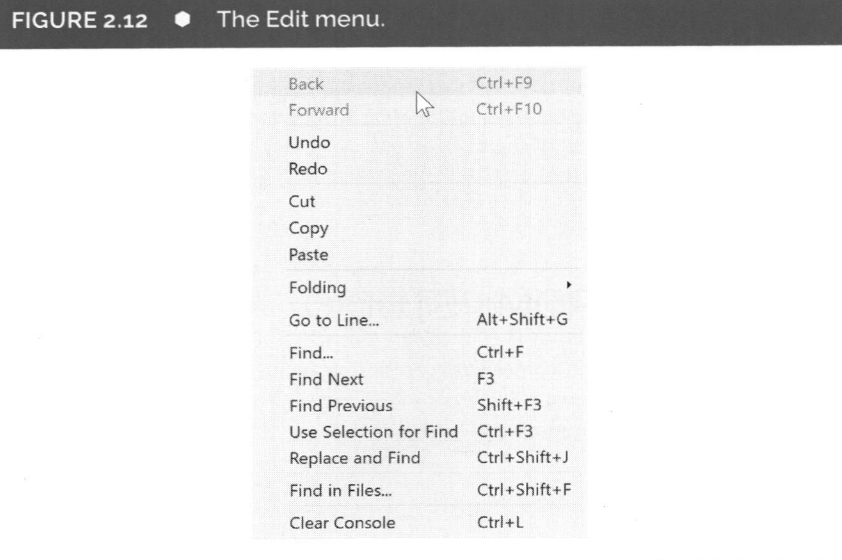

Code

Coding (the focus of the Code menu), in any programming environment, is the name of the game and such is surely the case with RStudio. In Figure 2.13, you can easily insert an entire section of script, find the definition of a function, have RStudio run only those lines of script you want to, and examine the Source File or the set of commands with which you are working.

FIGURE 2.13 ● The Code menu.

View

If you want to rearrange the way that RStudio panes are displayed on your monitor, commands on the View menu shown in Figure 2.14 are where you want to be. Additionally, you can increase or decrease the size of elements on the screen; show files, plots, and packages (and more); and use the cool Tab key to help you insert commands (more about that soon).

FIGURE 2.14 ● The View menu.

Rearranging Panes

If you find that you want to rearrange the way that RStudio panes appear on your screen, click View→Panes→Pane Layout and you will see an Options dialog box. There you can select which of the four RStudio panes you want in each of the four possible positions. You can even check the spelling or add a custom dictionary.

Plots

For those of us who are visual learners and for illustration purposes, RStudio provides an easy-to-use and powerful set of tools to create and manipulate plots through the Plot menu. You can save the plots you create as an image, in PDF or other formats, and copy the plot to the clipboard, where it can then be easily pasted into another application such as Word. See the lower right pane of RStudio for a visual of some of what the Plots menu can do after you select Next Plot as shown in Figure 2.15.

FIGURE 2.15 ● The Plots menu.

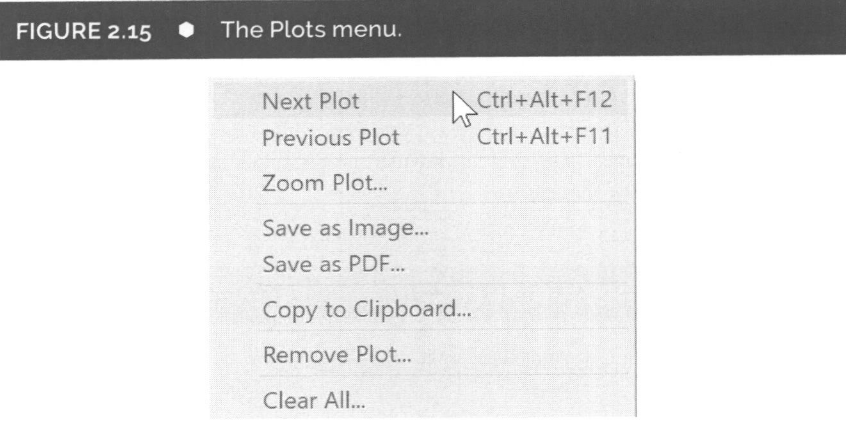

Session

Time to start a new session? Set the working directory, or clear the workspace? What do these things even mean? Stay tuned! We will talk about all of these things in the next chapter. Check out the Session menu shown in Figure 2.16.

FIGURE 2.16 ● The Session menu.

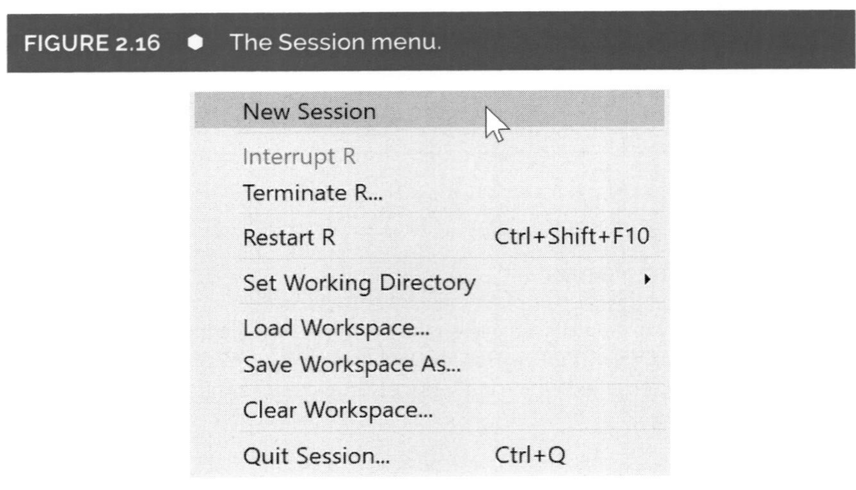

Build

You may not spend lots of time in the Build menu, but if you are looking to build a package or develop some kind of add-on to RStudio, this is where you want to be. The Build menu has one item on it—Configure Build Tools—so we will skip showing a picture of this menu.

Debug

Once that package is developed or a script developed, you want to use the debug tools found on the Debug menu shown in Figure 2.17.

FIGURE 2.17 ● The Debug menu.

Toggle Breakpoint Shift+F9
Clear All Breakpoints...
Execute Next Line F10
Step Into Function Shift+F4
Finish Function/Loop Shift+F6
Continue Shift+F5
Stop Debugging Shift+F8
On Error
Debugging Help

Profile

The Profile menu shown in Figure 2.18 is for the more advanced of us who are creating scripts, developing packages, and more. This menu helps the RStudio user to understand how R spends its time and resources in an effort to make things operate more efficiently.

FIGURE 2.18 ● The Profile menu.

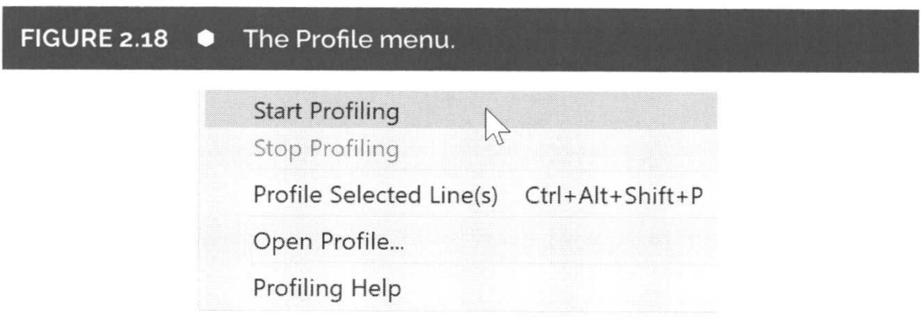

Tools

What's a good toolbox without tools? RStudio provides several on the Tools menu shown in Figure 2.19 that allow you to do such things as install packages, check that the packages that are installed are up-to-date, use RStudio add-ins, and define global options such as setting the default working directory.

FIGURE 2.19 ● The Tools menu.

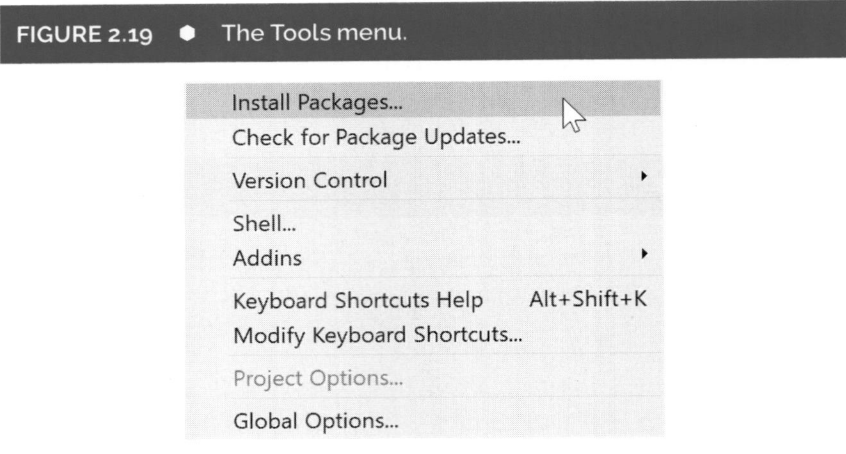

Help(!)

And, finally, RStudio offers a Help menu filled with options that can get you back on track. As shown in Figure 2.20, you can check for updates (and you should do this every so often), access RStudio Support, find out about keyboard shortcuts, and even diagnose what might be happening with the scripts you want to run.

FIGURE 2.20 ● The Help menu.

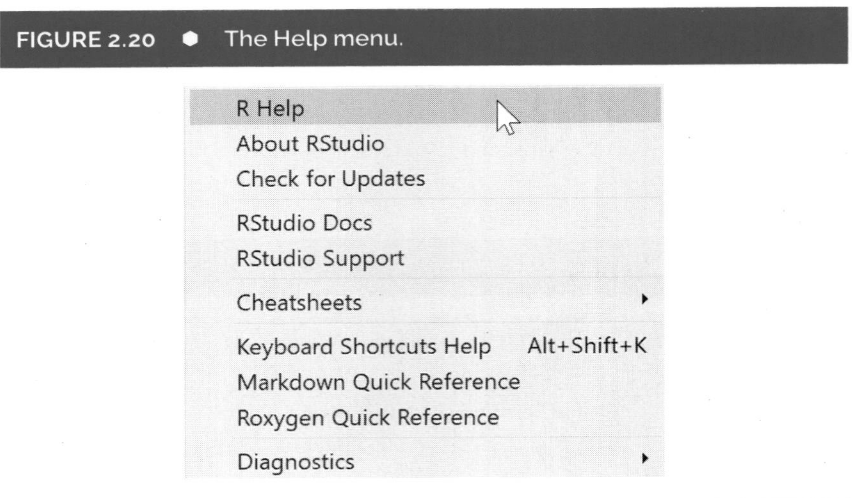

Summary

Well, some congratulations are in order.

Once you have finished this chapter and completed the Time to Practice exercises that follow, you will have installed R and RStudio, learned some new terms, and performed some simple arithmetic in the R Console window. Now, it takes practice using R and, most of all, just having some fun exploring different functions and seeing the results. Keep in mind that working with a study buddy (as we talked about in Chapter 1) is invaluable, especially when such details as remembering case and including quotes are concerned. In Chapter 3, we'll move on to learning more about R, RStudio, and its panes; revisit packages; start using R as a calculator (either the most or least expensive calculator you have ever owned); and enter data.

Time to Practice

1. What is R, and what are some of the advantages and disadvantages of using it for statistical analysis?
2. Describe two ways to get help in R.
3. Objects in R:
   a. What type of data can you store in a vector?
   b. Can you store both numbers and text in a vector?
   c. How are functions and packages related to each other?
4. In RStudio, run some of the functions we showed in the chapter.
   a. `library(help = "stats")`
   b. `data()`
   c. `help(help)`
   d. `library()`
5. Where did the help text show up once you tried the command for `library(help = "stats")`?
6. What is RStudio, and how does it differ from R?

Student Study Site

Get the tools you need to sharpen your study skills! Visit **edge.sagepub.com/salkindshaw** to access practice quizzes and eFlashcards, watch R tutorial videos, and download data sets!

USING RSTUDIO

Much Easier Than You Think

Difficulty Scale ☺ ☺
(easily doable—just practice along)

WHAT YOU WILL LEARN IN THIS CHAPTER

- Understanding the four panes of RStudio and what they do
- Using R like a calculator
- Creating, using, and importing data sets in RStudio
- Conducting a simple data analysis in R

This chapter in *Statistics for People Who (Think They) Hate Statistics Using R* will familiarize you with RStudio and show you how to use it in association with R to use R commands in a friendly way to get the results you want. We will start using R like a calculator, create our first objects, and learn some commands and concepts that will be mentioned throughout this book.

So, while R alone is very cool and, as we have mentioned several times in the last chapter, wide and deep, it's RStudio that really helps bring home the power for everyday users like us.

Get ready for some striking fun.

THE GRAND TOUR AND ALL ABOUT THOSE FOUR PANES

Let's explore the RStudio panes with an example for each one as shown in Figure 3.1, which is just chock full of good and interesting examples of how RStudio is structured and works.

FIGURE 3.1 ● The RStudio opening screen.

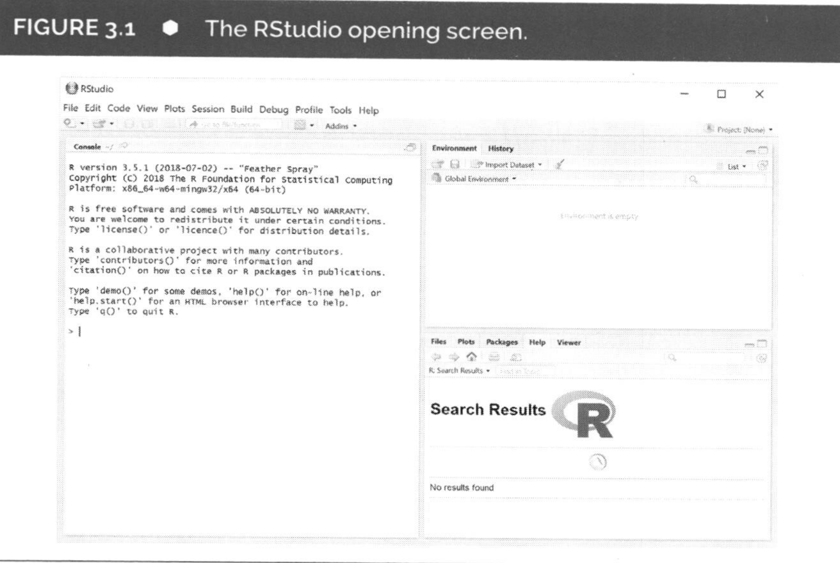

This screen is going to be similar to the RStudio screen you saw just after installing RStudio. Right now, there are three panes. Let's open one more, and then we will talk about all four in more detail. Follow these steps to open up the fourth pane:

1. Go to the File menu.
2. Point at New File and a submenu will pop up.
3. Select R Script. . . .

RStudio should now look something like Figure 3.2.

FIGURE 3.2 ● The four open panes of RStudio.

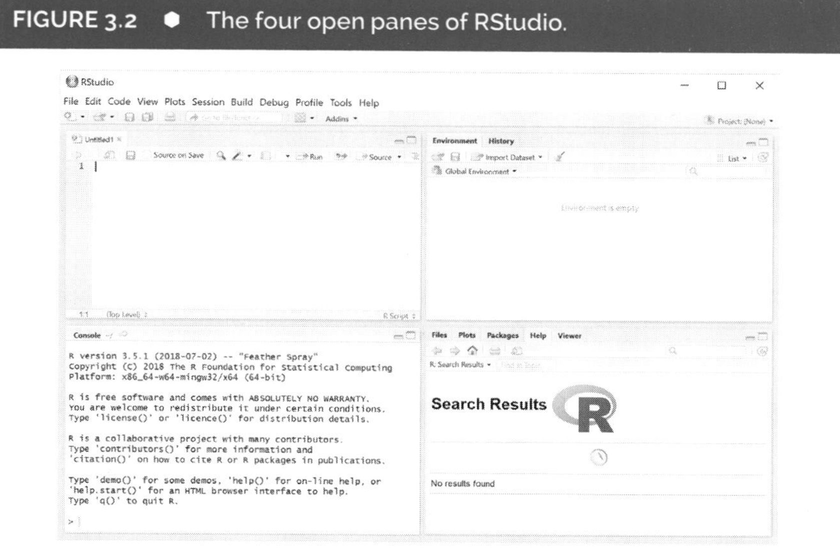

We now have four panes along with some options within the pane, like the ability to view either Environment or History in the top right pane. Let's learn what each pane is.

- The top left pane in Figure 3.2 is the *Source* pane (also called the *Syntax* pane) where you can enter RStudio commands to create R scripts. We often enter R commands in the Source pane along with comments, particularly about stuff that worked, and save our R scripts for later.
- To the right of the Syntax pane is the *Environment and History* pane with two tabs. The first one is the *Environment* tab that provides a listing of all the objects, like vectors or data frames, that you are currently working on in RStudio. The other tab, *History,* lists all of the RStudio commands that have been entered in your RStudio session. Session just refers to the time between starting and exiting RStudio. This *History* tab listing is not only terrific to track what you have done and find out what did or did not work but also to use the listing to reenter a command by simply double-clicking on that command.
- The lower left pane is called the *Console* and is RStudio central—it's where you enter RStudio commands and see the result of executing those commands as well. Commands can be entered directly in the Console, sent from the History tab to the Console, or sent from the Source pane to the Console.
- Finally, to the right of the Console (and the lower right-hand pane) is the *Files, Plots, Packages, Help, and Viewer* pane (sorry no short descriptive name), but there are many very useful things you can do here.
    - The *Files* tab lists the files that are currently in whatever directory you select or those that you have saved in your RStudio account.
    - The *Plots* tab shows the results of graphics commands.
    - The *Packages* tab shows you what packages are available for you to access in RStudio.
    - *Help* is exactly what you expect and need—help on using R.
    - And, finally, the *Viewer* tab, which allows you to view local web content, content that is sitting on your computer.

RSTUDIO PANE GOODIES

RStudio can do lots of things and do them much easier than in the RGui. That's the whole point of using an interface like RStudio rather than just sticking with the RGui.

What follows is a brief description in tabular form of the most important tools (which appear as icons) in each of the four panes that we described above along with the icon that you click on to make these things happen.

Be sure to notice that in every pane, there is a collapse/expand icon that collapses or expands the pane that is clicked. It's nice to give you more room with one pane, especially if you are not working in any of the others.

For example, in Figure 3.3, you can see how the Source pane was collapsed and is no longer visible. To make it visible, just click the expand button in that pane.

FIGURE 3.3 ● Collapsing the Source pane.

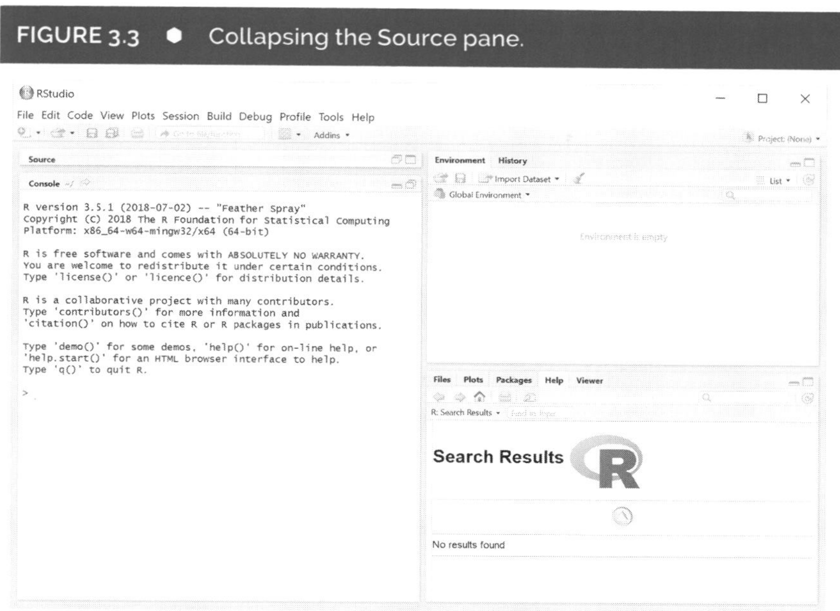

The Icon	What You See When You Mouse Over It	What It Does
The Source pane		
	Show in new window	Opens a new Script window
	Save current document	Saves the current document and allows you to name it
Source on Save	Source on save	Run every line in your R Script when you save the file (make sure this is unchecked!)
	Find/replace	Find and replace commands and syntax
	Code tools	Lists a comprehensive set of tools used to enter and adjust code
	Compile report	Provides tools to compile a report
Run	Run the current line or selection	Execute the command or commands that are selected
	Rerun the previous code region	Run the previous code again

(Continued)

(Continued)

The Icon	What You See When You Mouse Over It	What It Does
Source	Source the contents of the active document	Run every line in the open R Script
The Environment Tab in the Environment/History Pane		
	Open a workspace	Opens a dialog box from which you open a workspace
	Saves a workspace	Opens a dialog box for saving a workspace
Import Dataset	Import a data set	Allows you to import a data set in various formats
	Clears objects from the workspace	Clears the pane of any environment entries
List	List	Allows for viewing Environment entries as a list or as a grid
	Refresh the list of objects in the environment	Refreshes list of all those objects in the global environment
The History Tab in the Environment/History Pane		
	Load history from an existing file	Opens the history of commands from a file that already exists
	Save history into a file	Saves the current listing of commands
To Console	Send the selected commands to the R Console	Inserts commands from the History pane into the Console
To Source	Insert the selected commands into the current document	Inserts commands from the History pane into the current document
	Removes the selected history entries	Removes the selected R command from the History pane
	Clears all history entries	Removes all R commands from the History pane
	Search for history entries	Searches through the history pane for specific commands
The Files Tab in the Files, Plots, Packages, Help, and Viewer Pane		
New Folder	Create a new folder	Creates a new folder on your computer in the directory shown below

The Icon	What You See When You Mouse Over It	What It Does
Delete	Delete selected files or folders	Deletes those files or folders that have been selected
Rename	Rename selected file or folder	Renames a file or folder that has been selected
More ▾	More options	Allows for copying, moving, and working with directories
	Refresh file listing	Creates a new list based on any changes that have been made in the file listings
The Plots Tab in the Files, Plots, Packages, Help, and Viewer Pane		
	Previous/next plot	Goes to the previous or the next plot
Zoom	View a larger version of the plot in a new window	Allows you to increase the size of the plot and view it in a new window
Export ▾	Export a plot	Saves a plot as an image or a PDF or copies it to the clipboard
	Removes the current plot	Removes the current plot from the Plot pane
	Clears all plots	Clears all the plots in the Plot tab
Publish ▾	Publish plot	You may not see this icon until you create a plot. This button publishes a plot to the location you specify.
	Refresh current plot	Refreshes the plot currently in the Plot pane
The Packages Tab in the Files, Plots, Packages, Help, and Viewer Pane		
Install	Install R packages	Provides a dialog box for locating and installing R packages
Update	Check for package updates	Look on CRAN for packages that have versions different from what you have on your computer
	Search for packages	Search for an R package
	Refresh package listing	Refreshes the listing of packages that are available
The Help Tab in the Files, Plots, Packages, Help, and Viewer Pane		
	Previous/next topic	Goes to previous or next help topic

(Continued)

(Continued)

The Icon	What You See When You Mouse Over It	What It Does
	Show R help	Shows main R help screen
	Print topic	Prints the current topic
	Show in a new window	Shows help topic in a new window
	Find topic	Finds the searched-for topic
	Refresh topic	Refreshes the current help topic
The Viewer Tab in the Files, Plots, Packages, Help, and Viewer Pane[a]		
Viewer	See the Viewer pane	Reveals web content created using RStudio or existing on your computer

[a]Using the Viewer pane is beyond the scope of this book, but there is cool material online if you want to learn how to view and work with webpages in RStudio.

SHOWING YOUR STUFF—WORKING WITH MENUS AND TABS AND A SAMPLE DATA ANALYSIS USING RSTUDIO

There's really only one way to get to learn how to use RStudio and that's by doing it. So, here goes some sample data analysis using RStudio and three data sets. If you download the syntax files for each chapter, you will find that each line is documented using the # mark. We're showing you lots of examples so you can see how each command is entered and what the results are. Our History pane will help us keep track of everything we do (even the errors!). Let's start working in the Console.

Visit **edge.sagepub.com/salkindshaw** to watch an R tutorial video on this topic.

THE BASICS: +, –, ?, *, AND MORE: USING OPERATORS

At its most basic level, R is a calculator, and entering a command to calculate the value of a number is just like entering any other command.

For example, we entered the simple command to add the values of 4 and 6 and pressed the Enter key.

```
> 4 + 6
[1] 10
>
```

Using R as a simple calculator,

- > is the R prompt waiting for you to enter information.
- 4 + 6 is the expression you are asking R to solve.
- [1] is the line number, and the result is 10. Although this is only a one-line result, these numbers (such as [1]) help you track outcomes when there is more than one line.

Now, the above was a pretty simple calculation, but these calculations can become much more complex and use all the operators such as + (addition), – (subtraction), * (multiplication), / (division), and ^ as an exponential (such as the value of 2 squared).

Do you remember "Pretty please my dear Aunt Sally?" In math, this mnemonic reminds you of the order of operations to use when evaluating mathematical operations: parentheses, power, multiplication, division, addition, and subtraction. R reads left to write, but we can add parentheses to enforce some order to our operations.

Let's take $\frac{(3+5)^2}{17+21}$. Following the order, 3 + 5 = 8, which we then square. Our numerator equals 64. Add 17 to 21 to get 38 for the denominator. Then we divide 64 by 38. Your answer is 1.684211.

```
> (3 + 5)^2/17 + 21
[1] 24.76471
>
```

R evaluated left to right. The values within parentheses were added first and then squared. So, our numerator was 64 as we expected. The numerator was divided by 17 instead of 17 + 21 (38). Let's try this again with parentheses around the denominator 17 + 21.

```
> (3 + 5)^2/(17 + 21)
[1] 1.684211
>
```

Repeating Command Lines

R

Any time you enter a command in the R Console, you can easily repeat that command line once again by pressing the up arrow ↑ on your keyboard. So, if you goof and mistype, you can easily repeat what you have already entered and then edit it as you would any line of text. If you continue to press the up arrow, you will continue to scroll through previous command lines. And if you press the down arrow ↓, you can scroll through commands in the opposite direction.

(Continued)

(Continued)

Once you find the line you want to repeat, just hit Enter. If you want to make a change to the commands, use your left and right arrows to move within the line and edit as you would any line of text by adding or deleting characters.

Spaces, Spaces, Spaces

R doesn't care how many or how few spaces you use when entering your commands.

```
> 104+105
[1] 209
>
> 104 + 105
[1] 209
>
> 104 + 105
[1] 209
>
```

But odds are you are going to use R for class assignments, and spaces in your command will make your work easier to decipher (and grade), just as reading any sentence is simpler to do when written with spaces. Youwouldnotwriteasentencelikethis. You would add spaces. In the first command above, 104+105 is like writing "104plus105" while 104 + 105 is like writing "104 plus 105." Use spaces when you enter command lines in R. It makes the reading and review of commands much easier.

Visit **edge.sagepub.com/salkindshaw** to watch an R tutorial video on this topic.

WORKING WITH DATA

Real data are the currency that R needs to perform its magic, so let's focus on two important skills. The first is how to create a data set in R, and the second is how to read an existing data set (such as one of those many that come with R base) into R so we can show you some simple statistical analysis.

Creating a Data Set From One Vector

Let's begin by creating a vector or a data set named correct (not CORRECT or Correct—case matters, remember?), which represents the number of items that are correct on a 10-item test.

To create a vector or a data set using the `c()` function, follow these steps:

- At the R prompt, enter the following

```
> correct <- c(8, 6, 5, 8, 7, 8, 9, 6, 10, 8)
>
```

where

- `correct` is the name of the data set being created.
- `<-` are the characters that mean assign what follows to the object on the left
- `c` represents the R command called *concatenate,* which simply means ("treat whatever follows as a single vector"). We think it's easier to think of the c command as "combine" all that follows into an object.
- The 10 values (8, 6, etc.) represent the scores.
    1. Press the Enter or Return key, and you will then see nothing more than the R prompt. But fear not, this information is now part of the R Console. Want to check that? Enter correct at the prompt and nothing more—just the word `correct` (with a lowercase c of course) and you will see the output like in the example just above.

```
> correct
[1]  8  6  5  8  7  8  9  6 10  8
>
```

There are all 10 values as you entered them and ready for additional analysis.

If you look at the top right RStudio pane for Environment, you will now see the R object correct listed under values. You can also enter the function `ls()` to see a list of all objects in your environment:

```
> ls()
[1] "correct"
>
```

1. The `ls()` function we called with nothing in parentheses tells R to list every object it's aware of. Before, we added some numbers together but did not store them in anything so the `ls()` function knows nothing about those numbers.
2. `"correct"` is the one object listed in our environment.

If we want to list everything that starts with the letter c, we can enter `ls(pattern = "c")`. Give that a try to see what you get.

Some Simple RStudio Tasks

Where did we find out how to use the `ls` function to list the objects in our environment? We opened a web browser and entered "R list environment objects" in Google and got many results—over 91,000,000. There are lots and lots of responses to this simple question, but a bit of reading led us to the format `ls()`. Why not just use R Help? Because sometimes it can help to see how more than one person writes about a function.

Once we found the format of the `ls` function, we could then type `?ls` at the R prompt and get available help on listing objects through RStudio.

Clearing the Console

You may want to clear the Console as you start or at a later time, any time when you want a clean screen. Easy. In the Console pane, click Edit → Clear Console or use the Ctrl + L key combination.

More Vectors

First, let's stay simple and enter some data sets, calling them data1, data2, and data3, and then perform some simple tasks. As you can see below, each object contains 10 observations. And, as you can also see, there's a big *oops* or an error when we entered the second data set. We first entered data2 without the "c" command, and RStudio let us know that.

```
> data1 <- c(45, 56, 34, 56, 25, 74, 35, 68, 98, 56)
> data2 <- (7, 5, 3, 6, 4, 7, 6, 4, 5, 9)
Error: unexpected ',' in "data2 <- (7,"
```

Now, the error message ("unexpected ',' . . .") is not crystal clear as to what we need to correct, but some eyeballing and comparison of what did work (the entry of data1) and what did not (the entry of data2) shows us the answer.

```
> data2 <- c(7, 5, 3, 6, 4, 7, 6, 4, 5, 9)
> data3 <- c(1, 2, 1, 2, 2, 1, 2, 1, 2, 2)
>
```

LET'S SEE WHAT'S IN THE WORKSPACE

With the data sets read into RStudio, let's use the `ls()` function to see what's in that workspace.

```
> ls()
[1] "correct" "data1" "data2" "data3"
>
```

You can see in the output a listing of all the objects, including data1, data2, and data3. You can also click on the Environment tab to see the same information.

Looking With the Environment

The `ls()` function will certainly tell you what's in your workspace, but you can also just give a good look with the Environment tab in the Environment/History pane and see listed all the data sets that R has immediately accessible. And, you can click on any one of the data set names and you will see the data in the Source or Syntax pane (the upper left-hand pane) of RStudio.

Removing an Object From the Workspace

Use the `rm("name of object")` command and the object will be removed. So, for example, if we entered

```
> rm(data1)
```

and pressed the Enter or Return key and then typed `ls()`, data1 is no longer in the workspace.

```
> ls()
[1] "correct" "data2" "data3"
>
```

Returning an Object to the Workspace

Now, data1 is removed from the workspace. To return it to the workspace, we simply need to double-click in the History pane on that command [data1 = c(. . .)] that is being pointed to in Figure 3.4 or hit the up arrow until we get to the command we used to create data1 the first time around. Once you find that line of syntax, hit Enter. Magic!

Seeing the Contents of an Object

You want to make sure that the object contains what you think. Simply enter the name of the object such as

```
> data1
[1] 45 56 34 56 25 74 35 68 98 56
>
```

and, as you can see, the contents of the object are revealed. And if the magic is not working, return to the History tab and try double-clicking again on data1.

FIGURE 3.4 ● A view of the History pane.

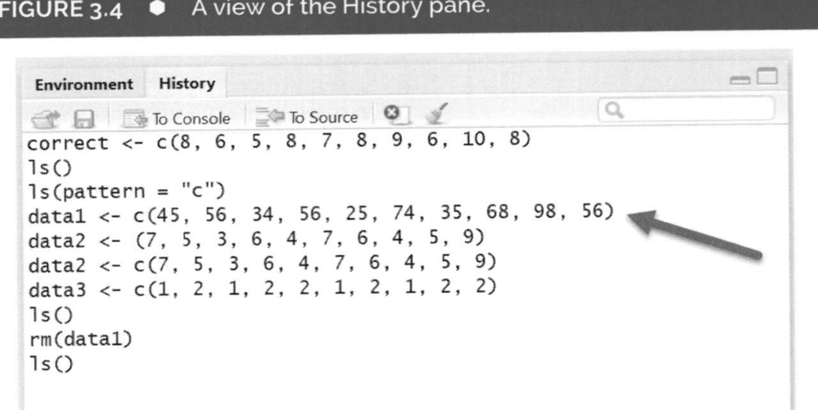

READING IN ESTABLISHED DATA SETS

Visit **edge.sagepub.com/salkindshaw** to watch an R tutorial video on this topic.

Here's the second situation where an existing data set is read into RStudio.

You may remember that in Chapter 2, we showed you how to use the *read.table* command. That's a perfectly good way to read a vector or a data set into R or RStudio, but we've two better ways to show you. Here goes.

Using the Easiest R Command in the Galaxy

There is a very easy way to enter the data set you want into RStudio.

Remember that we are working with files that are saved as .csv values. For example, in Figure 3.5, you can see the first 15 rows of a file named Sample Data Set.csv, consisting of 25 rows and five variables: ID, gender, treatment group, test 1, and test 2. The data are saved as a .csv file, which is available at the *Statistics for People Who (Think They) Hate Statistics Using R* website at edge.sagepub.com/salkindshaw.

To use this new command, we are going to call this new data set `example`. You can choose something else if you would like. Type the following in the Console:

```
> example <- read.csv(file.choose(), header = TRUE)
```

where

- `example` is the object name you want RStudio to assign the object in R.
- `<- read.csv` tells RStudio to read a .csv file.
- `file.choose()` is the R command to open the Select file dialog box.
- `header = TRUE` tells RStudio that the .csv table has column names in the first row of the file that it can use to label the variables (vectors).

FIGURE 3.5 ● A file created using Excel and saved in .csv format.

	A	B	C	D	E	F
1	ID	Gender	Treatment	Test1	Test2	
2	1	Male	Control	98	32	
3	2	Female	Experiment	87	33	
4	3	Female	Control	89	54	
5	4	Female	Control	88	44	
6	5	Male	Experiment	76	64	
7	6	Male	Control	68	54	
8	7	Female	Control	78	44	
9	8	Female	Experiment	98	32	
10	9	Female	Experiment	93	64	
11	10	Male	Experiment	76	37	
12	11	Female	Control	75	43	
13	12	Female	Control	65	56	
14	13	Male	Control	76	78	
15	14	Female	Control	78	99	
16	15	Female	Control	89	87	
17	16	Female	Experiment	81	56	

Sample Data Set

Then press the Enter or Return key.

If you are following along, the Select file window should look something like Figure 3.6.

FIGURE 3.6 ● Using the file.choose command to select a file to read into RStudio.

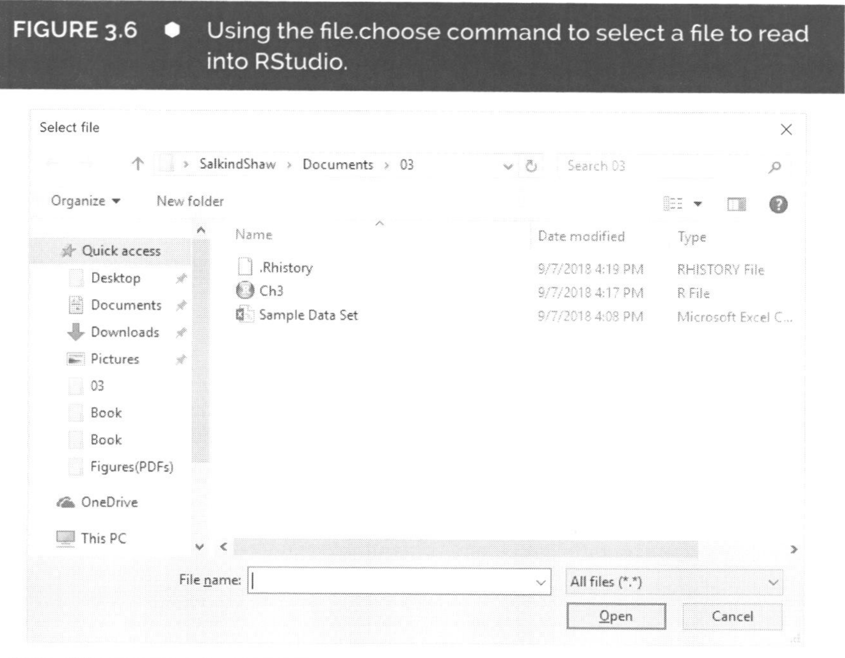

Now you need to find and select the .csv file that you created and put it on your computer. Hopefully you remember where you put the file. If you downloaded it from the website for this book, it may be in your Downloads folder. The file is now available to RStudio.

Okay, don't believe us. Just to be sure this all worked, we typed the name of the object **example** in the Console, and now all 25 rows of data are listed.

```
> example <- read.csv(file.choose(), header = TRUE)
> example
   ID Gender    Treatment Test1 Test2
1   1   Male      Control    98    32
2   2 Female Experimental    87    33
3   3 Female      Control    89    54
4   4 Female      Control    88    44
5   5   Male Experimental    76    64
6   6   Male      Control    68    54
7   7 Female      Control    78    44
8   8 Female Experimental    98    32
9   9 Female Experimental    93    64
10 10   Male Experimental    76    37
11 11 Female      Control    75    43
12 12 Female      Control    65    56
13 13   Male      Control    76    78
14 14 Female      Control    78    99
15 15 Female      Control    89    87
16 16 Female Experimental    81    56
17 17   Male      Control    78    78
18 18 Female      Control    83    56
19 19   Male      Control    88    67
20 20 Female      Control    90    88
21 21   Male      Control    93    81
22 22   Male Experimental    89    93
23 23 Female Experimental    86    87
24 24   Male      Control    77    80
25 25   Male      Control    89    99
>
```

Remember to save your files in a location where you can find them. Label your directory clearly so that the path is easily identifiable. Try creating a folder under Documents. R looks there first if you launch RStudio by clicking on the RStudio icon on your computer.

OOPS! HOW DO YOU CORRECT CONSOLE ERRORS?

More easily than you think, and there are several ways.

The first way is to use the up arrow key ↑ on your keyboard and scroll through the previous commands you have entered to find the command line you want to edit. You press the up arrow key, and the previous command will appear in the Console. You can then simply edit it by moving the insertion point and making a correction. You can use the down arrow key ↓ to scroll your way back.

The second way is to go to the History pane, find the command (or commands) you want to edit, and then double-click on it (or them) and it (or they) will appear in the Console. Or, yet a third way, highlight the command you want to restore to the Console and click the To Console button on the History tab. Voilà—the line appears in the Console and is ready for editing.

There are some very cool things about RStudio, and one of them is the Tab Completion feature that works like this. As you enter a command, RStudio guesses what you want to do next, so when we entered the *sqrt* and an open parenthesis like this (, RStudio came back with

```
sqrt()
```

and then if you press the Tab key again, you will see this next to the RStudio prompt:

```
sqrt(x = )
```

as if it knew that the next entry was the value of x, for which we wanted to find the square root.

As you can see in Figure 3.7, for the sqrt function, RStudio provides a drop-down menu of possibilities, including the name of the environment where the objects are located and more. Even better, as you can see, it also defines what the items in the drop-down list include. In fact, when you use a function in RStudio, you'll get this drop-down menu and as much autocompletion as RStudio can figure out, including names of files that you may have used before. So, if we enter

```
> data
```

and press the Tab key, RStudio will provide us with a list of all objects that start with the characters "data." Very helpful.

FIGURE 3.7 ● Using the Tab Completion feature in RStudio.

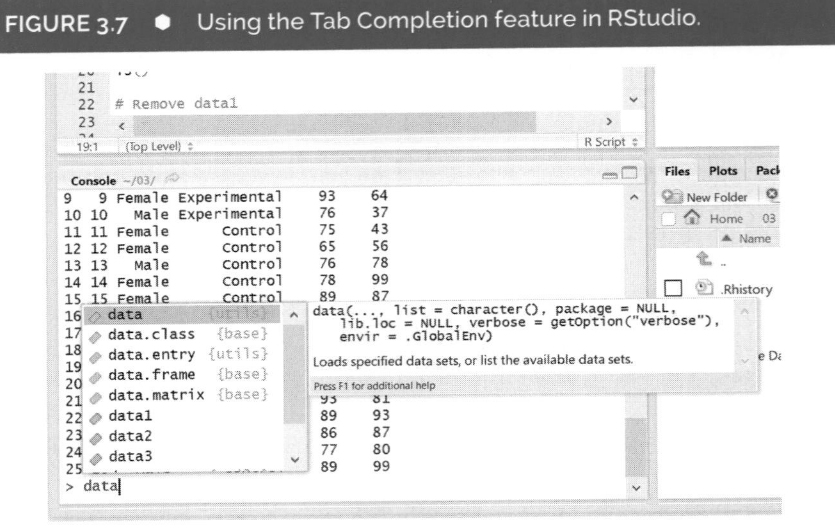

POINTING AND CLICKING TO OPEN A DATA SET

As if the previous command using file.choose was not easy enough, here's an even easier way and right out of Windows point and click.

To read a data set into RStudio, follow these steps:

1. File → Import Dataset → From Text (readr) and you will see the Import Text Data dialog box as shown in Figure 3.8. Remember, all the files we deal with in *Statistics for People Who (Think They) Hate Statistics Using R* are saved as .csv values and are available to you at edge.sagepub.com/salkindshaw.

FIGURE 3.8 ● The Import Text Data dialog box.

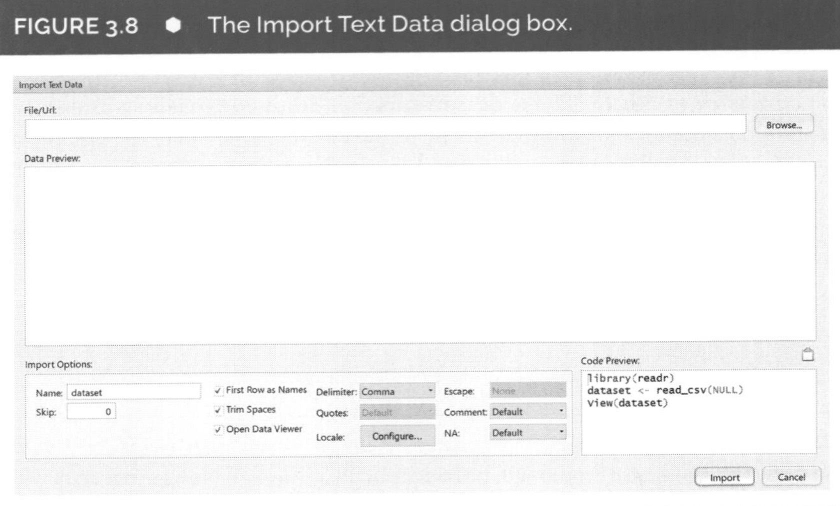

Text or CSV?

The dialog box for importing is named "Import Text Data" instead of "CSV Data" because .csv data are considered text data because they can be read and understood by any text editor. Now you can sleep without wondering about this.

2. Click the Browse button and locate the .csv file you want to read into RStudio. In this example, it was example.csv.
3. Double-click on the name of the .csv file and it will appear in the Import Text Data dialog box as you see in Figure 3.9. And note that in this dialog box, you have many options open to you, such as whether the first row is to be used as names and the name of the file, among others. And how did R name the object it is going to create?

FIGURE 3.9 ● The file imported in the RStudio dialog box.

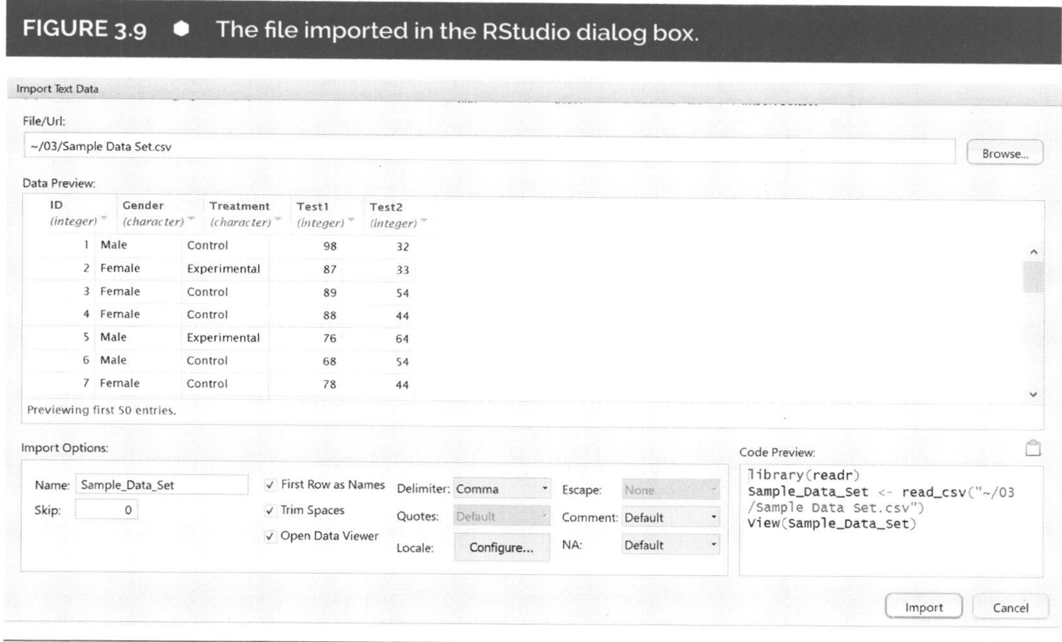

R cannot easily handle spaces, so the file name Sample data set.csv was used to create an object called `Sample_data_set` after import.

4. Click the Import button and it will be automatically read into RStudio, as you can see in the Syntax pane in Figure 3.10 ready for commands.

FIGURE 3.10 ● Importing a data set into RStudio.

Ch3.R × Sample_Data_Set ×

Filter

	ID	Gender	Treatment	Test1	Test2
1	1	Male	Control	98	32
2	2	Female	Experimental	87	33
3	3	Female	Control	89	54
4	4	Female	Control	88	44
5	5	Male	Experimental	76	64
6	6	Male	Control	68	54
7	7	Female	Control	78	44
8	8	Female	Experimental	98	32

Showing 1 to 9 of 25 entries

Sorting in RStudio

Now that you have the data set shown in the Syntax pane (the upper left pane), you can sort on any of the columns by clicking the ▲ or ▼ symbol at the top of the column next to the column headers.

COMPUTING SOME STATISTICS

Here's a grand finale to this chapter—just a touch into the world of computing simple statistics using RStudio. This kind of activity is what we will be doing for many chapters to come, but here's a preview, and once you can do these, you can do anything in the book.

Computing Some Simple Descriptive Statistics

The first step in most analyses is just getting a broad overview of what's going on in a data set. And, the data set that we will use as an example here is `example`, the one that we fooled around with earlier in this chapter. We'll be using the `summary()` function.

To see the basics about any data set, follow these steps:

1. At the RStudio prompt, type the following.

```
> summary(example)
```

2. Press the Enter or Return key.

In the R Console, it should look something like this:

```
> summary(example)
      ID          Gender            Treatment          Test1
Min.   : 1   Female:14   Control      :17   Min.   :65.00
1st Qu.: 7   Male  :11   Experimental: 8   1st Qu.:77.00
Median :13                                  Median :86.00
Mean   :13                                  Mean   :83.52
3rd Qu.:19                                  3rd Qu.:89.00
Max.   :25                                  Max.   :98.00
    Test2
Min.   :32.00
1st Qu.:44.00
Median :64.00
Mean   :64.24
3rd Qu.:81.00
Max.   :99.00
>
```

And as you can see, you get a nice neat summary of what the data set looks like, including lots of descriptive statistics (see the next two chapters for more about these) such as the mean and the median. Unfortunately, we also received the average ID, a value that really has no meaning, but R saw the first variable as a number and automatically did the calculations for us.

Wow . . . All Those Packages

There are hundreds of R packages out there, many of which will compute simple descriptive statistics, and each package has its own way of reporting the average. For example, in some RStudio packages, if you type `mean("name of some data set")`, you'll get the average of that data set. In other packages, `summary` does the trick. So, `summary()` or `mean()` provides similar information (presented differently). It's just a matter of what packages have been made available and what functions are being used.

Computing a Correlation Coefficient (Your First Time!)

And to get just the slightest bit fancier, here comes another type of statistic you will learn a great deal about in Chapters 7 and 17—the correlation coefficient. No need to understand the statistic in any great detail now, but using the command `cor()` to calculate correlation illustrates nicely how easy it is to compute in RStudio.

To compute a simple correlation coefficient, follow these steps:

1. Enter the following function (the text following >) at the RStudio prompt > and then press the Enter or Return key.

```
> cor(data1, data2)
[1] 0.1842457
>
```

You will see the simple correlation coefficient (.18) as shown in output. No worries about interpreting and such for now—just get the idea that these outcomes are pretty easy to create using RStudio.

Creating a Plot

Finally, for the end of this chapter, we'll use the `plot()` command to create a simple plot of data1 and data2 (both of which should be active data sets, and if not, just return to the History tab to find them, double-click on them to enter them into the Console, or just retype them).

To create a plot of two variables, follow these steps:

1. Enter the following function at the RStudio prompt > and then press the Enter or Return key.

```
> plot(data1, data2)
>
```

You can see the results in Figure 3.11, along with both the *x*- and *y*-axes being labeled using the names of the data set. This kind of simple command should increase your confidence that you can master enough of RStudio to be successful.

FIGURE 3.11 ● A simple plot of two variables named data1 and data2.

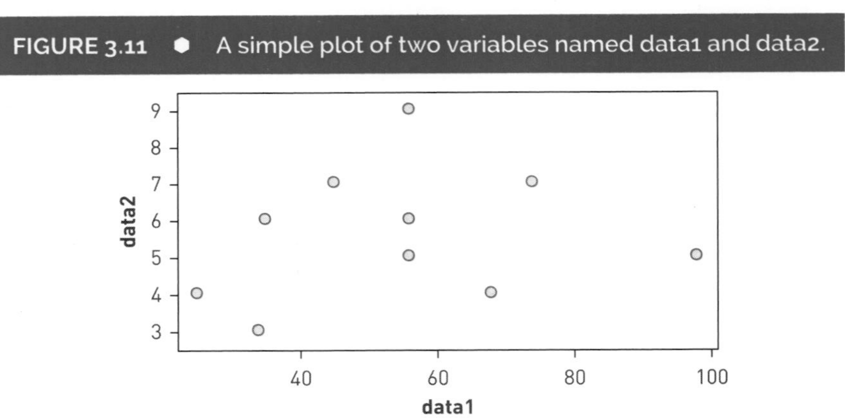

TEN IMPORTANT THINGS TO REMEMBER ABOUT R AND RSTUDIO (BUT NOT NECESSARILY IN ORDER OF IMPORTANCE)

Anyone new to R and RStudio is going to find that R can drive them nuts because it is easy to make "silly" errors. So, here are 10 things that you should look for when working in R and RStudio that will help make the drive (being nuts) a bit longer.

1. At the end of any R or RStudio command, always press the Enter or Return key.
2. Spelling really does count. If a command does not work, checking the spelling is the first thing to do.
3. Case really does count. If a command does not work, checking that the case is correct is the second thing to do.
4. In R and RStudio commands, spaces don't count, so no worries. But they very much count in the names that you assign to objects—there you can't have spaces.
5. Use the History tab to recall what you have already done and, if necessary, modify the command until the command works.
6. R and RStudio use the same commands.
7. To find out what packages are installed in R, use the `search()` command.
8. Always be sure you have the latest versions of R and RStudio installed.
9. Packages contain functions.
10. Use the up and down arrows to scroll through previous commands and the Tab key to complete a functions argument.

Whew. . . .

Summary

Well, congratulations are in order again.

You should now have sufficient familiarity with R and RStudio to use them as tools in learning about the basics of statistics and statistical analyses. Chapter 3 focuses on RStudio and how it can be used to manipulate data and perform some simple analyses. And, in Chapter 4, we will begin to talk in more depth about descriptive analyses and how you can get a good overall picture of what the data that you are working with look like. Stay the course, do the exercises, work with a buddy, and don't fall behind—all of which will help ensure success.

Time to Practice

1. What are the four panes in RStudio, and what is their function?
2. Which tab and in which pane would you click to see past commands that have been entered in the RStudio console?
3. Enter, and assign a name to, the following simple data set in RStudio.

513, 545, 354, 675, 873

- What is the RStudio command that you would use?
- List the objects in the workspace using the `ls()` function.
- Using the summary command, produce a summary of the data.

4. Read in Chapter 3 Data Set 1 (ch3ds1.csv) and name it ch3ds1. Now produce a summary of that data set.

Student Study Site

Get the tools you need to sharpen your study skills! Visit **edge.sagepub.com/salkindshaw** to access practice quizzes and eFlashcards, watch R tutorial videos, and download data sets!

ΣIGMA FREUD AND DESCRIPTIVE STATISTICS

PART III

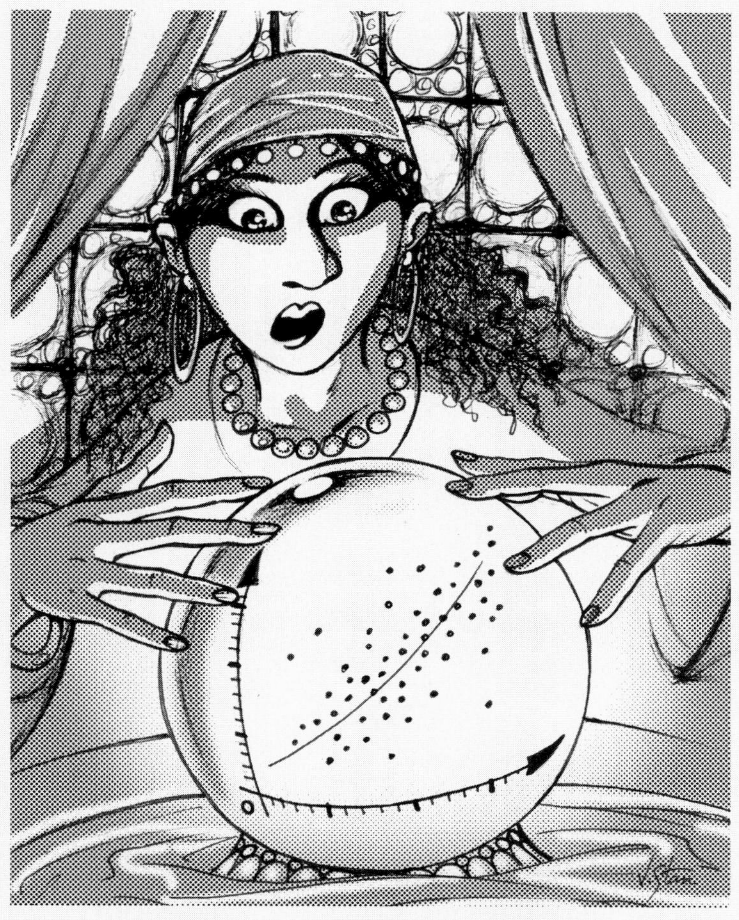

"Yes, it's all becoming clear."

One of the things that Sigmund Freud, the founder of psychoanalysis, did quite well was to observe and describe the nature of his patients' conditions. An astute observer, he used his skills to develop the first systematic and comprehensive theory of personality. Regardless of what you may think about the validity of his ideas, he was a good scientist.

Back in the early 20th century, courses in statistics (like the one you are taking) were not offered as part of undergraduate or graduate curricula. The field was relatively new, and the nature of scientific explorations did not demand the precision that this set of tools brings to the scientific arena.

But things have changed. Now, in almost any endeavor, numbers count (as Francis Galton, the inventor of correlation and a first cousin to Charles Darwin, said as well). This section of *Statistics for People Who (Think They) Hate Statistics Using R* is devoted to understanding how we can use statistics to describe an outcome and better understand it, once the information about the outcome is organized.

Chapter 4 discusses measures of central tendency, how computing one of several different types of averages gives you the one best data point that represents a set of scores and when to use what. Chapter 5 completes the coverage of tools we need to fully describe a set of data points in its discussion of variability, including the standard deviation and variance. When you get to Chapter 6, you will be ready to learn how distributions, or sets of scores, differ from one another and what this difference means. Chapter 7 deals with the nature of relationships between variables—namely, correlations. And finally, Chapter 8 introduces you to the importance of reliability and validity when we are describing some of the qualities of effective measurement tools.

When you finish Part III, you'll be in excellent shape to start understanding the role that probability and inference play in the social, behavioral, and other sciences.

COMPUTING AND UNDERSTANDING AVERAGES

Means to an End

Difficulty Scale ☺ ☺ ☺ ☺
(moderately easy)

WHAT YOU WILL LEARN IN THIS CHAPTER

- ✦ Understanding measures of central tendency
- ✦ Computing the mean for a set of scores
- ✦ Computing the median for a set of scores
- ✦ Computing the mode for a set of scores
- ✦ Understanding and applying scales or levels of measurement
- ✦ Selecting a measure of central tendency

You've been very patient, and now it's finally time to get started working with some real, live data. That's exactly what you'll do in this chapter. Once data are collected, a usual first step is to organize the information using simple indexes to describe the data. The easiest way to do this is through computing an average, of which there are several different types.

An **average** is the one value that best represents an entire group of scores. It doesn't matter whether the group of scores is the number correct on a spelling test for 30 fifth graders or the batting percentage of each of the New York Yankees (which, by the way, was not very good during the 2015 season) or the number of people who registered as Democrats or Republicans for the upcoming elections. In all of these examples, groups of data can be summarized using an average. You can also think of an average as the "middle" space or as a fulcrum on a seesaw. It's the point where all the values in a set of values are balanced.

Averages, also called **measures of central tendency**, come in three flavors: the mean, the median, and the mode. Each provides you with a different type of information about a distribution of scores and is simple to compute and interpret.

COMPUTING THE MEAN

The **mean** is the most common type of average that is computed. It is simply the sum of all the values in a group, divided by the number of values in that group. So, if you had the spelling scores for 30 fifth graders, you would simply add up all the scores to get a total and then divide by the number of students, which is 30.

The formula for computing the mean is shown in Formula 4.1.

$$\bar{X} = \frac{\Sigma X}{n}, \tag{4.1}$$

where

- the letter *X* with a line above it (also sometimes called "*X* bar") is the mean value of the group of scores or the mean;
- the Σ, or the Greek letter sigma, is the summation sign, which tells you to add together whatever follows it to obtain a total or sum;
- the *X* is each individual score in the group of scores; and
- the *n* is the size of the sample from which you are computing the mean.

To compute the mean, follow these steps:

1. List the entire set of values in one or more columns. These are all the *X*s.
2. Add all of the values together to obtain the total.
3. Divide the total by the number of values.

For example, if you needed to compute the average number of shoppers at three different locations, you would compute a mean for that value.

Location	Number of Annual Customers
Lanham Park Store	2,150
Williamsburg Store	1,534
Downtown Store	3,564

The mean or average number of shoppers in each store is 2,416. Formula 4.2 shows how this average was computed using the formula you saw in Formula 4.1:

$$\bar{X} = \frac{\sum X}{n} = \frac{2{,}150 + 1{,}534 + 3{,}564}{3} = \frac{7{,}248}{3} = 2{,}416. \tag{4.2}$$

Or, if you needed to compute the average number of students in kindergarten through Grade 6, you would follow the same procedure.

Grade	Number of Students
Kindergarten	18
1	21
2	24
3	23
4	22
5	24
6	25

The mean or average number of students in each class is 22.43. Formula 4.3 shows how this average was computed using the formula you saw in Formula 4.1:

$$\bar{X} = \frac{\sum X}{n} = \frac{18 + 21 + 24 + 23 + 22 + 24 + 25}{7} = \frac{157}{7} = 22.43. \tag{4.3}$$

See, we told you it was easy. No big deal. Let's repeat our two computations in R starting with the average number of customers.

```
> (2150 + 1534 + 3564)/3
[1] 2416
>
```

Let's break this down.

- `>`—the first character in a new line in the R Console.
- `(2150 + 1534 + 3564)/3`—we added the customer counts together and divided the total by the number of locations, 3.
- `[1] 2416`—the mean number of customers, also called the average.

Repeating this process to compute the mean of students across classrooms, the syntax in R is

```
> (18 + 21 + 24 + 23 + 22 + 24 + 25)/7
[1] 22.42857
>
```

Note that the average number of customers was a whole number, 2,416, but the average number of students did not divide evenly, so the answer was 22.42857. When we reported the average number of students, calculated with a calculator, we rounded to the second decimal place, giving us an average of 22.43 students per classroom. Like using a calculator, R will report numbers past two decimal places, so you will round to the number appropriate for your field. Psychologists follow reporting guidelines for the American Psychological Association (APA) in the APA style guide and round to two decimal places. Ask your instructor what is common practice in her or his field.

- The mean is sometimes represented by the letter *M* and is also called the typical or average score. If you are reading another statistics book or a research report and you see something like $M = 45.87$, it probably means that the mean is equal to 45.87.
- In the formula, a small *n* represents the sample size for which the mean is being computed. A large *N* (← like this) would represent the population size. In some books and in some journal articles, no distinction is made between the two.
- In the classroom example, we had a sample of elementary school classrooms. If we calculate a mean for all elementary school classrooms across the country, then we are computing the mean for the population of elementary classrooms in the country.
- The sample mean is the measure of central tendency that most accurately reflects the population mean.
- The mean is like the fulcrum on a seesaw. It's the centermost point where all the values on one side of the mean are equal in weight to all the values on the other side of the mean.
- Finally, for better or worse, the mean is very sensitive to extreme scores. An extreme score can pull the mean in one or the other direction and make it less representative of the set of scores and less useful as a measure of central tendency. This, of course, all depends on the values for which the mean is being computed. And, if you have extreme scores and the mean won't work as well as you want, we have a solution! More about that later.

The mean is also referred to as the **arithmetic mean**, and there are other types of means that you may read about, such as the harmonic mean. Those are used in special circumstances and need not concern you here. And if you want to be technical about it, the arithmetic mean (which is the one that we have discussed up to now) is also defined as the point about which the sum of the deviations is equal to zero (whew!). So, if you have scores like 3, 4, and 5 (whose mean is 4), the sum of the deviations about the mean (−1, 0, and +1) is 0.

Remember that the word *average* means only the one measure that best represents a set of scores and that there are many different types of averages. Which type of average you use depends on the question that you are asking and the type of data that you are trying to summarize. This is a levels-of-measurement issue, which we will cover later in this chapter when we talk about when to use which measure.

Computing a Weighted Mean

You've just seen an example of how to compute a simple mean. But there may be situations when you have the occurrence of more than one value and you want to compute a weighted mean. A weighted mean can be easily computed by multiplying the value by the frequency of its occurrence, adding the total of all the products, and then dividing by the total number of occurrences. It beats adding up every individual data point.

To compute a weighted mean, follow these steps:

1. List all the values in the sample for which the mean is being computed, such as those shown in the column labeled "Value" (the value of *X*) in the following table.
2. List the frequency with which each value occurs.
3. Multiply the value by the frequency, as shown in the third column.
4. Sum all the values in the Value × Frequency column.
5. Divide by the total frequency.

For example, here's a table that organizes the values and frequencies in a flying proficiency test for 100 airline pilots.

Value	Frequency	Value × Frequency
97	4	388
94	11	1,034
92	12	1,104

(Continued)

(Continued)

Value	Frequency	Value × Frequency
91	21	1,911
90	30	2,700
89	12	1,068
78	9	702
60 (Don't fly with this guy.)	1	60
Total	100	8,967

The weighted mean is 8,967/100, or 89.67. Computing the mean this way is much easier than entering 100 different scores into your calculator or computer program.

In basic statistics, an important distinction is made between those values associated with samples (a part of a population) and those associated with populations. To do this, statisticians use the following conventions. For a sample statistic (such as the mean of a sample), Roman letters are used. For a population parameter (such as the mean of a population), Greek letters are used. For example, the mean for the spelling score for a sample of 100 fifth graders is represented as $\bar{X}_5$, whereas the mean for the spelling score for the entire population of fifth graders is represented, using the Greek letter mu, as μ_5.

COMPUTING THE MEDIAN

The median is also a measure of central tendency but of a very different kind. The **median** is defined as the midpoint in a set of scores. It's the point at which one half, or 50%, of the scores fall above and one half, or 50%, fall below. It's got some special qualities that we will talk about later in this section, but for now, let's concentrate on how it is computed. There's no standard formula for computing the median.

To compute the median, follow these steps:

1. List the values in order, from either highest to lowest or lowest to highest.
2. Find the middle-most score. That's the median.

For example, here are the incomes from five different households:

$135,456

$25,500

$32,456

$54,365

$37,668

Here is the list ordered from highest to lowest:

$135,456

$54,365

$37,668

$32,456

$25,500

There are five values. The middle-most value is $37,668, and that's the median.

Now, what if the number of values is even? Let's add a value ($34,500) to the list so there are six income levels. Here they are sorted with the largest value first:

$135,456

$54,365

$37,668

$34,500

$32,456

$25,500

When there are an even number of values, the median is simply the mean of the two middle values. In this case, the middle two cases are $34,500 and $37,668. The mean of those two values is $36,084. That's the median for that set of six values.

What if the two middle-most values are the same, such as in the following set of data?

$45,678

$25,567

$25,567

$13,234

Then the median is same as both of those middle-most values. In this example, it's $25,567.

If we had a series of values that was the number of days spent in rehabilitation for a sports-related injury for seven different patients, the numbers might look like this:

43

34

32

12

51

6

27

As we did before, we can order the values (51, 43, 34, 32, 27, 12, 6) and then select the middle value as the median, which in this case is 32. So, the median number of days spent in rehab is 32.

Placing these numbers in order is straightforward when you have fewer than 10 numbers. Once you start dealing with data sets with more observations, like some used later in this chapter and the book, R can easily reorder your data. Let R sort your numbers from smallest to largest like this:

```
> sort(c(43, 34, 32, 12, 51, 6, 27))
[1] 6 12 27 32 34 43 51
>
```

The `sort()` function expects a vector of values, so we used the `c()` function to put all of our numbers together in a vector. What did we get back? A reordered vector of seven numbers, in which we can easily see the median is 32 because it is the middle value.

If you know about medians, you should also know about **percentile points**. Percentile points are used to define the percentage of cases equal to and below a certain point in a distribution or set of scores. For example, if a score is "at the 75th percentile," it means that the score is at or above 75% of the other scores in the distribution. The median is also known as the 50th percentile, because it's the point below which 50% of the cases in the distribution fall. Other percentiles are useful as well, such as the 25th percentile, often called Q_1, and the 75th percentile, referred to as Q_3. So what's Q_2? The median, of course.

Here comes the answer to the question you've probably had in the back of your mind since we started talking about the median. Why use the median instead of the mean?

For one very good reason. The median is unaffected by extreme scores, whereas the mean is affected by extreme values.

When you have a set of scores in which one or more scores are extreme, the median better represents the centermost value of that set of scores than any other measure of central tendency. Yes, even better than the mean.

What do we mean by *extreme?* It's probably easiest to think of an extreme score as one that is very different from the group to which it belongs. For example, consider the list of five incomes that we worked with earlier (shown again here):

$135,456

$54,365

$37,668

$32,456

$25,500

The value $135,456 is more different from the other four than is any other value in the set. We would consider that an extreme score.

The best way to illustrate how useful the median is as a measure of central tendency is to compute both the mean and the median for a set of data that contains one or more extreme scores and then compare them to see which one best represents the group. Here goes.

The mean of the set of five scores you see above is the sum of the set of five divided by 5, which turns out to be $57,089. On the other hand, the median for this set of five scores is $37,668. Which is more representative of the group? The value $37,668, because it clearly lies more in the middle of the group, and we like to think about "the average" (in this case, we are using the median as a measure of central tendency) as being representative or assuming a central position. In fact, the mean value of $57,089 falls above the fourth highest value ($54,365) and is not very central or representative of the distribution.

It's for this reason that certain social and economic indicators (often involving income) are reported using a median as a measure of central tendency—"The median income of the average American family is . . ."—rather than using the mean to summarize the values. There are just too many extreme scores that would **skew**, or significantly distort, what is actually a central point in the set or distribution of scores.

Another way to identify when the median might be more useful than the mean is to create a picture. We will spend more time in Chapter 6 talking about visualizing data and how to personalize those graphics, but let's look at one option now. The R function we are going to use is `hist()`. Let's input the numbers from the first income example to create a histogram like Figure 4.1.

```
> hist(c(135456, 25500, 32456, 54365, 37668))
>
```

FIGURE 4.1 ● Histogram of the vector of income numbers.

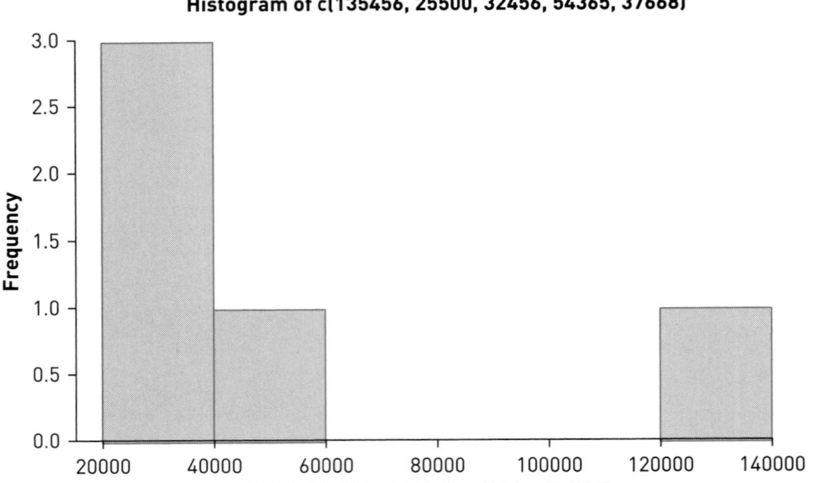

R created a title displayed across the top of the figure, "`Histogram of c(135456, 25500, 32456, 54365, 37668)`." It is not necessarily the best title in the world, but R lets us know what we are looking at. The *x*-axis ranges from 20,000 to 140,000 in 20,000 increments. R also described the vector of numbers used as input for the function. The *y*-axis shows the frequency (aka count) of observations in each block. What is most interesting about this histogram? The gap. Nothing is happening between 60,000 and 120,000, and that tells you the value on the far right is very different from the other items. Therefore, the median is probably a better measure of central tendency to use with these data.

With only six numbers, we can easily tell that 135,456 is extreme without the histogram. When someone gives you some data with 50, 100, or more values, the histogram can be quite helpful!

You learned earlier that sometimes the mean is represented by the capital letter *M* instead of $\bar{X}$. Well, other symbols are used for the median as well. We like the letter *M,* but some people confuse it with the mean, so they use *Med* or *Mdn* for median. Don't let that throw you—just remember what the median is and what it represents, and you'll have no trouble adapting to different symbols.

Here are some interesting and important things to remember about the median.

- Although the mean is the middle point of a set of values, the median is the middle point of a set of cases.
- Because the median deals with how many cases there are and not the values of those cases, extreme scores (sometimes called outliers) don't overly influence the median.

COMPUTING THE MODE

The third and last measure of central tendency that we'll cover, the mode, is the most general and least precise measure of central tendency, but it plays a very important part in understanding the characteristics of a set of scores. The **mode** is the value that occurs most frequently. There is no formula for computing the mode.

To compute the mode, follow these steps:

1. List all the values in a distribution but list each value only once.
2. Tally the number of times that each value occurs.
3. The value that occurs most often is the mode.

For example, an examination of the political party affiliation of 300 people might result in the following distribution of scores.

Party Affiliation	Number or Frequency
Democrats	90
Republicans	70
Independents	140

The mode is the value that occurs most frequently, which in the preceding example is Independents. That's the mode for this distribution.

If we were looking at the modal response on a 100-item multiple-choice test, we might find that A was chosen more frequently than any other choice. The data might look like this.

Response Choices Selected	A	B	C	D
Number of times	57	20	12	11

On this 100-item multiple-choice test where each item has four choices (A, B, C, and D), A was the answer selected 57 times. It's the modal response.

Want to know the easiest and most commonly made mistake when computing the mode? It's selecting the number of *times* a category occurs, rather than the *label* of the category itself. Instead of the mode being Independents (in our first example above), it's easy for someone to mistakenly conclude the mode is 140. Why? Because he or she is looking at the number of times the value occurred, not the value that occurred most often! This is a simple error to make, so be on your toes when you are asked about these things.

Apple Pie à la Bimodal

If every value in a distribution contains the same number of occurrences, then there really isn't a single mode. But if more than one value appears with equal frequency, the distribution is multimodal. The set of scores can be bimodal (with two modes), as the following set of data using pie flavors illustrates.

Slices of Pie Flavors	Number or Frequency
Apple	28
Cherry	17
Pecan	45
Pumpkin	28

In the above example, the distribution is bimodal because the frequency of the values of apple and pumpkin occurs equally. You can even have a bimodal distribution when the modes are relatively close together but not exactly the same, such as 45 slices of apple pie and 44 slices of pumpkin pie. The question becomes, "How much does one class of occurrences stand apart from another?"

Can you have a trimodal distribution? Sure—where three values have the same frequency. It's unlikely, especially when you are dealing with a large set of **data points**, or observations, but certainly possible. The real answer to the above stand-apart question is that categories have to be mutually exclusive—in a restaurant, you cannot order a slice of pie and get both apple and cherry pie, unless the chef created a new pie flavor that combines the two. In that case, you have a new flavor category to count.

WHEN TO USE WHAT MEASURE OF CENTRAL TENDENCY (AND ALL YOU NEED TO KNOW ABOUT SCALES OF MEASUREMENT FOR NOW)

Which measure of central tendency you use depends on certain characteristics of the data you are working with—specifically the **scale of measurement** at which those data occur. And that scale or level dictates the specific measure of central tendency you will use.

But let's step back for just a minute and make sure that we have some vocabulary straight, beginning with the idea of what measurement is.

Measurement is the assignment of values to outcomes following a set of rules—simple. The results are the different scales we'll define in a moment, and an outcome is anything we are interested in measuring, such as hair color, gender, test score, or height.

These scales of measurement, or rules, are the particular levels at which outcomes are observed. Each level has a particular set of characteristics, and scales of measurement come in four flavors (there are four types): nominal, ordinal, interval, and ratio.

Let's move on to a brief discussion and examples of the four scales of measurement and then discuss how these levels of scales fit with the different measures of central tendency discussed earlier.

A Rose by Any Other Name: The Nominal Level of Measurement

The **nominal level of measurement** is defined by the characteristics of an outcome that fit into one and only one class or category. For example, sex can be a nominal variable (female, male, and other), as can ethnicity (Caucasian or African American), as can political affiliation (Republican, Democrat, or Independent). Nominal-level variables are "names" (*nominal* in Latin), and the nominal level can be the least precise level of measurement. Nominal levels of measurement have categories that are mutually exclusive; for example, political affiliation cannot be both Republican and Democrat. Another commonly used word to describe a nominal variable is categorical.

Any Order Is Fine With Me: The Ordinal Level of Measurement

The *ord* in **ordinal level of measurement** stands for *order,* and the characteristic of things being measured here is that they are ordered. The perfect example is a rank of candidates for a job. If we know that Amy is ranked #1, Joe is ranked #2, and Hannah is ranked #3, then this is an ordinal arrangement. We have no idea how much higher on this scale Amy is relative to Joe than Joe is relative to Hannah. We just know that it's "better" to be #1 than #2 or #3, but not by how much.

1 + 1 = 2: The Interval Level of Measurement

Now we're getting somewhere. When we talk about the **interval level of measurement**, a test or an assessment tool is based on some underlying continuum such that we can talk about how much more a higher performance is than a lesser one. For example, if you get 10 words correct on a vocabulary test, that is twice as many as getting 5 words correct. A distinguishing characteristic of interval-level scales is that the intervals or spaces or points along the scale are equal to one another. Ten words correct is 2 more than 8 correct, which is 3 more than 5 correct.

Can Anyone Have Nothing of Anything? The Ratio Level of Measurement

Well, here's a little conundrum for you. An assessment tool at the **ratio level of measurement** is characterized by the presence of an absolute zero on the scale. What that zero means is the absence of any of the trait that is being measured. The conundrum? Are there outcomes we measure where it is possible to have nothing of what is being measured? In some disciplines, that can be the case. For example, in the physical and biological sciences, you can have the absence of a characteristic, such as absolute zero (no molecular movement) or zero light. In the social and behavioral sciences, it's a bit harder. Even if you score zero on that spelling test or miss every item of an IQ test (in Russian), that does not mean that you have no spelling ability or no intelligence, right? So, the chance of 0 occurring in real life and in your data may be quite small, but we are talking about the theoretical possibility of a 0 or even values below 0.

In Sum . . .

These scales of measurement, or rules, represent particular levels at which outcomes are measured. And, in sum, we can say the following:

- Any outcome can be assigned to one of four scales of measurement.
- Scales of measurement have an order, from the least precise being nominal to the most precise being ratio.
- The "higher up" the scale of measurement, the more precise the data being collected, and the more detailed and informative the data are. It may be enough to know that some people are rich and some poor (and that's a nominal or categorical distinction), but it's much better to know exactly how much money they make (ratio). We can always make the "rich" versus "poor" distinction if we want to once we have all the information.
- Finally, the more precise scales contain all the qualities of the scales below them; for example, the interval scale includes the characteristics of the ordinal and nominal scales. If you know that the Cubs' batting average is .350, you know it is better than that of the Tigers (who hit .250) by 100 points, but you also know that the Cubs are better than the Tigers (but not by how much) and that the Cubs are different from the Tigers (but there's no direction to the difference).

Okay, we've defined levels of measurement, discussed three different measures of central tendency, and given you fairly clear examples of each. But the most important question remains unanswered: "When do you use which measure?"

In general, which measure of central tendency you use depends on the type of data that you are describing, which in turn means at what level of measurement the data occur. Unquestionably, a measure of central tendency for qualitative, categorical, or nominal data (such as racial group, eye color, income bracket, voting preference, and neighborhood location) can be described using only the mode.

For example, you can't be interested in the most central measure that describes which political affiliation is most predominant in a group and use the mean—what in the world could you conclude, that everyone is half Republican? Rather, saying that out of 300 people, almost half (140) are Independent seems to be the best way to describe the value of this variable. In general, the median and mean are best used with quantitative data, such as height, income level in dollars (not categories), age, test score, reaction time, and number of hours completed toward a degree.

It's also fair to say that the mean is a more precise measure than the median and that the median is a more precise measure than the mode. This means that all other things being equal, use the mean, and indeed, the mean is the most often used measure of central tendency. However, we do have occasions when the mean would not be appropriate as a measure of central tendency—for example, when we have categorical or nominal data, such as hospitalized versus nonhospitalized people. Then we use the mode.

So, here is a set of three guidelines that may be of some help. And remember, there can always be exceptions.

1. Use the mode when the data are categorical in nature and values can fit into only one class, such as hair color, political affiliation, neighborhood location, and religion. When this is the case, these categories are called mutually exclusive.
2. Use the median when you have extreme scores and you don't want to distort the average (computed as the mean), such as when the variable of interest is income expressed in dollars.
3. Finally, use the mean when you have data that do not include extreme scores and are not categorical, such as the numerical score on a test or the number of seconds it takes to swim 50 yards.

USING THE COMPUTER TO COMPUTE DESCRIPTIVE STATISTICS

Visit **edge.sagepub .com/salkindshaw** to watch an R tutorial video on this topic.

If you haven't already, now would be a good time to go back to Chapter 2 to install R and RStudio and Chapter 3 to start practicing with R. Then come back here.

Let's use R to compute some descriptive statistics. The data set we are using is Chapter 4 Data Set 1, named ch4ds1.csv. There is a method to our file names. Let's take a moment to decipher it.

- ch—shorthand for chapter
- 4—the number of the chapter that will use the data set
- ds—shorthand for data set
- 1—the first data set
- .csv—this file extension refers to comma separated values

R can import data from files that have spaces in the filename, but the process is simpler when the filename doesn't have spaces. So in the spirit of keeping things simple, we will use this file-naming convention throughout the book.

The file ch4ds1.csv is a set of 20 scores on a test of prejudice (also listed in Appendix C as Chapter 4 Data Set 1). All of the data sets are available in Appendix C and from the SAGE website **edge.sagepub.com/salkindshaw**. There is one variable in this data set:

Variable	Definition
Prejudice	The value on a test of prejudice as measured on a scale from 1 to 100

In R, we are going to look at one example of each measure of central tendency, using a combination of built-in functions to calculate the mean, and then look at the mean function itself. For median, we already looked at the sort function to put all items in a vector in order from smallest to largest. Now, we will look at the function that will do all of the work for us. Last, we will look at `mode()` and talk about why we get something unexpected. We will then look at another function that will simplify finding the mode.

But first, let's read in our data with the read.csv function.

```
> ch4ds1 <- read.csv(file.choose())
>
```

This command launches a dialog box. In this example, I have all of my Chapter 4 data sets in the same folder as my R syntax file. Putting everything for this chapter in the same folder saves time. We then selected ch4ds1.csv and hit Open. Next, let's look at the data set we imported. You can double-click on ch4ds1 in the Global Environment (top left). In the R Console, RStudio will now show this command:

```
> View(ch4ds1)
```

By clicking on the ch4ds1 object in the Global Environment, RStudio is prompted to send the `View()` function to the R Console.

Calculating the Mean

Earlier in the chapter, we used R to compute the mean much like you would with a calculator. Let's now use some built-in functions to fill in the blanks for Formula 4.1. Starting with the numerator—the sum of all *X*s—we will use `sum()` to add up the Prejudice scores.

```
> sum(ch4ds1$Prejudice)
[1] 1694
>
```

The sum function adds up all items in the object, in this case our vector of Prejudice scores. Our total is 1,694. For the denominator, we need to know how many scores we have. And R has a function for that!

```
> length(ch4ds1$Prejudice)
[1] 20
>
```

Filling in Formula 4.1, we will divide 1,694 by 20, which can be entered directly in the R Console, or you could put both functions on the same line.

```
> sum(ch4ds1$Prejudice) / length(ch4ds1$Prejudice)
[1] 84.7
>
```

R returns 84.7. Now let's use the built-in function, `mean()`, to quickly get our answer.

```
> mean(ch4ds1$Prejudice)
[1] 84.7
>
```

You can use R to calculate the mean by filling in the values for the formula, something we encourage as you are learning this simple formula, or go straight to the function to easily obtain the answer.

Finding the 50th Percentile: The Median

To find the middle score by hand, we can ask R to display all scores.

```
> ch4ds1$Prejudice
[1] 87 99 87 87 67 87 77 89 99 96 76 55 64 81 94 81 82 99 93 94
>
```

Not so helpful. We could sort these numbers automatically like we did several pages ago. Or, we can just use the built-in function, `median()`.

```
> median(ch4ds1$Prejudice)
[1] 87
>
```

Recall, because we have an even number of observations, R needed to find the middle two scores and calculate the mean of those two numbers. In this example, the 10th and 11th scores were both 87, so the median is simply 87.

A Rose by Any Other Name: The Nominal Level of Measurement

Try this command for mode:

```
> mode(ch4ds1$Prejudice)
```

This time, we didn't get what we expected. R told us that the mode is "numeric." The function `mode()` in R returns the type of object; in this case, the Prejudice vector contains numbers. But what we really want to know is the most frequent response. Let's use `summary()` and `as.factor()`.

```
> summary(as.factor(ch4ds1$Prejudice))
55 64 67 76 77 81 82 87 89 93 94 96 99
1  1  1  1  1  2  1  4  1  1  2  1  3
>
```

Starting with the vector:

- `ch4ds1$Prejudice`—the vector of scores
- `as.factor`—treat the vector of scores as a nominal vector. Up to now, we have been treating our scores like a ratio-level set of values.
- `summary`—summarize the object in the parentheses, in this case nominal Prejudice scores

By inspecting the results, we can see that one number occurred four times, more frequent than any other score. And that Prejudice score is 87. We can figure out the mode with our Prejudice scores, but the mode isn't really that helpful as a measure of central tendency. More useful is the mean or the median with our scores because of the level of our data.

R output can be full of information or just give you the basics. It all depends on the type of analysis that you are conducting. In the above examples, we have just the basics and, frankly, just what we need. Throughout *Statistics for People Who (Think They) Hate Statistics Using R,* you will be seeing output and then learning about what it means, but in some cases, discussing the entire collection of output information is far beyond the scope of the book. We'll focus on output that is directly related to what you learned in the chapter.

There are other ways to compute the central tendency:

Package	Function	What It Tells You
Base	summary	Minimum, 25th percentile, 50th percentile (median), mean, 75th percentile, and maximum

```
> summary(ch4ds1$Prejudice)
Min.  1st Qu.  Median  Mean  3rd Qu.  Max.
55.0   80.0     87.0   84.7   94.0    99.0
>
```

REAL-WORLD STATS

Few applications of descriptive statistics would make more sense than using them in a survey or poll, and there have been literally millions of such surveys (as in every U.S. presidential election). In an article, Roger Morrell and his colleagues examined Internet use patterns in 550 adults in several age groups, including middle aged (ages 40–59), young-old (ages 60–74), and old-old (ages 75–92). With a response rate of 71%, which is pretty good, they found a few very interesting (but not entirely unexpected) outcomes:

- There are distinct age and demographic differences among individuals who use the Internet.
- Middle-aged and older web users are similar in their use patterns.
- The two primary predictors for not using the Internet are lack of access to a computer and lack of knowledge about the Internet.
- Old-old adults have the least interest in using the Internet compared with middle-aged and young-old adults.
- The primary content areas in learning how to use the Internet are using electronic mail and accessing health information and information about traveling for pleasure.

This survey, which primarily used descriptive statistics to reach its conclusions, was done almost 20 years ago, and many, many things have changed since then. But the reason we are including it in this example of real-world statistics is that it is a good illustration of a historical anchor point that can be used for comparative purposes in future studies—a purpose for which descriptive statistics and such studies are often used.

Want to know more? Go online or go to the library and read . . .

Morrell, R. W., Mayhorn, C. B., & Bennett, J. (2000). A survey of world wide web use in middle-aged and older adults. *Human Factors, 42,* 175–182.

Summary

No matter how fancy schmancy your statistical techniques are, you will almost always start by simply describing what's there—hence the importance of understanding the simple notion of central tendency. From here, we go to another important descriptive construct: variability, or how different scores are from one another. That's what we'll explore in Chapter 5!

Time to Practice

1. By hand, compute the mean, median, and mode for the following set of 40 chemistry final scores.

93	85	99	77
94	99	86	76
95	99	97	84
91	89	77	87
97	83	80	98
75	94	81	85
78	92	89	94
76	94	96	94
90	79	80	92
77	86	83	81

2. Compute the mean, median, and mode for the following three sets of scores in Chapter 4 Data Set 2 (ch4ds2.csv). Do it by hand or R. Show your work, and if you use R, print out a copy of the output from the R Console.

Score 1	Score 2	Score 3
3	34	154
7	54	167
5	17	132
4	26	145
5	34	154
6	25	145
7	14	113
8	24	156
6	25	154
5	23	123

3. Compute the means for the following set of scores in Chapter 4 Data Set 3 (ch4ds3.csv) using R. Print out a copy of the output from the R Console.

Number of Beds (Infection Rate)	Infection Rate (per 1,000 Admissions)
234	1.7
214	2.4
165	3.1
436	5.6
432	4.9
342	5.3
276	5.6
187	1.2
512	3.3
553	4.1

4. You are the manager of a fast-food restaurant. Part of your job is to report to the boss at the end of each day which special is selling best. Use your vast knowledge of descriptive statistics and write one paragraph to let the boss know what happened today. Here are the data. Don't use R to compute important values; rather, do it by hand. Be sure to include a copy of your work.

Special	Number Sold	Cost
Huge Burger	20	$2.95
Baby Burger	18	$1.49
Chicken Littles	25	$3.50
Porker Burger	19	$2.95
Yummy Burger	17	$1.99
Coney Dog	20	$1.99
Total specials sold	119	

5. Imagine you are the CEO of a huge corporation and you are planning an expansion. You'd like your new store to post similar numbers as the other three that are in your empire. By hand, provide some idea of what you want the store's financial performance to look like.

(Continued)

(Continued)

And remember that you have to select whether to use the mean, the median, or the mode as an average. Good luck, young Jedi.

Average	Store 1	Store 2	Store 3	New Store
Sales (in thousands of dollars)	323.6	234.6	308.3	
Number of items purchased	3,454	5,645	4,565	
Number of visitors	4,534	6,765	6,654	

6. Here are ratings (on a scale from 1 through 5) for various Super Bowl party foods. You have to decide which food is rated highest (5 is a winner and 1 a loser). Decide what type of average you will use and why. Do this by hand or use R.

Snack Food	North Fans	East Fans	South Fans	West Fans
Loaded Nachos	4	4	5	4
Fruit Cup	2	1	2	1
Spicy Wings	4	3	3	3
Gargantuan Overstuffed Pizza	3	4	4	5
Beer Chicken	5	5	5	4

7. Under what conditions would you use the median rather than the mean as a measure of central tendency? Why? Provide an example of two situations in which the median might be more useful than the mean as a measure of central tendency.

8. Suppose you are working with a data set that has some very "different" (much larger or much smaller than the rest of the data) scores. What measure of central tendency would you use and why?

9. For this exercise, use the following set of 16 scores (ranked) that consists of income levels ranging from about $50,000 to about $200,000. What is the best measure of central tendency and why?

$199,999	$76,564
$98,789	$76,465
$90,878	$75,643
$87,678	$66,768
$87,245	$65,654
$83,675	$58,768
$77,876	$54,678
$77,743	$51,354

10. Use the data in Chapter 4 Data Set 4 (ch4ds4.csv) and, manually, compute the average attitude scores (with a score of 10 being positive and 1 being negative) for three groups (little experience, moderate experience, and lots of experience) of individuals' attitudes reflecting their experience with urban transportation.
11. Take a look at the following number of pie orders from the Lady Bird Diner and determine the average number of orders for each week.

Week	Chocolate Silk	Apple	Douglas County Pie
1	12	21	7
2	14	15	12
3	18	14	21
4	27	12	15

Student Study Site

Get the tools you need to sharpen your study skills! Visit **edge.sagepub.com/salkindshaw** to access practice quizzes and eFlashcards, watch R tutorial videos, and download data sets!

UNDERSTANDING VARIABILITY

Vive la Différence

Difficulty Scale ☺ ☺ ☺ ☺
(moderately easy, but not a cinch)

WHAT YOU WILL LEARN IN THIS CHAPTER

- ✦ Understanding the value of variability as a descriptive tool
- ✦ Computing the range
- ✦ Computing the standard deviation
- ✦ Computing the variance
- ✦ Understanding what the standard deviation and variance have in common—and how they are different

WHY UNDERSTANDING VARIABILITY IS IMPORTANT

In Chapter 4, you learned about different types of averages, what they mean, how they are computed, and when to use them. But when it comes to descriptive statistics and describing the characteristics of a distribution, averages are only half the story. The other half is measures of variability.

In the simplest of terms, **variability** reflects how scores differ from one another. For example, the following set of scores shows some variability:

7, 6, 3, 3, 1

The following set of scores has the same mean (4) but has less variability than the previous set:

3, 4, 4, 5, 4

The next set has no variability at all—the scores do not differ from one another—but it also has the same mean as the other two sets we just showed you.

4, 4, 4, 4, 4

Variability (also called spread or dispersion) can be thought of as a measure of how different scores are from one another. It's even more accurate (and maybe even easier) to think of variability as how different scores are from one particular score. And what "score" do you think that might be? Well, instead of comparing each score to every other score in a distribution, the one score that could be used as a comparison is—that's right—the mean. So, variability becomes a measure of how much each score in a group of scores differs from the mean. More about this in a moment.

Remember what you already know about computing averages—that an average (whether it is the mean, the median, or the mode) is a representative score of a set of scores. Now, add your new knowledge about variability—that it reflects how different scores are from one another. Each is an important descriptive statistic. Together, these two (average and variability) can be used to describe the characteristics of a distribution and show how distributions differ from one another.

Three measures of variability are commonly used to reflect the degree of variability, spread, or dispersion in a group of scores. These are the range, the standard deviation, and the variance. Let's take a closer look at each one and how each one is used.

Actually, how data points differ from one another is a central part of understanding and using basic statistics. But when it comes to differences between individuals and groups (a mainstay of most social and behavioral sciences), the whole concept of variability becomes really important. Sometimes it's called fluctuation, or lability, or error, or one of many other terms, but the fact is, variety is the spice of life, and what makes people different from one another also makes understanding them and their behavior all the more challenging (and interesting). Without variability either in a set of data or between individuals and groups, things are just boring.

COMPUTING THE RANGE

The **range** is the most general measure of variability. It gives you an idea of how far apart scores are from one another. The range is computed simply by subtracting the lowest score in a distribution from the highest score in the distribution.

In general, the formula for the range is

$$r = h - l, \tag{5.1}$$

where

- r is the range,
- h is the highest score in the data set, and
- l is the lowest score in the data set.

Take the following set of scores, for example (shown here in descending order):

98, 86, 77, 56, 48

In this example, 98 – 48 = 50. The range is 50. In a set of 500 numbers, where the largest is 98 and the smallest is 37, the range is 61.

There really are two kinds of ranges. One is the *exclusive range,* which is the highest score minus the lowest score (or $h - l$), and the one we just defined. The second kind of range is the *inclusive range,* which is the highest score minus the lowest score plus 1 (or $h - l + 1$). You most commonly see the exclusive range in research articles, but the inclusive range is also used on occasion if the researcher prefers it.

The range tells you how different the highest and lowest values in a data set are from one another—that is, the range shows how much spread there is from the lowest to the highest point in a distribution. So, although the range is fine as a general indicator of variability, it should not be used to reach any conclusions regarding how individual scores differ from one another. And you will usually never see it reported as the only measure of variability but only as one of several—which brings us to. . . .

COMPUTING THE STANDARD DEVIATION

Now we get to the most frequently used measure of variability, the standard deviation. Just think about what the term implies—it's a deviation from something (guess what?) that is standard. Actually, the **standard deviation** (abbreviated as s or SD) represents the average amount of variability in a set of scores. In practical terms, it's the average distance from the mean. The larger the standard deviation, the larger the average distance each data point is from the mean of the distribution, and the more variable the set of scores is.

So, what's the logic behind computing the standard deviation? Your initial thoughts may be to compute the mean of a set of scores and then subtract each individual score from the mean. Then, compute the average of that distance.

That's a good idea—you'll end up with the average distance of each score from the mean. But it won't work (see if you know why, even though we'll show you why in a moment).

First, here's the formula for computing the standard deviation:

$$s = \sqrt{\frac{\sum\left(X_i - \bar{X}\right)^2}{n-1}}, \tag{5.2}$$

where

- s is the standard deviation;
- Σ is sigma, which tells you to find the sum of what follows;
- X_i is each individual (i) score;
- $\bar{X}$ is the mean of all the scores; and
- n is the sample size.

This formula finds the difference between each individual score and the mean $(X_i - \bar{X})$, squares each difference, and sums them all together. Then, it divides the sum by the size of the sample (minus 1) and takes the square root of the result. As you can see, and as we mentioned earlier, the standard deviation is an average deviation from the mean.

1. List each score. It doesn't matter whether the scores are in any particular order.
2. Compute the mean of the group.
3. Subtract the mean from each score. If done correctly, the column total is 0.
4. Square each individual difference.
5. Sum all the squared deviations about the mean. As you can see, the total is 28.
6. Divide the sum by $n - 1$, or $10 - 1 = 9$, so then $28/9 = 3.11$.
7. Compute the square root of 3.11, which is 1.76 (after rounding). That is the standard deviation for this set of 10 scores.

STEP-BY-STEP

Here are the data we'll use in the following step-by-step explanation of how to compute the standard deviation:

5, 8, 5, 4, 6, 7, 8, 8, 3, 6

To start, set up a table like the one below. In this example, the data in column 1 were rearranged from largest to smallest. And we have a row at the end that we will use when we total some columns. Follow Steps 2 through 5 above to fill in the rest of the table.

Step 1	Step 2	Step 3	Step 4
X_i	$\bar{X}$	$(X_i - \bar{X})$	$(X_i - \bar{X})^2$
8			
8			

(Continued)

(Continued)

Step 1	Step 2	Step 3	Step 4
8			
7			
6			
6			
5			
5			
4			
3			
	Sum =		

Once the table is filled in, your table should look something like this. Step 3 may just contain the number instead of showing the full calculation.

Step 1	Step 2	Step 3	Step 4
X_i	$\bar{X}$	$(X_i - \bar{X})$	$(X_i - \bar{X})^2$
8	6	8 − 6 = +2	4
8	6	8 − 6 = +2	4
8	6	8 − 6 = +2	4
7	6	7 − 6 = +1	1
6	6	6 − 6 = 0	0
6	6	6 − 6 = 0	0
5	6	5 − 6 = −1	1
5	6	5 − 6 = −1	1
4	6	4 − 6 = −2	4
3	6	3 − 6 = −3	9
	Sum =	0	28

With this table, we have everything we need for Formula 5.1. Following Steps 6 and 7 leads us to the answer.

What we now know from these results is that each score in this distribution differs from the mean by an average of 1.76 points.

First, why didn't we just add up the deviations from the mean? Because the sum of the deviations from the mean is always equal to zero. Try it by summing the deviations (2 + 2 + 2 + 1 + 0 + 0 − 1 − 1 − 2 − 3). In fact, that's the best way to check whether you computed the mean correctly. The only time the deviation won't sum to 0 is if you calculate the mean and round it to just a couple of decimal places before filling in your table. Then the sum will be close to 0 but not exactly 0.

There's another type of deviation that you may read about, and you should know what it means. The **mean deviation** (also called the mean absolute deviation) is the sum of the absolute value of the deviations from the mean divided by the number of scores. You already know that the sum of the deviations from the mean must equal zero (otherwise, the mean is computed incorrectly). Instead, let's take the *absolute* value of each deviation (which is the value regardless of the sign). Sum the absolute values and divide by the number of data points, and you have the mean deviation. So, if you have a set of scores such as 3, 4, 5, 5, 8 and the arithmetic mean is 5, the mean deviation is the sum of 2 (the absolute value of 5 – 3), 1, 0, 0, and 3, for a total of 6. Then divide this by 5 to get the result of 1.2. (Note: The absolute value of a number is usually represented as that number with a vertical line on each side of it, such as |5|. For example, the absolute value of –6, or |–6|, is 6.)

Second, why do we square the deviations? Because we want to get rid of the negative sign so that when we do eventually sum them, they don't add up to 0.

And third, why do we eventually end up taking the square root of the entire value in Step 7? Because we want to return to the same scale with which we originally started. We squared the deviations from the mean in Step 4 (to get rid of negative values) and then took the square root of their total in Step 7. Pretty tidy.

Why *n* – 1? What's Wrong With Just *n*?

You might have guessed why we square the deviations about the mean and why we go back and take the square root of their sum. But how about subtracting the value of 1 from the denominator of the formula? Why do we divide by $n - 1$ rather than just plain ol' n? Good question.

The answer is that s (the standard deviation) is an estimate of the population standard deviation, and it is an **unbiased estimate** at that, but only when we subtract 1 from n. By subtracting 1 from the denominator, we artificially force the standard deviation to be larger than it would be otherwise. Why would we want to do that? Because, as good scientists, we are conservative. Being conservative means that if we have to err (and there is always a pretty good chance that we will), we will do so on the side of overestimating what the standard deviation of the population is. Dividing by a smaller denominator lets us do so. Thus, instead of dividing by 10, we divide by 9. Or instead of dividing by 100, we divide by 99. On the other hand, if you are dealing with your whole population, then divide by n instead of $n - 1$.

Biased estimates are appropriate if your intent is only to describe the characteristics of the sample. But if you intend to use the sample as an estimate of a population parameter, then it's best to calculate the unbiased statistic.

Take a look at the following table and see what happens as the size of the sample gets larger (and moves closer to the population in size). The $n - 1$ adjustment has far less impact on the difference between the biased and the unbiased estimates of the standard deviation (the bold column in the table) as the sample size increases.

All other things being equal, then, the larger the size of the sample, the less difference there is between the biased and the unbiased estimates of the standard deviation.

Sample Size	Value of Numerator in Standard Deviation Formula	Biased Estimate of the Population Standard Deviation (dividing by n)	Unbiased Estimate of the Population Standard Deviation (dividing by $n - 1$)	Difference Between Biased and Unbiased Estimates
10	500	7.07	7.45	**0.38**
100	500	2.24	2.25	**0.01**
1,000	500	0.7071	0.7075	**0.0004**

The moral of the story? When you compute the standard deviation for a sample, which is an estimate of the population, the closer to the size of the population the sample is, the more accurate the estimate will be. And when someone talks about the sample standard deviation, you will know they are dividing by $n - 1$.

WHAT'S THE BIG DEAL?

The computation of the standard deviation is very straightforward. But what does it mean? As a measure of variability, all it tells us is how much each score in a set of scores, on the average, varies from the mean. But it has some very practical applications, as you will find out in Chapter 8. Just to whet your appetite, consider this: The standard deviation can be used to help us compare scores from different distributions, *even when the means and standard deviations are different.* Amazing! This, as you will see, can be very cool.

- The standard deviation is computed as the average distance from the mean. So, you will need to first compute the mean as a measure of central tendency. Always use the mean, not the median or the mode, in computing the standard deviation.
- The larger the standard deviation, the more spread out the values are, and the more different they are from one another.
- Just like the mean, the standard deviation is sensitive to extreme scores. When you are computing the standard deviation of a sample and you have extreme scores, note that fact somewhere in your written report and in your interpretation of what the data mean.
- If $s = 0$, there is absolutely no variability in the set of scores, and the scores are identical in value, like the third example at the beginning of this chapter. In real life, this will rarely happen.

So, what's the big deal about variability and its importance? As a statistical concept, you learned above that it is a measure of dispersion or how scores differ from one another. But, "shakin' it up" really is the spice of life, and as you may have learned in your biology or psychology classes or from your own personal reading, variability is *the* key component of evolution, for without change (which variability always accompanies), organisms cannot adapt. All very cool.

COMPUTING THE VARIANCE

Here comes another measure of variability and a nice surprise. If you know the standard deviation of a set of scores and you can square a number, you can easily compute the **variance** of that same set of scores. This third measure of variability, the variance, is simply the standard deviation squared.

In other words, it's the same formula you saw earlier but without the square root bracket, like the one shown in Formula 5.3:

$$s^2 = \frac{\sum\left(X_i - \bar{X}\right)^2}{n-1}. \quad (5.3)$$

If you take the standard deviation and never complete the last step (taking the square root), you have the variance. In other words, $s^2 = s \times s$, or the variance equals the standard deviation times itself (or squared). In our earlier example, where the standard deviation was equal to 1.76 (before rounding), the variance is equal to 1.76^2, or 3.11. As another example, let's say that the standard deviation of a set of 150 scores is 2.34. Then, the variance would be 2.34^2, or 5.48.

You are not likely to see the variance mentioned by itself in a journal article or see it used as a descriptive statistic. This is because the variance is a difficult number to interpret and apply to a set of data. After all, it is based on squared deviation scores.

But the variance is important because it is used both as a concept and as a practical measure of variability in many statistical formulas and techniques. You will learn about these later in *Statistics for People Who (Think They) Hate Statistics Using R.*

The Standard Deviation Versus the Variance

How are standard deviation and the variance the same, and how are they different?

Well, they are both measures of variability, dispersion, or spread. The formulas used to compute them are very similar. You see them (but mostly the standard deviation) reported all over the place in the "Results" sections of journals.

They are also quite different.

First, and most important, the standard deviation (because we take the square root of the average summed squared deviation) is stated in the original units from which it was derived. The variance is stated in units that are squared (the square root of the final value is never taken).

What does this mean? Let's say that we need to know the variability of a group of production workers assembling circuit boards. Let's say that they average 8.6 boards per hour and the standard deviation is 1.59. The value 1.59 means that the difference in the average number of boards assembled per hour is about 1.59 circuit boards from the mean. This kind of information is quite valuable when trying to understand the overall performance of groups.

Let's look at an interpretation of the variance, which is 1.59^2, or 2.53. This would be interpreted as meaning that the average difference between the workers is about 2.53 circuit boards *squared* from the mean. Which of these two makes more sense?

USING R TO COMPUTE MEASURES OF VARIABILITY

Visit **edge.sagepub.com/salkindshaw** to watch an R tutorial video on this topic.

Let's use R to compute some measures of variability. We are using the Chapter 5 Data Set 1 (ch5ds1.csv). Like in Chapter 4, we will use R to manually compute range, variance, and standard deviation. Then we will try out some built-in functions.

There is one variable in this data set:

Variable	Definition
Reaction.Time	Reaction time on a tapping task in seconds

First, let's read in the data set. We are hoping the syntax to read in a data set is starting to look familiar, so we won't bore you with all of the details around importing a data set. If you need to be reminded of the details of the read.csv function, revisit Chapter 3 or 4. Here, we will just read it in and start computing measures of variability.

```
> ch5ds1 <- read.csv(file.choose())
> View(ch5ds1)
>
```

If the file was read in correctly, Reaction.Time values in rows 1, 2, and 3 should show 0.4, 0.7, and 0.4, respectively.

Let's look at summary information for Reaction.Time.

```
> summary(ch5ds1$Reaction.Time)
   Min. 1st Qu.  Median    Mean 3rd Qu.    Max.
 0.2000  0.5000  0.7500  0.9567  1.1000  2.8000
>
```

To use Formula 5.1 to calculate the (exclusive) range, we need to know the highest and lowest values. In the output above, that translates to Max. and Min. Easy peasy! Using R as a calculator,

```
> 2.8 - 0.2
[1] 2.6
>
```

Another option for calculating the range is to use two functions, `min()` and `max()`, to subtract the lowest value from the highest value.

```
> max(ch5ds1$Reaction.Time) - min(ch5ds1$Reaction.Time)
[1] 2.6
>
```

This time around, we are going to compute variance and then standard deviation. Can you guess why? It's because we compute the variance on the way to computing the standard deviation.

Like we did with range, let's use R to manually walk through the steps to create what we need for Formula 5.3. In the tables used to calculate standard deviation, we started with X and the mean of X, represented as $\bar{X}$. In this example, X is Reaction.Time. Look at Reaction.Time:

```
> ch5ds1$Reaction.Time
[1] 0.4 0.7 0.4 0.9 0.8 0.7 0.3 1.9 1.2 2.8 0.8 0.9 1.1
1.3 0.2 0.6 0.8
[18] 0.7 0.5 2.6 0.5 2.1 2.3 0.2 0.5 0.7 1.1 0.9 0.6 0.2
>
```

If you are following along, the number of numbers that fit on one row in your R Console will probably be different from ours. We made our R Console narrow so it only shows 17 numbers in the first row. Now, calculate the mean of Reaction.Time and store it in RTmean (an abbreviation for Reaction.Time mean).

```
> RTmean <- mean(ch5ds1$Reaction.Time)
> RTmean
[1] 0.9566667
>
```

The next step is to subtract the Reaction.Time mean from every Reaction.Time to get $(X - \bar{X})$, the mean deviation. We use ch5ds1$Reaction.Time and subtract RTmean. Let's do that step and look at the result.

```
> RTminusMean <- ch5ds1$Reaction.Time - RTmean
> RTminusMean
 [1] -0.55666667 -0.25666667 -0.55666667 -0.05666667
 [5] -0.15666667 -0.25666667 -0.65666667  0.94333333
 [9]  0.24333333  1.84333333 -0.15666667 -0.05666667
[13]  0.14333333  0.34333333 -0.75666667 -0.35666667
[17] -0.15666667 -0.25666667 -0.45666667  1.64333333
[21] -0.45666667  1.14333333  1.34333333 -0.75666667
[25] -0.45666667 -0.25666667  0.14333333 -0.05666667
[29] -0.35666667 -0.75666667
>
```

After getting the mean deviation, we need to square it. In R we will use ^2, ^ for take the power and 2 for the number of times we will multiply something by itself.

```
> SqMeanDeviation <- RTminusMean^2
> SqMeanDeviation
 [1] 0.309877778 0.065877778 0.309877778 0.003211111
 [5] 0.024544444 0.065877778 0.431211111 0.889877778
 [9] 0.059211111 3.397877778 0.024544444 0.003211111
[13] 0.020544444 0.117877778 0.572544444 0.127211111
[17] 0.024544444 0.065877778 0.208544444 2.700544444
[21] 0.208544444 1.307211111 1.804544444 0.572544444
[25] 0.208544444 0.065877778 0.020544444 0.003211111
[29] 0.127211111 0.572544444
>
```

We get a little fancy in this last step by combining the last two steps in one. We are also choosing to divide by n instead of $n - 1$ to get what is referred to as population variance, or σ^2 (note the use of the Greek letter for s^2 to stand for population variance).

```
> RTvariance <- sum(SqMeanDeviation) /
length(SqMeanDeviation)
> RTvariance
[1] 0.4771222
>
```

What if we divide the sum by $n - 1$ instead to get s^2?

```
> RTvarianceS <- sum(SqMeanDeviation) /
(length(SqMeanDeviation) - 1)
> RTvarianceS
[1] 0.4935747
>
```

Recall, if we use $n - 1$ for a sample, we get a conservative estimate for the standard deviation in the population–in this case, a difference between the population and sample variance of less than 0.02. If we use the built-in function for variance, R returns variance calculated with $n - 1$.

```
> var(ch5ds1$Reaction.Time)
[1] 0.4935747
>
```

If we weren't sure which type of variance R would give us, we could actually ask R for help. Go to the R Console and type in this:

```
> ?var
>
```

The Help Viewer in the bottom left now displays the help information for Correlation, Variance, and Covariance (Matrices), like what is shown in Figure 5.1.

FIGURE 5.1 ● Help text for correlation, variance, and covariance.

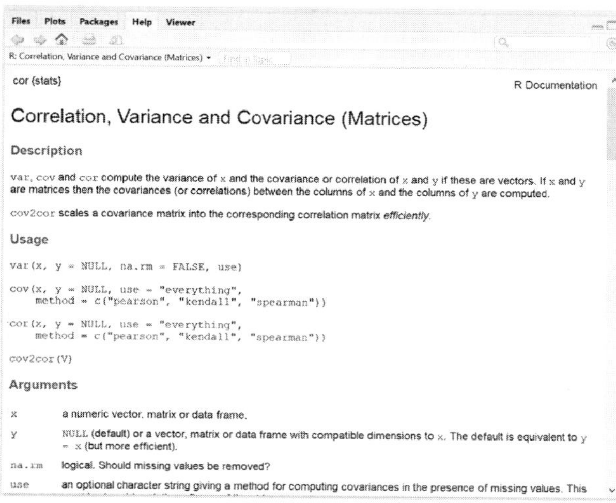

If you scroll down to the Details section, the sixth paragraph talks about $n - 1$ for the denominator to get an unbiased estimate of the population (co)variance.

To get population variance, you need to return to the steps above where we manually calculated variance. And why doesn't the var function in R give you the choice of population versus sample variance? That is because we rarely deal with the whole population of anything, particularly in education, psychology, marketing, political science, or any other field.

Whew! We took many steps to get the same answer as `var()` gave us, but hopefully you feel a little more comfortable with variance and standard deviation. To get to standard deviation, we need only one more line of syntax after computing variance. And let's use the sample variance, RTvarianceS—yes, *s* is for sample!

```
> sqrt(RTvarianceS)
[1] 0.7025487
>
```

The standard deviation is 0.70 seconds. Using the built-in R function `sd()` for *s*, we get

```
> sd(ch5ds1$Reaction.Time)
[1] 0.7025487
>
```

We received the same answer down to the seventh decimal place. The function is carrying out all of the steps we took, just carrying them out behind the scenes. And like variance, `sd()` used $n - 1$ in the denominator. If you want to make sure R used $n - 1$ instead of n, we can just ask!

Go to the R Console and type

```
> ?sd
>
```

On the bottom right of RStudio, the Help tab displays information about *Standard Deviation*. Scroll down to look at the first line in the Details section. The authors of this handy function tell us right there: "Like var this uses denominator n – 1." So, R is returning the unbiased, or sample, standard deviation.

We will go into much greater detail as to how this value is used in Chapter 8, but for now, the value of 0.70 represents the average amount each score is from the center-most point in the set of scores, or the mean. For these reaction time data, it means that the average reaction time varies from the mean by about 0.70 seconds.

Let's try another one, using Chapter 5 Data Set 2 (ch5ds2.csv). There are two variables in this data set:

Variable	Definition
Math_Score	Score on a mathematics test
Reading_Score	Score on a reading test

Follow the same set of instructions as given previously, only do it twice, once for each variable.

Other useful functions for variability:

Package	Function	What It Tells You
base	range	Minimum and maximum values in the data set are displayed so you can compute the inclusive or exclusive range

```
> range(ch5ds1$Reaction.Time)
[1] 0.2 2.8
>
```

Package	Function	What It Tells You
psych	describe	

```
> describe(ch5ds1$Reaction.Time)
   vars  n mean  sd median trimmed  mad min max range skew kurtosis   se
X1    1 30 0.96 0.7   0.75    0.85 0.44 0.2 2.8   2.6 1.26     0.58 0.13
>
```

REAL-WORLD STATS

If you were like a mega stats person, then you might be interested in the properties of measures of variability for the sake of those properties. That's what mainline statisticians spend lots of their time doing—looking at the characteristics and performance and assumptions (and the violation thereof) of certain statistics.

But we're more interested in how these tools are used, so let's take a look at one such study that actually focused on variability as an outcome. And, as you read earlier, variability among scores is interesting for sure, but when it comes to understanding the reasons for variability among substantive performances and people, then the topic becomes really interesting.

This is exactly what Nicholas Stapelberg and his colleagues in Australia did when they looked at variability in heart rate as it related to coronary heart disease. Now, they did not look at this phenomenon directly, but they entered the search terms *heart rate variability, depression,* and *heart disease* into multiple electronic databases and found that decreased heart rate variability is found in conjunction with both major depressive disorders and coronary heart disease.

Why might this be the case? The researchers think that both diseases disrupt control feedback loops that help the heart function efficiently. This is a terrific example of how looking at variability can be the focal point of a study, rather than an accompanying descriptive statistic.

Want to know more? Go online or to the library and read . . .

Stapelberg, N. J., Hamilton-Craig, I., Neumann, D. L., Shum, D. H., & McConnell, H. (2012). Mind and heart: Heart rate variability in major depressive disorder and coronary heart disease—a review and recommendations. *The Australian and New Zealand Journal of Psychiatry, 46,* 946–957.

Summary

Measures of variability help us even more fully understand what a distribution of data points looks like. Along with a measure of central tendency, we can use these values to distinguish distributions from one another and effectively describe what a collection of test scores, heights, or measures of personality looks like and what those individual scores represent. Now that we can think and talk about distributions, let's explore ways we can look at them.

Time to Practice

1. Why is the range the most convenient measure of dispersion, yet the most imprecise measure of variability? When would you use the range?
2. Fill in the exclusive and inclusive ranges for the following items.

High Score	Low Score	Inclusive Range	Exclusive Range
12.1	3		
92	51		
42	42		
7.5	6		
27	26		

3. Why would you expect more variability on a measure of personality in college freshmen than you would on a measure of height?

4. Why does the standard deviation get smaller as the individuals in a group score more similarly on a test? And why would you expect the amount of variability on a measure to be relatively less with a larger number of observations than with a smaller one?

5. For the following set of scores, compute the range, the unbiased and the biased standard deviations, and the variance. Do the exercise by hand.

   94, 86, 72, 69, 93, 79, 55, 88, 70, 93

6. In Question 5, why is the unbiased estimate greater than the biased estimate?

7. Use R to compute all the descriptive statistics for the following set of three test scores over the course of a semester. Which test had the highest average score? Which test had the smallest amount of variability?

Test 1	Test 2	Test 3
50	50	49
48	49	47
51	51	51
46	46	55
49	48	55
48	53	45
49	49	47
49	52	45
50	48	46
50	55	53

8. For the following set of scores, compute by hand the unbiased estimates of the standard deviation and variance.

58	76
56	78
48	45
76	66
69	

9. The variance for a set of scores is 36. What is the standard deviation, and what is the range?

(Continued)

(Continued)

10. Find the inclusive range, the sample standard deviation, and the sample variance of each of the following sets of scores:
    a. 5, 7, 9, 11
    b. 0.3, 0.5, 0.6, 0.9
    c. 6.1, 7.3, 4.5, 3.8
    d. 435, 456, 423, 546, 465
11. This practice problem uses the data contained in Chapter 5 Data Set 3 (ch5ds3.csv). There are two variables in this data set:

Variable	Definition
Height	Height in inches
Weight	Weight in pounds

Using R, compute all of the measures of variability you can for height and weight.

12. How can you tell whether R produces a biased or an unbiased estimate of the standard deviation?
13. Compute the biased and unbiased values of the standard deviation and variance for the set of accuracy scores shown in Chapter 5 Data Set 4 (ch5ds4.csv). Use R if you can; otherwise, do it by hand. Which one is smaller and why?
14. On a spelling test, the standard deviation is equal to 0.94. What does this mean?

Student Study Site

Get the tools you need to sharpen your study skills! Visit **edge.sagepub.com/salkindshaw** to access practice quizzes and eFlashcards, watch R tutorial videos, and download data sets!

CREATING GRAPHS

A Picture Really Is Worth a Thousand Words

Difficulty Scale ☺ ☺ ☺ ☺
(moderately easy, but not a cinch)

WHAT YOU WILL LEARN IN THIS CHAPTER

- Understanding why a picture is really worth a thousand words
- Creating a histogram and a polygon
- Understanding the different shapes of different distributions
- Using R to create incredibly cool charts
- Creating different types of charts and understanding their application and uses

WHY ILLUSTRATE DATA?

In the previous two chapters, you learned about two important types of descriptive statistics—measures of central tendency and measures of variability. Both categories of statistics provide you with the one best measure for describing a group of data (central tendency) and a measure of how diverse, or different, scores are from one another (variability).

What we did not do, and what we will do here, is examine how differences in these two measures result in different-*looking* distributions. Numbers alone (such as $\bar{X}$ and $s = 3$) may be important, but a visual representation is a much more effective way of examining the characteristics of a distribution as well as the characteristics of any set of data. And this is where R starts to shine. It's simple to create something like Figure 4.1 in Chapter 4 where we created our first histogram to highlight how one number was much larger than the rest. But what we didn't show you was how to easily create a figure that is sure to impress.

So, in this chapter, we'll learn how to visually represent a distribution of scores as well as how to use different types of graphs to represent different types of data. And because R creates figures easily, we are going to introduce functions throughout the chapter rather than waiting for the end, so open up RStudio and follow along.

TEN WAYS TO A GREAT GRAPHIC

Whether you create illustrations by hand or use a computer program, the same principles of decent design apply. Here are 10 to copy and put above your desk.

1. **Minimize chart or graph junk.** "Chart junk" (a close cousin to "word junk") happens when you use every function, every graph, and every feature a computer program has to make your charts busy, full, and uninformative. More is definitely less.
2. **Plan out your chart before you start creating the final copy.** Use graph paper even if you will be using a computer program to generate the graph. And, in fact, just use your computer to generate and print out graph paper (try www.printfreegraphpaper.com).
3. **Say what you mean and mean what you say—no more and no less.** There's nothing worse than a cluttered (with too much text and fancy features) graph to confuse the reader.
4. **Label everything so nothing is left to the misunderstanding of the audience.**
5. **A graph should communicate only one idea.**
6. **Keep things balanced.** When you construct a graph, center titles and axis labels.
7. **Maintain the scale in a graph.** The scale refers to the relationship between the horizontal and vertical axes. This ratio should be about 3 to 4, so a graph that is 3 inches tall will be about 4 inches wide.
8. **Simple is best and less is more.** Keep the chart simple but not simplistic. Convey one idea as straightforwardly as possible, with distracting information saved for the accompanying text. Remember, a chart or graph should be able to stand alone, and the reader should be able to understand the message.

9. **Limit the number of words you use.** Too many words, or words that are too large (both in terms of physical size and idea-wise), can detract from the visual message your chart should convey.
10. **A chart alone should convey what you want to say.** If it doesn't, go back to your plan and try it again.

FIRST THINGS FIRST: CREATING A FREQUENCY DISTRIBUTION

The most basic way to illustrate data is through the creation of a frequency distribution. A **frequency distribution** is a method of tallying and representing how often certain scores occur. In the creation of a frequency distribution, scores are usually grouped into class intervals, or ranges of numbers.

Here are 50 scores on a test of reading comprehension on which a frequency distribution is based:

47	10	31	25	20
2	11	31	25	21
44	14	15	26	21
41	14	16	26	21
7	30	17	27	24
6	30	16	29	24
35	32	15	29	23
38	33	19	28	20
35	34	18	29	21
36	32	16	27	20

And here's the frequency distribution. You can see that for each range of scores, there are associated frequency counts.

Class Interval	Frequency
45–49	1
40–44	2
35–39	4
30–34	8

(Continued)

(Continued)

Class Interval	Frequency
25–29	10
20–24	10
15–19	8
10–14	4
5–9	2
0–4	1

The Classiest of Intervals

As you can see from the above table, a **class interval** is a range of numbers, and the first step in the creation of a frequency distribution is to define how large each interval will be. As you can see in the frequency distribution that we created, each interval spans five possible scores, such as 5–9 (which includes scores 5, 6, 7, 8, and 9) and 40–44 (which includes scores 40, 41, 42, 43, and 44). How did we decide to have an interval that includes only five scores? Why not five intervals, each consisting of 10 scores? Or two intervals, each consisting of 25 scores?

Here are some general rules to follow in the creation of a class interval, regardless of the size of values in the data set you are dealing with.

- Select a class interval that has a range of 2, 5, 10, 15, or 20 data points. In our example, we chose 5.
- Select a class interval so that 7 to 10 such intervals cover the entire range of data. A convenient way to do this is to compute the range and then divide by a number that represents the number of intervals you want to use (between 7 and 10). In our example, there are 50 scores and we wanted 10 intervals: 50/10 = 5, which is the size of each class interval. We don't want fewer than 7 because it becomes harder to see what the distribution of numbers looks like.
- Begin listing the class interval with a multiple of that interval. In our frequency distribution of reading comprehension test scores, the class interval is 5, and we started the lowest class interval at 0.
- Finally, the largest interval goes at the top of the frequency distribution.

Simply put, there are no hard-and-fast rules about creating class intervals on the way to creating a frequency distribution. Here are six general rules:

1. Determine the inclusive range (range that includes both the largest and smallest numbers in your data).
2. Decide on the number of class intervals.

3. Decide on the size of the class interval.
4. Decide the starting point for the first class.
5. Create the class intervals.
6. Put the data into the class intervals.

Once class intervals are created, it's time to complete the frequency part of the frequency distribution. That's simply counting the number of times a score occurs in the raw data and entering that number in each of the class intervals represented by the count.

In the frequency distribution that we created for our reading comprehension data, the number of scores that occur between 30 and 34 and thus are in the 30–34 class interval is 8. So, an 8 goes in the column marked Frequency. There's your frequency distribution.

Sometimes it is a good idea to graph your data first and then do whatever calculations or analysis is called for. By first looking at the data, you may gain insight into the relationship between variables, what kind of descriptive statistic is the right one to use to describe the data, and so on. This extra step might increase your insights and the value of what you are doing.

THE PLOT THICKENS: CREATING A HISTOGRAM

Now that we've got a tally of how many scores fall in what class intervals, we'll go to the next step and create what is called a **histogram**, a visual representation of the frequency distribution where the frequencies are represented by bars.

Depending on the book or journal article or report you read and the software you use, visual representations of data are called plots (such as in R) or charts (such as in Microsoft Excel). It really makes no difference. All you need to know is that graphs, figures, plots, and charts are all visual representations of data.

To create a histogram, do the following:

1. Using a piece of graph paper, place values at equal distances along the *x*-axis, as shown in Figure 6.1. Now, identify the **midpoint** of each class interval, which is the middle point in the interval. It's pretty easy to just eyeball, but you can also just add the top and bottom values of the class interval and divide by 2. For example, the midpoint of the class interval 0–4 is the average of 0 and 4, or 4/2 = 2.

(Continued)

(Continued)

FIGURE 6.1 ● Class intervals along the x-axis.

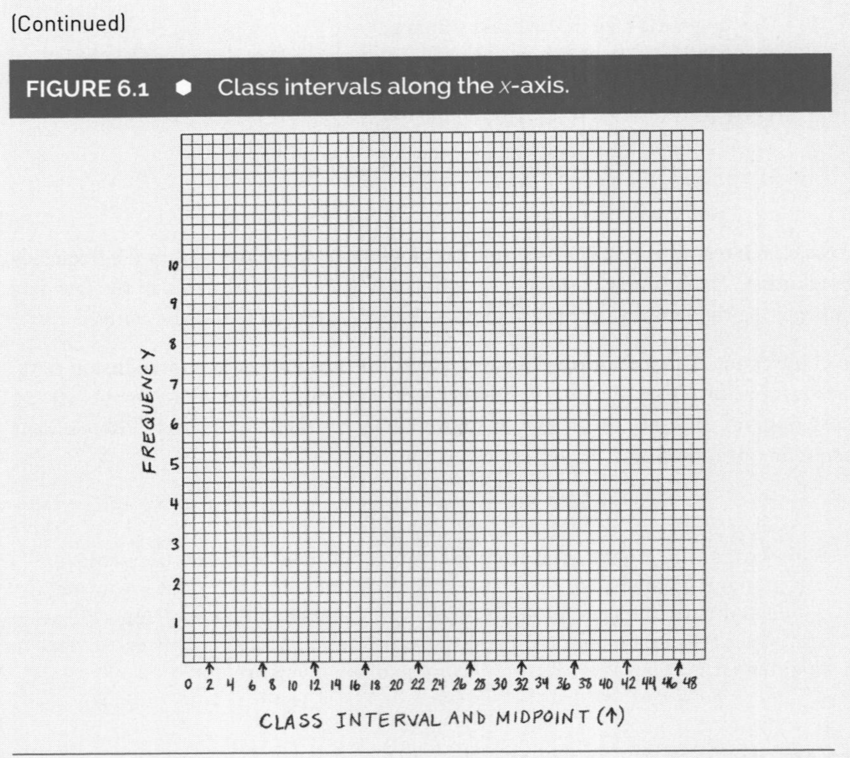

2. Draw a bar or column centered on each midpoint that represents the entire class interval to the height representing the frequency of that class interval. For example, in Figure 6.2, you can see that in our first entry, the class interval of 0–4 is represented by the frequency of 1 (representing the one time a value between 0 and 4 occurs). Continue drawing bars or columns until each of the frequencies for each of the class intervals is represented. Here's a nice hand-drawn (really!) histogram for the frequency distribution of the 50 scores that we have been working with so far.

Notice that each class interval is represented by a range of scores along the *x*-axis.

The Tallyho Method

You can see by the simple frequency distribution at the beginning of the chapter that you already know more about the distribution of scores than you'd learn from just a simple listing of them. You have a good idea of what values occur with what frequency. But another visual representation (besides a histogram) can be done by using tallies for each of the occurrences, as shown in Figure 6.3.

We used tallies that correspond with the frequency of scores that occur within a certain class. This gives you an even better visual representation of how often certain scores occur relative to other scores.

FIGURE 6.2 ● A hand-drawn histogram.

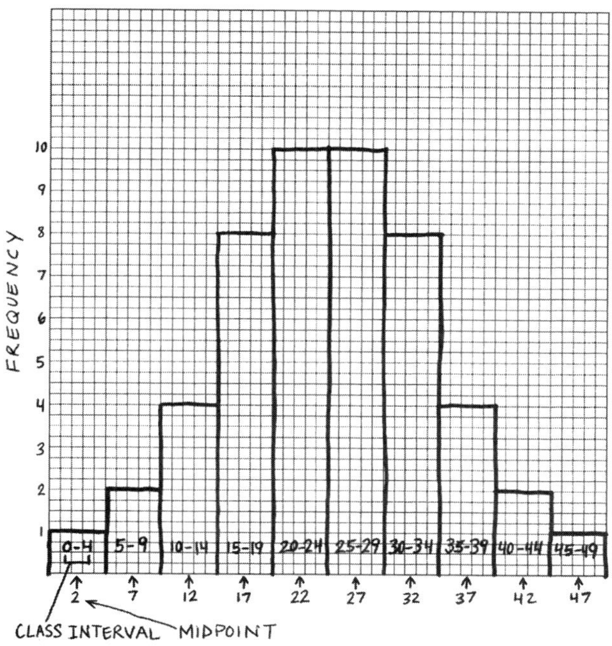

FIGURE 6.3 ● Tallying scores.

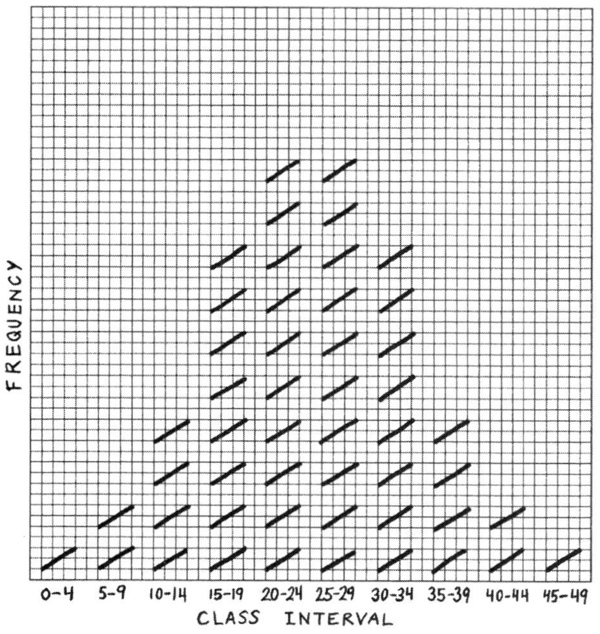

THE NEXT STEP: A FREQUENCY POLYGON

Creating a histogram or a tally of scores wasn't so difficult, and the next step (and the next way of illustrating data) is even easier. We're going to use the same data—and, in fact, the histogram that you just saw created—to create a frequency polygon. A **frequency polygon** is a continuous line that represents the frequencies of scores within a class interval, as shown in Figure 6.4.

FIGURE 6.4 ● A hand-drawn frequency polygon.

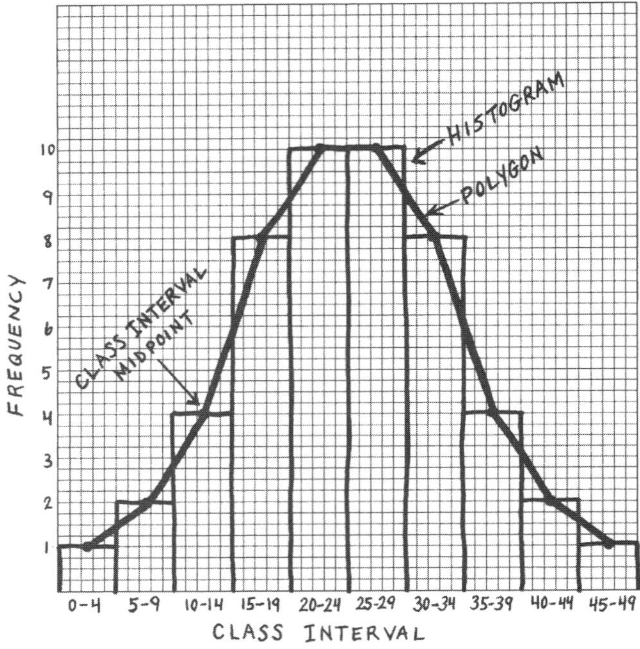

How did we draw this? Here's how.

1. Place a midpoint at the top of each bar or column in a histogram (see Figure 6.2).
2. Connect the lines and you've got it—a frequency polygon!

Note that in Figure 6.4, the histogram on which the frequency polygon is based is drawn using vertical and horizontal lines, and the polygon is drawn using curved lines. That's because, although we want you to see what a frequency polygon is based on, you usually don't see the underlying histogram.

Why use a frequency polygon rather than a histogram to represent data? It's more a matter of preference than anything else. A frequency polygon appears more dynamic than a histogram (a line that represents change in frequency always looks neat), but you are basically conveying the same information.

Now let R do the heavy lifting! We will start with a simple histogram of our reading scores.

```
> Reading <- c(47, 2, 44, 41, 7, 6, 35, 38, 35, 36,
+              10, 11, 14, 14, 30, 30, 32, 33, 34, 32,
+              31, 31, 15, 16, 17, 16, 15, 19, 18, 16,
+              25, 25, 26, 26, 27, 29, 29, 28, 29, 27,
+              20, 21, 21, 21, 24, 24, 23, 20, 21, 20)
> hist(Reading)
>
```

In the first line, we created our vector of reading scores that we stored in an object called `Reading`. In the following line to get a histogram, we used the function `hist()`. R returned Figure 6.5.

FIGURE 6.5 ● Histogram as drawn by R.

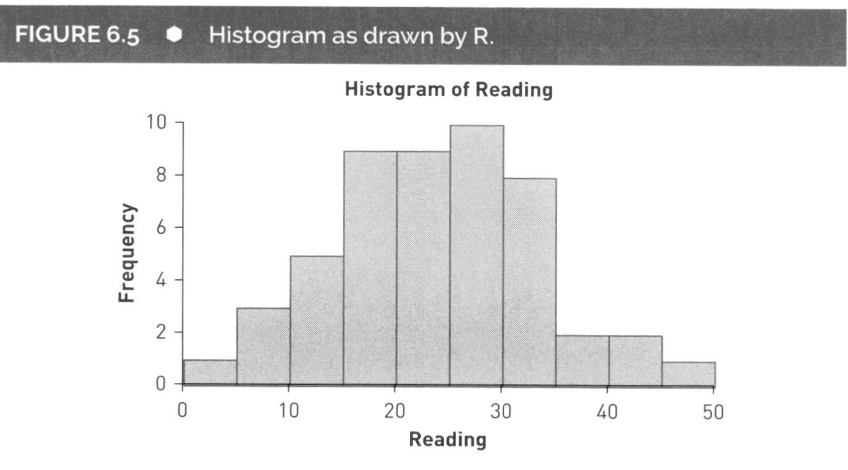

R created 10 intervals from our data. The difference is that R defines class intervals using its own method. Consequently, scores are allocated to different groups. The lesson here? How you group data makes a big difference in the way they look in a histogram. And, once you get to know R well, you can make all kinds of fine-tuned adjustments to make graphs appear exactly as you want them. Let's make our first adjustments now.

We can change the number of intervals by adding a little bit of syntax to our function. Specifically, we tell R how many breaks we want. In Figure 6.5, R gave us 10 intervals, which contains nine breaks. How many lines do we need to break up a continuous distribution into our desired number of intervals? Imagine a square brownie and you want to break it apart for sharing. If you are sharing with one other person, you break the brownie once to create two pieces. To share between three people, break the brownie in two places to get three pieces. Similarly, we pick how many intervals we want and subtract 1 to get the number of breaks—unfortunately, no chocolate is involved this time.

In this example we are going to pick a small number of intervals just to show you how to do it (too few intervals in practice!). We tell R we want five intervals so we set breaks to 5 – 1 = 4 to create Figure 6.6.

```
> hist(Reading, breaks = 4)
>
```

FIGURE 6.6 ● Histogram redrawn with four breaks.

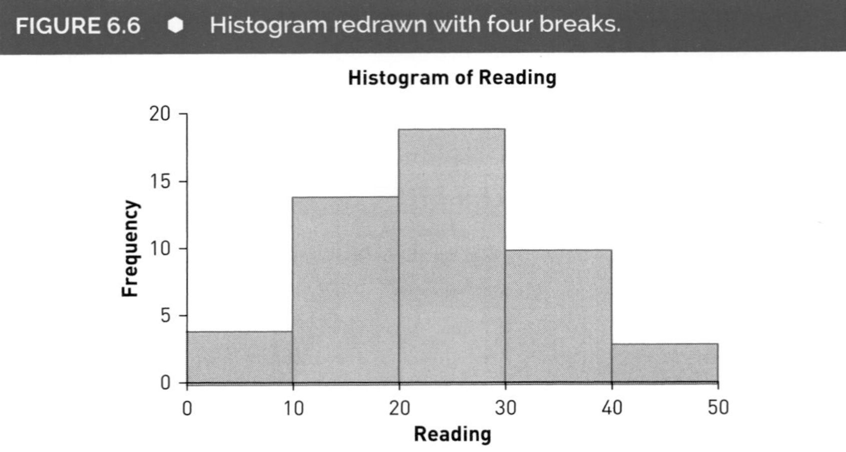

There are several ways to specify how many intervals you want R to create. We can use the default, which is a formula by Sturges that takes the logarithm (base 2) of our sample size and adds 1. If you have fewer than 30 scores, it doesn't work that well. In that case, you can specify the number of breaks you want and the exact breakpoints, like you did when you created the histogram by hand, or a function mimicking Rules 1 and 2 for creating a histogram:

```
(max(Reading) - min(Reading))/5
```

Type `?hist` in the R Console for more information about specifying breaks in a histogram.

Let's look at adding a frequency polygon. We will use a different option in `hist()` and then add one more line of syntax.

```
> hist(Reading, probability = TRUE)
> lines(density(Reading))
>
```

The plot you created should look like Figure 6.7.

FIGURE 6.7 ● Histogram and polygon.

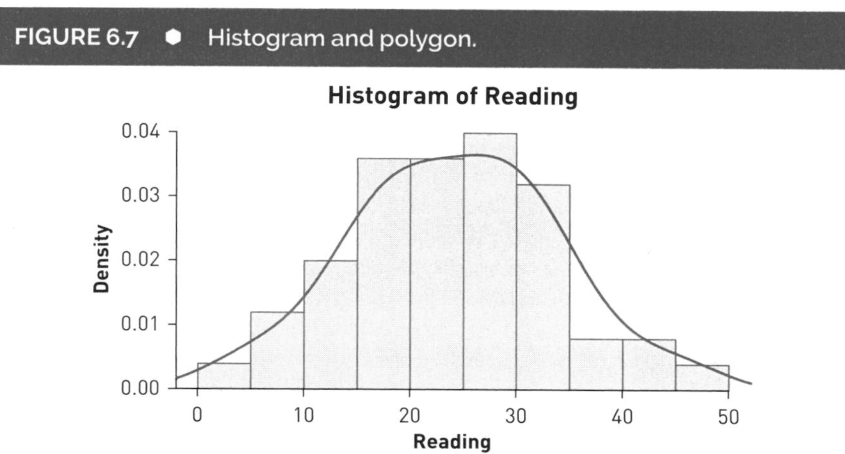

In this example, we changed the *y*-axis to track probability of a score falling in an interval, with `probability = TRUE`, so that R would draw the density polygon on top with the `line()` function. You can use `line()` after you have created an initial plot, in this case a histogram. But wait, is it really a line? Technically no because we asked for a drawing of the density, which follows the shape of our data. Line in this case returns a continuous mark across the plot rather than dots or other marks on the plot.

CUMULATING FREQUENCIES

Once you have created a frequency distribution and have visually represented those data using a histogram or a frequency polygon, another option is to create a visual representation of the cumulative frequency of occurrences by class intervals. This is called a **cumulative frequency distribution.**

A cumulative frequency distribution is based on the same data as a frequency distribution but with an added column (Cumulative Frequency), as shown below.

Class Interval	Frequency	Cumulative Frequency
45–49	1	50
40–44	2	49
35–39	4	47

(Continued)

(Continued)

Class Interval	Frequency	Cumulative Frequency
30–34	8	43
25–29	10	35
20–24	10	25
15–19	8	15
10–14	4	7
5–9	2	3
0–4	1	1

The cumulative frequency distribution begins with the creation of a new column labeled Cumulative Frequency. Then, we add the frequency in a class interval to all the frequencies below it. For example, for the class interval of 0–4, there is 1 occurrence and none below it, so the cumulative frequency is 1. For the class interval of 5–9, there are 2 occurrences in that class interval and 1 below it for a total of 3 (2 + 1) occurrences. The last class interval (45–49) contains 1 occurrence, and there is a total of 50 occurrences at or below that class interval.

Once we create the cumulative frequency distribution, then the data can be plotted just as they were in a histogram or a frequency polygon. Only this time, we'll skip right ahead and plot the midpoint of each class interval as a function of the cumulative frequency of that class interval. You can see the cumulative frequency distribution in Figure 6.8 based on the 50 scores from the beginning of this chapter.

FIGURE 6.8 ● A hand-drawn cumulative frequency distribution.

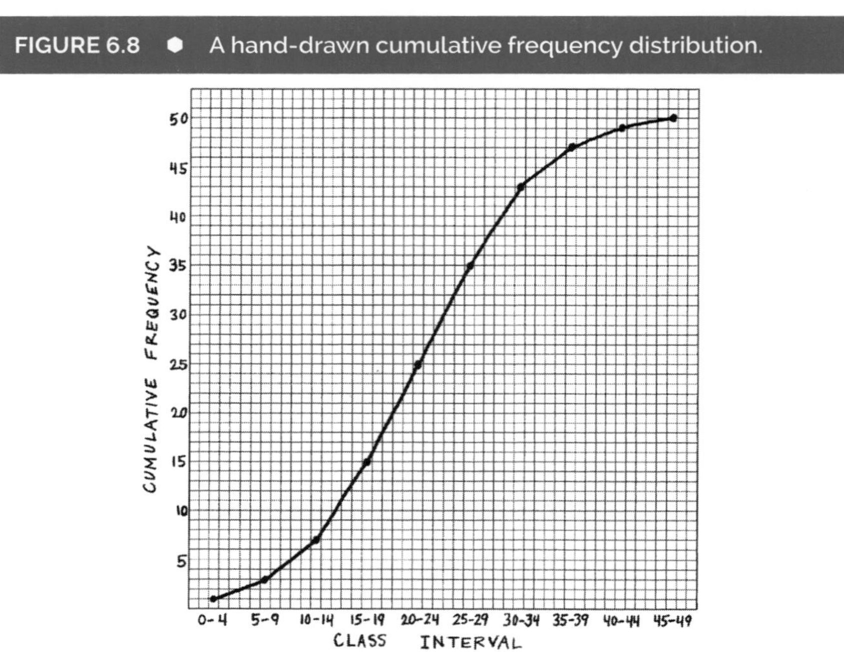

Another name for a cumulative frequency polygon is an **ogive**, pronounced "o jive." And, if the distribution of the data is normal or bell shaped (see Chapter 12 for more on this), then the ogive represents what is popularly known as a bell curve or a normal distribution. They are also referred to as probability plots.

OTHER COOL WAYS TO CHART DATA

What we did so far in this chapter is take some data and show how charts such as histograms and polygons can be used to communicate visually. But several other types of charts are also used in the behavioral and social sciences, and although it's not necessary for you to know exactly how to create them (manually), you should at least be familiar with their names and what they do. So here are some popular charts, what they do, and how they do it.

There are several very good personal computer applications for creating charts, among them the spreadsheet Excel (a Microsoft product)—the authors' personal favorite—and, of course, R. The charts in the "Using the Computer to Illustrate Data" section were created using R as well.

Bar Charts

A bar or column chart should be used when you want to compare the frequencies of different categories with one another. Categories are organized horizontally on the *x*-axis, and values are shown vertically on the *y*-axis. Here are some examples of when you might want to use a column chart:

- Number of participants in different water exercise activities
- The sales of three different types of products
- Number of children in each of six different grades

Figure 6.9 shows a graph of number of participants in different water activities.

Column Charts

A column chart is identical to a bar chart, but in this chart, categories are organized on the *y*-axis (which is the vertical one), and values are shown on the *x*-axis (the horizontal one).

Line Charts

A line chart should be used when you want to show a trend in the data at equal intervals. Here are some examples of when you might want to use a line chart:

- Number of cases of mononucleosis (mono) per season among college students at three state universities
- Toy sales for the T&K company over four quarters
- Number of travelers on two different airlines for each quarter

FIGURE 6.9 ● A bar chart that compares different water activities.

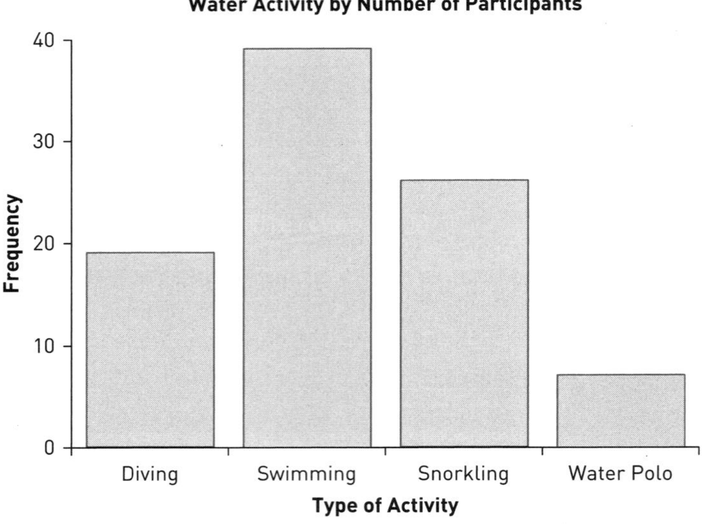

In Figure 6.10, you can see a chart of sales in units over four quarters.

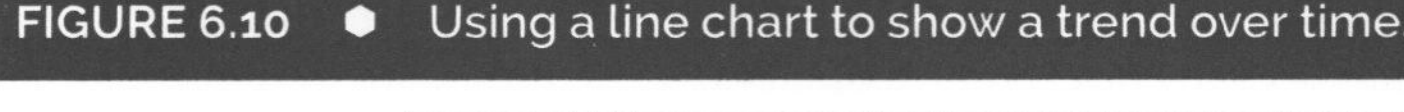
FIGURE 6.10 ● Using a line chart to show a trend over time.

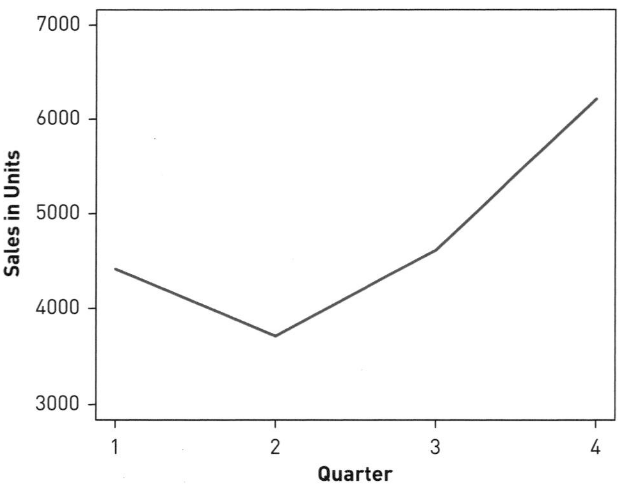

USING THE COMPUTER (R, THAT IS) TO ILLUSTRATE DATA

Visit **edge.sagepub.com/salkindshaw** to watch an R tutorial video on this topic.

Now let's use R and go through the steps in creating some of the charts that we explored in this chapter. First, let's read in our first data set, Chapter 6 Data Set 1 (ch6ds1.csv).

Let's start reading the data set that matches the one used for the earlier histogram example.

```
> ch6ds1 <- read.csv(file.choose())
> View(ch6ds1)
>
```

As should be familiar by now, we used the `file.choose()` option in the `read.csv` function. And after reading in our file, we looked at it to make sure we got what we expected. We got what we expected, an object titled `ch6ds1` with 50 observations of one variable. Did you?

Creating a Histogram

We are going to re-create the histogram but this time with `ch6ds1$Reading`. After creating the data set, we are going to circle back to our measures of central tendency and variability. To do so, we will use that handy little function called `summary()`.

1. Create the histogram.
2. Run the summary function on Reading in the object **ch6ds1**.
3. Run the function **sd()** on Reading in the object **ch6ds1**.
4. Locate the following statistics on the histogram:
   a. Mean
   b. Median
   c. −1 standard deviation
   d. +1 standard deviation

Here is the syntax for creating the histogram and getting the statistics we are interested in:

```
> hist(ch6ds1$Reading)
> summary(ch6ds1$Reading)
   Min.  1st Qu.  Median    Mean  3rd Qu.    Max.
   2.00    17.25   24.50   24.22    30.75   47.00
> sd(ch6ds1$Reading)
[1] 9.69597
>
```

FIGURE 6.11 ● Reading scores from our data set.

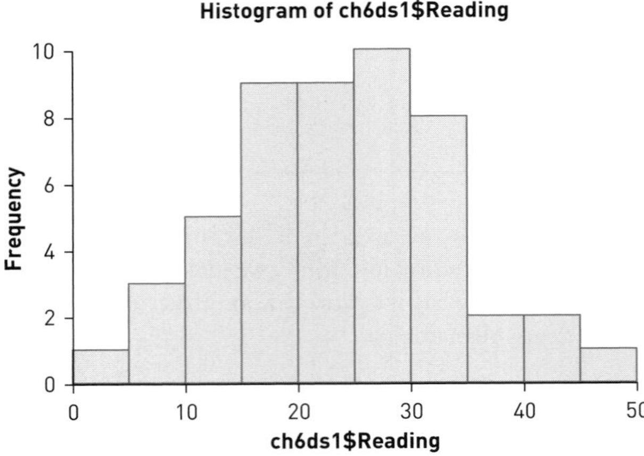

The histogram in Figure 6.11 looks a bit different from Figure 6.5, specifically the label for the *x*-axis and the main title of the histogram. We will show syntax to fix all of that and add some other features, but first let's talk about our plot and statistics.

If you were to mark the location of the mean on the histogram, what should you look at first? Right, the scores on the *x*-axis. The lowest score on the *x*-axis is 0 and the largest is 50 with every 10 points marked. The breaks in the histogram are every 5 points, so the mean of 24.22 is to the left of the interval break at 25 points. The median at 24.50 is close by, between the mean and the break at 25. How about –1 standard deviation? Let's use R as a calculator to help with that step.

```
> 24.22 - sd(ch6ds1$Reading)
[1] 14.52403
>
```

Now we can look for the break between intervals at 15 and know the location of 1 standard deviation below the mean. Repeating that process but adding instead of subtracting, we can find that +1 standard deviation is 33.92.

Let's use R to create a cleaned-up version of our histogram and add information about our statistics with the function `abline()` to get Figure 6.12.

```
> hist(ch6ds1$Reading, xlab = "Scores", main = "Reading")
> abline(v = 24.22)
> abline(v = 24.50, lty = 2)
> abline(v = 24.22 - 9.69567)
> abline(v = mean(ch6ds1$Reading) + sd(ch6ds1$Reading))
>
```

- `hist`: the function for histogram
- `chds1$Reading`: the variable we want displayed in our histogram
- `xlab = "Scores"`: the label for the *x*-axis
- `main = "Reading"`: the title for the histogram. If we did not want a main title, we could have set it to `main = ""`.
- `abline`: the function to draw a line on top of our histogram
- `v = 24.22`: v tells abline that we want a vertical line placed at 24.22, the mean.
- `lty = 2`: because the mean (24.22) and median (24.50) are so close together, we changed the type of line that abline drew by choosing a different number. The default, the value abline will use if not specified, is 1 for a straight line; 2 gives us a dashed line.
- `v = 24.22 - 9.69567`: we subtracted the standard deviation from the mean to place the line for 1 standard deviation below the mean.
- `v = mean(ch6ds1$Reading) + sd(ch6ds1$Reading)`: here we got a little fancy to show you what R can do. We didn't need to put in the numbers for the line 1 standard deviation above the mean. Instead, we used functions to do some calculations for us and called two functions, `mean` and `sd`, within the function `abline()`.

FIGURE 6.12 ● The histogram with mean, median, and standard deviations.

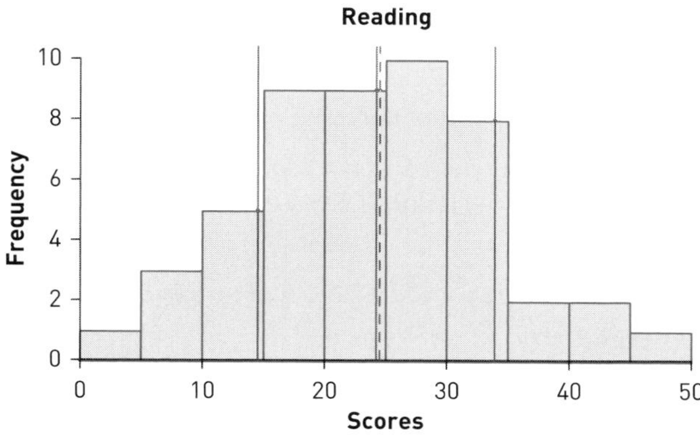

Creating a Bar Chart

To create a bar chart, follow these steps:

1. Count the number of observations for each category. In this example, count the number of Republican, Democrat, and Independent voters:

(Continued)

(Continued)

Republican	Democrat	Independent
54	63	19

2. Enter your labels in a vector for each category.
3. Enter your counts in a second vector.
4. Enter the vectors into the function **barplot()** to get Figure 6.13.

Here is the syntax for creating the bar chart:

```
> Party <- c("Republican", "Democrat", "Independent")
> Members <- c(54, 63, 19)
> barplot(height = Members, names.arg = Party, ylim = c(0, 70),
+         ylab = "Frequency")
>
```

- `Party`: the vector of our party names
- `Attitude`: the vector of counts of party membership
- `barplot`: the R function for drawing the barplot
- `height`: the vector that contains numbers for each bar
- `names.arg`: the vector of labels for each bar
- `ylim = c(0, 70)`: the lower and upper limits of the *y*-axis. Our largest count was 63, so we chose 70 to provide some extra white space between the tallest bar and the top of the chart.
- +: because the barplot syntax was not complete (no closing ")" on the first line), R displayed + to let us know it was expecting more syntax before it could draw our barplot.
- `ylab = "Frequency"`: add a label to the *y*-axis and call it Frequency.

FIGURE 6.13 ● The bar chart build with the function barplot().

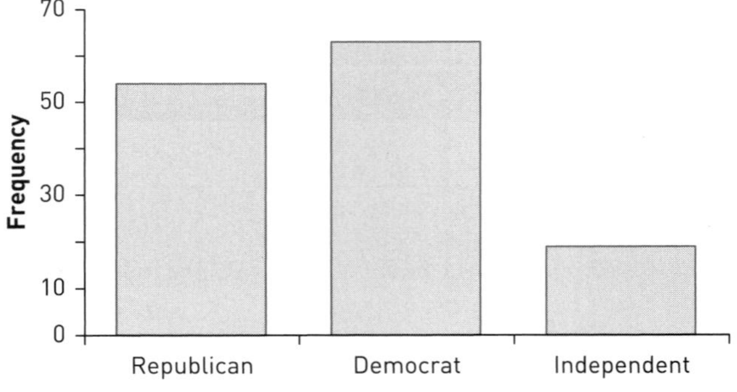

Creating a Line Graph

To create a line graph, follow these steps:

1. Create a vector for the *x*-axis to cover the range of attendance over a 10-year time period.

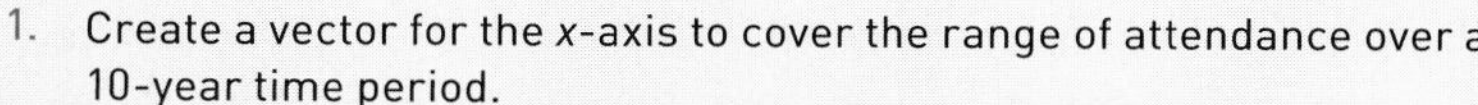

2. Create a second vector for the attendance numbers. These percentages are percent of whole membership who actually attended the event.
3. Create a line plot with labels to match the first row of the table to get Figure 6.14.

Year	Percent Attending
1	87
2	88
3	89
4	76
5	80
6	96
7	91
8	97
9	89
10	79

This is the syntax we used to create Figure 6.14. Syntax new to you is explained below.

```
> Year <- seq(1:10)
> Attendance <- c(87, 88, 89, 76, 80, 96, 91, 97, 89, 79)
> plot(x = Year, y = Attendance, type = "l",
ylab = "Percent Attending")
>
```

- `seq(1:10)`: seq is short for sequence that we want to start at 1 and end at 10. By default, the units between 1 and 10 increase by 1, returning the numbers 1 through 10.
- `Attendance:` a vector that we created with the function `c()` holding 10 numbers

- `plot`: the function to draw our plot based on `Year` on the *x*-axis and `Attendance` on the *y*-axis
- `type = "l"`: we told plot to draw a line by the type argument set to lowercase l.
- `ylab = "Percent Attending"`: because R objects cannot have spaces in their names but we wanted the *y*-axis label to match the name in the column, we added a label with `y-lab`, short for the *y*-axis label.

FIGURE 6.14 ● A line graph of percent attending.

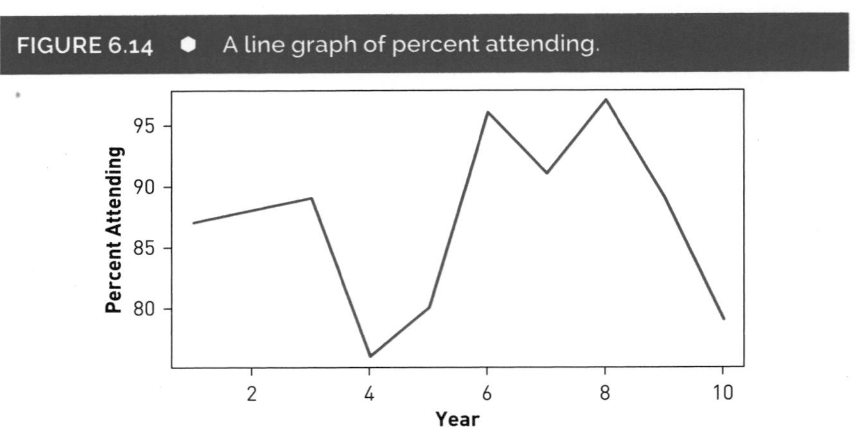

REAL-WORLD STATS

Graphs work, and a picture really is worth more than a thousand words.

In this article, an oldie but goodie still being referenced by researchers in environmental modeling, human-computer interactions, and business, to name just a few fields, the researchers examined how people perceive and process statistical graphs. Stephen Lewandowsky and Ian Spence reviewed empirical studies designed to explore how suitable different types of graphs are and how what is known about human perception can have an impact on the design and utility of these charts.

They focused on some of the theoretical explanations for why certain elements work and don't; the use of pictorial symbols (like a happy face symbol, which could make up the bar in a bar chart); and multivariate displays where more than one set of data needs to be represented. And, as is very often the case with any paper, they concluded that not enough data were available yet. Given the increasingly visual world in which we live (emoticons, anyone? ☹ ☺), this is interesting and useful reading to gain a historical perspective on how information was (and still is) discussed as a scientific topic.

Want to know more? Go online or to the library and find . . .

Lewandowsky, S., & Spence, I. (1989). The perception of statistical graphs. *Sociological Methods & Research, 18,* 200–242.

Summary

There's no question that charts are fun to create and can add enormous understanding to what might otherwise appear to be disorganized data. Follow our suggestions in this chapter and use charts well, but only when they enhance, not just add to, what's already there. And keep your eye out for more examples in the coming chapters. This chapter barely scratched the surface on what is possible when it comes to visualizing your data.

Time to Practice

1. A data set of 50 comprehension scores (named Comprehension Score) in Chapter 6 Data Set 2 (ch6ds2.csv) is available in Appendix C and on the website. Answer the following questions and/or complete the following tasks:
   a. Create a frequency distribution and a histogram for the set.
   b. Why did you select the class interval you used?
   c. Is this distribution skewed? How do you know?
2. Create a histogram by hand or by using R of data from Problem 1 and mark the location of the mean, median, + 1 standard deviation, and –1 standard deviation.
3. A third-grade teacher wants to improve her students' level of engagement during group discussions and instruction. She keeps track of each of the 15 third graders' number of responses every day for 1 week, and the data are available as ch6ds3.csv. Use R to create a line graph based on average engagement. Use 1 through 5 on the *x*-axis with 1 for Monday, 2 for Tuesday, and so on. Label the *x*-axis "Days of the Week" and the *y*-axis "Average Engagement."
4. Type `??lty` in the R Console. In the Help that comes up, click on the first entry, graphics::par.
   a. If we chose `lty = 4`, what type of a line would we draw?
   b. What are the two ways we could write the syntax to get a dashed line on our chart?
5. For each of the following, indicate whether you would use line or bar chart and why.
   a. The proportion of freshmen, sophomores, juniors, and seniors in a particular university
   b. Change in temperature over a 24-hour period
   c. Number of applicants for four different jobs
   d. Number of scores in each of 10 categories
6. Provide an example of when you might use each of the following types of charts. For example, you would use a pie chart to show the proportion of children in Grades 1 through 6 who receive a reduced-price lunch. When you are done, draw the fictitious chart by hand.
   a. Line
   b. Bar
   c. Scatter/dot (extra credit)

(Continued)

(Continued)

7. Go to the library and find a journal article in your area of interest that contains empirical data but does not contain any visual representation of them. Use the data to create a chart. Be sure to specify what type of chart you are creating and why you chose the one you did. You can create the chart manually or using R.

8. Create the worst-looking chart that you can, crowded with chart and font junk. Nothing makes as lasting an impression as a *bad* example.

9. And, finally, what is the purpose of a chart or graph?

Student Study Site

Get the tools you need to sharpen your study skills! Visit **edge.sagepub.com/salkindshaw** to access practice quizzes and eFlashcards, watch R tutorial videos, and download data sets!

COMPUTING CORRELATION COEFFICIENTS

Ice Cream and Crime

Difficulty Scale ☺ ☺
(moderately hard)

WHAT YOU WILL LEARN IN THIS CHAPTER

- ✦ Understanding what correlations are and how they work
- ✦ Computing a simple correlation coefficient
- ✦ Interpreting the value of the correlation coefficient
- ✦ Understanding what other types of correlations exist and when they should be used
- ✦ Computing a partial correlation
- ✦ Interpreting the value of a partial correlation

WHAT ARE CORRELATIONS ALL ABOUT?

Measures of central tendency and measures of variability are not the only descriptive statistics that we are interested in using to get a picture of what a set of scores looks like. You have already learned that knowing the values of the one most representative score (central tendency) and a measure of spread or dispersion (variability) is critical for describing the characteristics of a distribution.

However, sometimes we are as interested in the relationship between variables—or, to be more precise, how the value of one variable changes when the value of another variable changes. The way we express this interest is through the computation of a simple correlation coefficient. For example, what's the relationship between age and strength? Income and education? Memory skills and drug use? Voting preferences and attitude toward regulations?

A **correlation coefficient** is a numerical index that reflects the relationship between two variables. The value of this descriptive statistic ranges between −1.00 and +1.00. A correlation between two variables is sometimes referred to as a bivariate (for two variables) correlation. Even more specifically, the type of correlation that we will talk about in the majority of this chapter is called the Pearson product-moment correlation, named for its inventor, Karl Pearson.

The Pearson correlation coefficient is a statistic that quantifies the relationship between two variables, and both of those variables should be continuous in nature. In other words, they are variables that can assume any value along some underlying continuum; examples include height (you really can be 5 feet and 6.1938574673 inches tall), age, test score, and income. But a host of other variables are not continuous. They're called *discrete* or *categorical* variables, and examples are race (such as black and white); social class (such as high and low); and political affiliation (such as Democrat, Republican, and Independent). You need to use other correlational techniques, such as the point-biserial correlation, in these cases. These topics are for a more advanced course, but you should know they are acceptable and very useful techniques. We mention them briefly later on in this chapter.

Other types of correlation coefficients measure the relationship between more than two variables, and we'll leave those for the next statistics course (which you are looking forward to already, right?).

Types of Correlation Coefficients: Flavor 1 and Flavor 2

A correlation reflects the dynamic quality of the relationship between variables. In doing so, it allows us to understand whether variables tend to move in the same or opposite directions when they change. If variables change in the same direction, the correlation is called a **direct correlation** or a **positive correlation**. If variables change in opposite directions, the correlation is called an **indirect correlation** or a **negative correlation**. Table 7.1 shows a summary of these relationships.

Now, keep in mind that the examples in the table reflect generalities, for example, regarding time to complete a test and the number of correct items on that test. In general, the less time that is taken on a test, the lower the score. Such a conclusion is not rocket science, because the faster one goes, the more likely one is to make careless mistakes such as not reading instructions correctly. But of course, some people can go very fast and do very well. And other people go very slowly and don't do well at all. The point is that we are talking about the performance of a group of people on two different variables. We are computing the correlation between the two variables for the group, not for any one particular person.

TABLE 7.1 ● Types of Correlations.

What Happens to Variable *X*	What Happens to Variable *Y*	Type of Correlation	Value	Example
X increases in value.	*Y* increases in value.	Direct or positive	Positive, ranging from .01 to +1.00	The more time you spend studying, the higher your test score will be.
X decreases in value.	*Y* decreases in value.	Direct or positive	Positive, ranging from .01 to +1.00	The less money you put in the bank, the less interest you will earn.
X increases in value.	*Y* decreases in value.	Indirect or negative	Negative, ranging from −1.00 to −.01	The more you exercise, the less you will weigh.
X decreases in value.	*Y* increases in value.	Indirect or negative	Negative, ranging from −1.00 to −.01	The less time you take to complete a test, the more items you will get wrong.

There are several easy (but important) things to remember about the correlation coefficient:

- A correlation can range in value from −1.00 to +1.00.
- A correlation equal to 0 means there is no relationship between the two variables.
- The absolute value of the coefficient reflects the strength of the correlation. So, a correlation of −.70 is stronger than a correlation of +.50. One frequently made mistake regarding correlation coefficients occurs when students assume that a direct or positive correlation is always stronger (i.e., "better") than an indirect or negative correlation because of the sign and nothing else.
- A correlation always reflects a situation in which there are at least two data points (or variables) per case.
- Another easy mistake is to assign a value judgment to the sign of the correlation. Many students assume that a negative relationship is not good and a positive one is good. That's why, instead of using the terms *negative* and *positive,* we may prefer to use the terms *indirect* and *direct* to communicate meaning more clearly.
- The Pearson product-moment correlation coefficient is represented by the small letter *r* with a subscript representing the variables that are being correlated. For example,
  - r_{XY} is the correlation between variable *X* and variable *Y*.
  - $r_{\text{weight-height}}$ is the correlation between weight and height.
  - $r_{\text{SAT.GPA}}$ is the correlation between SAT scores and grade point average (GPA).

The correlation coefficient reflects the amount of variability that is shared between two variables and what they have in common. For example, you can expect an individual's height to be correlated with an individual's weight because these two variables share many of the same characteristics, such as the individual's nutritional and medical history, general health, and genetics. However, if one variable does not change in value and therefore has nothing to share, then the correlation between it and another variable is zero. For example, if you computed the correlation between age and number of years of school completed, and everyone was 25 years old, there would be no correlation between the two variables because there's literally nothing (no variability) in age available to share.

Likewise, if you constrain or restrict the range of one variable, the correlation between that variable and another variable will be less than if the range is not constrained. For example, if you correlate reading comprehension and grades in school for very high-achieving children, you'll find the correlation to be lower than if you computed the same correlation for children in general. That's because the reading comprehension score of very high-achieving students is quite high and much less variable than it would be for all children. The lesson? When you are interested in the relationship between two variables, try to collect sufficiently diverse data—that way, you'll get the truest representative result. And how do you do that? Measure a variable as precisely as possible.

Visit **edge.sagepub.com/salkindshaw** to watch an R tutorial video on this topic.

COMPUTING A SIMPLE CORRELATION COEFFICIENT

The computational formula for the simple Pearson product-moment correlation coefficient between a variable labeled *X* and a variable labeled *Y* is shown in Formula 7.1.

$$r_{XY} = \frac{n\sum XY - \sum X \sum Y}{\sqrt{\left[n\sum X^2 - \left(\sum X\right)^2\right]\left[n\sum Y^2 - \left(\sum Y\right)^2\right]}}, \quad (7.1)$$

where

- r_{XY} is the correlation coefficient between *X* and *Y*;
- *n* is the size of the sample;
- *X* is the individual's score on the *X* variable;
- *Y* is the individual's score on the *Y* variable;
- *XY* is the product of each *X* score times its corresponding *Y* score;
- X^2 is the individual's *X* score, squared; and
- Y^2 is the individual's *Y* score, squared.

Here are the steps to get the numbers needed to calculate the correlation coefficient:

1. List the two values for each participant like in Table 7.2. You should do this in a column format so as not to get confused. Use graph paper if working manually.

2. Compute the sum of all the *X* values and compute the sum of all the *Y* values.
3. Square each of the *X* values and square each of the *Y* values and sum the values for each column.
4. Find the sum of the *XY* products.

If you want to fill in the table manually, use the numbers in the columns for *X* and *Y* of Table 7.2 and follow the steps above. As a final step, check your work by comparing it to Table 7.3.

Another option? Instead of computing everything by hand, let's use R to compute *r*. We will first compute *r* the long way to get more practice with R and become more comfortable with Formula 7.1. Then we will use the function for correlation.

Let's start by first populating each column and then sum all numbers in a column to fill in the last row.

TABLE 7.2 ● Start With the Numbers for *X* and *Y*.

Respondent ID	*X*	*Y*	X^2	Y^2	*XY*
1	2	3			
2	4	2			
3	5	6			
4	6	5			
5	4	3			
6	7	6			
7	8	5			
8	5	4			
9	6	4			
10	7	5			
Total, sum, or $\sum$					

To start, let's create two vectors, one to hold the numbers for *X* and the other to hold the numbers for *Y*:

```
> X <- c(2, 4, 5, 6, 4, 7, 8, 5, 6, 7)
> Y <- c(3, 2, 6, 5, 3, 6, 5, 4, 4, 5)
```

To fill in the rest of the table, let's tell R to square and multiply some numbers for us. Starting with X,

```
> Xsq <- X^2
> Xsq
[1] 4 16 25 36 16 49 64 25 36 49
>
```

X^2 told R to square—multiply every number by itself—every value of X and store the result in Xsq. Now we will repeat that step with Y.

```
> Ysq <- Y^2
> Ysq
[1] 9 4 36 25 9 36 25 16 16 25
>
```

We have the numbers to fill in the next two columns of our table. To fill in the last column, let's multiply each row of numbers stored in X and Y to create a new vector called XY. For example, $X = 2$ in the first row and $Y = 3$. Multiply those two numbers and you get 6. With R, we get products for every row with a simple command:

```
> XY <- X*Y
> XY
[1] 6 8 30 30 12 42 40 20 24 35
>
```

We now have values for X^2, Y^2, and XY. Everything has been filled in except for the last row.

The last numbers we need to complete our table are the sum totals (Σ) of every number in each table column. Again, let R do the heavy lifting of summing all of the numbers in a vector. The function that we saw when using R to calculate the mean was sum(). To sum up the X vector, we will use the sum function on the X vector and store the result in sumX.

```
> sumX <- sum(X)
> sumX
[1] 54
```

Repeat this step with Y, Xsq, Ysq, and XY to create sumY, sumXsq, sumYsq, and sumXY to fill in the rest of the table and have the numbers we will plug into R to get r. Your table should now be complete and resemble Table 7.3.

TABLE 7.3 ● The Final Table.

Respondent ID	X	Y	X^2	Y^2	XY
1	2	3	4	9	6
2	4	2	16	4	8
3	5	6	25	36	30
4	6	5	36	25	30
5	4	3	16	9	12
6	7	6	49	36	42
7	8	5	64	25	40
8	5	4	25	16	20
9	6	4	36	16	24
10	7	5	49	25	35
Total, sum, or $\sum$	54	43	320	201	247

Before we plug the numbers into the formula both by hand and in R, let's make sure you understand what each one represents:

- $\sum X$, or the sum of all the X values, is 54.
- $\sum Y$, or the sum of all the Y values, is 43.
- $\sum X^2$, or the sum of each X value squared, is 320.
- $\sum Y^2$, or the sum of each Y value squared, is 201.
- $\sum XY$, or the sum of the products of X and Y, is 247.

It's easy to confuse the sum of a set of values squared and the sum of the squared values. The sum of a set of values squared is taking values such as 2 and 3, summing them (to be 5), and then squaring that (which is 25). The sum of the squared values is taking values such as 2 and 3; squaring them (to get 4 and 9, respectively); and then adding those together (to get 13). Just look for the parentheses as you work.

These values from the last row of the table are plugged into the equation you see in Formula 7.2:

$$r_{XY} = \frac{n\sum XY - \sum X \sum Y}{\sqrt{\left[n\sum X^2 - \left(\sum X\right)^2\right]\left[n\sum Y^2 - \left(\sum Y\right)^2\right]}}, \tag{7.2}$$

$$r_{XY} = \frac{(10 \times 247) - (54 \times 43)}{\sqrt{\left[(10 \times 320) - 54^2\right]\left[(10 \times 201) - 43^2\right]}}.$$

Ta-da! And you can see the answer in Formula 7.3:

$$r_{XY} = \frac{148}{213.83} = .692. \tag{7.3}$$

Instead of pulling out a calculator, let's enter the equation in R, using the R objects we created. We will create one more object to hold the size of our sample. Then we will re-create the formula.

```
> n <- 10
> rByHand <- ((n * sumXY) - (sumX * sumY))/
+ sqrt((((n * sumXsq) - (sumX^2)) * ((n * sumYsq) -
(sumY^2))))
> rByHand
[1] 0.6921331
```

What's really interesting about correlations is that they measure the amount of distance that one variable *covaries* in relation to another. So, if both variables are highly variable (have lots of wide-ranging values), the correlation between them is more likely to be high than if not. Now, that's not to say that lots of variability guarantees a higher correlation, because the scores have to vary in a systematic way. But if the variance is constrained in one variable, then no matter how much the other variable changes, the correlation will be lower. For example, let's say you are examining the correlation between academic achievement in high school and first-year grades in college and you only look at the top 10% of the class. Well, that top 10% is likely to have very similar grades, introducing no variability and no room for the one variable to vary as a function of the other. Guess what you get when you correlate one variable with another variable that does not change (that is, has no variability)? $r_{XY} = 0$, that's what. The lesson here? Variability works, and you should not artificially limit it.

A Visual Picture of a Correlation: The Scatterplot

There's a very simple way to visually represent a correlation: Create what is called a **scatterplot**, or **scattergram**. A scatterplot is simply a plot of each set of scores on separate axes.

Here are the steps to complete a scatterplot like the one you see in Figure 7.1, which plots the 10 sets of scores for which we computed the sample correlation earlier.

1. Draw the *x*-axis and the *y*-axis. Usually, the *X* variable goes on the horizontal axis and the *Y* variable goes on the vertical axis.
2. Mark both axes with the range of values that you know to be the case for the data. For example, the value of the *X* variable in our example ranges from 2 to 8, so we marked the *x*-axis from 0 to 9. There's no harm in marking

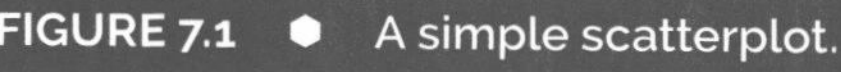

FIGURE 7.1 ● A simple scatterplot.

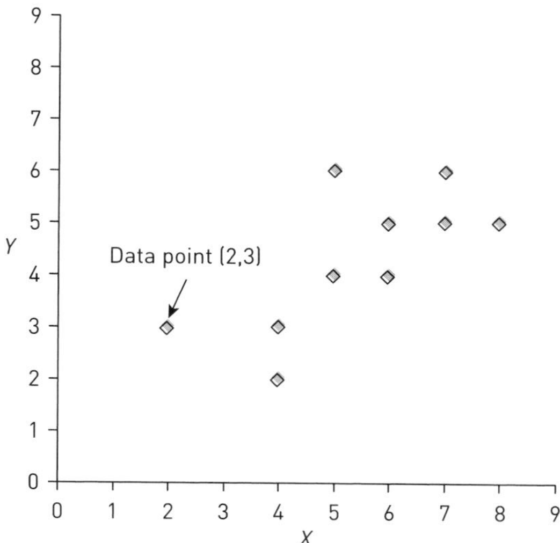

the axes a bit low or high—just as long as you allow room for the values to appear. The value of the *Y* variable ranges from 2 to 6, and we marked that axis from 0 to 9. Having similarly labeled (and scaled) axes can sometimes make the finished scatterplot easier to understand.

3. Finally, for each pair of scores (such as 2 and 3, as shown in Figure 7.1), we entered a dot on the chart by marking the place where 2 falls on the *x*-axis and 3 falls on the *y*-axis. The dot represents a data point, which is the intersection of the two values.

When all the data points are plotted, what does such an illustration tell us about the relationship between the variables? To begin with, the general shape of the collection of data points indicates whether the correlation is direct (positive) or indirect (negative).

A positive correlation occurs when the data points group themselves in a cluster from the lower left-hand corner on the *x*- and *y*-axes through the upper right-hand corner. A negative correlation occurs when the data points group themselves in a cluster from the upper left-hand corner on the *x*- and *y*-axes through the lower right-hand corner.

We can easily create a scatterplot with R. Try this command:

```
> plot(Y ~ X)
```

- `plot` is the name of the function.
- Y listed first tells R what variable we want represented with the vertical axis.
- ~ is a symbol that roughly means related.
- X is listed second and will be displayed on the horizontal axis.

Here are some scatterplots showing very different correlations where you can see how the grouping of the data points reflects the sign and strength of the correlation coefficient.

Figure 7.2 shows a perfect direct correlation where r_{XY} = 1.00 and all the data points are aligned along a straight line with a positive correlation.

FIGURE 7.2 ● A perfect positive correlation.

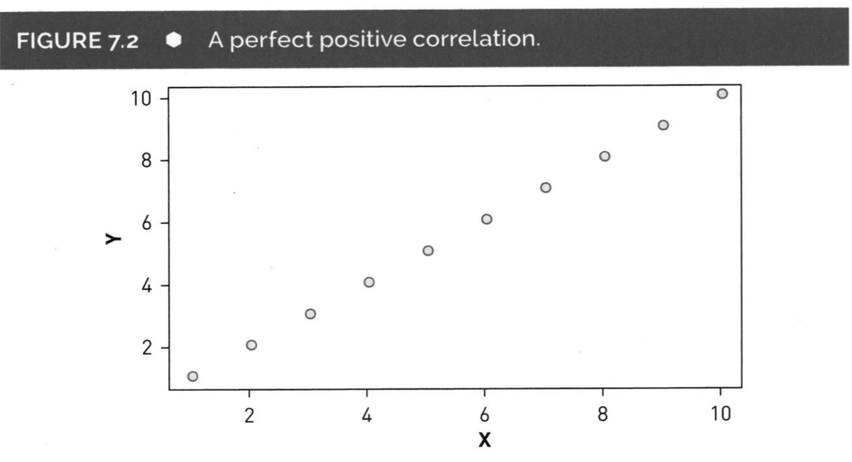

If the correlation were perfectly indirect, the value of the correlation coefficient would be −1.00, and the data points would align themselves in a straight line as well but from the upper left-hand corner of the chart to the lower right. In other words, the line that connects the data points would have a negative correlation.

Don't ever expect to find a perfect correlation between any two variables in the behavioral or social sciences. Such a correlation would say that two variables are so perfectly related, they share everything in common. In other words, knowing one is like knowing the other. Just think about your classmates. Do you think they all share any one thing in common that is perfectly related to another of their characteristics across all those different people? Probably not. In fact, *r* values approaching .7 and .8 are just about the highest you'll see.

In Figure 7.3, you can see the scatterplot for a strong (but not perfect) direct relationship where r_{XY} = .70. Notice that the data points align themselves along a positive line, although not perfectly. If you were to draw a circle around the data points, it would look like an ellipse.

Now, we'll show you a strong indirect, or negative, relationship in Figure 7.4, where r_{XY} = −.82. Notice that the data points align themselves on a negative line from the upper left-hand corner of the chart to the lower right-hand corner. Again, a circle drawn around the data points will look like an ellipse.

FIGURE 7.3 ● A strong, but not perfect, direct relationship.

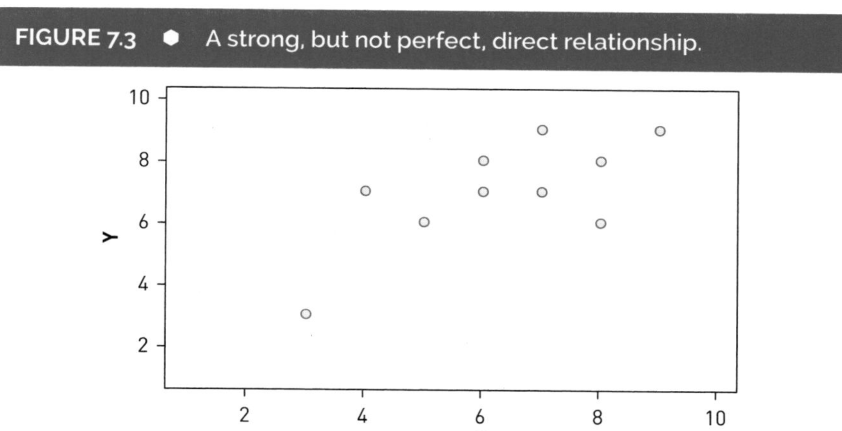

FIGURE 7.4 ● A strong, but not perfect, indirect relationship.

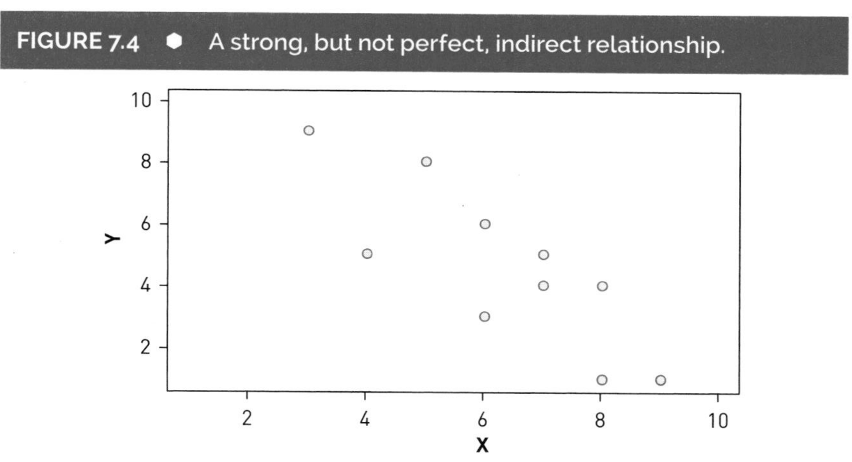

That's what different types of correlations look like, and you can really tell the general strength and direction by examining the way the points are grouped.

Not all correlations are reflected by a straight line showing the *X* and the *Y* values in a relationship called a **linear correlation** (see Chapter 17 for tons of fun stuff about this). The relationship may not be linear and may not be reflected by a straight line. Let's take the correlation between age and memory. For the early years, the correlation is probably highly positive—the older children get, the better their memories. Then, into young and middle adulthood, there isn't much of a change or much of a correlation, because most young and middle adults maintain a good (but not necessarily increasingly variable) memory. But with old age, memory begins to suffer, and there is an indirect relationship between memory and aging in the later years. If you take these together and look at the relationship over the life span, you find that the correlation between memory and age tends to look something like a curve where memory increases, levels off, and then decreases. It's a *curvilinear* relationship, and sometimes, the best description of a relationship is that it is curvilinear.

Bunches of Correlations: The Correlation Matrix

What happens if you have more than two variables? How are the correlations illustrated? Use a **correlation matrix** like the one shown in Table 7.4—a simple and elegant solution.

TABLE 7.4 ● Correlation Matrix.

	Income	Education	Attitude	Vote
Income	1.00	.574	−.08	−.291
Education	.574	1.00	−.149	−.199
Attitude	−.08	−.149	1.00	−.169
Vote	−.291	−.199	−.169	1.00

As you can see, there are four variables in the matrix: level of income (Income), level of education (Education), attitude toward voting (Attitude), and whether the individual voted in the most recent election (Vote).

For each pair of variables, there is a correlation coefficient. For example, the correlation between income level and education is .574. Similarly, the correlation between income level and whether the person participated in the most recent election is −.291 (meaning that the higher the level of income, the less likely people are to vote, and of course, the lower the level of income, the more likely it is people will vote).

In such a matrix with *four* variables, there are always $4!/[(4-2)!2!]$, or four things taken two at a time for a total of six correlation coefficients (recall $4! = 4 \times 3 \times 2 \times 1$). Because variables correlate perfectly with themselves (those are the 1.00s down the diagonal), and because the correlation between Income and Vote is the same as the correlation between Vote and Income, the matrix creates a mirror image of itself.

You will see such matrices (the plural of *matrix*) when you read journal articles that use correlations to describe the relationships among several variables.

UNDERSTANDING WHAT THE CORRELATION COEFFICIENT MEANS

Well, we have this numerical index of the relationship between two variables, and we know that the higher the value of the correlation (regardless of its sign), the stronger the relationship is. But because the correlation coefficient is a value that is not directly tied to the value of an outcome, just how can we interpret it and make it a more meaningful indicator of a relationship?

Here are different ways to look at the interpretation of that simple r_{XY}.

Using-Your-Thumb (or Eyeball) Method

Perhaps the easiest (but not the most informative) way to interpret the value of a correlation coefficient is by eyeballing it and using the information in Table 7.5.

TABLE 7.5 ● Interpreting a Correlation Coefficient.

Size of the Correlation	Coefficient General Interpretation
.8 to 1.0	Very strong relationship
.6 to .8	Strong relationship
.4 to .6	Moderate relationship
.2 to .4	Weak relationship
.0 to .2	Weak or no relationship

So, if the correlation between two variables is .5, you could safely conclude that the relationship is a moderate one—not strong, but certainly not weak enough to say that the variables in question don't share anything in common.

This eyeball method is perfectly acceptable for a quick assessment of the strength of the relationship between variables, such as when you briefly evaluate data presented visually. But because this rule of thumb depends on a subjective judgment (of what's "strong" or "weak"), we would like a more precise method. That's what we'll look at now.

These cutoff points may differ from cutoffs other researchers use. The exact cutoffs and what is considered strong versus weak depend on the field of research. Ask your professor what standards they use.

A DETERMINED EFFORT: SQUARING THE CORRELATION COEFFICIENT

Here's the much more precise way to interpret the correlation coefficient: computing the coefficient of determination. The **coefficient of determination** is the percentage of variance in one variable that is accounted for by the variance in the other variable. Quite a mouthful, huh? A simpler way would be to say the coefficient of determination is the amount of variance the two variables share.

Earlier in this chapter, we pointed out how variables that share something in common tend to be correlated with one another. If we correlated math and English grades for 100 fifth-grade students, we would find the correlation to be moderately strong, because many of the reasons why children do well (or poorly) in math tend to be the same reasons why they do well (or poorly) in English. The number of hours they study, how bright they are, how interested their parents are in their schoolwork, the number of books they have at home, and more are all related to both math and English performance and account for differences between children (and that's where the variability comes in).

The more these two variables share in common, the more they will be related. These two variables share variability—or the reason why children differ from one another. And on the whole, the brighter child who studies more will do better.

To determine exactly how much of the variance in one variable can be accounted for by the variance in another variable, the coefficient of determination is computed by squaring the correlation coefficient.

For example, if the correlation between GPA and number of hours of study time is .70 (or $r_{\text{GPA.time}} = .70$), then the coefficient of determination, represented by $r^2_{\text{GPA.time}}$, is $.70^2$, or .49. This means that 49% of the variance in GPA can be explained by the variance in studying time. And the stronger the correlation, the more variance can be explained (which only makes good sense). The more two variables share in common (such as good study habits, knowledge of what's expected in class, and lack of fatigue), the more information about performance on one score can be explained (and, as you will learn in Chapter 18, predicted) by the other score.

However, if 49% of the variance can be explained, this means that 51% cannot—so even for a strong correlation of .70, many of the reasons why scores on these variables tend to be different from one another go unexplained. This amount of unexplained variance is called the **coefficient of alienation** (also called the **coefficient of nondetermination**). Don't worry. No aliens here. This isn't *Avatar, Signs,* or *District 9* stuff—it's just the amount of variance in *Y* not explained by *X* (and, of course, vice versa since the relationship goes both ways).

How about a visual presentation of this sharing variance idea? Okay. In Figure 7.5, you'll find a correlation coefficient, the corresponding coefficient of determination, and a diagram that represents how much variance is shared between the two variables. The larger the shaded area in each diagram (and the more variance the two variables share), the more highly the variables are correlated.

- The first diagram in Figure 7.5 shows two circles that do not touch. They don't touch because they do not share anything in common. The correlation is zero.
- The second diagram shows two circles that overlap. With a correlation of .5 (and $r^2_{XY} = .25$), they share about 25% of the variance between them.
- Finally, the third diagram shows two circles placed almost on top of each other. With an almost perfect correlation of $r_{XY} = .90$ ($r^2_{XY} = .81$), they share about 81% of the variance between them.

FIGURE 7.5 ● Correlations and the resulting amount of variance shared.

Correlation	Coefficient of Determination	Variable *X*	Variable *Y*
$r_{XY} = 0$	$r^2_{XY} = 0$	0% shared	
$r_{XY} = .5$	$r^2_{XY} = .25$ or 25%	25% shared	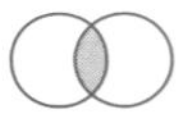
$r_{XY} = .9$	$r^2_{XY} = .81$ or 81%	81% shared	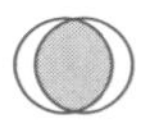

As More Ice Cream Is Eaten . . . the Crime Rate Goes Up (or Association vs. Causality)

Now here's the really important thing to be aware of, and very careful about, when computing, reading about, or interpreting correlation coefficients.

Imagine this. In a small Midwestern town, a phenomenon occurred that defied any logic. The local police chief observed that as ice cream consumption increased, crime rates tended to increase as well. Quite simply, if you measured both, you would find the relationship was direct, meaning that as people eat more ice cream, the crime rate increases. And as you might expect, as they eat less ice cream, the crime rate goes down. The police chief was baffled until he recalled the Stats 1 class he took in college and still fondly remembered.

He wondered how this could be turned into an aha! "Very easily," he thought. The two variables must share something or have something in common with one another. Remember that it must be something that relates to both level of ice cream consumption and level of crime rate. Can you guess what that is?

The *outside temperature* is what they both have in common. When it gets warm outside, such as in the summertime, more crimes are committed (it stays light longer, people leave the windows open, bad guys and girls are out more, etc.). And because it is warmer, people enjoy the ancient treat and art of eating ice cream. Conversely, during the long and dark winter months, less ice cream is consumed and fewer crimes are committed as well.

Joe, recently elected as a city commissioner, learns about these findings and has a great idea, or at least one that he thinks his constituents will love. (Keep in mind, he skipped the statistics offering in college.) Why not just limit the consumption of ice cream in the summer months to reduce the crime rate? Sounds good, right? Well, on closer inspection, it really makes no sense at all.

That's because of the simple principle that correlations express the *association* that exists between two or more variables; they have nothing to do with *causality*. In other words, just because level of ice cream consumption and crime rate increase together (and decrease together as well) does not mean that a change in one results in a change in the other.

For example, if we took all the ice cream out of all the stores in town and no more was available, do you think the crime rate would decrease? Of course not, and it's preposterous to think so. But strangely enough, that's often how associations are interpreted—as being causal in nature—and complex issues in the social and behavioral sciences are reduced to trivialities because of this misunderstanding. Did long hair and hippiedom have anything to do with the Vietnam conflict? Of course not. Does the rise in the number of crimes committed have anything to do with more efficient and safer cars? Of course not. But they all happen at the same time, creating the illusion of being associated.

Using RStudio to Compute the Correlation Coefficient

Let's use RStudio to compute the correlation coefficient. The data set we are using is Chapter 7 Data Set 1 (ch7ds1.csv).

There are two variables in this data set:

Variable	Definition
Income	Annual income in thousands of dollars
Education	Level of education measured in years

COMPUTING THE CORRELATION COEFFICIENT BY ENTERING DATA

To compute the Pearson correlation coefficient, follow these steps:

1. Enter the data from ch7ds1 by hand for Income and Education. We're using the `c` function to concatenate or combine the data that follow.

```
> Income <- c(36577, 54365, 33542, 65654, 45765, 24354,
43233, 44321, 23216, 43454, 64543, 43433, 34644, 33213,
55654, 76545, 21324, 17645, 23432, 44543)
> Education <- c(11, 12, 10, 12, 11, 7, 12, 13, 9, 12,
12, 14, 12, 10, 15, 14, 11, 12, 11, 15)
>
```

When you enter a command into R and don't complete it (you might have forgot a parenthesis, for example, like this . . .)

```
x <- c(3, 5
```

RStudio will let you know that you have more to enter by placing an empty line rather than the usual RStudio > prompt. RStudio is telling you that it needs more to complete the operation.

2. Calculate the correlation coefficient using the `cor` function.

```
> cor(Income, Education)
>
```

3. Press the Enter key.

The results [1] (0.5744407) are as shown in the R syntax for this whole example:

```
> Income <- c(36577, 54365, 33542, 65654, 45765, 24354,
+             43233, 44321, 23216, 43454, 64543, 43433,
+             34644, 33213, 55654, 76545, 21324, 17645,
+             23432, 44543)
> Education <- c(11, 12, 10, 12, 11, 7, 12, 13, 9, 12,
+               12, 14, 12, 10, 15, 14, 11, 12, 11, 15)
> cor(Income, Education) # Calculate correlation
[1] 0.5744407
>
```

R Output

The output shows the correlation coefficient to be equal to .574, and that's all the output shows. Nothing about the statistical significance of the correlation coefficient or sample size and other useful information, but we'll get to all that in Chapter 18. For now, we just want to compute the correlation coefficient, which `cor` does quite nicely.

The R Console output shows that the two variables are related to one another (directly) and that as level of income increases, so does level of education. Similarly, as level of income decreases, so does level of education (again, directly).

As for the meaningfulness of the relationship, the coefficient of determination is $.574^2$ or .33, meaning that 33% of the variance in one variable is accounted for by the other. According to our eyeball strategy, this is a relatively moderate relationship. Once again, remember that low levels of income do not cause low levels of education, nor does not finishing high school mean that someone is destined to a life of low income. That's causality, not association, and correlations speak only to association.

COMPUTING THE CORRELATION COEFFICIENT BY IMPORTING A FILE

We can also read a data set into RStudio by using the Import Dataset option on the file menu as you have seen earlier in *Statistics for People Who (Think They) Hate Statistics Using R*. See Chapter 3 if you need a refresher on how to do this.

Once the file is imported, use the `cor()` function to compute the correlation coefficient as you see below. Here the $ sign was used to reference the RStudio object (ch7ds1 separated from the vector names such as Income and Education). The command takes the following form:

```
> cor(data1$Income, data1$Education)
[1] 0.5744407
>
```

Creating a Scatterplot (or Scattergram or Whatever You Want to Call It)

To use RStudio to create a scatterplot, follow these steps. This is a really easy procedure and the same function we used to plot *X* and *Y*. Be sure that Income and Education are both objects in the workspace by looking in your Global Environment on the Environment/History pane or using the `ls()` command to check their availability. If they are not available, add them.

1. At the RStudio prompt, enter the following command.

```
> plot(Income, Education)
```

2. Press the Enter key.

The R syntax above produces the plot you see below in Figure 7.6, although minus the attractive axis labels. We learned how to fancy up plots in Chapter 6.

FIGURE 7.6 ● A scatterplot of Income and Education.

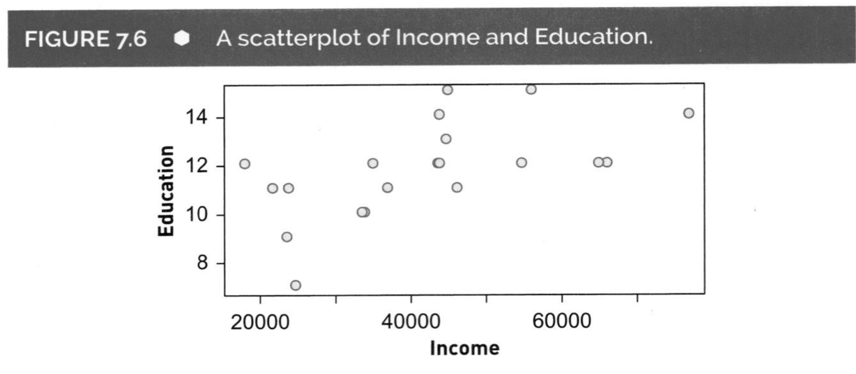

Another Scatterplot

Remember way back in Chapters 2 and 3 that we talked about the many different ways R and RStudio can be used to accomplish a similar task? Well, take a look at Figure 7.7, where we used the scatterplot function from the *car* package (we had to download this package because it is not a part of R base). It provides the same visual information (and much more). Remember that with R, there are many different ways to accomplish the same goal.

Here is the syntax we used to install and reference the car package and then use the `scatterplot()` function:

```
> install.packages("car")
> library(car)
> scatterplot(Income, Education)
>
```

FIGURE 7.7 ● A scatterplot using the *scatterplot* function from the car package.

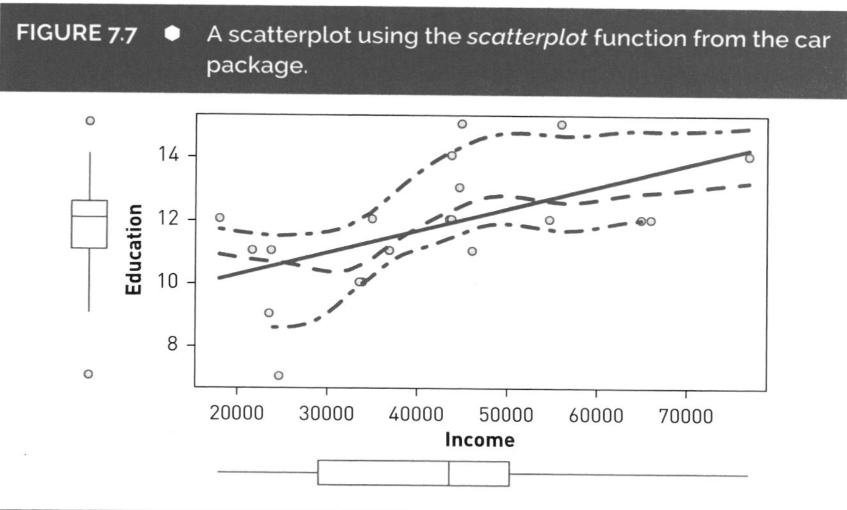

In addition to the data points, the line representing the correlation is the solid line running from the bottom left to the top right. We will talk about the dotted and dashed lines in the next paragraph. What is really different is the rectangular boxes on the *x*-axis and *y*-axis. They are boxplots with the middle line at the median.

Things Don't Have to Be Linear Part 2

Above, we mentioned that the relationship between two variables is not always linear. One way to investigate how linear the relationship is? Use the scatterplot function to get a line that follows the data, called a lowess line. Lowess stands for Locally Weighted Scatterplot Smoothing. In this case, for income below 30,000, the relationship appears negative and weak. For income from 30,000 to 50,000, the relationship appears positive and strong. For income above 50,000, the relationship appears positive and weak. The dashed lines above and below represent a confidence interval allowing us to show how uncertain we are about the lowess line. Meaning, if we collected another sample of 20 observations and created a scatterplot, its lowess line is probably (95% of the time) somewhere between the two dashed lines.

OTHER COOL CORRELATIONS

There are different ways in which variables can be assessed. For example, nominal-level variables are categorical in nature; examples are race (Black or White) and political affiliation (Independent or Republican). Or, if you are measuring income and age, you are measuring interval-level variables, because the underlying continuum on which they are based has equally appearing intervals. As you continue your studies, you're likely to come across correlations between data that occur at different levels of measurement. And to compute these correlations, you need some specialized techniques. Table 7.6 summarizes what these different techniques are and how they differ from one another.

TABLE 7.6 ● Correlation Coefficient Shopping, Anyone?

Level of Measurement and Examples			
Variable *X*	**Variable *Y***	**Type of Correlation**	**Example**
Nominal (voting preference, such as Republican or Democrat)	Nominal (sex, such as male or female)	Phi coefficient	The correlation between voting preference and sex
Nominal (social class, such as high, medium, or low)	Ordinal (rank in high school graduating class)	Rank biserial coefficient	The correlation between social class and rank in high school
Nominal (family configuration, such as two-parent or single-parent)	Interval (grade point average)	Point biserial	The correlation between family configuration and grade point average
Ordinal (height converted to rank)	Ordinal (weight converted to rank)	Spearman rank coefficient	The correlation between height and weight
Interval (number of problems solved)	Interval (age in years)	Pearson correlation coefficient	The correlation between number of problems solved and age in years

Using RStudio to Compute Other Correlations

As you already know, the command for computing a simple correlation coefficient is cor(). And the default here is to compute the Pearson correlation coefficient. But you can also compute other kinds of correlations by defining a method. So, if you wanted to compute Kendall's tau correlation coefficient (and that would be used for the correlation between two ordered variables such as finishing first, second, etc. in a race), you would enter this command at the RStudio prompt—and remember the quotes!

```
> cor(x, y, method = "kendall")
```

where x and y represent the two variables you want to correlate. You can do the same with the Spearman rank correlation coefficient.

PARTING WAYS: A BIT ABOUT PARTIAL CORRELATION

Okay, now you have the basics about simple correlation, but there are many other correlational techniques that are specialized tools to use when exploring relationships between variables.

A common "extra" tool is called **partial correlation**, where the relationship between two variables is explored, but the impact of a third variable is removed from the relationship between the two. Sometimes that third variable is called a *confounding* variable.

For example, let's say that we are exploring the relationship between level of depression and incidence of chronic disease and we find that, on the whole, the relationship is positive. In other words, the more chronic disease is evident, the higher the likelihood that depression is present as well (and of course vice versa).

Now remember, one variable does not "cause" the other, and the presence of one variable does not mean that the other will be present as well. The positive correlation is just an assessment of the relationship between these two variables, the key idea being that they share some variance in common.

And that's exactly the point—it's what they share in common that we want to control and, in some cases, remove from the relationship.

For example, how about level of family support? Nutritional habits? Severity or length of illness? These and many more variables can all be responsible for the relationship between these two variables, or they may at least account for some of the variance.

And think back a bit. That's exactly the same argument we made when focusing on the relationship between consumption of ice cream and level of crime. Once outside temperature (the mediating or confounding variable) is removed from the equation . . . boom! The relationship between consumption of ice cream and crime level plummets. Let's take a look.

USING R TO COMPUTE PARTIAL CORRELATIONS

Let's use some data and R to illustrate the computation of a partial correlation. Here are the raw data we mentioned earlier about ice cream and crime.

City	Ice Cream Consumption	Crime Rate	Average Outside Temperature
1	3.4	62	88
2	5.4	98	89
3	6.7	76	65
4	2.3	45	44

(Continued)

(Continued)

City	Ice Cream Consumption	Crime Rate	Average Outside Temperature
5	5.3	94	89
6	4.4	88	62
7	5.1	90	91
8	2.1	68	33
9	3.2	76	46
10	2.2	35	41

Here are the steps in computing a partial correlation coefficient using R.

1. Create three vectors using the data in the above table as shown here.

```
> IceCreamConsumption <- c(3.4, 5.4, 6.7, 2.3, 5.3, 4.4,
5.1, 2.1, 3.2, 2.2)
> CrimeRate <- c(62, 98, 76, 45, 94, 88, 90, 68, 76, 35)
> AverageTemperature <- c(88, 89, 65, 44, 89, 62, 91,
33, 46, 41)
```

One was named IceCreamConsumption, the second was named CrimeRate, and the third was named AverageTemperature. You can, of course, name them what you want, and these are a bit long, but we wanted to use highly descriptive names to make this exercise easy to follow.

2. Create a data frame (named IceCream) that combines these three vectors or variables into a data frame.

```
> IceCream <- data.frame(IceCreamConsumption, CrimeRate,
AverageTemperature)
>
```

3. Using the `cor()` function, enter the following command to compute the simple correlation on the whole data frame to get a correlation matrix on the three variables.

```
> cor(IceCream)
                    IceCreamConsumption CrimeRate AverageTemperature
IceCreamConsumption 1.0000000 0.7429317          0.7038434
CrimeRate           0.7429317 1.0000000          0.6552779
AverageTemperature  0.7038434 0.6552779          1.0000000
>
```

Computing the Correlation Between Three Variables

As you can see by these values, there's a pretty healthy relationship between ice cream consumption and outside temperature (.703) and between crime rate and outside temperature (.655). We're interested in the question, "What's the correlation between ice cream consumption and crime rate with the effects of outside temperature removed or *partialed out?*"

That's what partial correlation does. It looks at the relationship between two variables (in this case, consumption of ice cream and crime rate) as it removes the influence of a third (in this case, outside temperature). And, the all-important relationship between consumption of ice cream and crime rate is .7429. This too (remember, at this point, it is a simple correlation coefficient) is a pretty healthy relationship, accounting for more than 50% of the variance between the two variables ($.7429^2 =$ .5519 or 55%). Pretty respectable (but not to be trusted!—read on).

4. If you have not already, install the package named ppcor using the Install tab on the Files, Plots . . . pane in RStudio. If you have questions about how to install packages, see the section on Installing Packages in Chapter 2.

Making Packages Work

Remember that when you install a package, the functions in that package do not become active and available until you enter the following command `library(package name)`, such as

```
> library(ppcor)
>
```

Otherwise, RStudio will not be able to find and execute any of the functions.

5. Enter the following command at the RStudio prompt to compute the partial correlations for all three variables.

```
> pcor(IceCream)
```

You will see the results of the partial correlation analysis as shown below. The variable that is partialed out is AverageTemperature (the farthest column to the right), so the first two columns and rows represent the correlation without the influence of AverageTemperature.

```
> pcor(IceCream)
$estimate
                    IceCreamConsumption  CrimeRate  AverageTemperature
IceCreamConsumption           1.0000000  0.5250130           0.4291989
CrimeRate                     0.5250130  1.0000000           0.2783881
AverageTemperature            0.4291989  0.2783881           1.0000000
```

Understanding the R Output for Partial Correlation

As you can see in the R output, the correlation of IceCreamConsumption and CrimeRate with AverageTemperature removed or controlled is .5250. If you look back at the results of the simple correlation obtained from the `cor()` function, you can see that the removal of that one variable (AverageTemperature) reduced the correlation from .74 to .53. In terms of the way we interpret correlations (remember the coefficient of determination), the amount of variance accounted for goes from 54% (that's $.74^2$) to 27% (that's $.52^2$)—it's quite a difference in explanatory power.

Our conclusion? With the removal of the confounding variable of outside temperature, the relationship decreases and much less variance is accounted for. In fact, removing the variable of AverageTemperature decreases the amount of explained variance by 100% (it's just about reduced by half). Yikes—that's a big difference.

And, the most important implication of this analysis is that we don't need to stop selling ice cream to try to reduce crime. Breathe easy.

Other Ways to Compute the Correlation Coefficient

Package	Function	What It Tells You
`Hmisc`	`rcorr`	The correlation between *x* and *y*, the number of pairs of data, and the statistical significance of *r*.

```
> rcorr(X, Y)
     x     y
x 1.00  0.69
y 0.69  1.00
n = 10
P
  x    y
x      0.0266
y 0.0266
```

REAL-WORLD STATS

Nicholas Derzis and his colleagues examined the relationship between career thoughts and career interests in a group of incarcerated males as part of a reentry program for prisoners in their last 90 days in a medium-security prison.

Negative career thoughts were assessed on three subscales, decision-making confusion, external conflict, and commitment anxiety, that make up the Career Thoughts Inventory. Career interests were assessed by the Self-Directed Search, which gauges likes and dislikes in six career domains: realistic, investigative, conventional, artistic, enterprising, and social.

Career Thoughts Inventory scores were converted to *T* scores (something you will learn about in Chapter 10), and means on the subscales and overall ranged from

54.20 to 57.19. Self-Directed Search results indicated that the most popular jobs were those in which people prefer to work with things rather than other people (realistic).

The researchers used Kendall's tau to examine the relationship between normal scores on the Career Thoughts Inventory and categories on the Self-Directed Search. Looking at Table 7.5, all correlations would be rated as weak or no relationship with values that ranged from .08 to .18.

Want to know more? Go online or to the library and find . . .

Derzis, N. C., Meyer, J., Curtis, R. S., & Shippen, M. E. (2017). An analysis of career thinking and career interests of incarcerated males. *Journal of Correctional Education, 68*(1), 52–70.

Summary

The idea of showing how things are related to one another and what they have in common is a very powerful one, and the correlation coefficient is a very useful descriptive statistic (one used in inference as well, as we will show you later). Keep in mind that correlations express a relationship that is only associative and not causal, and you'll be able to understand how this statistic gives us valuable information about relationships between variables and how variables change or remain the same in concert with others. Now it's time to change speeds just a bit and wrap up Part III with a focus on reliability and validity. You need to know about these ideas because you'll be learning about how to determine what differences in outcomes, such as scores and other variables, represent.

Time to Practice

1. Use these data to answer Questions 1a and 1b. These data are saved in Chapter 7 Data Set 2 (ch7ds2.csv).
   a. Compute the Pearson product-moment correlation coefficient by hand and show all your work.
   b. Construct a scatterplot for the following 10 pairs of values by hand. Based on the scatterplot, would you predict the correlation to be direct or indirect? Why?

Number Correct (out of a possible 20)	Attitude (out of a possible 100)
17	94
13	73
12	59

(Continued)

(Continued)

Number Correct (out of a possible 20)	Attitude (out of a possible 100)
15	80
16	93
14	85
16	66
16	79
18	77
19	91

2. Use Chapter 7 Data Set 3 (ch7ds3.csv) to answer Questions 2a and 2b.
   a. Using either a calculator or a computer, compute the Pearson correlation coefficient.
   b. Interpret these data using the general range of very weak to very strong. Also compute the coefficient of determination. How does the subjective analysis compare with the value of r^2?

Speed (to complete a 50-yard swim)	Strength (number of pounds bench-pressed)
21.6	135
23.4	213
26.5	243
25.5	167
20.8	120
19.5	134
20.9	209
18.7	176
29.8	156
28.7	177

3. Rank the following correlation coefficients on strength of their relationship (list the weakest first).

.71 .47

+.36 −.62

−.45

4. For the following set of scores, calculate the Pearson correlation coefficient and interpret the outcome. These data are saved in Chapter 7 Data Set 4 (ch7ds4.csv).

Achievement Increase Over 12 Months	Classroom Budget Increase Over 12 Months
0.07	0.11
0.03	0.14
0.05	0.13
0.07	0.26
0.02	0.08
0.01	0.03
0.05	0.06
0.04	0.12
0.04	0.11

5. For the following set of data, use R to correlate minutes of exercise with GPA. What do you conclude given your analysis? These data are found in Chapter 7 Data Set 5 (ch7ds5.csv).

Exercise	GPA
25	3.6
30	4.0
20	3.8
60	3.0
45	3.7
90	3.9
60	3.5
0	2.8
15	3.0
10	2.5

(Continued)

(Continued)

6. Calculate the correlation between hours of studying and grade point average for these honor students. Why is the correlation so low?

Hours of Studying	GPA
23	3.95
12	3.90
15	4.00
14	3.76
16	3.97
21	3.89
14	3.66
11	3.91
18	3.80
9	3.89

7. The coefficient of determination between two variables is .64. Answer the following questions:
   a. What is the Pearson correlation coefficient?
   b. How strong is the relationship?
   c. How much of the variance in the relationship between these two variables is unaccounted for?

8. Here is a set of three variables for each of 20 participants in a study on recovery from a head injury. Create a data frame (and name it what you want) and create the correlation matrix for each pair of variables. These data are found in Chapter 7 Data Set 6 (ch7ds6.csv).

Age at Injury	Level of Treatment	12-Month Treatment Score
25	1	78
16	2	66
8	2	78
23	3	89
31	4	87
19	4	90
15	4	98
31	5	76
21	1	56

Age at Injury	Level of Treatment	12-Month Treatment Score
26	1	72
24	5	84
25	5	87
36	4	69
45	4	87
16	4	88
23	1	92
31	2	97
53	2	69
11	3	79
33	2	69

9. Look at Table 7.4. What type of correlation coefficient would you use to examine the relationship between sex (defined as male or female) and political affiliation? How about family configuration (two-parent or single-parent) and high school GPA? Explain why you selected the answers you did.
10. When two variables are correlated (such as strength and running speed), they are associated with one another. But if they are associated with one another, then why doesn't one cause the other?
11. Provide three examples of an association between two variables where a causal relationship makes perfect sense conceptually but, since correlations do not imply causality, makes little sense statistically until further examination.
12. Why can't correlations be used as a tool to prove a causal relationship between variables, rather than just an association?
13. When would you use partial correlation?

Student Study Site

Get the tools you need to sharpen your study skills! Visit **edge.sagepub.com/salkindshaw** to access practice quizzes and eFlashcards, watch R tutorial videos, and download data sets!

AN INTRODUCTION TO UNDERSTANDING RELIABILITY AND VALIDITY

Just the Truth

Difficulty Scale ☺ ☺ ☺
(not so hard)

WHAT YOU WILL LEARN IN THIS CHAPTER

- ✦ Defining reliability and validity and understanding why they are important
- ✦ This is a stats class! What's up with this measurement stuff?
- ✦ Understanding scales of measurement
- ✦ Computing and interpreting various types of reliability coefficients
- ✦ Computing and interpreting various types of validity coefficients

AN INTRODUCTION TO RELIABILITY AND VALIDITY

Ask any parent, teacher, pediatrician, or almost anyone in your neighborhood what the five top concerns are about today's children, and there is sure to be a group who identifies obesity as one of those concerns. Sandy Slater and her colleagues developed and tested the reliability and validity of a self-reported questionnaire on home, school, and neighborhood physical activity environments for youth located in low-income urban minority neighborhoods and rural areas. In particular, the researchers looked at variables such as information on the presence of electronic and play equipment in youth participants' bedrooms and homes and outdoor play equipment at schools. They also looked at what people close to the children thought about being active.

A total of 205 parent–child pairs completed a 160-item take-home survey on two different occasions, a perfect model for establishing test–retest reliability. The researchers found that 90% of the measures had good reliability and validity. The researchers hope that this survey can be used to help identify opportunities and develop strategies to encourage underserved youth to be more physically active.

Want to know more? Go online or to the library and find . . .

Slater, S., Full, K., Fitzgibbon, M., & Uskali, A. (2015, June 4). Test–retest reliability and validity results of the Youth Physical Activity Supports Questionnaire. *SAGE Open, 5*(2). doi: 10.1177/2158244015586809

What's Up With This Measurement Stuff?

An excellent question, and one that you should be asking. After all, you enrolled in a stats class, and up to now, that's been the focus of the material that has been covered. Now it looks like you're faced with a topic that belongs in a tests and measurements class. So, what's this material doing in a stats book?

Well, much of what we have covered so far in *Statistics for People Who (Think They) Hate Statistics Using R* has to do with the collection and description of data. And if we are collecting data, we want to make sure that the data we are collecting are what we think they are—that the data represent what it is you want to know about. You could be using a test like your teacher to test knowledge, a ruler or thermometer, a career interest inventory, a stopwatch, or any other tool. For example, if you're studying poverty, you want to make sure that the measure you use to assess poverty actually measures poverty and that it works time after time. Or, if you are studying aggression in middle-aged males, you want to make sure that whatever tool you use to assess aggression measures aggression and not assertiveness and that it works time after time rather than providing a different result each time it is measured.

More really good news: Should you continue in your education and want to take a class on tests and measurements, this introductory chapter will give you a real jump on understanding the scope of the area and what topics you'll be studying.

And to make sure that the entire process of collecting data and making sense out of them works, you first have to make sure that what you use to collect data works as well. The fundamental questions that will be answered in this chapter are "How do I know that the test, scale, instrument, etc. I use gives me the same score every time I use it?" (that's **reliability**) and "How do I know that the test, scale, instrument, etc. I use measures what it is supposed to?" (that's **validity**).

Anyone who does research will tell you about the importance of establishing the reliability and validity of your test tool, whether it's a simple observational instrument of consumer behavior or one that measures a complex psychological construct such as attachment. However, there's another very good reason. If the tools that you use to collect data are unreliable or invalid, then the results of any test or any hypothesis, as well as the conclusions you may reach based on those results, are necessarily inconclusive. If you are not sure that the test does what

(Continued)

(Continued)

it is supposed to do and that it does so consistently, how do you know that the nonsignificant results you got aren't a function of the lousy test tools rather than an actual rejection of the null hypothesis when it is true (the Type I error you will learn about in Chapter 11)? Want a clean test of the research hypothesis? Make reliability and validity an important part of your research.

In the article at the beginning of the chapter, you were reading about physical activity. Physical activity would be referred to as the **dependent variable**. In an experiment, this is the outcome variable, or what the researcher looks at to see whether any change has occurred as a function of the treatment that has taken place. And guess what? The treatment has a name as well—the **independent variable**. For example, if a researcher examined the effect of different reading programs on comprehension, the independent variable would be the reading program, and the dependent or outcome variable would be reading comprehension score. Although these terms will not be used often throughout the remainder of this book, you should have some familiarity with them.

RELIABILITY: DOING IT AGAIN UNTIL YOU GET IT RIGHT

Reliability is pretty easy to understand and figure out. It's simply whether a test, or whatever you use as a measurement tool, measures something consistently. If you administer a test of personality type before a special treatment occurs, will the administration of that same test 4 months later be reliable? That, my friend, is one of the questions. And that is one reason why there are different types of reliability, each of which we will get to after we define reliability just a bit more.

Test Scores: Truth or Dare?

When you take a test in this class, you get a score, such as 89 (good for you) or 65 (back to the books!). That test score consists of several elements, including the **observed score** (or what you actually get on the test, such as 89 or 65) and a **true score** (the true, 100% accurate reflection of what you *really* know). We can't directly measure true score because it is a theoretical reflection of the actual amount of the trait or characteristic possessed by the individual.

Nothing about this tests and measurement stuff is clear-cut, and this true score stuff surely qualifies. Here's why. We just defined true score as the real, real, real value associated with some trait or attribute. So far, so good. But there's another point of view as well. Some psychometricians (the people who do tests and measurement for a living) believe that true score (variance) is what is left over if we could take out all of the error (variance) from the data that was actually collected or observed. Now, one would hope that the typical level of performance would reflect the thing we are interested in studying, but that's another question (a validity one at that). The distinction here is that a test is reliable if it consistently produces whatever score a person would get on average, regardless of what the test is measuring. In fact, a perfectly reliable test might not produce a score that has anything to do with the construct of interest, such as "what you really know."

Why aren't true scores and observed scores the same? Well, they can be if the test (and the accompanying observed score) is a perfect (and we mean absolutely perfect) reflection of what's being measured.

But the Yankees don't always win, the bread sometimes falls on the buttered side, and Murphy's law tells us that the world is not perfect. So, what you see as an observed score may come close to the true score, but rarely are they the same because there will always be noise in our data. We can only measure something as precisely as our tool. Rather, the difference you see is the amount of noise we call error that is introduced.

Observed Score = True Score + Error Score

Error? Yes—in all its glory. For example, let's suppose for a moment that someone gets an 85 on a stats test, but his or her true score (which we never really know but only theorize about) is 89. That means the 4-point difference (that's the **error score**) is due to error, or the reason why individual test scores vary from being 100% true.

What might be the source of such error? Well, perhaps the room in which the test was taken was so warm that it caused some students to fall asleep. That would certainly have an impact on a test score. Or perhaps the test taker didn't study for the test as much as he or she should have. Ditto. Both of these examples would reflect testing situations or conditions rather than qualities of the trait being measured, right?

Our job is to reduce those errors as much as possible by having, for example, good test-taking conditions and making sure the test takers are encouraged to get enough sleep. Reduce the error and you increase the reliability, so the observed score will more closely match the true score.

The less error, the more reliable—it's that simple.

DIFFERENT TYPES OF RELIABILITY

There are several types of reliability, and we'll cover the four most important and most often used in this section. They are all summarized in Table 8.1, and as you will see, the most common statistic used to assess reliability is correlation, the statistic you learned about in Chapter 7.

Visit **edge.sagepub.com/salkindshaw** to watch an R tutorial video on this topic.

Test–Retest Reliability

Test–retest reliability is used when you want to examine whether a test is reliable over time.

For example, let's say that you are developing a test that will examine preferences for different types of vocational programs. You may administer the test in September and then readminister the same test (and it's important for it to be the same test) again in June. Then, the two sets of scores (remember, the same people took it twice) are correlated (just like we did in Chapter 7), and you have a measure of reliability. Test–retest reliability is a must when you are examining differences or changes over time.

TABLE 8.1 ● Different Types of Reliability, When They Are Used, How They Are Computed, and What They Mean.

Type of Reliability	When You Use It	How You Do It	An Example of What You Can Say When You're Done
Test–retest reliability	When you want to know whether a test is reliable over time	Correlate the scores from a test given at Time 1 with scores from the same test given at Time 2.	The Bonzo test of identity formation for adolescents is reliable over time.
Parallel forms reliability	When you want to know if several different forms of a test are reliable or equivalent	Correlate the scores from one form of the test with the scores from a second form of the same test of the same content (but not the exact same test).	The two forms of the Regular Guy test are equivalent to one another and have shown parallel forms reliability.
Internal consistency reliability	When you want to know if the items on a test assess one, and only one, dimension	Correlate each individual item score with the total score.	All of the items on the SMART Test of Creativity assess the same construct.
Interrater reliability	When you want to know whether there is consistency in the rating of some outcome	Examine the percentage of agreement between raters.	The interrater reliability for the Best-Dressed Football Player judging was .91, indicating a high degree of agreement between judges.

You must be very confident that what you are measuring has been measured in a reliable way such that the results you are getting come as close as possible to the individual's score each and every time.

Computing Test–Retest Reliability. Here are some scores from a test at Time 1 and Time 2 for the Mastering Vocational Education (MVE) test, which is under development. Our goal is to compute the Pearson correlation coefficient as a measure of the test–retest reliability of the instrument.

ID	Scores From Time 1	Scores From Time 2
1	54	56
2	67	77
3	67	87

ID	Scores From Time 1	Scores From Time 2
4	83	89
5	87	89
6	89	90
7	84	87
8	90	92
9	98	99
10	65	76

The first and last steps in this process are to compute the Pearson product-moment correlation (see Chapter 7 for a refresher on this). Another opportunity to practice R! Let's start with entering our data and move straight to the function for correlation.

First, create your vectors for Time 1 and Time 2.

```
> Time1 <- c(54, 67, 67, 83, 87, 89, 84, 90, 98, 65)
> Time2 <- c(56, 77, 87, 89, 89, 90, 87, 92, 99, 76)
>
```

If you are looking for more practice before a quiz or test, you can use these numbers and compare your result to the answer R gives us from `cor()`. Using `cor()`,

```
> cor(Time1, Time2)
[1] 0.9005792
>
```

The function `cor()` returned `0.9005792`, which for reporting the final answer we will round to two decimal places. Presenting the following result lets the reader know test–retest reliability was calculated with r based on variables Time1 and Time2:

$$r_{\text{Time1.Time2}} = .90$$

What does .90 mean as far as test–retest reliability? We'll get to the interpretation of this value shortly.

Parallel Forms Reliability

Parallel forms reliability is used when you want to examine the equivalence or similarity between two different forms of the same test.

For example, let's say that you are doing a study on memory and part of the task is to look at 10 different words, memorize them as best you can, and then recite them back after 20 seconds of study and 10 seconds of rest. Because this study takes place over a 2-day period and involves some training of memory skills, you want to have another set of items that is exactly similar in task demands, but it obviously cannot be the same as far as content. So, you create another list of words that is hopefully similar to the first. In this example, you want the consistency to be high across forms—the same ideas are being tested, just using a different form.

Computing Parallel Forms Reliability. Here are some scores from the I Remember Memory Test (IRMT) on Form A and Form B. Our goal is to compute the Pearson correlation coefficient as a measure of the parallel forms reliability of the instrument.

ID	Scores From Form A	Scores From Form B
1	4	5
2	5	6
3	3	5
4	6	6
5	7	7
6	5	6
7	6	7
8	4	8
9	3	7
10	3	7

The first and last steps in this process are to compute the Pearson product-moment correlation (again, see Chapter 7 for a refresher on this). Using R again,

```
> FormA <- c(4, 5, 3, 6, 7, 5, 6, 4, 3, 3)
> FormB <- c(5, 6, 5, 6, 7, 6, 7, 8, 7, 7)
> cor(FormA, FormB)
[1] 0.1286979
>
```

Rounding that result of calculating the correlation between scores on FormA and FormB, we get $r_{\text{FormA.FormB}} = .13$.

Internal Consistency Reliability

Internal consistency reliability is quite different from the two previous types that we have explored. It is used when you want to know whether the items on a test are consistent with one another. In other words, that they represent one—and only one—idea, dimension, construct, or area of interest.

Let's say that you are developing a test of attitudes toward different types of health care and you want to make sure that the set of five items measures just that—and nothing else. You would look at the score for each item (for a group of test takers) and see if the individual score correlates with the total score. You would expect that people who scored high on certain items (e.g., "I like my HMO") would score low on others (e.g., "I don't like spending money on health care") and that this would be consistent across all the people who took the test.

Based on work by Louis Guttman, Cronbach developed a test that we refer to as Cronbach's alpha (or α). This reliability test is a special measure of reliability known as internal consistency. The more consistently individual item scores relate to the total score on the test, the higher the value of Cronbach's alpha. And the higher the value, the more confidence you can have that this test is internally consistent, or measures one thing, and that one thing is the sum of what each item evaluates.

For example, here's a five-item test that has lots of internal consistency:

1. 4 + 4 = ?
2. 5 − ? = 3
3. 6 + 2 = ?
4. 8 − ? = 3
5. 1 + 1 = ?

All of the items seem to measure the same thing, regardless of what that same thing is (which is a validity question—stay tuned).

Now, here's a five-item test that doesn't quite come up to speed as far as being internally consistent:

1. 4 + 4 = ?
2. Who is the fattest of the three little pigs?
3. 6 + 2 = ?
4. 8 − ? = 3
5. So, just what did the wolf want?

It's obvious why. These questions are inconsistent with one another, with three questions assessing addition and subtraction and two questions assessing fairytale knowledge. These five questions are measuring two different ideas, violating the key criterion for internal consistency.

COMPUTING CRONBACH'S ALPHA

Here are some sample data for 10 people on this five-item attitude test (the I♥HMO test) where scores are between 1 (*strongly disagree*) and 5 (*strongly agree*) on each item.

When you compute Cronbach's alpha (named after Lee Cronbach), you are actually correlating the score for each item with the total score for each individual and then comparing that with the variability present for all individual item scores. The logic is that any individual test taker with a high total test score should have a high(er) score on each item (such as 5, 5, 3, 5, 3, 4, 4, 2, 4, 5 for a total score of 40) and that any individual test taker with a low(er) total test score should have a low(er) score on each individual item (such as 4, 1, 2, 1, 3, 2, 4, 1, 2, 1).

ID	Item 1	Item 2	Item 3	Item 4	Item 5
1	3	5	1	4	1
2	4	4	3	5	3
3	3	4	4	4	4
4	3	3	5	2	1
5	3	4	5	4	3
6	4	5	5	3	2
7	2	5	5	3	4
8	3	4	4	2	4
9	3	5	4	4	3
10	3	3	2	3	2

And here's the formula to compute Cronbach's alpha:

$$\alpha = \left(\frac{k}{k-1}\right)\left(\frac{s_y^2 - \sum s_i^2}{s_y^2}\right), \tag{8.1}$$

where

- k = the number of items,
- s_y^2 = the variance associated with the observed score, and
- $\sum s_i^2$ = the sum of all the variances for each item.

Here's the same set of data with the values (the variance associated with the observed score, or s_y^2, and the sum of all the variances for each item, or $\sum s_i^2$) needed to complete the preceding equation.

ID	Item 1	Item 2	Item 3	Item 4	Item 5	Total Score
1	3	5	1	4	1	14
2	4	4	3	5	3	19
3	3	4	4	4	4	19

ID	Item 1	Item 2	Item 3	Item 4	Item 5	Total Score
4	3	3	5	2	1	14
5	3	4	5	4	3	19
6	4	5	5	3	2	19
7	2	5	5	3	4	19
8	3	4	4	2	4	17
9	3	5	4	4	3	19
10	3	3	2	3	2	13
						$s_y^2 = 6.4$
Item Variance	0.32	0.62	1.96	0.93	1.34	$\Sigma s_i^2 = 5.17$

And when you plug all these figures into the equation and get

$$\alpha = \left(\frac{5}{5-1}\right)\left(\frac{6.40-5.17}{6.40}\right) = .24, \tag{8.2}$$

you find that coefficient alpha is .24 and you're done (except for the interpretation—that comes later!).

If we told you that there were many other types of internal consistency validity, you would not be surprised, right? This is especially true for measures of internal consistency. Not only is there Cronbach's coefficient alpha, but there are also split-half reliability, Spearman–Brown, Kuder–Richardson 20 and 21 (KR_{20} and KR_{21}), and still others that basically do the same thing—examine the one-dimensional nature of a test—only in different ways.

USING R TO CALCULATE CRONBACH'S ALPHA

Once you know how to compute Cronbach's alpha by hand and want to move on to using R, the transition is very easy. We are using the data set shown above minus the Total Score, the five-item test with 10 people's responses.

1. Load the psych package into our R environment.
2. Import the data for Chapter 8 Data Set 1 (ch8ds1.csv). You should have 10 observations with six variables.
3. Use the function called `alpha()`.

Start with loading the psych package so we can get to the function **alpha()**:

```
> library(psych)
>
```

Next, import the data set that matches the example above:

```
> ch8ds1 <- read.csv(file.choose())
>
```

Now use the function **alpha()** to obtain Cronbach's alpha.

```
> alpha(ch8ds1)
Some items ( Item3 Item5 ) were negatively correlated with the
total scale and
probably should be reversed.
To do this, run the function again with the 'check.keys=TRUE'
option
Reliability analysis
Call: alpha(x = ch8ds1[, c(1:5)])

  raw_alpha std.alpha G6(smc) average_r S/N ase mean sd median_r
      0.24      0.23      0.43      0.057 0.3 0.37   3.4 0.51   0.08

lower alpha upper     95% confidence boundaries
-0.49 0.24 0.97

Reliability if an item is dropped:

    raw_alpha std.alpha G6(smc) average_r   S/N alpha se  var.r   med.r
Item1  0.309     0.345    0.43     0.117 0.528     0.35 0.066  0.1567
Item2  0.091     0.044    0.32     0.011 0.046     0.45 0.094  0.0035
Item3  0.326     0.316    0.38     0.104 0.462     0.33 0.056  0.1567
Item4  0.263     0.097    0.19     0.026 0.107     0.32 0.054 -0.0047
Item5 -0.082     0.109    0.26     0.030 0.122     0.58 0.068 -0.0047

Item statistics
       n raw.r std.r r.cor  r.drop mean   sd
Item1  10  0.14  0.35 0.081 -0.086  3.1 0.57
Item2  10  0.53  0.61 0.409  0.255  4.2 0.79
Item3  10  0.58  0.38 0.173  0.031  3.8 1.40
Item4  10  0.42  0.57 0.512  0.040  3.4 0.97
Item5  10  0.70  0.56 0.446  0.328  2.7 1.16
```

```
Non missing response frequency for each item
        1   2   3   4   5 miss
Item1 0.0 0.1 0.7 0.2 0.0    0
Item2 0.0 0.0 0.2 0.4 0.4    0
Item3 0.1 0.1 0.1 0.3 0.4    0
Item4 0.0 0.2 0.3 0.4 0.1    0
Item5 0.2 0.2 0.3 0.3 0.0    0
```

UNDERSTANDING THE R OUTPUT

As you can see in the output above, R is doing many things for us, and some items are beyond the scope of this book, so don't worry. But let's talk about a few of the lines of output like the very first:

```
Some items ( Item3 Item5 ) were negatively correlated
with the total scale and probably should be reversed.
```

What is R telling us here? Sometimes people will write a question like "I like my HMO" and another question like "I don't mind having a large co-pay for office visits." Responses on these two questions are probably negatively correlated—high responses on one question would correspond to low responses on another question. For reliability to be correctly calculated, all questions need to run in the same direction. A person who likes his or her HMO, an economical choice for health care, probably likes to pay little in co-pays. So, we would recode questions running in the wrong direction so that all questions run in the same direction and were all positively correlated. In this case, R tells us we can add `check.keys=TRUE` to the function to calculate alpha as if those negatively correlated items were recoded to run in the same direction. If we want it to, the function temporarily does the recoding work for us.

Looking at the next section, let's look at the first two statistics in the output. We get to `raw_alpha` and `std.alpha`, which means standardized alpha. Standardized alpha is based on correlations

```
raw_alpha std.alpha G6(smc) average_r S/N  ase mean   sd median_r
     0.24      0.23    0.43     0.057 0.3 0.37  3.4 0.51     0.08
```

Raw alpha is based on item covariances, like we calculated by hand above. R tells us that $\alpha = 0.24$ and standardized $\alpha = 0.23$. If you want to read more about the rest of the output, enter `?alpha` in the R Console to get the help file.

Interrater Reliability

Interrater reliability is the measure that tells you how much two raters agree on their judgments of some outcome.

For example, let's say you are interested in a particular type of social interaction during a transaction between a banker and a potential checking account customer, and you observe both people in real time (you're observing behind a one-way mirror) to see if the new and improved customer relations course that the banker took resulted in increased smiling and pleasant types of behavior toward the potential customer. Your job is to note every 10 seconds whether the banker is demonstrating one of the three different behaviors he has been taught—smiling, leaning forward in his chair, or using his hands to make a point. Each time you see any one of those behaviors, you mark it on your scoring sheet as an *X*. If you observe nothing, you score a dash (–).

As part of this process, and to be sure that what you are recording is a reliable measure, you will want to find out what the level of agreement is between observers as to the occurrence of these behaviors. The more similar the ratings are, the higher the level of interrater agreement and interrater reliability.

COMPUTING INTERRATER RELIABILITY

In this example, the really important variable is whether a customer-friendly act occurred within a set of 10-second time frames across 2 minutes (or twelve 10-second periods). So, what we are looking at is the rating consistency across a 2-minute period broken down into twelve 10-second periods. An *X* on the scoring sheet means that the behavior occurred, and a dash (–) means it did not.

For a total of 12 periods (and 12 possible agreements), there are 7 where both Dave and Maureen agreed that friendly behavior did take place (Periods 1, 3, 4, 5, 7, 8, and 12) and 3 where they agreed it did not (Periods 2, 6, and 9), for a total of 10 agreements and 2 disagreements.

	Time Period	1	2	3	4	5	6	7	8	9	10	11	12
Rater 1	Dave	X	–	X	X	X	–	X	X	–	–	X	X
Rater 2	Maureen	X	–	X	X	X	–	X	X	–	X	–	X

Interrater reliability is computed using the following simple formula:

$$\text{Interrater reliability} = \frac{\text{Number of agreements}}{\text{Number of possible agreements}}.$$

And when we plug in the numbers as you see here,

$$\text{Interrater reliability} = \frac{10}{12} = .833.$$

The resulting interrater reliability coefficient is .83.

HOW BIG IS BIG? FINALLY: INTERPRETING RELIABILITY COEFFICIENTS

Okay, now we get down to business, and guess what? Remember all you learned about interpreting the value of the correlation coefficient in Chapter 5? It's almost the same as when you interpret reliability coefficients, with a (little) bit of a difference.

We want only two things, and here they are:

- Reliability coefficients to be positive and not to be negative
- Reliability coefficients that are as large as possible (between .00 and +1.00)

So, the interpretation is left to you. The interrater reliability coefficient of .83 that we just computed is certainly high and represents a strong level of agreement between the two sets of observations. The earlier Cronbach value of .24—not so strong.

And If You Can't Establish Reliability . . . Then What?

The road to establishing the reliability of a test is not a smooth one at all—it takes a good deal of work. What if the test is not reliable?

Here are a few things to keep in mind. Remember that reliability is a function of how much error contributes to the observed score. Lower that error, and you increase the reliability.

- Make sure that the instructions are standardized and clear across all settings in which the test is administered.
- Increase the number of items or observations because the larger the sample from the universe of behaviors you are investigating, the more likely the sample is representative and reliable. This is especially true for achievement tests.
- Delete unclear items because some people will respond in one way and others will respond in a different fashion, regardless of their knowledge or ability level or individual traits.
- For an achievement test especially (such as a spelling or history test), moderate the easiness and difficulty of the test. Any test that is too difficult or too easy does not reflect an accurate picture of the test taker's performance.
- Minimize the effects of external events and standardize directions. For example, if a particularly important event, such as Mardi Gras or graduation, occurs near the time of testing, you might postpone an assessment.

Just One More Thing

The first step in creating an instrument that has sound *psychometric* (how's that for a big word?) properties is to establish its reliability (and we just spent some good time on that). Why? Well, if a test or measurement instrument is not reliable, is not consistent, and does not do the same thing time after time after time, it does not matter what it measures (and that's the validity question), right?

On the Kids Are Cool at Spelling (KACAS) test of introductory spelling, the first three items could be as follows:

$$16 + 12 = ?$$

$$21 + 13 = ?$$

$$41 + 33 = ?$$

This is surely a highly reliable test, but surely not a valid one. Now that we have reliability well understood, let's move on to an introduction to validity.

VALIDITY: WHOA! WHAT IS THE TRUTH?

Validity is, most simply, the property of an assessment tool that indicates that the tool does what it says it does. A valid test is a test that measures what it is supposed to. If an achievement test is supposed to measure knowledge of history, then that's what it does. If an intelligence test is supposed to measure whatever intelligence is defined as by the test's creators, then it does just that.

Different Types of Validity

Just as there are different types of reliability, so there are different types of validity, and we'll cover the three most important categories and most often used in this section. They are all summarized in Table 8.2.

TABLE 8.2 ● Different Types of Validity, When They Are Used, How They Are Computed, and What They Mean.

Type of Validity	When You Use It	How You Do It	An Example of What You Can Say When You're Done
Content validity	When you want to know whether a sample of items truly reflects an entire universe of items on a certain topic	Ask Mr. or Ms. Expert to make a judgment that the test items reflect the universe of items on the topic being measured.	My weekly quiz in my stats class fairly assesses the chapter's content.
Criterion validity	When you want to know whether test scores are systematically related to other criteria that indicate that the test taker is competent in a certain area	Correlate the scores from the test with some other measure that is already valid and that assesses the same set of abilities.	The EATS test (of culinary skills) has been shown to be correlated with being a fine chef 2 years after culinary school (an example of predictive validity).

Type of Validity	When You Use It	How You Do It	An Example of What You Can Say When You're Done
Construct validity	When you want to know whether a test measures some underlying psychological construct	Correlate the set of test scores with some theorized outcome that reflects the construct for which the test is being designed.	It's true—men who participate in body contact and physically dangerous sports score higher on the TEST(osterone) test of aggression.

Content Validity

Content validity is the property of a test such that the test items sample the universe of items for which the test is designed. Content validity is most often used with achievement tests (e.g., everything from your first-grade spelling test to the Scholastic Aptitude Test [SAT]).

Establishing Content Validity. Establishing content validity is actually very easy. All you need to do is locate your local (and cooperative) content expert. For example, if we were designing a test of introductory physics, we would go to the local physics expert (perhaps the teacher at the local high school or a professor at the university who teaches physics), and we would say, "Hey, Leonard, do you think this set of 100 multiple-choice questions accurately reflects all the possible topics and ideas that we would expect the students in my introductory class to understand?"

We would probably tell Leonard what the topics were, and then he would look at the items and provide a judgment as to whether they met the criterion we established—a representation of the entire universe of all items that are introductory in physics. If the answer is yes, we're done (at least for now). If the answer is no, it's back to the drawing board and either the creation of new items or the refinement of existing ones (until the content is deemed correct by the expert).

Criterion Validity

Criterion validity assesses whether a test reflects a set of abilities in a current or future setting. If the criterion is taking place in the here and now, we talk about **concurrent criterion validity**. If the criterion is taking place in the future, we talk about **predictive validity**. For criterion validity to be present, one need not establish both concurrent and predictive validity but only the one that works for the purposes of the test.

Establishing Concurrent Validity. For example, you've been hired by the Universal Culinary Institute to design an instrument that measures culinary skills. Some part of culinary training has to do with straight knowledge (for example, what's a roux?). And that's left to the achievement test side of things.

So, you develop a test that you think does a good job of measuring culinary skills, and now you want to establish the level of concurrent validity. To do this, you design the COOK scale (whose score can range from 1 to 100 by your design), a set of 5-point items across a set of criteria (presentation, food safety, cleanliness, etc.) that each judge will use. As a criterion (and that's the key here), you have another set of judges rank each student from 1 to 10 on overall cooking ability. Then, you simply correlate the COOK scores with the judges' rankings. If the validity coefficient (a simple correlation) is high, you're in business—if not, it's back to the drawing board.

Establishing Predictive Validity. Let's say that the cooking school has been percolating (heh-heh) along just fine for 10 years and you are interested not only in how well people cook (and that's the concurrent validity part of this exercise that you just established) but in the test's predictive validity as well. Now, the criterion changes from a here-and-now score (the one that judges give) to one that looks to the future.

Here, we are interested in developing a test that *predicts* success as a chef 10 years down the line. To establish the predictive validity of the COOK test, you go back and locate graduates of the program who have been out cooking for 10 years and administer the test to them. The criterion that is used here is their level of success, and you use as measures (a) whether they own their own restaurant and (b) whether it has been in business for more than 1 year (given that the failure rate for new restaurants is more than 80% within the first year). The rationale here is that if a restaurant is in business for more than 1 year, then the chef must be doing something right.

To complete this exercise, you correlate the COOK score with a value of 1 (if the restaurant is in business for more than a year and owned by the graduate) with the previous (10 years earlier) COOK score. A high correlation coefficient indicates predictive validity, and a low correlation coefficient indicates a lack thereof.

Construct Validity

Construct validity is the most interesting and the most difficult of all the validities to establish because it is based on some underlying construct, or idea, behind a test or measurement tool.

You may remember from your extensive studies in Psych 1 that a construct is a group of interrelated variables. For example, aggression is a construct (consisting of such variables as inappropriate touching, violence, lack of successful social interaction, etc.), as are intelligence, mother–infant attachment, and hope. And keep in mind that these constructs are generated from some theoretical position that the researcher assumes. For example, he or she might propose that aggressive men have more trouble with law enforcement officials than nonaggressive men.

Establishing Construct Validity. So, you have the FIGHT test (of aggression), an observational tool that consists of a series of items. It is an outgrowth of your theoretical view about what the construct of aggression consists of. You know from the criminology literature that males who are aggressive do certain types of things more than others—for example, they get into more arguments, they are more physically aggressive (pushing and such), they commit more crimes of violence against others, and they have fewer successful interpersonal relationships. The FIGHT scale includes items that describe different behaviors, some that are theoretically related to aggressive behaviors and some that are not.

Once the FIGHT scale is completed, you examine the results to see whether positive scores on the FIGHT scale correlate with the presence of the kinds of behaviors you would predict given your theory (level of involvement in crime, quality of personal relationships, etc.) and don't correlate with the kinds of behaviors that should not be related (such as handedness or preferences for certain types of food). And, if the correlation is high for the items that you predict should correlate and low for the items that should not, then you can conclude that there is something about the FIGHT scale (probably the items you designed to assess elements of aggression) that works. Congratulations.

And If You Can't Establish Validity . . . Then What?

Well, this is a tough one, especially because there are so many different types of validity.

In general, if you don't have the validity evidence you want, it's because your test is not doing what it should. If it's an achievement test and a satisfactory level of content validity is what you seek, then you probably have to rewrite the questions on your test to make sure they are more consistent with the opinion of the expert you consulted.

If you are concerned with criterion validity, then you probably need to reexamine the nature of the items on the test and answer the question, "How well do I expect these responses to these questions to relate to the criterion?" And, of course, this assumes that the criterion you are using makes sense.

And finally, if it is construct validity that you are seeking and can't seem to find, better take a close look at the theoretical rationale that underlies the test you developed. Perhaps our definition and model of aggression are wrong, or perhaps the definition and conceptualization of intelligence need some critical rethinking. Your aim is to establish consistency between the theory and the test items based on the theory.

A LAST FRIENDLY WORD

This measurement stuff is pretty cool. It's intellectually interesting, and, in these times of accountability, everyone wants to know about the progress of students, stockbrokers, professors(!), social welfare agency programs, and more.

Because of this strong and growing interest in accountability and the measurement of outcomes, there's a great temptation for undergraduate students working on their honors thesis or semester project or graduate students working on their thesis or dissertation to design an instrument for their final project.

But be aware that what sounds like a good idea might lead to a disaster. The process of establishing the reliability and validity of any instrument can take years of intensive work. And what can make matters even worse is when the naive or unsuspecting individual wants to create a new instrument to test a new hypothesis. That means that on top of everything else that comes with testing a new hypothesis, there is also the work of making sure the instrument works as it should.

If you are doing original research of your own, such as for your thesis or dissertation requirement, be sure to find a measure that has already had reliability and validity evidence well established. That way, you can get on with the main task of testing your hypotheses and not fool with the huge task of instrument development—a career in and of itself. Want a good start? Try the Buros Center for Testing, available online at http://buros.org.

VALIDITY AND RELIABILITY: REALLY CLOSE COUSINS

Let's step back for a moment and recall one of the reasons that you're even reading this chapter.

It was assigned to you.

No, really. This chapter is important because you need to know something about reliability and the validity of the instruments you are using to measure outcomes. Why? If these instruments are not reliable *and* valid, then the results of your experiment will always be in doubt.

As we have mentioned earlier in this chapter, you can have a test that is reliable but not valid. However, you cannot have a valid test without it first being reliable. Why? Well, a test can do whatever it does over and over (that's reliability) but still not do what it is supposed to (that's validity). But if a test does what it is supposed to, then it has to do it consistently to work.

You've read about the relationship between reliability and validity in several places in this chapter, but there's a very cool relationship lurking out there that you may read about later in your coursework that you should know about now. This relationship says that the maximum level of validity is equal to the square root of the reliability coefficient. For example, if the reliability coefficient for a test of mechanical aptitude is .87, the validity coefficient can be no larger than .93 (which is the square root of .87). What this means in tech talk is that the validity of a test is constrained by how reliable it is. And that makes perfect sense if we stop to think that a test must do what it does consistently before we are sure it does what it says it does. But the relationship is closer as well. You cannot have a valid instrument without it first being reliable, because in order for something to do what it is supposed to do, it must first do it consistently, right? So, the two work hand in hand.

REAL-WORLD STATS

Here's a classic example of why validity is such an important concept to understand and to make sure is present when doing any kind of research or using the results of research to inform actions by professionals. In this case, the study has to do with the assessment of attention-deficit/hyperactivity disorder (ADHD).

Often, this diagnosis is biased by the subjectivity of symptoms and reports of parents and teachers. The relatively new use of continuous performance tests (which measure sustained and selective attention) increased expectations that the diagnosis of ADHD would be more standardized and accurate, both qualities of any reliable and valid test. In this study, Nathanel Zelnik and his colleagues looked at scores from the Test of Variables of Attention in 230 children who were referred to their ADHD clinic. Among the 179 children with diagnosed ADHD (the criterion group), the Test of Variables of Attention was suggestive of ADHD in 163 participants (91.1% sensitivity), but it was also suggestive for ADHD in 78.4% of the children without ADHD. In sum, it is just not a reliable enough measure to accurately discriminate between the two groups.

Want to know more? Go online or to the library and find . . .

Zelnik, N., Bennett-Back, O., Miari, W., Geoz, H. R., & Fattal-Valevski, A. (2012). Is the Test of Variables of Attention reliable for the diagnosis of attention-deficit hyperactivity disorder (ADHD)? *Journal of Child Neurology, 27,* 703–707.

Summary

Yep, this is a stats course, so what's the measurement stuff doing here? Once again, almost any use of statistics revolves around some outcome being measured. Just as you read basic stats to make sense of lots of data, you need basic measurement information to make sense out of how behaviors, test scores, and rankings and ratings are assessed.

Time to Practice

1. Go to the library and find five journal articles in your area of interest in which reliability and validity data are reported. Discuss the outcome measures that are used. Identify the type of reliability that was established and the type of validity and comment on whether you think that the levels are acceptable. If not, how can they be improved?
2. Provide an example of when you would want to establish test–retest and parallel forms reliability.
3. You are developing an instrument that measures vocational preferences (what people want to do for a living), and you need to administer the test several times during the year to students who are attending a vocational program. You need to assess the test–retest reliability of the test and the data from two administrations with Chapter 8 Data Set 2 (ch8ds2.csv)—one in the fall and one in the spring. Would you call this a reliable test? Why or why not?

(Continued)

(Continued)

4. How can a test be reliable and not valid? Provide an example. Why is a test not valid unless it is reliable?
5. Here's the situation. You are in charge of the test development program for the office of state employment, and you need at least two forms of the same test to administer on the same day. What kind of reliability will you want to establish? Use Chapter 8 Data Set 3 (ch8ds3.csv) to compute the reliability coefficient between the first and second form of the test for the 100 people who took it. Did you reach your goal?
6. In general terms, describe what a test would be like if it were reliable but not valid. Now, do the same for a test that is valid but not reliable.
7. When testing any experimental hypothesis, why is it important that the test you use to measure the outcome be both reliable and valid?
8. Describe the differences among content, predictive, and construct validity. Give examples of how each of these is measured.
9. Describe the steps that you would take to establish the construct validity of an observational paper-and-pencil test that assesses "thinking outside the box."

Student Study Site

Get the tools you need to sharpen your study skills! Visit **edge.sagepub.com/salkindshaw** to access practice quizzes and eFlashcards, watch R tutorial videos, and download data sets!

PART IV

TAKING CHANCES FOR FUN AND PROFIT

"And this is my statistically significant other."

What do you know so far, and what's next? To begin with, you've got a really solid basis for understanding how to describe the characteristics of a set of scores and how distributions can differ from one another, using R to lift the heavy statistical weight. That's what you learned in Chapters 4, 5, and 6 of *Statistics for People Who (Think They) Hate Statistics Using R.* In Chapter 7, you learned how to describe the relationship between variables using correlations as tools. And, in Chapter 8, you learned about the importance of reliability and validity for understanding the integrity of any test score or other kind of outcome.

Now it's time to bump up the ante a bit and start playing for real. In Part IV of *Statistics for People Who (Think They) Hate Statistics Using R,* you will be introduced in Chapter 9 to the importance, and nature, of hypothesis testing, including an in-depth discussion of what a hypothesis is, what different types of hypotheses there are, the function of the hypothesis, and why and how hypotheses are tested.

Then, in Chapter 10, we'll get to the all-important topic of probability, represented by our discussion of the normal curve and the basic principles underlying probability. This is the part of statistics that helps us define how likely it is that some event (such as a specific score on a test) will occur. We'll use the normal curve as a basis for these arguments, and you'll see how any score or occurrence within any distribution has a likelihood associated with it.

After some fun with probability and the normal curve, we'll be ready to start our extended discussion in Part IV regarding the application of hypothesis testing and probability theory to the testing of specific questions regarding relationships between variables. It only gets better from here!

HYPOTHETICALS AND YOU

Testing Your Questions

Difficulty Scale ☺ ☺ ☺ ½
(don't plan on going out tonight)

WHAT YOU WILL LEARN IN THIS CHAPTER

- ✦ Understanding the difference between a sample and a population
- ✦ Understanding the importance of the null and research hypotheses
- ✦ Using criteria to judge a good hypothesis

SO YOU WANT TO BE A SCIENTIST

You might have heard the term *hypothesis* used in other classes. You may even have had to formulate one for a research project you did for another class, or you may have read one or two in a journal article. If so, then you probably have a good idea what a hypothesis is. For those of you who are unfamiliar with this often-used term, a **hypothesis** is basically "an educated guess." Its most important role is to reflect the general problem statement or question that was the motivation for asking the research question in the first place.

That's why taking the care and time to formulate a really precise and clear research question is so important. This research question will guide your creation of a hypothesis, and in turn, the hypothesis will determine the techniques you will use to test it and answer the question that was originally asked.

So, a good hypothesis translates a problem statement or a research question into a form that is more amenable to testing. This form is called a hypothesis. We will talk about what makes a hypothesis a good one later in this chapter. Before that, let's turn our attention to the difference between a sample and a population. This is an important distinction, because hypothesis testing deals with a sample and then the results are generalized to the larger population. We also address the two main types of hypotheses (the null hypothesis and the research hypothesis). But first, let's formally define some simple terms that we have used earlier in *Statistics for People Who (Think They) Hate Statistics Using R.*

SAMPLES AND POPULATIONS

As a good scientist, you would like to be able to say that if Method A is better than Method B in your study, this is true forever and always and for all people in the universe, right? Indeed. And, if you do enough research on the relative merits of Methods A and B and test enough people, you may someday be able to say that.

But don't get too excited, because it's unlikely you will ever be able to speak with such confidence. It takes too much money ($$$) and too much time (all those people!) to do all that research, and besides, it's not even necessary. Instead, you can just select a representative sample from the population and test your hypothesis about the relative merits of Methods A and B.

Given the constraints of never enough time and never enough research funds, with which almost all scientists live, the next best strategy is to take a portion of a larger group of participants and do the research with that smaller group. In this context, the larger group is referred to as a *population,* and the smaller group selected from that population is referred to as a *sample.* In Chapter 5, we distinguished between population standard deviation and sample standard deviation. We changed the denominator to divide by $n - 1$ instead of n to get a better estimate of the population standard deviation from our sample data. And we did that because we are usually hoping to generalize from our representative sample to the population the sample comes from.

A measure of how well a sample approximates the characteristics of a population is called **sampling error**. Sampling error is basically the difference between the values of the sample statistic and the population parameter. The higher the sampling error, the less precision you have in sampling, and the more difficult it will be to make the case that what you find in the sample indeed reflects what you expected to find in the population. Just as there are measures of variability regarding distributions, so there are measures of the variability of this difference between a sample measure and a population measure. And if your sample is truly representative of the population, you will still have some sampling error due to the random nature of collecting any data from a sample. You just hope that the size of the sampling error is small.

Samples should be selected from populations in such a way that the sample matches as closely as possible the characteristics of the population. The goal is to have the sample be as much like the population as possible. The most important implication of ensuring similarity between the two is that the research results based on the sample can be generalized to the population. When the sample accurately represents the population, the results of the study are said to have a high degree of generalizability.

A high degree of generalizability is an important quality of good research because it means that the time and effort (and $$$) that went into the research may have implications for groups of people other than the original participants.

It's easy to equate "big" with "representative." Keep in mind that it is far more important to have an accurately representative sample than it is to have a big sample (people often think that big is better—only true on Thanksgiving, by the way). Having lots and lots of participants in a sample may be very impressive, but if the participants do not represent the larger population, the research will have little value.

THE NULL HYPOTHESIS

Okay. So we have a sample of participants selected from a population, and to begin the test of our research hypothesis, we first formulate the **null hypothesis**.

The null hypothesis is an interesting little creature. If it could talk, it would say something like "I represent no relationship between the variables that you are studying." In other words, null hypotheses are statements of equality demonstrated by the following real-life null hypotheses taken from a variety of popular social and behavioral science journals. Names have been changed to protect the innocent.

- There will be *no difference* between the average score of 9th graders and the average score of 12th graders on the ABC memory test.
- There is *no difference* between the effectiveness of community-based, long-term care and the effectiveness of in-home, long-term care in promoting the social activity of older adults when measured using the Margolis Scale of Social Activities.
- There is *no relationship* between reaction time and problem-solving ability.
- There is *no difference* between White and Black families in the amount of assistance families offer their children in school-related activities.

What these four null hypotheses have in common is that they all contain a statement that two or more things are equal or unrelated (that's the "no difference" and "no relationship" part) to each other.

The Purposes of the Null Hypothesis

What are the basic purposes of the null hypothesis? The null hypothesis acts as both a starting point and a benchmark against which the actual outcomes of a study can be measured.

Let's examine each of these purposes in more detail.

First, the null hypothesis acts as a starting point because it is the state of affairs that is accepted as true in the absence of any other information. For example, let's look at the first null hypothesis we stated earlier:

> There will be no difference between the average score of 9th graders and the average score of 12th graders on the ABC memory test.

Given absolutely no other knowledge of 9th and 12th graders' memory skills, you have no reason to believe that there will be differences between the two groups, right? If you know nothing about the relationship between these variables, the best you can do is guess. And that's taking a chance. You might speculate as to why one group might outperform another, but if you have no evidence a priori (before the fact), then what choice do you have but to assume that they are equal?

This lack of a relationship as a starting point is a hallmark of this whole topic. In other words, until you prove that there is a difference, you have to assume that there is no difference. And a statement of no difference or no relationship is exactly what the null hypothesis is all about. Such a statement assures us (as members of the scientific community) that we are starting on a level playing field with no bias toward one or the other direction as to how the test of our hypothesis will turn out.

Furthermore, if there are any differences between these two groups, you have to assume that these differences are due to the most attractive explanation for differences between any groups on any variable—chance! That's right: Given no other information, chance is always the most likely and attractive explanation for the observed differences between two groups or the relationship between variables. Chance explains what we cannot. You might have thought of chance as the odds of winning that $5,000 nickel jackpot at the slots, but we're talking about chance as all that other "stuff" that clouds the picture and makes it even more difficult to understand the "true" nature of relationships between variables.

For example, you could take a group of soccer players and a group of football players and compare their running speeds, thinking about whether playing soccer or playing football makes athletes faster. But look at all the factors we don't know about that could contribute to differences. Who is to know whether some soccer players practice more, or whether some football players are stronger, or whether both groups are receiving additional training of different types?

What's more, perhaps the way their speed is being measured leaves room for chance; a faulty stopwatch or a windy day can contribute to differences unrelated to *true* running speed. As good researchers, our job is to eliminate chance factors from explaining observed differences and to evaluate other factors that might contribute to group differences, such as intentional training or nutrition programs, and see how they affect speed.

The point is, if we find differences between groups and the differences are not due to training, we have no choice but to attribute the difference to chance. And, by the way, you might find it useful to think of *chance* as being somewhat equivalent to the idea of *error*. When we can control sources of error, the likelihood that we can offer a meaningful explanation for some outcome increases.

The second purpose of the null hypothesis is to provide a benchmark against which observed outcomes can be compared to see if these differences are due to some other factor. The null hypothesis helps to define a range within which any observed differences between groups can be attributed to chance (which is the null hypothesis's contention) or are due to something other than chance (which perhaps would be the result of the manipulation of some variable, such as training in our example of the soccer and football players).

Most research studies have an implied null hypothesis, and you may not find it clearly stated in a research report or journal article. Instead, you'll find the research hypothesis clearly stated, and this is where we now turn our attention.

THE RESEARCH HYPOTHESIS

Whereas a null hypothesis is a statement of no relationship between variables, a **research hypothesis** is a definite statement that a relationship exists between variables. For example, for each of the null hypotheses stated earlier, here is a corresponding research hypothesis. Notice that we said "a" and not "the" corresponding research hypothesis because there certainly could be more than one research hypothesis for any one null hypothesis.

- The average score of 9th graders *is different* from the average score of 12th graders on the ABC memory test.
- The effectiveness of community-based, long-term care *is different* from the effectiveness of in-home, long-term care in promoting the social activity of older adults when measured using the Margolis Scale of Social Activities.
- Slower reaction time and problem-solving ability *are positively related.*
- There *is a difference* between White and Black families in the amount of assistance families offer to their children in school-related activities.

Each of these four research hypotheses has one thing in common: They are all statements of inequality. They posit a relationship between variables and not an equality, as does the null hypothesis.

The nature of this inequality can take two different forms—a directional or a nondirectional research hypothesis. If the research hypothesis posits no direction to the inequality (such as "different from"), the hypothesis is a nondirectional research hypothesis. If the research hypothesis posits a direction to the inequality (such as "more than" or "less than"), the research hypothesis is a directional research hypothesis.

The Nondirectional Research Hypothesis

A **nondirectional research hypothesis** reflects a difference between groups, but the direction of the difference is not specified.

For example, the following research hypothesis is nondirectional in that the direction of the difference between the two groups is not specified: The average score of 9th graders is different from the average score of 12th graders on the ABC memory test. The hypothesis is a research hypothesis because it states that there is a difference, and it is nondirectional because it says nothing about the direction of that difference.

A nondirectional research hypothesis, like this one, would be represented by the following equation:

$$H_1 : \bar{X}_9 \neq \bar{X}_{12}, \tag{9.1}$$

where

- H_1 represents the symbol for the first (of possibly several) research hypotheses,
- $\bar{X}_9$ represents the average memory score for the sample of 9th graders,
- $\bar{X}_{12}$ represents the average memory score for the sample of 12th graders, and
- $\neq$ means "is not equal to."

The Directional Research Hypothesis

A **directional research hypothesis** reflects a difference between groups, and the direction of the difference is specified.

For example, the following research hypothesis is directional because the direction of the difference between the two groups is specified: The average score of 12th graders is greater than the average score of 9th graders on the ABC memory test. One is hypothesized to be greater than (not just different from) the other.

Examples of two other directional hypotheses are these:

A is greater than B (or A > B).

B is greater than A (or A < B).

These both represent inequalities (greater than or less than). A directional research hypothesis such as the one described above, where 12th graders are hypothesized to score better than 9th graders, would be represented by the following equation:

$$H_1 : \bar{X}_{12} > \bar{X}_9, \tag{9.2}$$

where

- H_1 represents the symbol for the first (of possibly several) research hypotheses,
- $\bar{X}_9$ represents the average memory score for the sample of 9th graders,
- $\bar{X}_{12}$ represents the average memory score for the sample of 12th graders, and
- > means "is greater than."

What is the purpose of the research hypothesis? It is this hypothesis that is directly tested as an important step in the research process. The results of this test are compared with what you expect by chance alone (reflecting the null hypothesis) to see which of the two is the more attractive explanation for any differences between groups or variables you might observe.

Table 9.1 gives the four null hypotheses and accompanying directional and nondirectional research hypotheses.

Another way to talk about directional and nondirectional hypotheses is to talk about one- and two-tailed tests. A **one-tailed test** (reflecting a directional hypothesis) posits a difference in a particular direction, such as when we hypothesize that Group 1 will score higher than Group 2. A **two-tailed test** (reflecting a nondirectional hypothesis) posits a difference but in no particular direction. The importance of this distinction begins when you test different types of hypotheses (one- and two-tailed) and establish probability levels for rejecting or not rejecting the null hypothesis. More about this in Chapters 10 and 11. Promise.

TABLE 9.1 ● Null Hypotheses and Corresponding Research Hypotheses.

Null Hypothesis	Nondirectional Research Hypothesis	Directional Research Hypothesis
There will be **no difference** in the average score of 9th graders and the average score of 12th graders on the ABC memory test.	Twelfth graders and 9th graders will **differ** on the ABC memory test.	Twelfth graders will have a **higher** average score on the ABC memory test than will 9th graders.
There is **no difference** between the effectiveness of community-based, long-term care for older adults and the effectiveness of in-home, long-term care for older adults when measured using the Margolis Scale of Social Activities.	The effect of community-based, long-term care for older adults is **different** from the effect of in-home, long-term care for older adults when measured using the Margolis Scale of Social Activities.	Older adults exposed to community-based, long-term care score **higher** on the Margolis Scale of Social Activities than do older adults receiving in-home, long-term care.
There is **no relationship** between reaction time and problem-solving ability.	There **is a relationship** between reaction time and problem-solving ability.	There **is a positive relationship** between reaction time and problem-solving ability.
There is **no difference** between White and Black families in the amount of assistance families offer their children in educational activities.	The amount of assistance offered by White families to their children in educational activities is **different** from the amount of support offered by Black families to their children in educational activities.	The amount of assistance offered by White families to their children in educational activities is **more** than the amount of support offered by Black families to their children in educational activities.

Some Differences Between the Null Hypothesis and the Research Hypothesis

Besides the null hypothesis representing an equality and the research hypothesis representing an inequality, the two types of hypotheses differ in several other important ways.

First, for a bit of review, the two types of hypotheses differ in that one (the null hypothesis) states that there is no relationship between variables (an equality), whereas the research hypothesis states that there is a relationship between the variables (an inequality). This is the primary difference.

Second, null hypotheses always refer to the population, whereas research hypotheses always refer to the sample. We select a sample of participants from a much larger population. We then try to generalize the results from the sample back to the population. If you remember your basic philosophy and logic (you did take these courses, right?), you'll remember that going from small (as in a sample) to large (as in a population) is a process of inference.

Third, because the entire population cannot be directly tested (again, it is impractical, uneconomical, and often impossible), you can't say with 100% certainty that there is no real difference between segments of the population on some variable. Rather, you have to infer it (indirectly) from the results of the test of the research hypothesis, which is based on the sample. Hence, the null hypothesis must be indirectly tested, and the research hypothesis can be directly tested.

Fourth, the null hypothesis is written with an equal sign, while the research hypothesis is written with a not equal to, greater than, or less than sign.

Fifth, null hypotheses are always written using Greek symbols, and research hypotheses are always written using Roman symbols. Thus, the null hypothesis that the average score for 9th graders is equal to that of 12th graders is represented like this:

$$H_0 : \mu_9 = \mu_{12}, \tag{9.3}$$

where

- H_0 represents the null hypothesis,
- μ_9 represents the theoretical average for the population of 9th graders, and
- μ_{12} represents the theoretical average for the population of 12th graders.

The research hypothesis that the average score for a sample of 12th graders is greater than the average score for a sample of 9th graders is shown in Formula 9.2.

Finally, because you cannot directly test the null hypothesis, it is an *implied* hypothesis. But the research hypothesis is explicit and is stated as such. This is another reason why you rarely see null hypotheses stated in research reports and will almost always see a statement (be it in symbols or words) of the research hypothesis.

WHAT MAKES A GOOD HYPOTHESIS?

You now know that hypotheses are educated guesses—a starting point for a lot more to come. As with any guess, some hypotheses are better than others right from the start. We can't stress enough how important it is to ask the question you want answered and to keep in mind that any hypothesis you present is a direct extension of the original question you asked. This question will reflect your personal interests and motivation and your understanding of what research has been done previously. With that in mind, here are criteria you might use to decide whether a hypothesis you read in a research report or one that you formulate is acceptable.

To illustrate, let's use an example of a study that examines the effects of providing afterschool child care to employees who work late on the parents' adjustment to work. Here is a well-written directional research hypothesis:

> Parents who enroll their children in afterschool programs will miss fewer days of work in 1 year and will have a more positive attitude toward work, as measured by the Attitude Toward Work survey, than will parents who do not enroll their children in such programs.

Here are the criteria.

First, a good hypothesis is stated in declarative form and not as a question. Although the above hypothesis may have started in the researcher's mind as a question ("Are parents better employees . . . ?"), the question was not used because hypotheses are most effective when they make a clear and forceful statement, like the hypothesis above.

Second, a good hypothesis posits an expected relationship between variables. The hypothesis in our example clearly describes the expected relationships among afterschool child care, parents' attitude, and absentee rate. These variables are being tested to see if one (enrollment in the afterschool program) has an effect upon the others (absentee rate and attitude).

Notice the word *expected* in the above criterion. Defining an expected relationship is intended to prevent a fishing trip to look for any relationships that may be found (sometimes called the "shotgun" approach), which may be tempting but is not very productive. You do get somewhere using the shotgun approach, but because you don't know where you started, you have no idea where you end up.

In the fishing-trip approach, you throw out your line and take anything that bites. You collect data on as many things as you can, regardless of your interest or even whether collecting the data is a reasonable part of a scientific investigation. Or, to use a shotgun analogy, you load up them guns and blast away at anything that moves, and you're bound to hit something. The problem is, you may not want what you hit, and worse, you may miss what you want to hit, and worst of all (if possible), you may not know what you hit! Good researchers do not want just anything they can catch or shoot. They want specific results. To get them, researchers need their opening questions and hypotheses to be clear, forceful, and easily understood.

Third, hypotheses reflect the theory or literature on which they are based. As you read in Chapter 1, the accomplishments of scientists rarely can be attributed to just their own hard work. Their accomplishments are always due, in part, to many other researchers who came before them and laid the framework for later explorations. A good hypothesis reflects this, in that it has a substantive link to existing literature and theory. In the aforementioned example, let's assume that there is literature indicating that parents are more comfortable knowing their children are being cared for in a structured environment and parents can then be more productive at work. Knowing this would allow one to hypothesize that an afterschool program would provide the security parents are looking for. In turn, this allows them to concentrate on working rather than calling or texting to find out whether Rachel or Gregory got home safely.

Fourth, a hypothesis should be brief and to the point. You want your hypothesis to describe the relationship between variables in a declarative form and to be as direct and explicit as possible. The more to the point it is, the easier it will be for others (such as your master's thesis or doctoral dissertation committee members!) to read your research and understand exactly what you are hypothesizing and what the important variables are. In fact, when people read and evaluate research (as you will learn more about later in this chapter), the first thing many of them do is find the hypotheses to get a good idea as to the general purpose of the research and how things will be done. A good hypothesis tells you both of these things.

Fifth, good hypotheses are testable hypotheses—and testable hypotheses contain variables that can be measured. This means that you can actually carry out the intent of the question reflected by the hypothesis. You can see from our example hypothesis that the important comparison is between parents who have enrolled their child in an afterschool program and those who have not. Then, such things as attitude and workdays missed will be measured. Identifying these two groups of parents and measuring the variables attitude and absenteeism are both reasonable objectives. Attitude is measured by the Attitude Toward Work survey (a fictitious title, but you get the idea), and absenteeism (the number of days missed at work) is an easily recorded and unambiguous measure almost always available in payroll records (assuming you've been granted access). Think how much harder things would be if the hypothesis were stated as *Parents who enroll their children in afterschool care feel better about their jobs.* Although you might get the same message, the results might be more difficult to interpret given the ambiguous nature of the phrase *feel better.*

In sum, hypotheses should

- be stated in declarative form,
- posit a relationship between variables,
- reflect a theory or a body of literature on which they are based,
- be brief and to the point, and
- be testable.

When a hypothesis meets each of these five criteria, you know that it is good enough to continue with a study that will accurately test the general question from which the hypothesis was derived.

REAL-WORLD STATS

You might think that the scientific method and the use of null and research hypotheses is beyond question in the world of scientific research. Well, you would be wrong. Here's just a sampling of some of the articles published in professional journals over the past few years that raise concerns. No one is yet ready to throw out the scientific method as the best approach for testing hypotheses, but it's not a bad idea to question every now and then whether the method always and forever is the best model to use.

Want to know more? Go online or to the library and find . . .

- Walter Schumm of Kansas State University highlights issues with null hypothesis testing, including sample size and statistical power, our inability to prove the null hypothesis, lack of true random assignment in many cases, and other design issues. Examples in the article draw on research conducted in medical, psychiatric, and psychological research. The biggest takeaway is the recommendation to always report effect sizes, something we discuss in Chapter 12. You can find the article by looking for this reference: Schumm, W. (2010). Statistical requirements for properly investigating a null hypothesis. *Psychological Reports, 107*(3), 953–971.

- Howard Wainer and Daniel Robinson take these criticisms one step further and suggest that the historical use of such procedures was reasonable but that modifications to significance testing and the interpretations of outcomes would serve modern science well. Basically, they are saying that other tools (such as effect size, which we discuss in Chapter 12) should be used to evaluate outcomes. Read all about it in Wainer, H., & Robinson, D. H. (2003). Shaping up the practice of null hypothesis significance testing. *Educational Researcher, 32,* 22–30.

- Finally, in the really interesting article "A Vast Graveyard of Undead Theories: Publication Bias and Psychological Science's Aversion to the Null," Christopher Ferguson and Moritz Heene raise the very real issue that many journals refuse to publish outcomes where a null result is found (such as no difference between groups). They believe that when such outcomes are not published, false theories are never taken to task and never tested for their truthfulness. Thus, the replicability of science (a very important aspect of the entire scientific process) is compromised. You can find more about this in Ferguson, C. J., & Heene, M. (2012). A vast graveyard of undead theories: Publication bias and psychological science's aversion to the null. *Perspectives on Psychological Science, 7,* 555–561.

We hope you get the idea from the above examples that science is not black-and-white, cut-and-dried, or any other metaphor indicating there is only a right way and only a wrong way of doing things. Science is an organic and dynamic process that is always changing in its focus, methods, and potential outcomes.

Summary

A central component of any scientific study is the hypothesis, and the different types of hypotheses (null and research) help form a plan for answering the questions asked by the purpose of our research. The null hypothesis provides a starting point and benchmark for research, and we use it as a comparison as we evaluate the acceptability of the research hypothesis. Now let's move on to how null hypotheses are actually tested.

Time to Practice

1. Go to the library and select five empirical research articles (those that contain actual data) from your area of interest. For each one, list the following:
   a. What is the null hypothesis (implied or explicitly stated)?
   b. What is the research hypothesis (implied or explicitly stated)?
   c. And what about those articles with no hypothesis clearly stated or implied? Identify those articles and see if you can write a research hypothesis for them.
2. While you're at the library, select two other articles from an area in which you are interested and write a brief description of the sample and how it was selected from the population. Be sure to include some words about whether the researchers did an adequate job of selecting the sample; be able to justify your answer.
3. For the following research questions, create one null hypothesis, one directional research hypothesis, and one nondirectional research hypothesis.
   a. What are the effects of attention span on out-of-seat classroom behavior?
   b. What is the relationship between the quality of a marriage and the quality of the spouses' relationships with their siblings?
   c. What is the best way to treat an eating disorder?
4. Go back to the five hypotheses that you found in Question 1 above and evaluate each using the five criteria that were discussed at the end of the chapter.
5. What kinds of problems might using a poorly written or ambiguous research hypothesis introduce?
6. What is the null hypothesis, and what is one of its important purposes? How does it differ from the research hypothesis?
7. What is *chance* in the context of a research hypothesis? And what do we do about chance in our experiments?
8. Why does the null hypothesis presume no relationship between variables?

Student Study Site

Get the tools you need to sharpen your study skills! Visit **edge.sagepub.com/salkindshaw** to access practice quizzes and eFlashcards, watch R tutorial videos, and download data sets!

PROBABILITY AND WHY IT COUNTS

Fun With a Bell-Shaped Curve

Difficulty Scale ☺ ☺ ☺
(not too easy and not too hard, but very important)

WHAT YOU WILL LEARN IN THIS CHAPTER

- Understanding probability and why it is basic to the understanding of statistics
- Applying the characteristics of the normal, or bell-shaped, curve
- Computing and interpreting *z* scores and understanding their importance

WHY PROBABILITY?

And here you thought this was a statistics class! Ha! Well, as you will learn in this chapter, the study of probability is the basis for the normal curve (much more on that later) and the foundation for inferential statistics.

Why? First, the normal curve provides us with a basis for understanding the probability associated with any possible outcome (such as the probability of getting a certain score on a test or the odds of getting a head on one flip of a coin).

Second, the study of probability is the basis for determining the degree of confidence we have in stating that a particular finding or outcome is "true." Or, better said, that an outcome (like an average score) may not have occurred due to chance alone. For example, let's compare Group A (which participates in 3 hours of extra swim practice each week) and Group B (which has no extra swim practice each week). We find that Group A differs from Group B on a test of fitness, but can we say that the difference is due to the extra practice? Or might it be due to something else? The tools that the study of probability provides allow us to determine the exact mathematical likelihood that the difference is due to practice (and practice only) versus something else (such as chance).

All that time we spent on hypotheses in the previous chapter was time well spent. Once we put together our understanding of what a null hypothesis and a research hypothesis are with the ideas that are the foundation of probability, we'll be in a position to discuss how likely certain outcomes (formulated by the research hypothesis) are.

THE NORMAL CURVE (A.K.A. THE BELL-SHAPED CURVE)

What is a normal curve? Well, the **normal curve** (also called a **bell-shaped curve**, or bell curve) is a visual representation of a distribution of scores that has three characteristics. Each of these characteristics is illustrated in Figure 10.1.

FIGURE 10.1 ● The normal, or bell-shaped, curve.

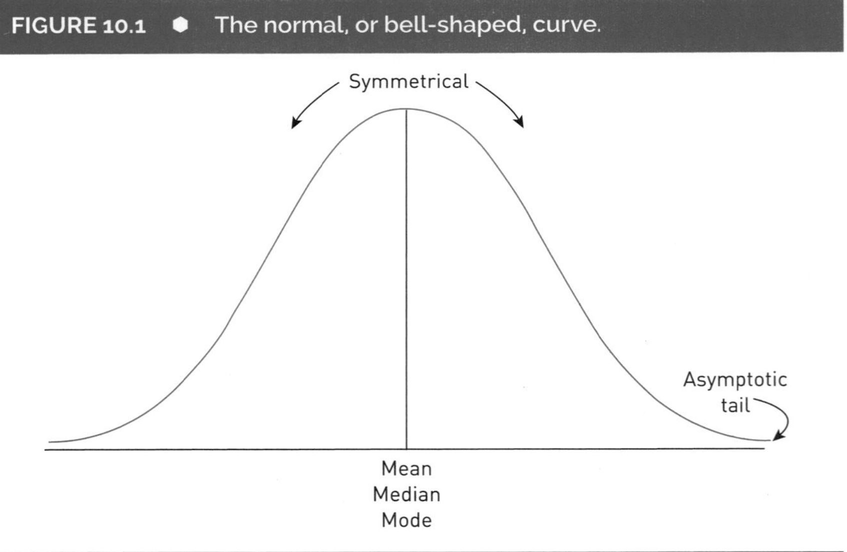

The normal curve represents a distribution of values in which the mean, median, and mode are equal to one another. You probably remember from Chapter 4 that if the median and the mean are different, then the distribution is skewed in one direction or the other. The normal curve is not skewed. It's got a nice hump (only one), and that hump is right in the middle.

Second, the normal curve is perfectly symmetrical about the mean. If you fold one half of the curve along its center line, the two halves would lie perfectly on top of each other. They are identical. One half of the curve is a mirror image of the other.

Finally (and get ready for a mouthful), the tails of the normal curve are **asymptotic**—a big word. What it means is that they come closer and closer to the horizontal axis but never touch because theoretically the line extends from negative infinity to positive infinity. See if you have some idea (in advance, because we will talk about it later) why this is so important, because it's really a cornerstone of all this probability stuff.

The normal curve's shape of a bell also gives the graph its other name, the bell-shaped curve.

When one of your authors was knee-high, he always wondered how the tail of a normal curve can approach the horizontal or *x*-axis yet never touch it. Try this. Place two pencils one inch apart and then move them closer (by half) so they are one-half inch apart, and then closer (one-quarter inch apart), and closer (one-eighth inch apart). They continually get closer, right? But they never (and never will) touch. Same thing with the tails of the curve. The tail slowly approaches the axis on which the curve "rests," but the tail and the axis can never really touch.

Why is this important? As you will learn later in this chapter, the fact that the tails never touch the *x*-axis means that there is an infinitely small likelihood that a score can be obtained that is very extreme (way out under the left or right tail of the curve). If the tails did touch the *x*-axis, then the likelihood that a very extreme score could be obtained would be nonexistent.

Hey, That's Not Normal!

We hope your next question is "But there are plenty of sets of scores where the distribution is not normal or bell shaped, right?" Yes (and it's a big *but*).

When we deal with large sets of data (more than 30), and as we take repeated samples of the data from a population, the values in the curve closely approximate the shape of a normal curve. This is very important, because a lot of what we do when we talk about inferring from a sample to a population is based on the assumption that the sample taken from the population is distributed normally. And that's just another way to say that the sample's characteristics continue to approach those characteristics of the population.

And as it turns out, in nature in general, many things are distributed with the characteristics that we call normal. That is, there are lots of events or occurrences right in the middle of the distribution but relatively few on each end, as you can see in Figure 10.2, which shows the distribution of IQ and height in the general population.

For example, there are very few people who are brilliant and very few who are intellectually or cognitively at the absolute bottom of the group. There are lots who are right in the middle and fewer as we move toward the tails of the curve. Likewise, there are *relatively* few very tall people and relatively few very short people, but lots

FIGURE 10.2 ● How scores can be distributed.

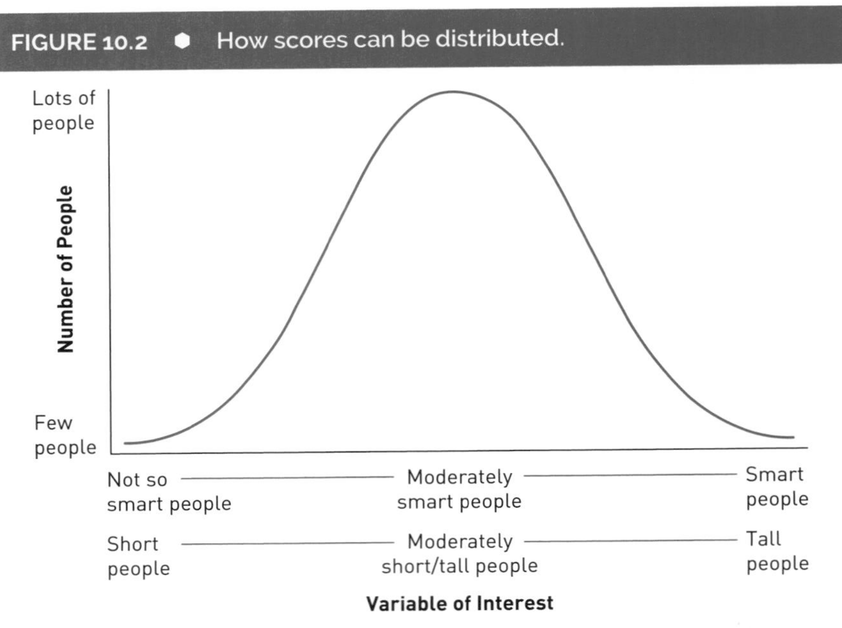

of people fall right in the middle. In both of these examples, the distribution of intellectual skills and of height approximates a normal distribution.

Consequently, those events that tend to occur in the extremes of the normal curve have a smaller probability associated with each occurrence. We can say with a great deal of confidence that the odds of any one person (whose height we do not know beforehand) being very tall (or very short) are just not very great. But we know that the odds of any one person being average in height, or right around the middle, are pretty good. Those events that tend to occur in the middle of the normal curve have a higher probability of occurring than do those in the extreme. And this is true for height, weight, general intelligence, weight-lifting ability, number of apps on your smartphone, number of Star Wars action figures owned, and on and on.

More Normal Curve 101

You already know the three main characteristics that make a curve normal or make it appear bell shaped, but there's more to it than that. Take a look at the curve in Figure 10.3.

The distribution represented here has a mean of 100 and a standard deviation of 10. We've added numbers across the *x*-axis that represent the distance in standard deviations from the mean for this distribution. You can see that the *x*-axis (representing the scores in the distribution) is marked from 70 through 130 in increments of 10 (which is the standard deviation for this distribution), the value of 1 standard deviation. We made up these numbers (100 and 10), so don't go nuts trying to find out where we got them from.

So, a quick review tells us that this distribution has a mean of 100 and a standard deviation of 10. Each vertical line within the curve separates the curve into a section,

FIGURE 10.3 ● A normal curve divided into different sections.

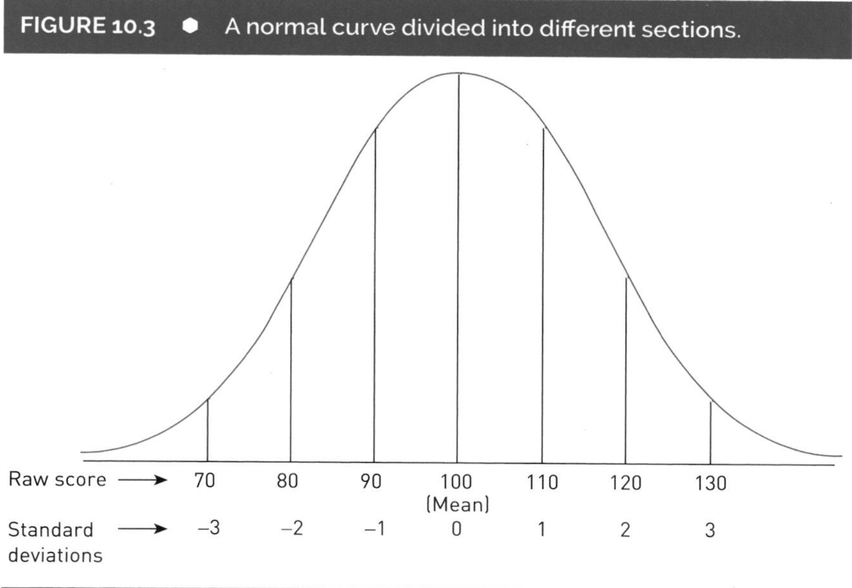

and each section is bound by particular scores. For example, the first section to the right of the mean of 100 is bound by the scores 100 and 110, and this section represents 1 standard deviation from the mean (which is 100).

And below each raw score (70, 80, 90, 100, 110, 120, and 130), you'll find a corresponding standard deviation (–3, –2, –1, 0, +1, +2, and +3). As you may have figured out already, each standard deviation in our example is 10 points. So 1 standard deviation from the mean (which is 100) is the mean plus 10 points or 110. Not so hard, is it?

If we extend this argument further, then you should be able to see how the range of scores represented by a normal distribution with a mean of 100 and a standard deviation of 10 is 70 through 130, which includes –3 to +3 standard deviations.

Now, here's a big fact that is always true about normal distributions, means, and standard deviations: For any distribution of scores (regardless of the value of the mean and standard deviation), if the scores are distributed normally, almost 100% of the scores will fit between -3 and +3 standard deviations from the mean. This is very important, because it applies to all normal distributions. Because the rule does apply (once again, regardless of the value of the mean or standard deviation), distributions can be compared with one another. We'll get to that again later.

With that said, we'll extend our argument a bit more. If the distribution of scores is normal, we can also say that between different points along the *x*-axis (such as between the mean and 1 standard deviation), a certain percentage of cases will fall. In fact, between the mean (which in this case is 100—got that yet?) and 1 standard deviation above the mean (which is 110), about 34% (actually 34.13%) of all cases in the distribution of scores will fall. This is a fact you can take to the bank because it will always be true.

Want to go further? Take a look at Figure 10.4. Here, you can see the same normal curve in all its glory (the mean equals 100 and the standard deviation equals 10) and the percentage of cases that we would expect to fall within the boundaries defined by the mean and standard deviation.

FIGURE 10.4 ● A normal curve divided into different sections.

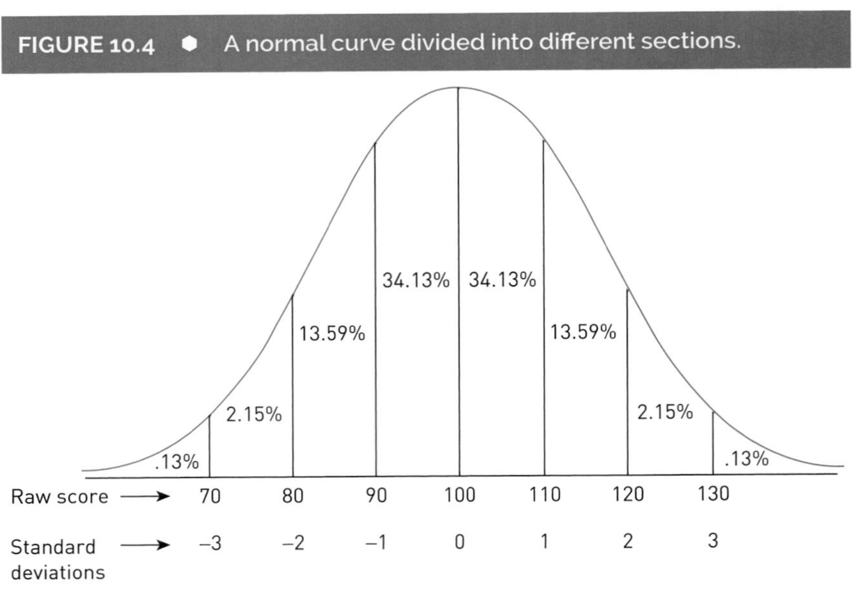

Here's what we can conclude:

The distance between . . .	includes . . .	and the scores that are included (if the mean = 100 and the standard deviation = 10) are . . .
the mean and 1 standard deviation	34.13% of all the cases under the curve	from 100 to 110
1 and 2 standard deviations	13.59% of all the cases under the curve	from 110 to 120
2 and 3 standard deviations	2.15% of all the cases under the curve	from 120 to 130
3 standard deviations and above	0.13% of all the cases under the curve	130 and above

If you add up all the values in either half of the normal curve, guess what you get? That's right, (just about almost) 50%. Why? The distance between the mean and all the scores to the right of the mean underneath the normal curve includes 50% of all the scores.

And because the curve is symmetrical about its central axis (each half is a mirror image of the other), the two halves together represent 100% of all the scores. Not rocket science, but important to point out, nonetheless.

Now, let's extend the same logic to the scores to the left of the mean of 100.

The distance between . . .	includes . . .	and the scores that are included (if the mean = 100 and the standard deviation = 10) are . . .
the mean and −1 standard deviation	34.13% of all the cases under the curve	from 90 to 100
−1 and −2 standard deviations	13.59% of all the cases under the curve	from 80 to 90
−2 and −3 standard deviations	2.15% of all the cases under the curve	from 70 to 80
−3 standard deviations and below	0.13% of all the cases under the curve	70 and below

Now, be sure to keep in mind that we are using a mean of 100 and a standard deviation of 10 only as a particular example. Obviously, not all distributions (not most distributions!) have a mean of 100 and a standard deviation of 10.

All of this is pretty neat, especially when you consider that the values of 34.13% and 13.59% and so on are absolutely independent of the actual values of the mean and the standard deviation. These percentages are due to the shape of the curve and do not depend on the value of any of the scores in the distribution or the value of the mean or standard deviation. In fact, you could draw a normal curve on a piece of cardboard and cut it out, so you had a bell-shaped piece of cardboard. Then if you cut out the area between the mean and +1 standard deviation and weighed it, it would tip the scale at exactly 34.13% of the entire piece of bell-shaped cardboard. (Try it—it's true.)

In our example, this means that (roughly) 68% (34.13% doubled) of the scores fall between the raw score values of 90 and 110. What about the other 32%? Good question. One half (16%, or 13.59% + 2.15% + 0.13%) fall above (to the right of) 1 standard deviation above the mean, and one half fall below (to the left of) 1 standard deviation below the mean. And because the curve slopes, and the amount of area decreases as you move farther away from the mean, it is no surprise that the likelihood that a score will fall more toward the extremes of the distribution is less than the likelihood it will fall toward the middle. That's why the curve has a bump in the middle and is not skewed in either direction. And that's why scores that are farther from the mean have a lower probability of occurring than scores that are closer to the mean.

OUR FAVORITE STANDARD SCORE: THE *z* SCORE

You have read more than once that distributions differ in their measures of central tendency and variability.

But in the general practice of applying statistics (and using them in research activities), we find ourselves working with distributions that are indeed different because each measure is on its own scale, yet we will be required to compare them with one another. And to do such a comparison, we need some kind of a standard.

Say hello to **standard scores**. These are scores that are comparable because they are standardized in units of standard deviations. For example, a standard score of 1 in a distribution with a mean of 50 and a standard deviation of 10 means the same as a standard score of 1 from a distribution with a mean of 100 and a standard deviation of 5; they both represent 1 standard score and are an equivalent distance from their respective means. Also, we can use our knowledge of the normal curve and assign a probability to the occurrence of a value that is 1 standard deviation from the mean. We'll do that later.

Although there are other types of standard scores, the one that you will see most frequently in your study of statistics is called a ***z* score**. This is the result of dividing the amount that a raw score differs from the mean of the sample scores by the standard deviation, as shown in Formula 10.1:

$$z = \frac{X - \bar{X}}{s}, \tag{10.1}$$

where

- z is the z score,
- X is the individual score,
- $\bar{X}$ is the mean of the distribution, and
- s is the distribution standard deviation.

For example, in Formula 10.2, you can see how the z score is calculated if the mean is 100, the raw score is 110, and the standard deviation is 10.

$$z = \frac{110 - 100}{10} = 1.0. \tag{10.2}$$

It's just as easy to compute a raw score given a z score as the other way around. You already know the formula for a z score given the raw score, mean, and standard deviation. But if you know only the z score and the mean and standard deviation, then what's the corresponding raw score? Easy: Just use the formula $X = z(s) + \bar{X}$. You can easily convert raw scores to z scores and back again if necessary. For example, a z score of −0.5 in a distribution with a mean of 50 and an s of 5 would equal a raw score of $X = (-0.5)(5) + 50$, or 47.5.

As you can see in our formula (Formula 10.1), we use $\bar{X}$ and s for the mean and standard deviation, respectively. In some books (and in some lectures), the population mean is represented by the Greek letter *mu*, or μ, and the standard deviation is represented by the Greek letter *sigma*, or σ. One can be strict about when to use what, but for our purposes, we will use letters of the Roman alphabet.

Statistical Term	Greek—Population	Roman—Sample
Mean	μ	$\bar{X}$
Standard deviation	σ	s

The following data show the original raw scores plus the z scores for a sample of 10 scores that has a mean of 12 and a standard deviation of 2. Any raw score above the mean will have a corresponding z score that is positive, and any raw score below the mean will have a corresponding z score that is negative. For example, a raw score of 15 has a corresponding z score of +1.5, and a raw score of 8 has a corresponding z score of –2.0. And of course, a raw score of 12 (or the mean) has a z score of 0 (because 12 is no distance from the mean).

X	$X - \bar{X}$	z Score
12	0	0.0
15	3	1.5
11	-1	-0.5
13	1	0.5
8	-4	-2.0
14	2	1.0
12	0	0.0
13	1	0.5
12	0	0.0
10	-2	-1.0

Following are just a few observations about these scores, as a little review.

First, those scores below the mean (such as 8 and 10) have negative z scores, and those scores above the mean (such as 13 and 14) have positive z scores.

Second, positive z scores always fall to the right of the mean and are in the upper half of the distribution. And negative z scores always fall to the left of the mean and are in the lower half of the distribution.

Third, when we talk about a score being located 1 standard deviation above the mean, it's the same as saying that the score is 1 z score above the mean. For our purposes, when comparing scores across distributions, *z* scores and standard deviations are equivalent. In other words, a *z* score is simply the number of standard deviations from the mean.

Finally (and this is very important), *z* scores across different distributions are comparable. Here's another table, similar to the one above, that will illustrate this last point. These 10 scores were selected from a set of 100 scores, with the scores having a mean of 59 and a standard deviation of 14.5.

Raw Score	$X - \bar{X}$	*z* Score
67	8	0.55
54	-5	-0.34
65	6	0.41
33	-26	-1.79
56	-3	-0.21
76	17	1.17
65	6	0.41
33	-26	-1.79
48	-11	-0.76
76	17	1.17

In the first distribution you saw, with a mean of 12 and a standard deviation of 2, a raw score of 12.8 has a corresponding *z* score of +0.4, which means that a raw score of 12.8 is 0.4 standard deviations from the mean. In the second distribution, with a mean of 59 and a standard deviation of 14.5, a raw score of 64.8 has a corresponding *z* score of +0.4 as well. A miracle? No—just a good idea that is a huge aid in comparing scores from different sets of data or distributions. And if you look at the standard deviation marks for 0 and 1 in Figure 10.4, where you would place your *z* score is the same in both cases.

Both raw scores of 12.8 and 64.8, *relative to one another,* are equal distances (and equally distant) from the mean. When these raw scores are represented as standard scores, they are directly comparable to one another in terms of their relative location in their respective distributions.

What *z* Scores Represent

You already know that a particular *z* score not only represents a raw score but also represents a particular location along the *x*-axis of a distribution. And the more extreme the *z* score (such as –2.0 or +2.6), the farther it is from the mean.

Because you already know the percentage of area that falls between certain points along the *x*-axis (such as about 34% between the mean and a standard deviation of

+1, for example, or about 14% between a standard deviation of +1 and a standard deviation of +2), we can make the following true statements as well:

- Eighty-four percent of all the scores fall below a *z* score of +1 (the 50% that fall below the mean plus the 34% that fall between the mean and the +1 *z* score).
- Sixteen percent of all the scores fall above a *z* score of +1 (because the total area under the curve has to equal 100%, and 84% of the scores fall below a score of +1.0).

Think about both of these facts for a moment.

Moment passes.

What we are saying is that, given the normal distribution, different areas of the curve are encompassed by different numbers of standard deviations or *z* scores.

Okay—here it comes. These percentages or areas can also easily be seen as representing *probabilities* of a certain score occurring. For example, here's a big sample question of the kind you can now ask and answer (drum roll, please):

> In a distribution with a mean of 100 and a standard deviation of 10, what is the probability that any one score will be 110 or above?

The answer? The probability is 16% or 16 out of 100 or .16. How did we get this?

First, we computed the corresponding *z* score, which is +1 [(110 – 100)/10]. Then, given the knowledge we already have (see Figure 10.4), we know a *z* score of 1 represents a location on the *x*-axis below which 84% (50% plus 34%) of all the scores in the distribution fall. Above that is 16% of the scores or a probability of .16.

In other words, because we already know the areas between the mean and 1, 2, or 3 standard deviations above or below the mean, we can easily figure out the probability that the value of any one *z* score has of occurring.

Now the method we just went through is fine for *z* values of 1, 2, and 3. But what if the value of the *z* score is not a whole number like 2 but is instead 1.23 or –2.01? We need to find a way to be more precise.

How do we do that? Simple—learn calculus and apply it to the curve to compute the area underneath it at almost every possible point along the *x*-axis, or (and we like this alternative much more) use Table B.1 in Appendix B (the normal distribution table). This is a listing of all the values (except the very most extreme) for the areas under a curve that correspond to different *z* scores.

Table B.1 has two columns. The first column, labeled "*z* Score," is simply the *z* score that has been computed. The second column, "Area Between the Mean and the *z* Score," is the exact area underneath the curve that is contained between the two points.

For example (and you should turn to Table B.1 and try this as you read along), if we wanted to know the area between the mean and a *z* score of +1, we would find the value 1.00 in the column labeled "*z* Score" and read across to the second column, where we would find the area between the mean and a *z* score of 1.00 to be 34.13. Seen that before?

Why aren't there any plus or minus signs in this table (such as –1.00)? Because the curve is symmetrical, it does not matter whether the value of the *z* score is positive or negative. The area between the mean and 1 standard deviation in any direction is *always* 34.13%.

Here's the next step. Let's say that for a particular *z* score of 1.38, you want to know the probability associated with that *z* score. If you wanted to know the percentage of the area between the mean and a *z* score of 1.38, you would find in Table B.1 the corresponding area for the *z* score of 1.38, which is 41.62, indicating that more than 41% of all the cases in the distribution fall between a *z* score of 0 and 1.38. Then we know that about 92% (50% plus 41.62%) will fall at or below a *z* score of 1.38. Now, you should notice that we did this last example without any raw scores at all. Once you get to this table, they are just no longer needed.

But are we always interested only in the amount of area between the mean and some other *z* score? What about between two *z* scores, neither of which is the mean? For example, what if we were interested in knowing the amount of area between a *z* score of 1.5 and a *z* score of 2.5, which translates to a probability that a score falls between the two *z* scores? How can we use the table to compute the answer to such questions? It's easy. Just find the corresponding amount of area each *z* score encompasses and subtract one from the other. Often, drawing a picture helps, as in Figure 10.5.

FIGURE 10.5 ● Using a drawing to figure out the difference in area between two *z* scores.

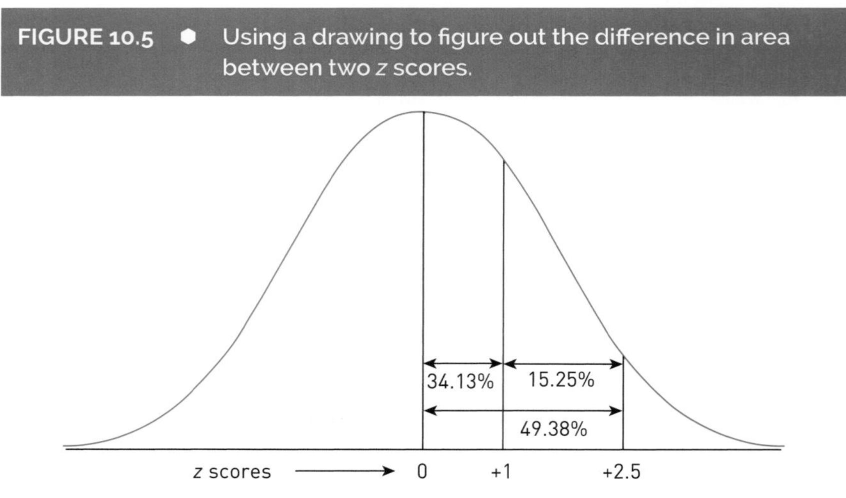

For example, let's say that we want to find the area between raw scores of 110 and 125 in a distribution with a mean of 100 and a standard deviation of 10. Here are the steps we would take.

1. Compute the z score for a raw score of 110, which is (110 − 100)/10, or +1.
2. Compute the z score for a raw score of 125, which is (125 − 100)/10, or +2.5.
3. Using Table B.1 in Appendix B, find the area between the mean and a z score of +1, which is 34.13%.
4. Using Table B.1 in Appendix B, find the area between the mean and a z score of +2.5, which is 49.38%.
5. Because you want to know the distance between the two, subtract the smaller from the larger: 49.38 − 34.13 = 15.25%. Here's the picture that's worth a thousand words, in Figure 10.5.

Okay—so we can be pretty confident that the probability of a particular score occurring can be best understood by examining where that score falls in a distribution relative to other scores. In this example, the probability of a score occurring between a z score of +1 and a z score of +2.5 is about 15%.

Here's another example. In a set of scores with a mean of 100 and a standard deviation of 10, a raw score of 117 has a corresponding z score of 1.70. This z score corresponds to an area under the curve of 95.54% (50% + 45.54%), meaning that the probability of this score occurring between a score of negative infinity and a score of 1.70 is 95.54% or 95.5 out of 100 or .955.

Just two things about standard scores. First, even though we are focusing on z scores, there are other types of standard scores as well. For example, a T score is a type of standard score that is computed by multiplying the z score by 10 (T score standard deviation) and adding 50 (T score mean). One advantage of this type of score is that you rarely have a negative T score. As with z scores, T scores allow you to compare standard scores from different distributions.

Second, a *standard* score is a whole different animal from a *standardized* score. A standardized score is one that comes from a distribution with a predefined mean and standard deviation. Standardized scores from tests such as IQ, the SAT, and the GRE (Graduate Record Exam) are used so that comparisons can easily be made between scores from different forms or administrations of the test, which all have the same mean and standard deviation.

What *z* Scores Really Represent

The name of the statistics game is being able to estimate the probability of an outcome. If we take what we have talked about and done so far in this chapter one step further, we can determine the probability of some event occurring. Then, we will use some criterion to judge whether we think that event is as likely, more likely, or less likely than what we would expect by chance. The research hypothesis presents a statement of the expected event, and we use our statistical tools to evaluate how likely that event is.

That's the 20-second version of what inferential statistics is, but that's a lot. So let's take everything from this paragraph and go through it again with an example.

Let's say that your lifelong friend, trusty Lew, gives you a coin and asks you to determine whether it is a "fair" one—that is, if you flip it 10 times, you should come up with 5 heads and 5 tails.

We would expect 5 heads (or 5 tails) because the probability is .5 of a head or a tail on any one flip (if it's a legit coin). On 10 independent flips (meaning that one flip does not affect another), we should get 5 heads, and so on. Now the question is, "How many heads would disqualify the coin as being fake or rigged?"

Let's say the criterion for fairness we will use is that if, in flipping the coin 10 times, we get heads (or heads turn up) less than 5% of the time, we'll say the coin is rigged and call the police on Lew. This 5% criterion is one standard that is used by statisticians. If the probability of the event (be it the number of heads or the score on a test or the difference between the average scores for two groups) occurs in the extreme (and we're saying the extreme is defined as less than 5% of all such occurrences), it's an unlikely, or in this case an unfair, outcome.

Back to the coin and Lew.

Because there are 2 possible outcomes (heads or tails) and we are flipping the coin 10 times, there are 2^{10} or 1,024 possible outcomes, such as 9 heads and 1 tail, 7 heads and 3 tails, 10 heads and 0 tails, and on and on. Here's the distribution of how many heads you can expect, just by chance alone, on 10 flips. For example, the probability associated with getting 6 heads in 10 flips is about 21%.

Number of Heads	Probability
0	0.00
1	0.01
2	0.04
3	0.12
4	0.21
5	0.25
6	0.21
7	0.12
8	0.04
9	0.01
10	0.00

So, the likelihood of any particular outcome is known. The likelihood of 6 heads from 10 tosses? About .21, or 21%. Now it's decision time. Just how many heads would one have to get on 10 flips to conclude that the coin is fixed, biased, busted, broken, or loony?

Well, as all good statisticians do, we'll define the criterion as 5%, which we discussed. If the probability of the observed outcome (the results of all our flips) is less than

5%, we'll conclude that it is so unlikely that something other than chance must be responsible—and that something is a bogus coin.

If you look at the table, you can see that 8, 9, or 10 heads all represent outcomes that have less than 5% probability of occurring. So if the result of 10 coin flips was 8, 9, or 10 heads, the conclusion would be that the coin is not a fair one. (Yep—you're right: 0, 1, and 2 qualify for the same decision. Sort of the other side of the coin—groan.)

The same logic applies to our discussion of *z* scores earlier. Just how extreme a *z* score would we expect before we could proclaim that an outcome is not due just to chance but to some other factor? If you look at the normal curve table in Appendix B, you'll see that the cutoff point for a *z* score of 1.65 includes about 45% of the area under the curve. If you add that to the other 50% of the area on the other side of the curve, you come up with a total of 95%. That leaves just 5% above that point on the *x*-axis. Any score that represents a *z* score of 1.65 or above is then into pretty thin air—or at least in a location that has a much smaller chance of occurring than others. Likewise, a *z* score of –1.65 has 5% of the area below –1.65 and 95% of the area above –1.65.

HYPOTHESIS TESTING AND *z* SCORES: THE FIRST STEP

What we showed you here is that any event can have a probability associated with it. And we use those probability values to decide how unlikely we think an event might be. For example, getting only 1 head and 9 tails in 10 tosses of a coin is highly unlikely. We also said that if an event seems to occur only 5 out of 100 times (5%), we will deem that event to be rather *unlikely* relative to all the other events that could occur.

It's much the same with any outcome related to a research hypothesis. The null hypothesis, which you learned about in Chapter 9, claims that there is no difference between groups (or variables) and that the likelihood of no difference occurring is 100%. We try to test the armor of the null for any chinks that might be there.

In other words, if, through the test of the research hypothesis, we find that the likelihood of an event that occurred is somewhat extreme, then the research hypothesis is a more attractive explanation than the null. So, if we find a *z* score (and remember that *z* scores have probabilities of occurrence associated with them as well) that is extreme (how extreme?—less than a 5% chance of occurring), we like to say that the reason for the extreme score is something to do with treatments or relationships and not just chance. We'll go into much greater detail on this point in the following chapter.

Using R to Compute *z* Scores

Visit **edge.sagepub.com/salkindshaw** to watch an R tutorial video on this topic.

R does lots of really cool things, but it's the little treats like the one you'll see here that make the program such a great time-saver. Now that you know how to compute *z* scores by hand, let's let R do the work to calculate Formula 10.1.

To have R compute *z* scores for the set of data you see in the first column in the following table (which you also saw earlier in this chapter), follow these steps:

1. Create a vector of the raw scores.

```
> rawScores <- c(67, 54, 65, 33, 56, 76, 65, 33, 48, 76)
>
```

2. Calculate the mean of the raw scores.

```
> rsMean <- mean(rawScores)
> rsMean
[1] 57.3
>
```

After computing and saving the mean, we asked R to show us the mean by entering `rsMean` (shorthand name for raw scores mean) on a line by itself. In this case, the mean is 57.30 with no remainder.

3. Calculate the standard deviation of the raw scores.

```
> rsSD <- sd(rawScores)
> rsSD
[1] 15.60662
>
```

Like with the mean, we asked R to show us the standard deviation of our raw scores. R returned 15.60662 that we stored in `rsSD`, short for raw scores standard deviation. If you were calculating these *z* scores by hand, you would want to keep at least four decimal places to get the same answers as found in the following table—never round until you get to the final answer!

4. Calculate *z* for each row.

```
> zScores <- (rawScores - rsMean) / rsSD
> zScores
[1] 0.62153102 -0.21144870 0.49338029 -1.55703132
-0.08329797 1.198209
[7] 28 0.49338029 -1.55703132 -0.59590087 1.19820928
>
```

In this last step, we used Formula 10.1 and plugged in the vector we created along with the mean and standard deviation. The cool part is that we provided the vector of 10 numbers, and R performed the calculations for each number in the vector. The following table shows the *z* scores, rounded to the second decimal place. No need to keep more than two digits because we don't plan to do anything else with these numbers.

Raw Score	*z* Score
67	0.62
54	-0.21
65	0.49
33	-1.56
56	-0.08
76	1.20
65	0.49
33	-1.56
48	-0.60
76	1.20

Like most everything else in R, there is a function for that! Let's try the function called `scale` to calculate *z* scores.

```
> getZ <- scale(rawScores)
> getZ
            [,1]
 [1,]  0.62153102
 [2,] -0.21144870
 [3,]  0.49338029
 [4,] -1.55703132
 [5,] -0.08329797
 [6,]  1.19820928
 [7,]  0.49338029
 [8,] -1.55703132
 [9,] -0.59590087
[10,]  1.19820928
attr(,"scaled:center")
[1] 57.3
attr(,"scaled:scale")
[1] 15.60662
>
```

We used the vector we created in Step 1, `rawScores`, and asked `scale` to give us *z* scores. In this function, R returned eight numbers to the right of the decimal point because the person who created this function wanted to show that many numbers. We also see the mean and standard deviation of our raw scores, 57.3 and 15.60662.

Do you see the items called `scaled:center` and `scaled:scale`? The first, `scaled:center`, refers to the setting that we want to scale each value by its mean. If all we were doing to our raw scores was subtracting the mean from each entry, the new mean for our raw scores would be 0. This would be our new vector of scores:

```
> rawScores - rsMean
[1] 9.7 -3.3 7.7 -24.3 -1.3 18.7 7.7 -24.3 -9.3 18.7
>
```

Before, the smallest number was 33 and the largest was 76, with a range of 43. By subtracting 57.3 from each value, our new smallest number is −24.3 and the largest number is 18.7, and the range is still 43. So, all `scale:center` is telling us is that 57.3 was subtracted from each value, and provided we did not tell the function to use another number, that value will be the mean.

Based on what we see for `scale:scale`, each value was divided by the standard deviation. Essentially, by using the defaults, `scale` computed *z* scores for us.

FAT AND SKINNY FREQUENCY DISTRIBUTIONS

You could certainly surmise by now that distributions can be very different from one another in a variety of ways. In fact, there are four different ways in which they can differ: average value (you know—the mean, median, or mode); variability (range, variance, and standard deviation); skewness; and kurtosis. Those last two are new terms, and we'll define them as we show you what they look like. Let's discuss each of the four characteristics and then illustrate them.

Average Value

We're back once again to measures of central tendency. You can see in Figure 10.6 how three different distributions can differ in their average value. Notice that the average for Distribution C is more than the average for Distribution B, which, in turn, is more than the average for Distribution A.

Variability

In Figure 10.7, you can see three distributions that all have the same average value but differ in variability. The variability in Distribution A is less than that in Distribution B and, in turn, less than that found in Distribution C. Another way to say this is that Distribution C has the largest amount of variability of the three distributions and Distribution A has the least.

FIGURE 10.6 ● How distributions can differ in their average score.

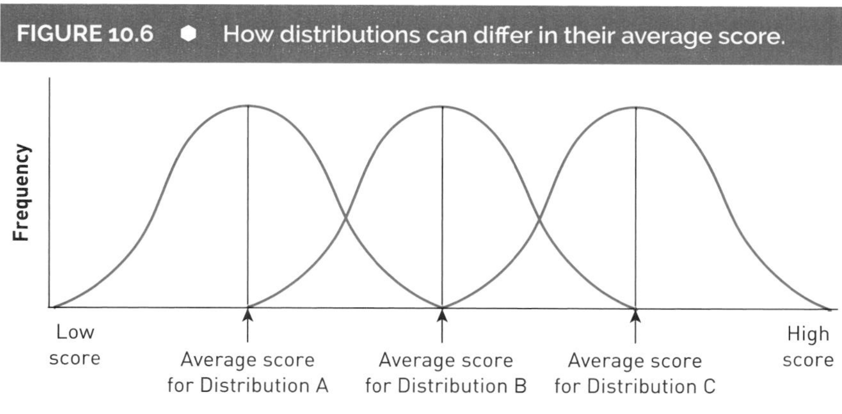

FIGURE 10.7 ● How distributions can differ in variability.

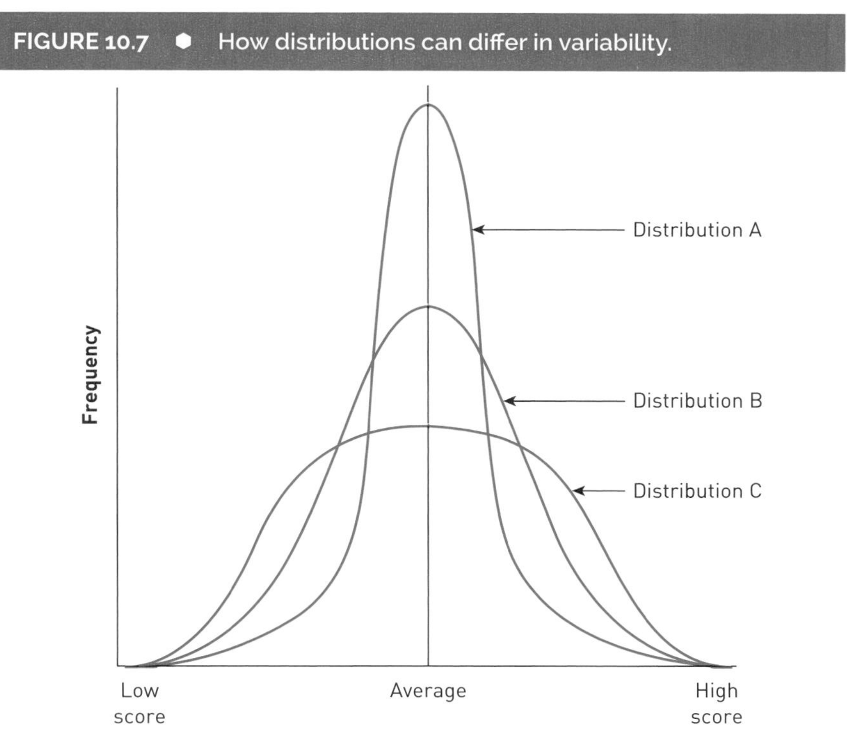

Skewness

Skewness is a measure of the lack of symmetry, or the lopsidedness, of a distribution. In other words, one "tail" of the distribution is longer than another. For example, in Figure 10.8, Distribution A's right tail is longer than its left tail, corresponding to a smaller number of occurrences at the high end of the distribution. This is a positively skewed distribution. This might be the case when you have a test that is very difficult, such that only a few people get scores that are relatively high and many more get scores that are relatively low. Distribution C's right tail is shorter than its left tail, corresponding to a larger number of occurrences at the high end of the distribution. This is a negatively skewed distribution and would be the case for an easy test (lots of high scores and relatively few low scores). And Distribution B—well, it's just right, with equal lengths of tails and no skewness.

FIGURE 10.8 ● Degree of skewness in different distributions.

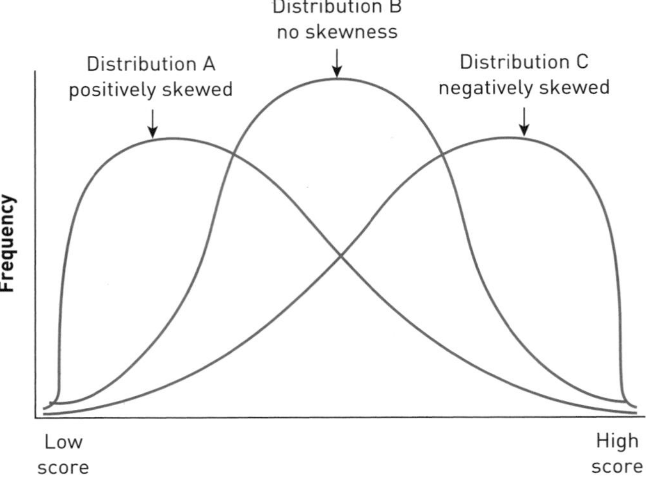

FIGURE 10.9 ● Degrees of kurtosis in different distributions.

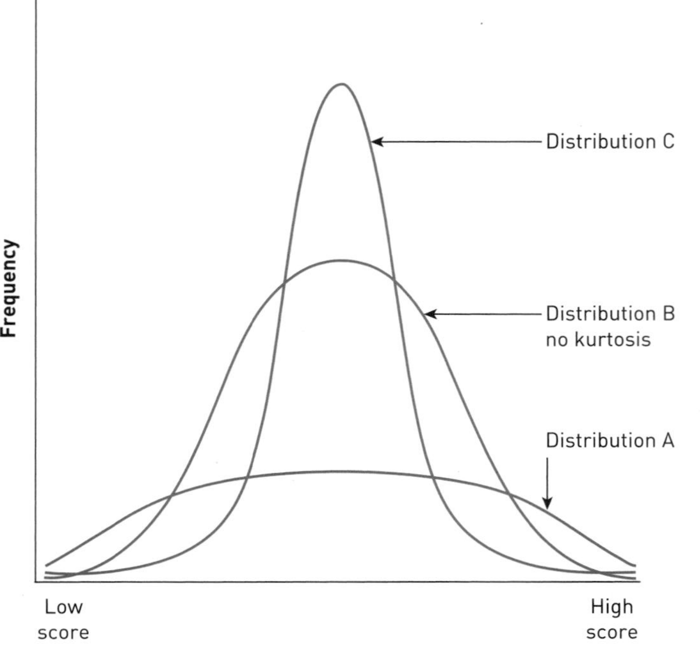

Kurtosis

Even though this sounds like a medical condition, it's the last of the four ways in which we can classify how distributions differ from one another. **Kurtosis** has to do with how flat or peaked a distribution appears, and the terms used to describe this characteristic are relative ones.

For example, the term **platykurtic** refers to a distribution that is relatively flat compared with a normal, or bell-shaped, distribution. The term **leptokurtic** refers to a distribution that is relatively peaked compared with a normal, or bell-shaped, distribution. In Figure 10.8, Distribution A is platykurtic compared with Distribution B. Distribution C is leptokurtic compared with Distribution B. Figure 10.9 looks similar to Figure 10.7 for a good reason—distributions that are platykurtic, for example, are relatively more dispersed than those that are not. Similarly, a distribution that is leptokurtic is less variable or dispersed relative to others.

While skewness and kurtosis are used mostly as descriptive terms (such as "That distribution is negatively skewed"), there are mathematical indicators of how skewed or kurtotic a distribution is. For example, skewness is computed by subtracting the value of the median from the mean. If the mean of a distribution is 100 and the median is 95, the skewness value is 100 – 95 = 5, and the distribution is positively skewed. If the mean of a distribution is 85 and the median is 90, the skewness value is 85 - 90 = –5, and the distribution is negatively skewed. There's an even more sophisticated formula, which uses the standard deviation of the distribution so that skewness indicators can be compared with one another (see Formula 10.3).

$$Sk = \frac{3(\bar{X} - M)}{s}, \qquad (10.3)$$

where

- Sk is Pearson's (he's the correlation guy you learned about in Chapter 7) measure of skewness,
- $\bar{X}$ is the mean,
- M is the median, and
- s is the sample standard deviation

Here's an example: The mean of Distribution A is 100, the median is 105, and the standard deviation is 10. For Distribution B, the mean is 120, the median is 116, and the standard deviation is 10. Using Pearson's formula, the skewness of Distribution A is –1.5, and the skewness of Distribution B is 1.2. Distribution A is negatively skewed, and Distribution B is positively skewed. However, Distribution A is more skewed than Distribution B, regardless of the direction.

Let's not leave kurtosis out of this discussion. It, too, can be computed using a fancy formula as follows:

$$K = \frac{\frac{\sum (X - \bar{X})^4}{n}}{s^2} - 3, \qquad (10.4)$$

(Continued)

(Continued)

where

- K = measure of kurtosis,
- $\sum$ = sum,
- X = the individual score,
- $\bar{X}$ = the mean of the sample,
- s = the sample standard deviation, and
- n = the sample size.

This is a pretty complicated formula that basically looks at how flat or peaked a set of scores is. You can see that if each score is the same, then the numerator is zero and $K = 0$, indicating no skewness. K equals zero when the distribution is normal or *mesokurtic* (now there's a new word to throw around). If the individual scores (the Xs in the formula) differ greatly from the mean (and there is lots of variability), then the curve will probably be quite flat.

So why do we care if our set of numbers is skewed or is lepto- or platykurtic? It all goes back to what we know about the normal curve and probabilities of our z score. Looking back at Figure 10.4, we know 34.13% of scores should fall between 0 and 1 standard deviation, 13.59% should fall between 1 and 2, and 2.28% (50% − 34.14% − 13.59%) from 2 to + ∞. Although no set of data you will collect or examine is perfectly normal, we expect it to be approximately normal. If the data are approximately normal, then we can use Table B.1 to look up probabilities for our zs. But if the data are too skewed ($Sk < -2$ or $Sk > 2$) or leptokurtic with $K > 7$, then we can't use Table B.1 with any confidence in our results.

REAL-WORLD STATS

More about obesity in children. . . .

You have probably heard about all the concerns regarding childhood obesity. These researchers investigated the possible reduction of obesity in children by focusing on physical activity as an intervention. What might this have to do with z scores? A z score was one of their primary outcome or dependent variables: mean body mass index (BMI) z score = 3.24, $SD = 0.49$.

The participants were invited to participate in a 1-week sports camp, and after the camp, a coach from a local sports club supported the children during participation in a chosen activity for 6 months. Weight, height, body composition, and lifestyle were measured at baseline and after 12 months. The results? Children who participated in the intervention had a significant decrease in their BMI z score.

Why did the researchers use z scores? Because the children who were being compared with one another came from different distributions of scores—different BMIs because BMI tables differ by sex and age. By using a standard score, those differences (at least in the variability of the scores) were eliminated.

Want to know more? Go online or to the library and find . . .

Nowicka, P., Lanke, J., Pietrobelli, A., Apitzsch, E., & Flodmark, C. E. (2009). Sports camp with six months of support from a local sports club as a treatment for childhood obesity. *Scandinavian Journal of Public Health, 37,* 793–800.

Summary

Being able to figure out a *z* score and estimate how likely it is to occur in a sample of data is the first and most important skill for understanding the whole notion of inference. Once we know how likely a test score or a difference between groups is, we can compare that likelihood with what we would expect by chance and then make informed decisions. As we start Part V of *Statistics for People Who (Think They) Hate Statistics Using R,* we'll apply this model to specific examples of testing questions about the difference.

Time to Practice

1. What are the characteristics of the normal curve? What human behavior, trait, or characteristic can you think of that is distributed normally? What makes you think it may be distributed normally?
2. To compute a standard score, what three bits of information do you need?
3. Standard scores, such as *z* scores, allow us to make comparisons across different samples. Why?
4. Why is a *z* score a standard score, and why can standard scores be used to compare scores from different distributions with one another?
5. The mean of a set of test scores is 50, and the standard deviation is 5. For a raw score of 55, the corresponding *z* score is +1. What's the *z* score when the standard deviation is half as much, or 2.5? From this example, what can you conclude the effect of decreasing the amount of variability in a set of scores is on a standard score (given all else is equal, such as the same raw score), and why is this effect important?
6. For the following set of scores, fill in the cells. The mean is 74.13, and the standard deviation is 9.98.

(Continued)

(Continued)

Raw Score	z Score
68.0	?
?	−1.6
82.0	?
?	1.8
69.0	?
?	−0.5
85.0	?
?	1.7
72.0	?

7. For the following set of scores, compute standard scores. Do it using R (easy) and do it manually to keep R honest (not as easy as using R but once you get the hang of it—easy enough). Notice any differences?

18	27
19	22
15	34
20	29
25	40
31	33
17	21
35	

8. Questions 8a through 8d are based on a distribution of scores with $\bar{X} = 75$ and standard deviation = 6.38. Draw a small picture to help you see what's required.
   a. What is the probability of a score falling between a raw score of 70 and 80?
   b. What is the probability of a score falling above a raw score of 80?
   c. What is the probability of a score falling between a raw score of 81 and 83?
   d. What is the probability of a score falling below a raw score of 63?

9. Identify whether these distributions are negatively skewed, positively skewed, or not skewed at all and explain why you describe them that way.
   a. This talented group of athletes scored very high on the vertical-jump task.
   b. On this incredibly crummy test, everyone received the same score.

c. On the most difficult spelling test of the year, the third graders wept as the scores were delivered and then their parents complained.

10. Jake needs to score in the top 10% of his class to earn a physical fitness certificate. The class mean is 78, and the standard deviation is 5.5. What raw score does he need to get that valuable piece of paper?

11. Imagine you are in charge of a program in which members are evaluated on five different tests at the end of the program. Why doesn't it make sense to simply compute the average of the five scores as a measure of performance rather than compute a *z* score for each test for each individual and average those?

12. Who is the better student, relative to his or her classmates? Here's all the information you ever wanted to know:

	Math		
Class mean	81		
Class standard deviation	2		
	Reading		
Class mean	87		
Class standard deviation	10		
	Raw Scores		
	Math Score	**Reading Score**	**Average**
Noah	85	88	86.5
Talya	87	81	84.0
	z Scores		
	Math Score	**Reading Score**	**Average**
Noah	________	________	________
Talya	________	________	________

13. Here's an interesting extra-credit question. As you know, one of the defining characteristics of the normal curve is that the tails do not touch the *x*-axis. Why don't they touch?

Student Study Site

Get the tools you need to sharpen your study skills! Visit **edge.sagepub.com/salkindshaw** to access practice quizzes and eFlashcards, watch R tutorial videos, and download data sets!

PART V

SIGNIFICANTLY DIFFERENT

USING INFERENTIAL STATISTICS

"Talk about a sum of squares."

You've gotten this far and you're still alive and kicking, so congratulate yourself. At this point, you should have a good understanding of what descriptive statistics is all about, how chance figures as a factor in making decisions about outcomes, and how likely outcomes are to have occurred due to chance or some treatment.

You're an expert on creating and understanding the role that hypotheses play in social and behavioral science research. Now it's time for the rubber to meet the road. Let's see what you're made of in the next part of *Statistics for People Who (Think They) Hate Statistics Using R.* The hard work you've put in will shortly pay off with an understanding of applied problems!

This part of the book deals exclusively with understanding and applying certain types of statistics to answer certain types of research questions, and we'll cover the most common statistical tests. Then, in Part VI, we'll even cover a few that are a bit more sophisticated and tests that are useful when you can't rely on the normal distribution.

Let's start with a brief discussion of what the concept of significance is and go through the steps for performing an inferential test. Then we'll go on to examples of specific tests. We have lots of hands-on work ahead of us, so let's get started.

SIGNIFICANTLY SIGNIFICANT

What It Means for You and Me

Difficulty Scale ☺ ☺
(somewhat thought provoking
and key to it all!)

WHAT YOU WILL LEARN IN THIS CHAPTER

- ✦ Understanding the concept of significance and why it is important
- ✦ Distinguishing between Type I and Type II errors
- ✦ Understanding how inferential statistics work
- ✦ Selecting the appropriate statistical test for your purposes

THE CONCEPT OF SIGNIFICANCE

Probably no term or concept causes the beginning statistics student more confusion than *statistical significance*. But it doesn't have to be that way for you. Although it's a powerful idea, it is also relatively straightforward and can be understood by anyone in a basic statistics class.

We need an example of a study to illustrate the points we want to make. Let's take E. Duckett and M. Richards's "Maternal Employment and Young Adolescents' Daily Experiences in Single Mother Families" (paper presented at the Society for Research in Child Development, Kansas City, MO, 1989—a long time ago in a galaxy far away [Kansas City, Missouri . . .]). These two authors examined the attitudes of 436 fifth- through ninth-grade adolescents toward maternal employment. Even though the presentation took place some years ago, it's a perfect example for illustrating many of the important ideas at the heart of this chapter.

Specifically, the two researchers investigated whether differences are present between the attitudes of adolescents whose mothers work and the attitudes of adolescents whose mothers do not work. They also examined some other factors, but for this example, we'll stick with the mothers-who-work and mothers-who-don't-work groups. One more thing. Let's add the word *significant* to our discussion of differences, and we have a research hypothesis something like this:

> There is a significant difference in attitude toward maternal employment between adolescents whose mothers work and adolescents whose mothers do not work, as measured by a test of emotional state.

What we mean by the word *significant* is that any difference between the attitudes of the two groups is due to some systematic influence and not due to chance. In this example, that influence is whether or not mothers work. We assume that all of the other factors that might account for any differences between groups were controlled. Thus, the only thing left to account for the differences between adolescents' attitudes is whether or not their mothers work. Right? Yes. Finished? Not quite.

If Only We Were Perfect

Because our world is not a perfect one, we must allow for some leeway in how confident we are that only those factors we identify could cause any difference between groups. In other words, you need to be able to say that although you are pretty sure the difference between the two groups of adolescents is due to maternal employment, you cannot be absolutely, 100%, positively, unequivocally, indisputably (get the picture?) sure. There's always a chance, no matter how small, that you are wrong. The improbable is probable: So said Aristotle, and he was right. No matter how small the chance, there's always a chance.

> And, by the way, the whole notion of the normal curve's tails never, ever really touching the *x*-axis—asymptotic (as we mentioned in the last chapter)—is directly relevant to our discussion here. If the tails did touch, the probability of an event being very extreme in one or the other tail would be absolutely zero. But since they do not touch, there is always a chance, no matter how perfect we might be, that an event can occur—no matter how small and unlikely its probability might be.

Why? Many reasons. For example, you could just be wrong. Maybe during this one experiment, differences between adolescents' attitudes were not due to whether their mothers worked or didn't work but were due to some other factor that was inadvertently not accounted for, such as a speech given by the local Mothers Who Work Club that several students attended. How about if the people in one group were mostly adolescent males and the people in the other group were mostly adolescent females? That could be the source of a difference as well. If you are a good researcher and do your homework, you can account for such differences, but it's always possible that you can't. And as a good researcher, you have to take that possibility into account.

So what do you do? In most scientific endeavors that involve testing hypotheses (such as the group differences example here), there is bound to be a certain amount of error that cannot be controlled—this is the chance factor that we have been talking about in the past few chapters. The level of chance or risk you are willing to take is expressed as a *significance level,* a term that unnecessarily strikes fear in the hearts of even strong men and women.

Significance level (here's the quick-and-dirty definition) is the risk associated with not being 100% confident that what you observe in an experiment is due to the treatment or what was being tested—in our example, whether or not mothers worked. If you read that significant findings occurred at the .05 level (or $p < .05$ in tech talk and what you regularly see in professional journals), the translation is that there is 1 chance in 20 or 5 in 100 (or .05 or 5%) that any differences found were not due to the hypothesized reason (whether mom works) but to some other, unknown reason or reasons (yep—or chance). Your job is to reduce this likelihood as much as possible by removing all of the competing reasons for any differences that you observed. Because you cannot fully eliminate the likelihood (because no one can control every potential factor), you assign some level of probability and report your results with that caveat.

In sum (and in practice), the researcher defines a level of risk that he or she is willing to take. If the results fall within the region that says, "This could not have occurred by chance alone—something else is going on," the researcher knows that the null hypothesis (which states an equality, nothing is going on) is not the most attractive explanation for the observed outcomes. Instead, the research hypothesis (that there is an inequality or a difference) is the favored explanation.

Let's take a look at another example, this one hypothetical.

A researcher is interested in seeing whether there is a difference between the academic achievement of children who participated in a preschool program and that of children who did not participate. The null hypothesis is that the two groups are equal to each other on some measure of achievement.

The research hypothesis is that the mean score for the group of children who participated in the program is higher than the mean score for the group of children who did not participate in the program.

As a good researcher, your job is to show (as best you can—and no one is so perfect that he or she can account for everything) that *any* difference that exists between the two groups is due only to the effects of the preschool experience and no other factor or combination of factors. Through a variety of techniques (that you'll learn about in your next statistics or research methods class!), you control or eliminate all the possible sources of difference, such as the influence of parents' education, number of children in the family, and so on. Once these other potential explanatory variables are removed, the only remaining alternative explanation for differences is the effect of the preschool experience itself.

But can you be absolutely (which is pretty darn) sure? No, you cannot. Why? First, because you can never be sure that you are testing a sample that identically reflects the profile of the population. And even if the sample perfectly represents the population, there are always other influences that might affect the outcome and that you inadvertently missed when designing the experiment. There's *always* the possibility of error (another word for chance).

By concluding that the differences in test scores are due to differences in treatment, you accept some risk. This degree of risk is, in effect (drumroll, please), the level of statistical significance at which you are willing to operate.

Statistical significance (here's the formal definition) is the degree of risk you are willing to take that you will reject a null hypothesis when it is actually true. In our preceding example, the null says that there is no difference between the two sample groups (remember, the null is always a statement of equality). In your data, however, you did find a difference. That is, given the evidence you have so far, group membership seems to have an effect on achievement scores. In reality, however, maybe there is no difference. If you reject the null you stated, you would be making an error. The probability of making a Type I error is referred to as α, and α is also the level of significance we set to make a decision about our null hypothesis. We will explain more in the coming pages.

So the next step is to develop a set of steps to test whether our findings indicate that error is responsible for differences or actual differences are responsible.

The World's Most Important Table (for This Semester Only)

Here's what it all boils down to.

A null hypothesis can be rejected or not for lack of evidence. Either there is no evidence of difference between groups, or there really and truly is an inequality (such as the difference between two groups). But remember, you'll never know this true state because the null cannot be tested directly because the null is about the population and we only have some evidence (for a variety of reasons we have talked about, the population can rarely be directly tested).

And, as a crackerjack statistician, you can choose to either reject or fail to reject the null hypothesis. Right? These four different conditions create the table you see in Table 11.1.

Let's look at each cell.

More About Table 11.1

Table 11.1 has four important cells that describe the relationship between the nature of the null (whether it's true or not) and your action (fail to reject or reject the null hypothesis). As you can see, the null can be either true or false, and you can either reject or fail to reject it.

The most important thing about understanding this table is the fact that the researcher never really knows the true nature of the null hypothesis and whether there really is or is not a difference between groups. Why? Because the population (which the null represents) is almost never directly tested. Why? Because in many fields like psychology, sociology, and education, it's impractical to do so, and that's why we have inferential statistics.

TABLE 11.1 ● Different Types of Errors

		Action You Take	
		Fail to Reject the Null Hypothesis	**Reject the Null Hypothesis**
True nature of the null hypothesis	The null hypothesis is really true.	1 ☺ Bingo, you failed to reject a null when it is true and there is really no difference between groups.	2 ☹ Oops—you made a Type I error and rejected a null hypothesis even when there really is no difference between groups. Type I errors are also represented by the Greek letter alpha, or α.
	The null hypothesis is really false.	3 ☹ Uh-oh—you made a Type II error by failing to reject a false null hypothesis. Type II errors are also represented by the Greek letter beta, or β.	4 ☺ Good job, you rejected the null hypothesis when there really are differences between the two groups. This is also called power, or $1 - \beta$.

- ☺ Cell 1 in Table 11.1 represents a situation in which the null hypothesis is really true (there's no difference between groups), and the researcher made the correct decision in failing to reject the null. No problem here. In our example, our results would show that there is no difference between the two groups of children, and we have acted correctly by failing to reject the null when there is no difference.
- ☹ Oops. Cell 2 represents a serious error. Here, we have rejected the null hypothesis (that there is no difference) when it is really true (there is no difference between groups). Even though there is no difference between the two groups of children, we will conclude there is, and that's an error—clearly a boo-boo called a **Type I error (α)**, also known as the level of significance.
- ☹ Uh-oh, another type of error. Cell 3 represents a serious error as well. Here, we have failed to reject the null hypothesis (that there is no difference) when it is really false (and, indeed, there is a difference between groups). We have said that even though there is a difference between the two groups of children, we will conclude there is not—also clearly a boo-boo, this time known as a **Type II error (β)**.
- ☺ Cell 4 represents a situation where the null hypothesis is really false and the researcher made the correct decision in rejecting it. No problem here. In our example, our results show that there is a difference between the two groups of children, and we have acted correctly by rejecting the null that states there is no difference.

So, if .05 is good and .01 is even "better," why not set your Type I level of risk at .000001? For the very good reason that you would be so rigorous in your rejection of false null hypotheses that you might reject a null when it was actually true. Such a stringent Type I error rate allows for little leeway—indeed, the research hypothesis might be true but the associated probability might be .015—still quite rare and probably very useful information, but missed with the too-rigid Type I level of error.

Why do we say fail to reject the null hypothesis? Why can't we accept the null hypothesis? Remember, the null hypothesis is about the population, and the reason we are testing hypotheses is because we cannot directly measure our population. If we could directly measure our population, like some political scientists and economists can when their data are based on the 50 U.S. states, we would just describe our sample. We wouldn't need to make inferences from our sample to our population. But because we are making inferences from our sample to our population, we can only collect evidence about what is happening in the population. We never know the true nature of the population. We can only test, test, and test again, collecting evidence for our theory that there is a difference. If we fail to reject the null, we are saying we don't have enough evidence to reject the null. At least, not with these data at this time.

Back to Type I Errors

Let's focus a bit more on Cell 2, where a Type I error was made, because this is the focus of our discussion.

This Type I error has certain values associated with it that define the risk you are willing to take in any test of the null hypothesis, and we do so by setting the level at which we are willing to say something more than chance is occurring. The conventional levels set are between .01 and .05.

For example, if the level of significance is .01, it means that on any one test of the null hypothesis, there is a 1% chance you will reject the null hypothesis when the null is true and conclude that there is a group difference when there really is no group difference at all.

If the level of significance is .05, it means that on any one test of the null hypothesis, there is a 5% chance you will reject it (and conclude that there is a group difference) when the null is true and there really is no group difference at all. Notice that the level of significance is associated with an independent test of the null, and it is not appropriate to say that "on 100 tests of the null hypothesis, I will make an error only 5 times, or 5% of the time."

In a research report, statistical significance is usually represented as $p < .05$, read as "the probability of observing that outcome is less than .05," and can be expressed in a report or journal article simply as "significant at the .05 level," although that phrase should be used only in summary text in which you are referring to multiple tests, all of which had $p < .05$. When possible, report the exact p associated with your statistical test and set your level when you are deciding which test to use, not after you have run the test.

With the introduction of fancy-schmancy software such as R that can do statistical analysis, there's no longer the worry about the imprecision of such statements as "$p < .05$" or "$p < .01$." For example, $p < .05$ can mean anything from .000 to .049999, right? Instead, software gives you the *exact* probability, such as .013 or .158, of the risk you are willing to take that you will commit a Type I error. So, when you see in a research article the statement that "$p < .05$," it means that the value of p is equal to anything from .00 to .049999999999 . . . (you get the picture). Likewise, when you see "$p > .05$" or "$p = ns$" (for nonsignificant), it means that the probability of rejecting a true null exceeds .05 and, in fact, can range from .0500001 to 1.00. So, it's actually terrific when we know the exact probability of an outcome because we can measure more precisely the risk we are willing to take. But what to do if the p value is exactly .05? Well, given what you've already read, if you want to play by the rules, then the outcome is not significant. A result either is statistically significant or is not. So, .04999999999 is and .05 is not. But, if R (or any other program) generates a value of .05, extend the number of decimal places—it may really be .04999999999.

As discussed earlier, there is another kind of error you can make, which, along with the Type I error, is shown in Table 11.1. A Type II error (Cell 3 in the chart) occurs when you inadvertently accept a false null hypothesis. For example, there may really be differences between the populations represented by the sample groups, but you mistakenly conclude there are not.

When talking about the significance of a finding, you might hear the word *power* used. Power is a construct that has to do with how well a statistical test can detect differences or an effect and reject a null hypothesis when it is false. Mathematically, it's calculated by subtracting the value of the Type II error from 1. A more powerful test is always more desirable than a less powerful test, because the more powerful one lets you get to the heart of what's false and what's not. Powerful tests have two desirable properties that we talked about in Chapter 8—high validity and reliability.

Ideally, you want to minimize both Type I and Type II errors, but doing so is not always easy or under your control. You have complete control over the Type I error level or the amount of risk that you are willing to take (because you actually set the level itself). Type II errors, however, are not as directly controlled but instead are related to factors such as sample size. Type II errors are particularly sensitive to the number of subjects in a sample, and as that number increases, Type II error decreases. In other words, as the sample characteristics more closely match those of the population (achieved by increasing the sample size), the likelihood that you will accept a false null hypothesis decreases.

SIGNIFICANCE VERSUS MEANINGFULNESS

What an interesting situation arises for the researcher when he or she discovers that the results of an experiment indeed are statistically significant! You know technically what statistical significance means—that the research was a technical success and the null hypothesis is not a reasonable explanation for what was observed. Now, if your experimental design and other considerations were well taken care of, statistically significant results are unquestionably the first step toward making a contribution to the literature in your field. However, the value of statistical significance and its importance or meaningfulness must be kept in perspective.

For example, let's take the case where a very large sample of illiterate adults (say, 10,000) is divided into two groups. One group receives intensive training to read using traditional teaching, and the other receives intensive training to read using computers. The average score for Group 1 (which learned in the traditional way) is 75.6 on a reading test, the dependent variable. The average score on the reading test for Group 2 (which learned using the computer) is 75.7. The amount of variance in both groups is about equal. As you can see, the difference in score is only one tenth of 1 point or 0.1 (75.6 vs. 75.7), but when a *t* test for the significance between independent means is applied, the results are significant at the .01 level, indicating that computers work better than traditional teaching methods. (Chapters 13 and 14 discuss *t* tests, the kind we would use in such a situation.)

The difference of 0.1 is indeed statistically significant at the .01 level, but is it meaningful? Does the improvement in test scores (by such a small margin) provide sufficient rationale for the $300,000 it costs to fund the program? Or is the difference negligible enough that it can be ignored, even if it is statistically significant?

Here are some conclusions about the importance of statistical significance that we can reach, given this and the countless other possible examples:

- Statistical significance, in and of itself, is not very meaningful unless the study that is conducted has a sound conceptual base that lends some meaning to the significance of the outcome.
- Statistical significance cannot be interpreted independently of the context within which the outcomes occur. For example, if you are the superintendent in a school system, are you willing to retain children in Grade 1 if the retention program significantly raises their standardized test scores by one half point?
- Although statistical significance is important as a concept, it is not the end-all and certainly should not be the only goal of scientific research. That is the reason why we set out to *test* hypotheses rather than *prove* them. If our study is designed correctly, then even null results tell you something very important. If a particular treatment does not work, this is important information that others need to know about. If your study is designed well, then you should know why the treatment does not work, and the next person down the line can design his or her study taking into account the valuable information you have provided.

Researchers treat the reporting of statistical significance in many different ways in their written reports. Some use words such as *significant* (assuming that if something is significant, it is statistically so) or the entire phrase *statistically significant*. But some also use the phrase *marginally significant*, where the probability associated with a finding might be .051 or .053 and include any result below .10 in that category. What to do? Best practice is to stick by your preset cutoff of .05 and do not refer to those results as marginally significant. But you can also provide your reader with more information that we will talk about later in this chapter and the next—confidence intervals and effect sizes (we will talk more about these in the next chapter). This additional information will provide that all-important context.

Almost every discipline has "other" terms for this *significant* versus *meaningful* distinction, but the issue is generally considered to concern the same elements. For example, health care professionals refer to the meaningful part of the equation as "clinical significance" rather than "meaningfulness." It's the same idea—they just use a different term given the setting in which their outcomes occur.

Ever hear of "publication bias"? It's where a preset significance value of .05 is used as the *only* criterion in the serious consideration of a paper for publication. It's not exactly .05 or bust, but in times past and even today, some editorial boards hold up significance values such as .05 or .01 as the holy grail of getting things right. If those values are not reached, then the findings cannot be significant, let alone meaningful, according to some people's judgment. Now, there's something to be said for consistency throughout a field, but today's cool stats tools such as R allow us to pinpoint the exact probability associated with an outcome rather than an all-or-nothing criterion such as .05, which dooms some meaningful work before it is even discussed. Be sophisticated—make up your own mind based on all the evidence.

AN INTRODUCTION TO INFERENTIAL STATISTICS

Whereas descriptive statistics are used to describe a sample's characteristics, inferential statistics are used to infer something about the population based on the sample's characteristics.

At several points throughout the first half of *Statistics for People Who (Think They) Hate Statistics Using R*, we have emphasized that a hallmark of good scientific research is choosing a sample in such a way that it is representative of the population from which it was selected. The process then becomes an inferential one, in which you infer from the smaller sample to the larger population based on the results of tests (and experiments) conducted using the sample.

Before we start discussing individual inferential tests, let's go through the logic of how the inferential method works.

How Inference Works

Here are the general steps of a research project to see how the process of inference might work. We'll stay with adolescents' attitudes toward mothers working as an example.

Here's the sequence of events that might happen:

1. The researcher selects representative samples of adolescents who have mothers who work and adolescents who have mothers who do not work. These are selected in such a way that the samples represent the populations from which they are drawn.
2. Each adolescent is administered a test to assess his or her attitude. The mean scores for groups are computed and compared using some test.
3. A conclusion is reached as to whether the difference between the scores is the result of chance (meaning some factor other than moms working is responsible for the difference) or the result of "true" and statistically significant differences between the two groups (meaning the results are due to moms working).
4. A conclusion is reached as to the relationship between maternal employment and adolescents' attitudes in the population from which the sample was originally drawn. In other words, an inference, based on the results of an analysis of the sample data, is made about the population of all adolescents.

How to Select What Test to Use

Step 3 above brings us to ask, "How do I select the appropriate statistical test to determine whether a difference between groups exists?" Heaven knows, there are plenty of them, and you have to decide which one to use and when to use it.

Well, the best way to learn which test to use is to be an experienced statistician who has taken lots of courses in this area and participated in lots of research. Experience is still the greatest teacher. In fact, there's no way you can really learn what to use and when to use it unless you've had the real-life, applied opportunity to actually use these tools. And as a result of taking this course, you are learning how to use these very tools.

So, for our purposes and to get started, we've created this nice little flowchart (a.k.a. cheat sheet) of sorts that you see in Figure 11.1. You have to have some idea of what you're doing, so selecting the correct statistical test does not put the rest of your study on autopilot, but it certainly is a good place to get started.

FIGURE 11.1 ● A quick (but not always great) approach to determining which statistical test to use.

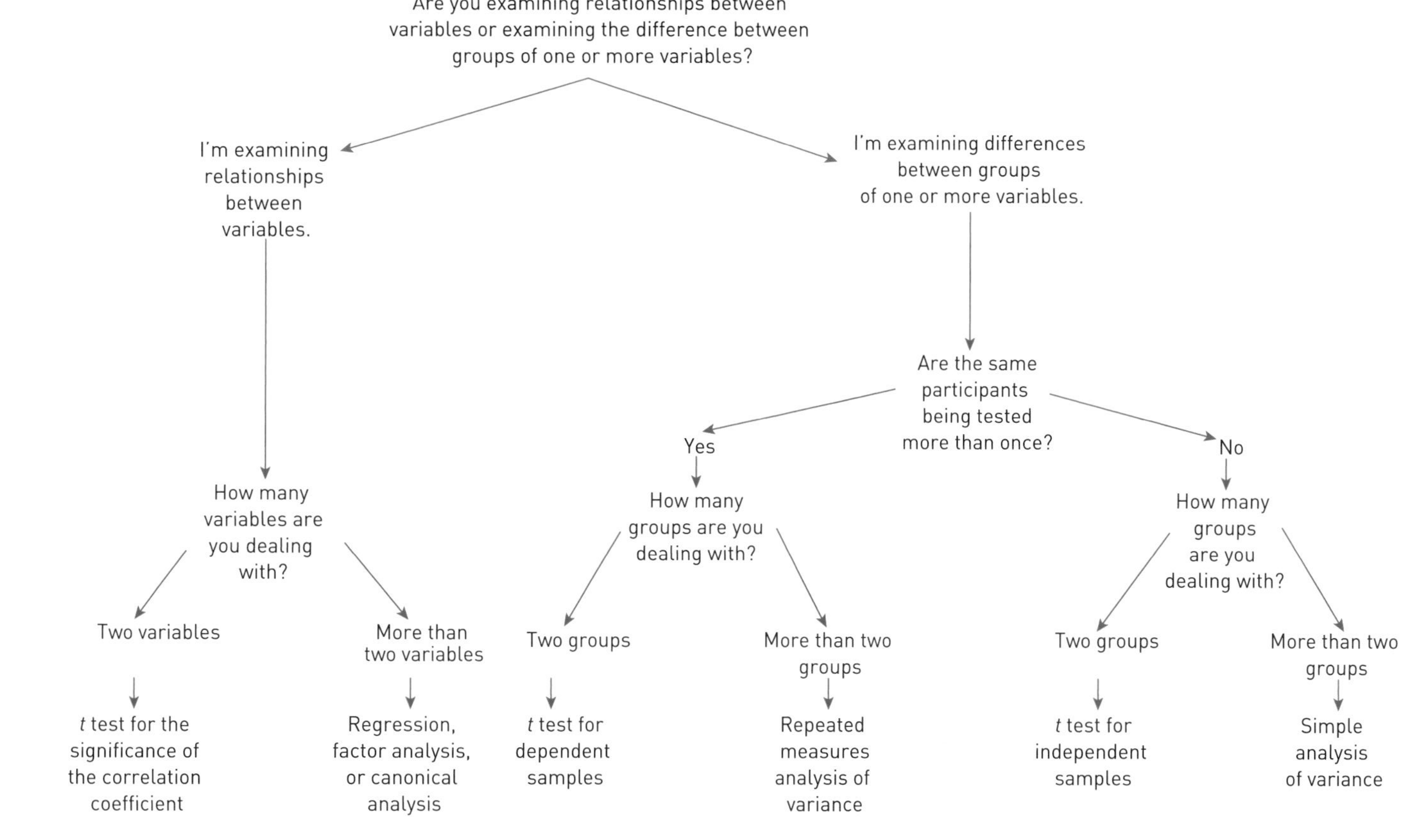

Don't think for a second that Figure 11.1 takes the place of your need to learn about when these different tests are appropriate. The flowchart is here only to help you get started.

This is really important. We just wrote that selecting the appropriate statistical test is not necessarily an easy thing to do. And the best way to learn how to do it is to do it, and that means practicing and even taking more statistics courses. The simple flowchart we present here works, in general, but use it with caution. When you make a decision, check with your professor or some other person who has been through this stuff and feels more confident than you might (and who also knows more!).

Here's How to Use the Chart

1. Assume that you're very new to this statistics stuff (which you are) and that you have some idea of what these tests of significance are, but you're pretty lost as far as deciding which one to use when.
2. Answer the question at the top of the flowchart.
3. Proceed down the chart by answering each of the questions until you get to the end of the chart. That's the statistical test you should use. This is not rocket science, and with some practice (which you will get throughout this part of the book), you'll be able to quickly and reliably select the appropriate test. Each of the remaining chapters in this part of the book will begin with a chart like the one you see in Figure 11.1 and take you through the specific steps to get to the test statistic you should use.

Does the cute flowchart in Figure 11.1 contain all the statistical tests there are? Not by a long shot. There are hundreds, but the ones in Figure 11.1 are the ones used most often. And if you are going to become familiar with the research in your own field, you are bound to run into these.

AN INTRODUCTION TO TESTS OF SIGNIFICANCE

What inferential statistics does best is allow decisions to be made about populations based on information about samples. One of the most useful tools for doing this is a test of statistical significance that can be applied to different types of situations, depending on the nature of the question being asked and the form of the null hypothesis.

For example, do you want to look at the difference between two groups, such as whether boys score significantly differently than girls on some test? Or the relationship between two variables, such as number of children in a family and average score on intelligence tests? The two cases call for different approaches, but both will result in a test of a null hypothesis using a specific test of statistical significance.

How a Test of Significance Works: The Plan

Tests of significance are based on the fact that each type of null hypothesis has associated with it a particular type of statistic. And each of the statistics has associated with it a special distribution that you compare with the data you obtain from a sample. A comparison between the characteristics of your sample and the characteristics of the test distribution allows you to conclude whether the sample characteristics are different from what you would expect by chance.

Here are the general steps to take in the application of a statistical test to any null hypothesis. These steps will serve as a model for each of the chapters in Part V.

1. *A statement of the null hypothesis.* Do you remember that the null hypothesis is a statement of equality? The null hypothesis is the "true" state of affairs given no other information on which to make a judgment.
2. *Setting the level of risk (or the level of significance or Type I error) associated with the null hypothesis.* With any research hypothesis comes a certain degree of risk that you are wrong. The smaller this error is (such as .01 compared with .05), the less risk you are willing to take. No test of a hypothesis is completely risk free because you never really know the "true" relationship between variables in the population. Remember that it is traditional to set the Type I error rate at .01 or .05; most R functions tell you the exact level.
3. *Selection of the appropriate test statistic.* Each null hypothesis has associated with it a particular test statistic. You can learn what test is related to what type of question in this part of the book.
4. *Computation of the test statistic value.* The **test statistic value** (also called the *estimated value*) is the result or product of a specific statistical test. For example, there are test statistics for the significance of the difference between the averages of two groups, for the significance of the difference of a correlation coefficient from zero, and for the significance of the difference between two proportions. You'll actually compute the test statistic and come up with a numerical value.
5. *Determination of the value needed for rejection of the null hypothesis using the appropriate table of critical values for the particular statistic.* Each test statistic (along with group size and the risk you are willing to take) has a **critical value** associated with it. This is the cutoff value you would expect the test statistic to be less than if the null hypothesis is indeed true.
6. *Comparison of the obtained value with the critical value.* This is the crucial step. Here, the value you obtained from the test statistic (the one you computed) is compared with the value (the critical value) you would expect to find by chance alone.

7. *If the obtained value is more extreme than the critical value, the null hypothesis can be rejected.* That is, the null hypothesis's statement of equality (reflecting chance) is not the most attractive explanation for differences that were found. Here is where the real beauty of the inferential method shines through. Only if your obtained value is more extreme than what would happen by chance (meaning that the result of the test statistic is not a result of some chance fluctuation) can you say that any differences you obtained are not due to chance and that the equality stated by the null hypothesis is not the most attractive explanation for any differences you might have found. Instead, the differences must be due to the treatment. What if the two values are equal (and you were about to ask your instructor that question, right?)? Nope—due to chance.
8. *If the obtained value does not exceed the critical value, the null hypothesis cannot be rejected.* If you cannot show that the difference you obtained is due to something other than chance (such as the treatment), then the difference must be due to chance or something you have no control over. In other words, the null, that there is no difference, is the best explanation.

Here's the Picture That's Worth a Thousand Words

What you see in Figure 11.2 represents the eight steps we just went through. This is a visual representation of what happens when the obtained and critical values are compared. In this example, the significance level is set at .05, or 5%. It could have been set at .01, or 1%. And note that all 5% is grouped together on the right side of the distribution, indicating that we are dealing with a one-tailed test (direction matters). If the 5% were divided evenly between the two tails, we would have a two-tailed test (direction doesn't matter).

FIGURE 11.2 ● Comparing obtained values with critical values and making decisions about rejecting or failing to reject the null hypothesis.

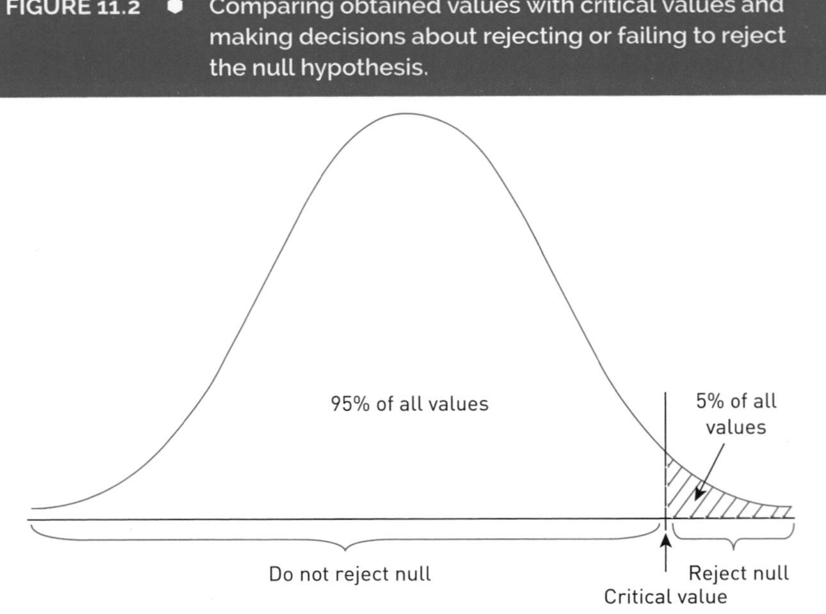

In examining Figure 11.2, note the following:

1. The entire curve represents all the possible outcomes based on a specific null hypothesis, such as the difference between two groups or the significance of a correlation coefficient.
2. The critical value is the point beyond which the obtained outcomes are judged to be so rare that the conclusion is that the obtained outcome is not due to chance but to some other factor. In this example, we define *rare* as having a less than 5% chance of occurring.
3. If the outcome representing the obtained value falls to the left of the critical value (it is less extreme), the conclusion is that the null hypothesis is the most attractive explanation for any differences that are observed. In other words, the obtained value falls in the region (95% of the area under the curve) where we expect only outcomes due to chance to occur.
4. If the obtained value falls to the right of the critical value (it is more extreme), the conclusion is that the research hypothesis is the most attractive explanation for any differences that are observed. In other words, the obtained value falls in the region (5% of the area under the curve) where we would expect only outcomes due to something other than chance to occur.

BE EVEN MORE CONFIDENT

You now know that probabilities can be associated with outcomes—that's been an ongoing theme for the past two chapters. Now we are going to say the same thing in a bit different way and introduce a new idea called confidence intervals.

A **confidence interval** (or CI) is the best estimate of the range of a population value (or population parameter) that we can come up with given the sample value (or sample statistic representing the population parameter). Say we knew the mean spelling score for a sample of 20 third graders (of all the third graders in a school district). How much confidence could we have that the population mean will fall between two scores? A 95% confidence interval would be correct 95% of the time.

Let's walk through the steps for finding our 95% confidence interval in the normal curve.

1. Go to Table B.1 in Appendix B for the areas beneath the normal curve.
2. To get the 95% confidence interval, find the area between the mean and the *z* score for the upper half of that confidence interval by dividing 95 by 2. That gives us 47.5.
3. Look in the columns labeled "Area Between the Mean and the *z* Score" for the number 47.5. Once you find that entry, look at the *z* score in the column to the left. It should say 1.96.

The *z* score is 1.96 for the upper half of the normal curve and −1.96 for the bottom half of the normal curve. The amount of area under the curve between those two numbers is 95%. We can now use this number to calculate our 95% confidence interval. How would you change those steps to get the 99% confidence interval? If you follow those steps, you should find the answer to ±2.56 *z* scores.

Let's fool around with some real numbers.

Let's say that the mean spelling score for a random sample of 100 sixth graders is 64 (out of 80 words) and the standard deviation is 5. What confidence can we have in predicting the population mean for the average spelling score for the entire population of sixth graders?

The 95% confidence interval is equal to

$$64 \pm 1.96(5)$$

or a range from 54.2 to 73.8, so at the least you can say with 95% confidence that the population mean for the average spelling score for all sixth graders falls between 54.2 and 73.8.

Want to be more confident? The 99% confidence interval would be computed as follows:

$$64 \pm 2.56(5)$$

or a range from 51.2 to 76.8, so you can conclude with 99% confidence that the population mean falls between those two scores.

Do keep in mind that some people use the standard error of the mean to compute confidence intervals and that the use of either the standard deviation or the standard error of the mean is correct. See what your instructor prefers you do. What is the standard error? Read the technical section that follows this paragraph to find out more.

While we are using the standard deviation in this chapter to compute confidence intervals, many people choose to use the standard error of the mean or SEM (see Chapter 12). The standard error of the mean is the standard deviation of all the sample means that could, in theory, be selected from the population. Remember that both the standard deviation and the standard error of the mean are "errors" in measurement that surround a certain "true" point (which in our case would be the true mean and the true amount of variability). The use of the SEM is a bit more complex, but it is an alternative way of computing and understanding confidence intervals.

Why does the confidence interval itself get larger as the probability of your being correct increases (from, say, 95% to 99%)? Because the larger range of the confidence interval (in this case, 19.6 [73.8–54.2] for a 95% confidence interval vs. 25.6 [76.8–51.2] for a 99% confidence interval) allows you to encompass a larger number of possible outcomes and you can thereby be more confident. Ha! Isn't this stuff cool?

REAL-WORLD STATS

It's really interesting how different disciplines can learn from one another when they share, and it's a shame that this does not happen more often. This is one of the reasons why interdisciplinary studies are so vital—they create an environment where new and old ideas can be used in new and old settings.

One such discussion took place in a medical journal that devotes itself to articles on anesthesia. The focus was a discussion of the relative merits of statistical versus clinical significance, and Drs. Timothy Houle and David Stump pointed out that many large clinical trials obtain a high level of statistical significance with minuscule differences between groups (just as we talked about earlier in the chapter), making the results clinically irrelevant. However, the authors pointed out that with proper marketing, billions can be made from results of dubious clinical importance. This is really a caveat emptor or buyer-beware state of affairs. Clearly, there are a few very good lessons here about whether the significance of an outcome is really meaningful or not. How to know? Look at the substance behind the results and the context within which the outcomes are found.

Want to know more? Go online or to the library and find . . .

Houle, T. T., & Stump, D. A. (2008). Statistical significance versus clinical significance. *Seminars in Cardiothoracic and Vascular Anesthesia, 12,* 5–6.

Summary

So, now you know exactly how the concept of significance works, and all that is left is to apply it to a variety of research questions. That's what we'll start with in the next chapter and continue with throughout this part of the book.

Time to Practice

1. Why is significance an important construct in the study and use of inferential statistics?
2. What is statistical significance?
3. What does the (idea of the) critical value represent?
4. Given the following information and setting the level of significance at .05 for decision making, would your decision be to reject or fail to reject the null hypothesis? Provide an explanation for your conclusions.
    a. The null hypothesis that there is no relationship between the type of music a person listens to and his or her propensity for crime ($p < .05$)

(Continued)

(Continued)

b. The null hypothesis that there is no relationship between the amount of coffee consumption and GPA ($p = .62$)

c. The research hypothesis that a negative relationship exists between the number of hours worked and level of job satisfaction ($p = .51$)

5. What's wrong with the following statements?

   a. A Type I error of .05 means that 5 times out of 100 experiments, we will reject a true null hypothesis.

   b. It is possible to set the Type I error rate to zero.

   c. The smaller the Type I error rate, the better the results.

6. Why is it "harder" to find a significant outcome (all other things being equal) when the research hypothesis is being tested at the .01 rather than the .05 level of significance?

7. Why should we think in terms of "failing to reject" the null, rather than just accepting it?

8. What is the difference between *significance* and *meaningfulness?*

9. Here's more exploration of the significance versus meaningfulness debate:

   a. Provide an example of a finding that may be both statistically significant and meaningful.

   b. Now provide an example of a finding that may be statistically significant but not meaningful.

10. What does chance have to do with testing the research hypothesis for significance?

11. In Figure 11.2, there is a striped area on the right side of the illustration.

    a. What does that entire striped area represent?

    b. If the striped area were a larger portion underneath the curve, what would that represent?

Student Study Site

Get the tools you need to sharpen your study skills! Visit **edge.sagepub.com/salkindshaw** to access practice quizzes and eFlashcards, watch R tutorial videos, and download data sets!

THE ONE-SAMPLE *z* TEST

Only the Lonely

Difficulty Scale ☺ ☺ ☺
(not too hard—this is the first chapter of this kind, but you know more than enough to master it)

WHAT YOU WILL LEARN IN THIS CHAPTER

- ✦ Deciding when the *z* test for one sample is appropriate to use
- ✦ Computing the observed *z* value
- ✦ Interpreting the *z* value
- ✦ Understanding what the *z* value means
- ✦ Understanding what effect size is and how to interpret it

INTRODUCTION TO THE ONE-SAMPLE *z* TEST

Lack of sleep can cause all kinds of problems, from grouchiness to fatigue and, in rare cases, even death. So, you can imagine health care professionals' interest in seeing that their patients get enough sleep. This is especially the case for patients who are ill and have a real need for the healing and rejuvenating qualities that sleep has. Dr. Joseph Cappelleri and his colleagues looked at the sleep difficulties of patients with a particular illness, fibromyalgia, to evaluate the usefulness of the Medical Outcomes Study (MOS) Sleep Scale as a measure of sleep problems. Although other analyses were completed, including one that compared a treatment group and a control group with one another, the important analysis (for our discussion) was the comparison of participants' MOS scores with national MOS norms. Such a comparison between a sample's score (the MOS score for participants in this study) and a population's score (the norms) necessitates the use of a one-sample *z* test. And the researchers' findings? MOS Sleep Scale scores were statistically significant ($p < .001$). In other words, the null hypothesis that the sample average and the population average were equal could be rejected.

So why use the one-sample *z* test? Cappelleri and his colleagues wanted to know whether the sample values were different from population (national) values collected using the same measure. The researchers were, in effect, comparing a sample statistic with a population parameter and seeing if they could conclude that the sample was (or was not) representative of the population.

Want to know more? Check out . . .

Cappelleri, J. C., Bushmakin, A. G., McDermott, A. M., Dukes, E., Sadosky, A., Petrie, C. D., & Martin, S. (2009). Measurement properties of the Medical Outcomes Study Sleep Scale in patients with fibromyalgia. *Sleep Medicine, 10,* 766–770.

THE PATH TO WISDOM AND KNOWLEDGE

Here's how you can use Figure 11.1, the flowchart introduced in Chapter 11, to select the appropriate test statistic, the **one-sample *z* test**. Follow along the highlighted sequence of steps in Figure 12.1. Now this is pretty easy (and they are not all this easy) because this is the only inferential procedure in all of Part V of this book where we have only one group. Plus, there's lots of stuff here that will take you back to Chapter 10 and standard scores, and because you're an expert on those.

1. We are examining differences between a sample and a population.
2. There is only one group being tested.
3. The appropriate test statistic is a one-sample *z* test.

COMPUTING THE *z* TEST STATISTIC

The formula used for computing the value for the one-sample *z* test is shown in Formula 12.1. Remember that we are testing whether a sample mean belongs to or represents a population mean. The difference between the sample mean ($\bar{X}$) and the population mean (μ) makes up the numerator for the *z* test value. The denominator, an error term, is called the *standard error of the mean* and is the

FIGURE 12.1 ● Determining that a one-sample z test is the correct statistic.

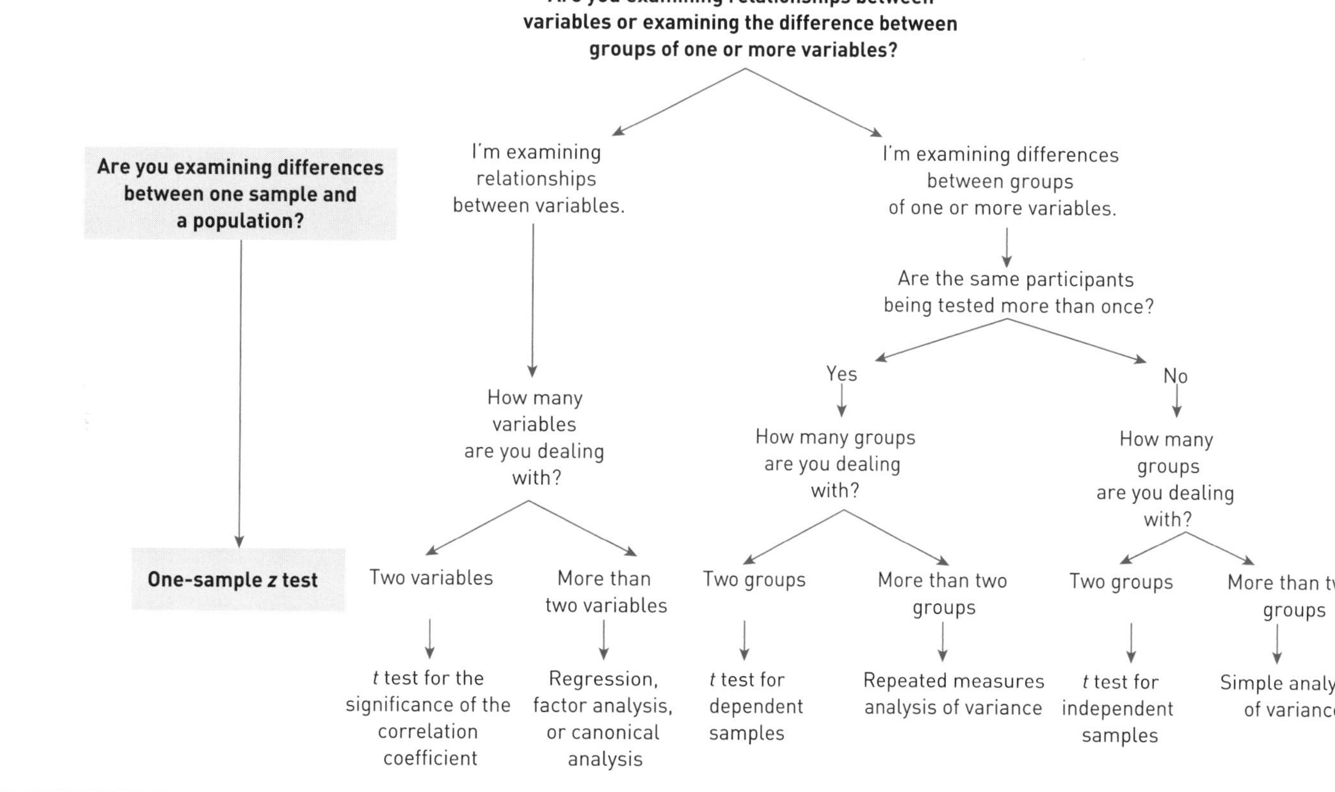

value we would expect by chance, given all the variability that surrounds the selection of all possible sample means from a population. Using this standard error of the mean (and the key term here is *standard*) allows us once again (as we talked about in Chapter 11) to use the table of z scores to determine the probability of an outcome.

$$z = \frac{\bar{X} - \mu}{SEM}, \tag{12.1}$$

where

- $\bar{X}$ is the mean of the sample,
- μ is the population average, and
- *SEM* is the standard error of the mean.

Now, to compute the standard error of the mean, which you need in Formula 12.1, use Formula 12.2:

$$SEM = \frac{\sigma}{\sqrt{n}}, \tag{12.2}$$

where

- σ is the standard deviation for the population, and
- n is the size of the sample.

The standard error of the mean is the standard deviation of all the possible means selected from the population. It's the best *estimate* we can come up with, given that it is impossible to compute *all* the possible means. If our sample selection were perfect, the difference between the sample and the population averages would be zero, right? Right. If the sampling from a population were not done correctly (randomly and representatively), however, then the standard deviation of all the means of all these samples could be huge, right? Right. So we try to select the perfect sample, but no matter how diligent we are in our efforts, there's always some error. The standard error of the mean reflects what that value would be for the entire population of all mean values. And yes, Virginia, this is the standard error of the mean. There can be (and are) standard errors for other measures as well.

Time for an example.

Dr. McDonald thinks that his group of earth science students is particularly special (in a good way), and he is interested in knowing whether their class average falls within the boundaries of the average score for the larger group of students who have taken earth science over the past 20 years. Because he's kept good records, he knows the means and standard deviations for both his group of 36 students and the larger group of 1,000 past enrollees. Here are the data.

	Size	Mean	Standard Deviation
Sample	36	100	5.0
Population	1,000	99	2.5

Here are the famous eight steps and the computation of the *z* test statistic.

1. State the null and research hypotheses.

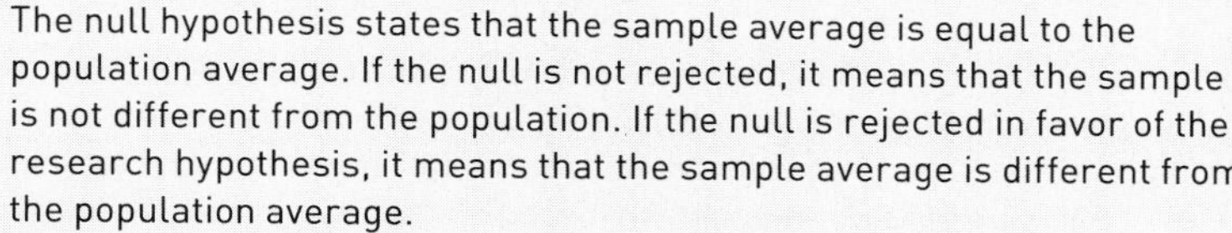

The null hypothesis states that the sample average is equal to the population average. If the null is not rejected, it means that the sample is not different from the population. If the null is rejected in favor of the research hypothesis, it means that the sample average is different from the population average.

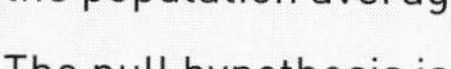

The null hypothesis is

$$H_0 : \bar{X} = \mu. \qquad (12.3)$$

The research, or alternate, hypothesis in this example is

$$H_A : \bar{X} \neq \mu. \qquad (12.4)$$

2. Set the level of risk (or the level of significance or Type I error) associated with the null hypothesis.

The level of risk or Type I error or level of significance (any other names?) here is .05, but this is totally at the discretion of the researcher.

3. Select the appropriate test statistic.

Using the flowchart shown in Figure 12.1, we determine that the appropriate test is a one-sample *z* test.

4. Compute the test statistic value (called the estimated value).

Now's your chance to plug in values and do some computation. The formula for the *z* value was shown in Formula 12.1. The specific values are plugged in (first for *SEM* in Formula 12.5 and then for *z* in Formula 12.6). With the values plugged in, we get the following results:

$$SEM = \frac{2.5}{\sqrt{36}} = \frac{2.5}{6} = 0.4167. \qquad (12.5)$$

$$z = \frac{100-99}{0.41667} = 2.40. \qquad (12.6)$$

After computing the *SEM*, we rounded at the fourth decimal place (always keep at least four decimal places or use the unrounded value in your calculations). The *z* value for a comparison of the sample mean to this population mean, given Dr. McDonald's data, is 2.40.

(Continued)

(Continued)

5. Determine the value needed for rejection of the null hypothesis using the appropriate table of critical values for the particular statistic.

   Here's where we go to Table B.1 in Appendix B, which lists the probabilities associated with specific *z* values, which are the critical values for the rejection of the null hypothesis. This is exactly the same thing we did with several examples in Chapter 11.

   We can use the values in Table B.1 to see if two means "belong" to one another by comparing what we would expect by chance (the tabled or critical value) with what we observe (the obtained value).

   From our work in Chapter 11, we know that a *z* value of +1.96 has associated with it a probability of .025 and .475 between the mean and the *z* score. If we consider that the sample mean could be bigger, or smaller, than the population mean for a two-tailed test, we need to consider both ends of the distribution (and a range of ±1.96) and a total Type I error rate of .05.

6. Compare the obtained value and the critical value.

   The obtained *z* value is 2.38. So, for a test of this null hypothesis at the .05 level with 36 participants, the critical value is ±1.96. This value represents the value at which chance is the most attractive explanation of why the sample mean and the population mean differ. A result beyond that critical value in either direction (remember that the research hypothesis is nondirectional and this is a two-tailed test) means that we need to provide an explanation as to why the sample and the population means differ.

7. and 8. Decision time!

   If the obtained value is more extreme than the critical value like we discussed in Chapter 11 when we talked about Figure 11.2, the null hypothesis cannot be accepted. If the obtained value does not exceed the critical value, the null hypothesis is the most attractive explanation. In this case, the obtained value (2.38) does exceed the critical value (1.96), and it is absolutely extreme enough for us to say that the sample of 36 students in Dr. McDonald's class is different from the previous 1,000 students who have also taken the course. If the obtained value were less than 1.96, it would mean that there is no difference between the test performance of the sample and that of the 1,000 students who have taken the test over the past 20 years. If we failed to reject the null, we are saying the 36 students have performed basically at the same level as the previous 1,000.

   And the final step? Why, of course. We wonder why this group of students differs? Perhaps McDonald is right in that they are smarter, but they may also be better users of technology or more motivated. Perhaps they just studied harder. All these are questions to be tested some other time.

So How Do I Interpret $z = 2.40, p < .05$?

- *z* represents the test statistic that was used.
- 2.40 is the obtained value, calculated using the formulas we showed you earlier in the chapter.

- $p < .05$ (the really important part of this little phrase) indicates that the probability is less than 5% that on any one test of the null hypothesis, the sample and the population averages will differ.

USING R TO PERFORM A z TEST

Visit **edge.sagepub.com/salkindshaw** to watch an R tutorial video on this topic.

We're going to use R in two ways. First, we will use R as a calculator, entering our sample into a vector, and then plug numbers into Formula 12.1. Second, we will use built-in functions to obtain the p associated with our z statistic.

Using the one-sample z test, we will evaluate whether the sample is different from the population average score $\mu = 13$ and standard deviation $\sigma = 3$. Our null hypothesis says that there is no difference, and our research hypothesis says the means are different. Here's the entire sample:

12	15
9	16
7	8
10	9
11	12

1. Enter the data in a vector.
2. Calculate the *SEM*.
3. Calculate the z statistic.
4. Obtain the probability of our z statistic.

1. Starting with the numbers above, let's create a vector:

```
> sampleScores <- c(12, 9, 7, 10, 11, 15, 16, 8, 9, 12)
>
```

2. We are told the population standard deviation is 3, and we know our sample size is 10. Calculate the *SEM* using Formula 12.2 and look at the results:

```
> sem <- 3/sqrt(10)
> sem
[1] 0.9486833
>
```

We used the square root function, `sqrt()`, right in our formula, and R returned `0.9486833` for the *SEM.*

3. The population mean is 13. Plug the *SEM,* the population mean, and the sample mean into Formula 12.1 to get z and look at the results:

```
> zStat <- (mean(sampleScores) - 13) / sem
> zStat
[1] -2.213594
>
```

Our z statistic is −2.213594. The statistic is negative because the sample mean is smaller than our population mean.

4. Because the normal distribution is symmetric, the probability of $z = -2.213594$ is the same as the probability of $z = 2.213594$. Taking the symmetric quality of the normal distribution into account and the fact that we hypothesized that the sample and population means were different, not one larger or smaller than the other, we need to double the probability that we are going to get from R:

```
> pnorm(abs(zStat))
[1] 0.9865717
>
```

This bit of R syntax is a starting point. By just asking for the absolute probability of the absolute value of our z statistic, we find out the probability for `zStat` = |−2.213594| is 98.66%. That means the area between 2.213594 and the mean is 48.66%; we also know the area below the mean is 50%, which added together gives you 98.66%. This is the same information you can get from Table B.1 but not exactly what we are interested in. We want to know the probability associated with getting our z or something more extreme. Let's change this to ask for that:

```
> 1 - pnorm(abs(zStat))
[1] 0.01342835
>
```

We now know the probability of getting $z = 2.213594$ or something larger. But what about something as small as −2.213594 or smaller? How can we get that? Easy! Just double the value:

```
> (1 - pnorm(abs(zStat))) * 2
[1] 0.0268567
>
```

Using our predetermined $\alpha = .05$ and a probability for our z score that is smaller than .05, we now know the probability that our sample mean is different from the population mean is equal to 0.0268567. Now that we have this information, how do we report our result?

Based on $z = -2.21$, $p = .03$, we reject the null hypothesis that the sample mean and population mean are equal and accept the research hypothesis that they are different.

SPECIAL EFFECTS: ARE THOSE DIFFERENCES FOR REAL?

Okay, time for you to entertain a whole new idea, that of effect size, and learn how to use it to make your analysis of any inferential test all that much more interesting and valuable.

In general, using various inferential tools, you may find differences between samples and populations, two samples or more, and so on, but the $64,000 question is not only whether that difference is (statistically) significant but also whether it is *meaningful*. That is, does enough of a separation exist between the distributions that represent each sample or group you test that the difference is really a difference worth discussing!

Hmm. . . . Welcome to the world of effect size.

Effect size is a measure of how different two groups are from one another—it's a measure of the magnitude of the treatment. Kind of like, "How big is big?" And what's especially interesting about computing effect size is that sample size is not taken into account. Calculating effect size, and making a judgment about it, adds a whole new dimension to understanding significant outcomes. Another interesting note about effect size is that many different inferential tests use different formulas to compute the effect size (as you will see through the next few chapters), but the same metric (called Cohen's *d*, and we'll get to that shortly) tends to be used whenever we are talking about mean differences. It's like if you use a ruler or a yardstick to measure two different sizes of lumber—you're still dealing with inches.

As an example, let's take the data from Dr. McDonald and the earth science test. Here are the means and standard deviations again.

	Size	Mean	Standard Deviation
Sample	36	100	5.0
Population	1,000	99	2.5

Here's the formula for computing Cohen's *d* for the effect size for a one-sample *z* test:

$$d = \frac{\bar{X} - \mu}{\sigma}, \tag{12.7}$$

where

$\bar{X}$ is the sample mean,

μ is the population mean, and

σ is the population standard deviation.

This formula looks a whole lot like the formula for the *z* statistic (12.1). What differs is the denominator. When computing effect sizes, we don't adjust for the size of the sample. So, if you have a sample the size of 10, 100, 1,000, or more, the effect size in this example remains the same.

If we substitute Dr. McDonald's values in Formula 12.7, we get this:

$$d = \frac{100 - 99}{2.5} = .4.$$

We know from our previous calculations that the obtained *z* score of 2.40 is significant, meaning that, indeed, the performance of Dr. McDonald's class is different from that of the population. Now we have figured out the effect size (.4), so let's turn our attention to what this statistically significant outcome might mean regarding the size of the effects.

Understanding Effect Size

The great pooh-bah of effect size was Jacob Cohen, who wrote some of the most influential and important articles on this topic. He authored a very important and influential book (your stats teacher has it on his or her shelf!) that instructs researchers in how to figure out the effect size for a variety of different questions that are asked about differences and relationships between variables. And the book also gives some guidelines as to what different sizes of effects might represent for understanding differences. You remember that for our example, the effect size is .4.

What does this mean? To help us understand what the values mean, Cohen (and others) assigned names to different values for *d* to say just what a small, medium, and large effect size is. They used the following guidelines:

- A small effect size ranges from 0 to .2.
- A medium effect size ranges from .2 to .5.
- A large effect size is any value above .5.

Our example, with an effect size of .4, is categorized as medium. But what does it *really* mean?

Effect size gives us an idea about the relative positions of one group to another, or how far apart the means are. For example, if the effect size is zero, that means that both groups tend to be very similar—there is no mean difference between the two distributions of scores. On the other hand, an effect size of 1 means that the two groups overlap about 45% (having that much in common) and the means are 1 standard deviation apart. And, as you might expect, as the effect size gets larger, it reflects an increasing lack of overlap between the two groups.

Jacob Cohen's book *Statistical Power Analysis for the Behavioral Sciences,* first published in 1967 with the latest edition (1988, Lawrence Erlbaum) available in reprint from Taylor and Francis, is a must for anyone who wants to go beyond the very general information that is presented here. It is full of tables and techniques for allowing you to understand how a statistically significant finding is only half the story—the other half is the magnitude of that effect.

Cohen's *d* is just one type of effect size that is particularly useful when your original scores are on a scale that has little meaning in the real world. Cohen's *d* is a standardized measure that allows us to communicate how meaningful the difference is, not just the statistical significance of the difference. What if your scores were actually money spent? Would calculating Cohen's *d* provide something that is more meaningful for your reader? Probably not. Our reader would probably be interested in the mean difference in dollars. And that is really the goal with effect sizes—make the results meaningful for your reader.

REAL-WORLD STATS

Been to the doctor lately? Had your test results explained to you? Know anything about the use of electronic medical records? In this study, Noel Brewer and his colleagues compared the usefulness of tables and bar graphs for reporting the results of medical tests.

Using a z test, the researchers found that participants required less viewing time when using bar graphs rather than tables. The researchers attributed this difference to superior performance of bar graphs in communicating essential information (and you well remember from Chapter 6, where we stressed that a picture, such as a bar graph, is well worth a thousand words). Also, not very surprisingly, when participants viewed both formats, those with experience with bar graphs preferred bar graphs, and those with experience with tables found bar graphs equally easy to use. Next time you visit your doc and he or she shows you a table, say you want to see the results as a bar graph. Now that's stats applied to real-world, everyday occurrences!

Want to know more? Go online or to the library and find . . .

Brewer, N. T., Gilkey, M. B., Lillie, S. E., Hesse, B. W., & Sheridan, S. L. (2012). Tables or bar graphs? Presenting test results in electronic medical records. *Medical Decision Making, 32,* 545–553.

Package	Function	What It Tells You
BSDA	z.test	The *z* test results with *p* value, the research hypothesis (referred to as alternative hypothesis here), the 95% confidence interval, and the sample mean

```
> z.test(x = sampleScores, mu = 13, sigma.x = 3)

  One-sample z-Test

data:  sampleScores
z = -2.2136, p-value = 0.02686
alternative hypothesis: true mean is not equal to 13
95 percent confidence interval:
   9.040615 12.759385
sample estimates:
mean of x
     10.9
>
```

Summary

The one-sample *z* test is a simple example of an inferential test, and that's why we started off this long section of the book with an explanation of what this test does and how it is applied. The (very) good news is that most (if not all) of the steps we take as we move on to more complex analytic tools are exactly the same as those you saw here. In fact, in the next chapter, we move on to a very common inferential test that is an extension of the *z* test we covered here, the *t* test between the means of two different groups.

Time to Practice

1. When is it appropriate to use the one-sample *z* test?
2. What does the *z* in *z* test represent? What similarity does it have to a simple *z* or standard score?
3. For the following situations, write out in words a research hypothesis and then write out in words the corresponding null hypothesis:
   a. Bob wants to know whether the weight loss for his group on the chocolate-only diet is representative of weight loss in a large population of middle-aged men.

b. The health department is charged with finding out whether the rate of flu per thousand citizens during this past flu season is comparable to the average rate during the past 50 seasons.

c. Blair is almost sure that his monthly costs for the past year are not representative of his average monthly costs over the past 20 years.

4. Flu cases this past flu season in the Remulak school system ($n = 500$) were 15 per week. For the entire state, the weekly average was 16, and the standard deviation was 15.1. Are the kids in Remulak as sick as the kids throughout the state?

5. The night-shift workers in three of Super Bo's specialty stores stock about 500 products in about 3 hours. How does this rate compare with the stocking done in the other 97 stores in the chain, which average about 496 products stocked in 3 hours? Are the stockers at the specialty stores doing a "better than average" job? Here's the info that you need:

	Size	Average Number of Products Stocked	Standard Deviation
Specialty stores	3	500	12.56
All stores	100	496	22.13

6. A major research study investigated how representative a treatment group's decrease in symptoms was when a certain drug was administered as compared with the response of the entire population. It turns out that the test of the research hypothesis resulted in a *z* test score of 1.67. What conclusion might the researchers put forth? Hint: Notice that the Type I error rate or significance level is *not* stated (as perhaps it should be). What do you make of all this?

7. Millman's golfing group is terrific for a group of amateurs. Are they ready to turn pro? Here are the data. (Hint: Remember that the lower the score [in golf], the better!)

	Size	Average Score	Standard Deviation
Millman's Group	9	82	2.6
The Pros	500	71	3.1

8. Here's a list of units of toys sold by T&K over a 12-month period during 2015. Were the average sales of $31,456 ($\sigma = \$3,287$) for 2016 significantly different from monthly sales in 2015? What is Cohen's *d*? What is the mean difference between 2015 and 2016 sales? Which is easier to understand?

Units Sold in 2015	
January	34,518
February	29,540
March	34,889

(Continued)

(Continued)

Units Sold in 2015	
April	26,764
May	31,429
June	29,962
July	31,084
August	30,506
September	28,546
October	29,560
November	29,304
December	25,852

Student Study Site

Get the tools you need to sharpen your study skills! Visit **edge.sagepub.com/salkindshaw** to access practice quizzes and eFlashcards, watch R tutorial videos, and download data sets!

t(EA) FOR TWO

Tests Between the Means of Different Groups

Difficulty Scale ☺ ☺ ☺
(A little longer than the previous chapter, but basically the same kind of procedures and very similar questions. Not too hard, but you have to pay attention.)

WHAT YOU WILL LEARN IN THIS CHAPTER

- Using the *t* test for independent means when appropriate
- Computing the observed *t* value
- Interpreting the *t* value and understanding what it means
- Computing the effect size for a *t* test for independent means

INTRODUCTION TO THE *t* TEST FOR INDEPENDENT SAMPLES

How do we navigate our world? What do we notice when we are traveling from one place to another, particularly in a world when many of us use our favorite app on our smartphone to give us directions? Aida Afrooz and colleagues at the University of New South Wales (UNSW) Sydney in Australia wondered the same thing. They designed a randomized control trial where 54 people in the experimental condition were asked to navigate with the help of a map a pre-defined route through UNSW Sydney's campus and 54 people in the control condition were asked to follow someone on that same route; they were shown the map once but were instructed to pay attention to their surroundings. Participants ranged in age from 17 to 58 with an average age of 23.9 (SD = 7.07), and all were partially familiar or familiar with the campus. The people asked to navigate their own route were referred to as active, and the people who followed another person on the route were called passive. They were then given a questionnaire asking them about things they saw on their route, called a scene recognition test to test their memory. This test showed them 27 scenes from the campus and 27 scenes from other Sydney locations. The active group scored higher than the passive group indicating the active group remembered more scenes on campus than their passive peers, $t_{(96)} = 2.00$, $p = .04$.

Now just what does all this mean? Read on.

Why was the t test for independent means used? Afrooz and her colleagues were interested in finding out whether there was a difference in the average scores of one (or more) variable(s) between the two groups that were independent of one another. By *independent,* we mean that the two groups were not related in any way. Each participant in the study was tested only once. The researchers applied a t test for independent means, arriving at the conclusion that for each of the outcome variables, the differences between the two groups were significant with a probability, or p value, at or beyond the .05 level. Such a small significance level means that there is very little chance that the difference in scores between the two groups was due to something other than group membership, in this case representing nationality, culture, or ethnicity.

Want to know more? Go online or to the library and find . . .

Afrooz, A., White, D., & Parolin, B. (2018). Effects of active and passive exploration of the built environment on memory during wayfinding. *Applied Geography, 101,* 68–74.

THE PATH TO WISDOM AND KNOWLEDGE

Here's how you can use Figure 13.1, the flowchart introduced in Chapter 11, to select the appropriate test statistic, the t test for independent means. Follow along the highlighted sequence of steps in Figure 13.1.

1. The differences between using a map to navigate (Group 1) and those following someone else (Group 2) are being explored.
2. Participants are being tested only once.
3. There are two groups.
4. The appropriate test statistic is the t test for independent samples.

FIGURE 13.1 ● Determining that a *t* test is the correct statistic.

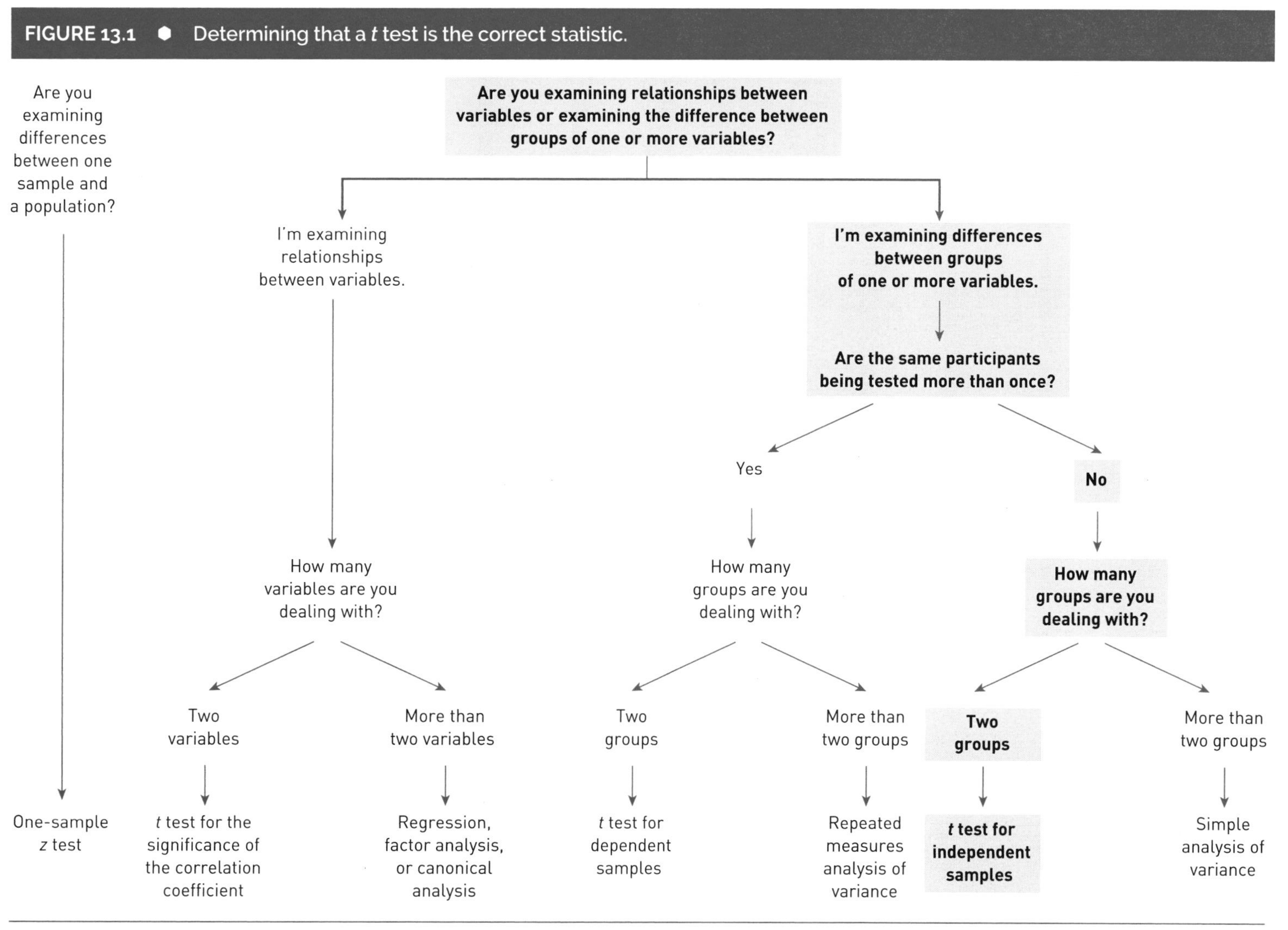

As we mentioned earlier, there are hundreds of statistical tests. The only inferential one that uses one sample that we cover in this book is the one-sample *z* test (see Chapter 12). But there is also the one-sample *t* test, which compares the mean score of a sample with another score, and sometimes that score is, indeed, the population mean, just as with the one-sample *z* test. We need to use the one-sample *t* test when we don't know the population standard deviation. In that case, we use the standard deviation of our sample instead. Following the flowchart, you can use the one-sample *z* test or one-sample *t* test to test the same hypothesis, and you will reach similar conclusions (although you will be using different values and tables—the *t* table in Table B.2 instead of the normal curve Table B.1—to do so).

COMPUTING THE *t* TEST STATISTIC

The formula for computing the *t* value for the *t* test for independent means is shown in Formula 13.1. The difference between the means makes up the numerator; the amount of variation within and between each of the two groups makes up the denominator.

$$t = \frac{\bar{X}_1 - \bar{X}_2}{\sqrt{\left[\frac{(n_1 - 1)s_1^2 + (n_2 - 1)s_2^2}{n_1 + n_2 - 2}\right]\left[\frac{n_1 + n_2}{n_1 n_2}\right]}}, \qquad (13.1)$$

where

- $\bar{X}_1$ is the mean for Group 1,
- $\bar{X}_2$ is the mean for Group 2,
- n_1 is the number of participants in Group 1,
- n_2 is the number of participants in Group 2,
- s_1^2 is the variance for Group 1, and
- s_2^2 is the variance for Group 2.

This is a bigger formula than we've seen before, but there's really nothing new here at all. It's just a matter of plugging in the correct values.

Time for an Example

Here are some data reflecting the number of words remembered following a program designed to help Alzheimer's patients remember the order of daily tasks. Group 1 was taught using visuals, and Group 2 was taught using visuals and intense verbal rehearsal. We'll use the data to compute the test statistic in the following example.

Group 1			Group 2		
7	5	5	5	3	4
3	4	7	4	2	3
3	6	1	4	5	2
2	10	9	5	4	7
3	10	2	5	4	6
8	5	5	7	6	2
8	1	2	8	7	8
5	1	12	8	7	9
8	4	15	9	5	7
5	3	4	8	6	6

Here are the famous eight steps and the computation of the *t* test statistic.

1. State the null and research hypotheses.

   As represented by Formula 13.2, the null hypothesis states that there is no difference between the means for Group 1 and Group 2. For our purposes, the research hypothesis (shown as Formula 13.3) states that there is a difference between the means of the two groups. The research hypothesis is two-tailed and nondirectional because it posits a difference, but in no particular direction.

   The null hypothesis is

$$H_0: \mu_1 = \mu_2. \tag{13.2}$$

   The research hypothesis is

$$H_1: \bar{X}_1 \neq \bar{X}_2. \tag{13.3}$$

2. Set the level of risk (or the level of significance or Type I error) associated with the null hypothesis.

   The level of risk or Type I error or level of significance (any other names?) here is .05, but this is totally the decision of the researcher.

3. Select the appropriate test statistic.

   Using the flowchart shown in Figure 13.1, we determined that the appropriate test is a *t* test for independent means. It is not a *t* test for dependent means (a common mistake beginning students make) because the groups are independent of one another.

4. Compute the test statistic value (called the estimate).

   Now's your chance to plug in values and do some computation. The formula for the t statistic was shown in Formula 13.1, which is repeated here so you can more easily see what numbers are getting plugged into the formula.

$$t = \frac{\bar{X}_1 - \bar{X}_2}{\sqrt{\left[\frac{(n_1 - 1)s_1^2 + (n_2 - 1)s_2^2}{n_1 + n_2 - 2}\right]\left[\frac{n_1 + n_2}{n_1 n_2}\right]}}.$$

   When the specific values are plugged in, we get the equation shown in Formula 13.4. (We already computed the mean and standard deviation.)

$$t = \frac{5.43 - 5.53}{\sqrt{\left[\frac{(30-1)3.42^2 + (30-1)2.06^2}{30+30-2}\right]\left[\frac{30+30}{30 \times 30}\right]}}. \quad (13.4)$$

   With the numbers plugged in, Formula 13.5 shows how we get the final value of −.137. The value is negative because a larger value (the mean of Group 2, which is 5.53) is being subtracted from a smaller number (the mean of Group 1, which is 5.43). Remember, though, that because the test is nondirectional—the research hypothesis is that any difference exists—the sign of the difference is meaningless.

$$t = \frac{-0.1}{\sqrt{\left[\frac{339.20 + 123.06}{58}\right]\left[\frac{60}{900}\right]}} = -0.14. \quad (13.5)$$

When a nondirectional test is discussed, you may find that the t value is represented as an absolute value looking like this, $|t|$ or $t = |0.137|$, which ignores the sign of the value altogether. And we can ignore the sign if our research hypothesis is nondirectional because the t distribution, like the normal curve, is symmetric. Your teacher may even express the t statistic with a sign to emphasize that the sign is relevant for a one-directional test.

5. Determine the value needed for rejection of the null hypothesis using the appropriate table of critical values for the particular statistic.

   Here's where we go to Table B.2 in Appendix B, which lists the critical values for the t test. We use this distribution to see whether two independent means from samples differ from one another by comparing what we would expect by chance (the tabled or critical value) with what we observe (the obtained value).

   Our first task is to determine the **degrees of freedom** (*df*), which approximates the sample size. For this particular statistic, the degrees of freedom is $n_1 - 1 + n_2 - 1$ or $n_1 + n_2 - 2$ (putting the terms in either order results in the same value). So for each group, add the size of the two samples and subtract 2. In this example, 30 + 30 – 2 = 58. This is the degrees of freedom for this test statistic and not necessarily for any other.

The idea of degrees of freedom means pretty much the same thing no matter what statistical test you use. But the way that the degrees of freedom is computed for specific tests can differ from teacher to teacher and from book to book. We tell you as we go along the most common way of computing degrees of freedom for each test. For the independent samples *t* test, the correct degrees of freedom is computed as $n_1 - 1 + n_2 - 1$.

Using this number (58), the level of risk you are willing to take (earlier defined as .05), and a two-tailed test (because there is no direction to the research hypothesis), you can use the *t* test table to look up the critical value. At the .05 level, with 58 degrees of freedom for a two-tailed test, the value needed for rejection of the null hypothesis is . . . oops! There's no 58 degrees of freedom in the table! What do you do?

Well, if you select the value that corresponds to 55, you're being conservative in that you are using a value for a sample smaller than what you have (and the critical *t* value will be larger). If you go for 60 degrees of freedom (the closest to your value of 58), you will be closer to the size of the population, but you'll be a bit liberal in that 60 is larger than 58. Although statisticians differ in their viewpoint as to what to do in this situation, let's always go with the value that's smaller than the actual sample size to get the more conservative cutoff. So, the value needed to reject the null hypothesis with 58 degrees of freedom at the .05 level of significance is 2.004.

6. Compare the obtained value and the critical value.

The obtained value is –0.14 (–0.137 rounded to the nearest hundredth), and the critical value for rejection of the null hypothesis that Group 1 and Group 2 performed differently is 2.004. The critical value of 2.004 represents the value at which chance is the most attractive explanation for any of the observed differences between the two groups, given 30 participants in each group and the willingness to take a .05 level of risk.

7. and 8. Decision time!

Now comes our decision. If the obtained value is more extreme than the critical value (remember Figure 11.2), the null hypothesis will be rejected. If the obtained value does not exceed the critical value, the null hypothesis is the most attractive explanation. In this case, the obtained value (–0.14) does not exceed the critical value (2.004)—it is not extreme enough for us to say that the difference between Groups 1 and 2 occurred due to anything other than chance. If the value were greater than 2.004, that would be just like getting 8, 9, or 10 heads in a coin toss—too extreme a result for us to believe that mere chance is at work. In the case of the coin, the cause would be an unfair coin; in this example, there would be a better way to teach memory skills to these older people.

So, to what can we attribute the small difference between the two groups? If we stick with our current argument, then we could say the difference is due to anything from sampling error to rounding error to simple variability in participants' scores. Most important, we're pretty sure (but, of course, not 100% sure—that's what level of significance and Type I errors are all about, right?) that the difference is not due to anything in particular that one group or the other experienced to make its scores better.

So How Do I Interpret $t_{(58)} = -0.14$, $p > .05$?

- t represents the test statistic that was used.
- 58 is the number of degrees of freedom.
- −0.14 is the obtained value, calculated using the formula we showed you earlier in the chapter.
- $p > .05$ (the really important part of this little phrase) indicates that the probability is greater than 5% that on any one test of the null hypothesis, the two groups do not differ because of the way they were taught. Note that $p > .05$ can also appear as $p = ns$ for nonsignificant or the exact p if you are using R to do your computations.

THE EFFECT SIZE AND *t*(EA) FOR TWO

You learned in Chapter 12 that effect size is a measure of how different two groups are from one another—it's a measure of the magnitude of the treatment. Kind of like "How big is big?"

What's especially interesting about computing effect size is that sample size is not taken into account. Calculating effect size, and making a judgment about it, adds a whole new dimension to understanding significant outcomes.

Let's take the following example. A researcher tests whether participation in community-sponsored services (such as card games, field trips, etc.) increases the quality of life (as rated from 1 to 10) for older Americans. The researcher implements the treatment over a 6-month period and then, at the end of the treatment period, measures quality of life in the two groups (each consisting of 50 participants over the age of 80 where one group got the services and one group did not). Here are the results.

	No Community Services	Community Services
Mean	6.90	7.46
Standard deviation	1.03	1.53

And the verdict is that the difference is significant at the .034 level (which is $p < .05$, right?). So there's a significant difference, but what about the magnitude of the difference?

Computing and Understanding the Effect Size

As we showed you in Chapter 12, the most direct and simple way to compute effect size is to simply divide the difference between the means by any one of the standard deviations. Danger, Will Robinson (ever heard of *Lost in Space?*)—this does assume that the standard deviations (and the amount of variance) between groups are equal to one another and that your groups are equal in size.

For our example, we'll do this:

$$ES = \frac{\bar{X}_1 - \bar{X}_2}{\sqrt{\left[\frac{s_1^2 + s_2^2}{2}\right]}}, \tag{13.6}$$

where

- ES is the effect size,
- $\bar{X}_1$ is the mean for Group 1,
- $\bar{X}_2$ is the mean for Group 2,
- s_1^2 is the variance for Group 1, and
- s_2^2 is the variance for Group 2.

So, in our example,

$$ES = \frac{7.46 - 6.90}{\sqrt{\left[\frac{1.03^2 + 1.53^2}{2}\right]}} = \frac{0.56}{\sqrt{1.70}} = 0.43. \tag{13.7}$$

The effect size for this example is 0.43.

You saw from our guidelines in Chapter 12 that an effect size of .43 is categorized as medium. In addition to the difference between the two means being statistically significant, one might conclude that the difference also is *meaningful* in that the effect size is not negligible. In fact, the means are 0.43 standard deviations apart. Now, how meaningful you wish to make it in your interpretation of the results depends on many factors, including the context within which the research question is being asked.

So, you really want to be cool about this effect size thing. If you have equally sized groups, you can do it the simple way, as we just showed you. The grown-up formula for the effect size uses the pooled variance in the denominator of the *ES* equation that you saw previously, and this pooled variance is needed if the groups are not equal in size. The pooled standard deviation is an average of the standard deviation from Group 1 and the standard deviation from Group 2 that adjusts the amount of variance each group contributes based on its size. Here's the formula:

(Continued)

(Continued)

$$ES = \frac{\bar{X}_1 - \bar{X}_2}{\sqrt{\left[\frac{(n_1-1)s_1^2 + (n_2-1)s_2^2}{n_1+n_2-2}\right]}}, \quad (13.8)$$

where

- ES is the effect size;
- $\bar{X}_1$ is the mean of Group 1,
- $\bar{X}_2$ is the mean of Group 2,
- s_1^2 is the variance of Group 1,
- s_2^2 is the variance of Group 2,
- n_1 is the size of Group 1, and
- n_2 is the size of Group 2.

Doesn't Formula 13.8 look familiar? Hopefully it does. It is very close to Formula 13.1 for our independent sample *t* test. What's different is the denominator. We are missing the part under the square root sign (the radical) where we added the two group sizes together and then divided by their product ($\frac{n_1+n_2}{n_1 n_2}$). This missing piece is why we say the sample size is not taken into account. Yes, the sample size is part of the formula but only in relation to the variance, so we can proportionally control for how much variance each group is contributing.

Two Very Cool Effect Size Calculators

Why not take the A train and just go right to http://www.uccs.edu/~lbecker/, where statistician Lee Becker from the University of California developed an effect size calculator? Or ditto for the one located at http://www.psychometrica.de/effect_size.html created by Drs. Wolfgang and Alexandra Lenhard? With these calculators, you just plug in the values, click Compute, and the program does the rest, as you see in Figure 13.2.

FIGURE 13.2 ● The very cool effect size calculator.

Group 1		Group 2	
M_1	7.4	M_2	6.9
SD_1	1.53	SD_2	1.03
Compute		Reset	
Cohen's *d*	0.38338	effect-size *r*	0.18826

Source: Lee Becker, http://www.uccs.edu/~lbecker/

USING R TO PERFORM A *t* TEST

R is willing and ready to help you perform these inferential tests. Here's how to perform the one that we just discussed and interpret the output. We are using the data set named Chapter 13 Data Set 1 (ch13ds1.csv). From your examination of the data, you can see how the grouping variable (Group 1 or Group 2) is in column 1 and the test variable (Memory) is in column 2.

1. Import the data set and view what you imported.
2. Run a *t* test.

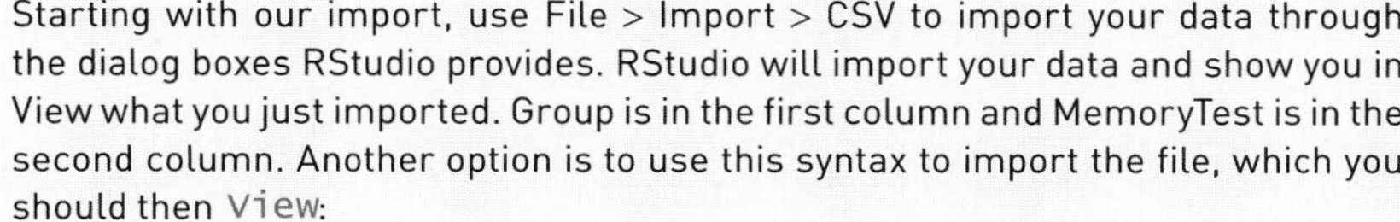

Starting with our import, use File > Import > CSV to import your data through the dialog boxes RStudio provides. RStudio will import your data and show you in View what you just imported. Group is in the first column and MemoryTest is in the second column. Another option is to use this syntax to import the file, which you should then `View`:

```
> ch13ds1 <- read.csv(file.choose())
> View(ch13ds1)
>
```

To run our *t* test, we can use this syntax:

```
> t.test(MemoryTest ~ Group, data = ch13ds1, var.equal =
TRUE)
```

where

- `MemoryTest ~ Group`: `MemoryTest` is the score we are comparing across our groups, represented by 1s for treatment and 2s for control in our `Group` column.
- `data = ch13ds1`: this is the R object that contains our data.
- `var.equal = TRUE`: we are telling the `t.test()` function that our groups have equal variance, an important assumption that we will talk more about below.

The output from the function `t.test()` is as follows:

```
  Two Sample t-test
data: MemoryTest by Group
t = -0.1371, df = 58, p-value = 0.8914
alternative hypothesis: true difference in means is not equal to 0
95 percent confidence interval:
-1.560009  1.360009
sample estimates:
mean in group 1 mean in group 2
      5.433333        5.533333
```

(Continued)

(Continued)

The output tells us that we conducted a two-sample *t* test and what data were used to run the test. The results, $t = -0.1371$, $df = 58$, $p = .8914$, tell us the *t*, the degrees of freedom for our test, and the exact *p*. When we did the calculations by hand and used Table B.2 to get our cutoff, all we knew was that $p > .05$. Now we know the probability of getting our result was .89. The confidence interval is like the confidence interval we talked about in Chapter 11, but this 95% confidence interval is around our mean difference of 0.1 (the numerator in Formula 13.5) and adjusted for the sample size. The last thing we are told is the mean for each group, which matches what we plugged into Formula 13.4, although we rounded down to two decimal places for that example.

With this little bit of syntax, we got the same answer as we did computing *t* by hand. R is handy like that. But in the process, we have learned something new and that has to do with variances for the memory test. We assumed they were equal. Are our results the same if variances are not equal?

The short answer is no. The *t* values in Table B.2 that we use for rejection of the null hypothesis do not hold up if variances are not equal across groups. Let's first look at our scores with a function called `boxplot`. And what we are going to get is exactly that—a plot that looks like a box! Let's save our results to an object named `memory` so we can look at the statistics used to create this fun plot.

```
> memory <- boxplot(MemoryTest ~ Group, data = ch13ds1,
+           main = "Memory Test Scores",
+           xlab = "Groups", ylab = "Scores")
> memory$stats
     [,1] [,2]
[1,]    1  2.0
[2,]    3  4.0
[3,]    5  5.5
[4,]    8  7.0
[5,]   15  9.0
attr(,"class")
        1
"integer"
>
```

We generate a boxplot with the `boxplot` function. Let's talk about the function.

- `memory <-`: stores the function output in the object memory
- `boxplot`: the name of the function
- `MemoryTest ~ Group`: our dependent variable MemoryTest is broken out by group membership

- `data = ch13ds1`: the data set used in the function
- `main = "Memory Test Scores"`: the title at the top of the boxplot
- `xlab = "Groups"`: the *x*-axis label
- `ylab = "Scores"`: the *y*-axis label

We then looked at the statistics generated from our data so we could see what numbers were used to create our boxplots. We used `memory$stats` to show these numbers.

The bottom whisker, representing the lower bound for our data, in Group 1 is drawn at 1. The lower whisker is at 2 for Group 2. These numbers are found on the line with `[1,]`. The next row of numbers is the first quartile (25%) and is used to start drawing the box. The third row is the median, and the fourth row is the third quartile (75%). So, the middle 50% of your data is represented by the box itself. The upper whisker on the line for `[5,]` is for the upper bound on your data. Compare those numbers to the boxplot in Figure 13.3.

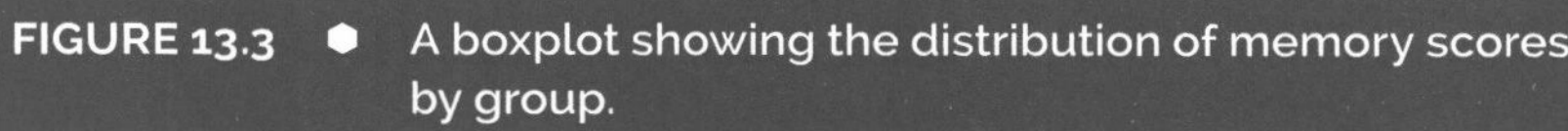
FIGURE 13.3 ● A boxplot showing the distribution of memory scores by group.

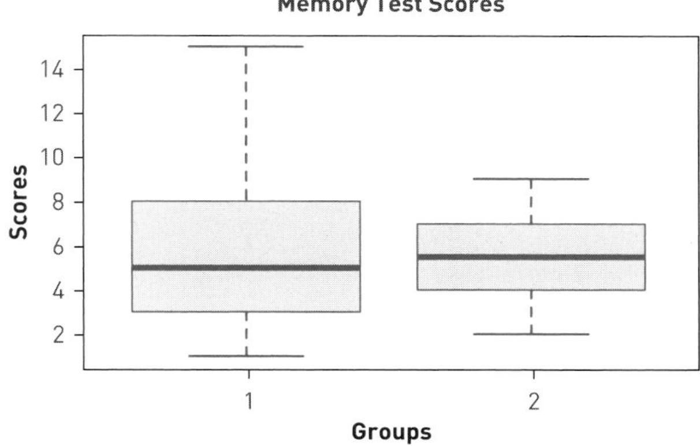

Based on the boxplots, you can probably see how the variance is different, but is it very different? Well, we have a statistic to help us answer that! And that statistic is called Levene's test. We are not going to show and explain the full formula but instead focus on what the statistic is telling us and use those results to correctly test our group differences.

Turning to R, we first need to load the `car` library so that R can find the function called `leveneTest`.

```
> library(car)
>
```

Next, we use the function `leveneTest()`. Inside the function, we are also telling R that group is a factor, essentially a categorical variable. The null hypothesis for this test is that the variances are equal, and the research hypothesis is that they are different. And like a good statistician, we need to decide upfront at what point we would reject our null hypothesis. For this test, we will use $p < .05$ to signal that we should reject our null hypothesis.

```
> leveneTest(MemoryTest ~ as.factor(Group), data = ch13ds1)
Levene's Test for Homogeneity of Variance (center = median)
      Df F value  Pr(>F)
group  1  3.3429 0.07264 .
      58
---
Signif. codes: 0 '***' 0.001 '**' 0.01 '*' 0.05 '.' 0.1 ' ' 1
>
```

In this case, Levene's test is $F_{(1, 58)} = 3.34$, $p = .07$. The p for Levene's test exceeds .05, so we fail to reject the null, and we can compare the memory scores exactly as we did above. So all is right with the world.

What if we had rejected the null? If you have been following along in R, try running the *t* test without `var.equal = TRUE`. What changed in the output? What stayed the same?

```
> t.test(MemoryTest ~ Group, data = ch13ds1)
      Welch Two Sample t-test
data: MemoryTest by Group
t = -0.1371, df = 47.635, p-value = 0.8915
alternative hypothesis: true difference in means is not equal to 0
95 percent confidence interval:
 -1.566803  1.366803
sample estimates:
mean in group 1 mean in group 2
       5.433333        5.533333
>
```

The first thing to note is the title of the test changed from the "Two Sample t test" to "Welch Two Sample t-test." Let's ask R for help to see what is going on.

```
> ?t.test
>
```

You should see help text for the function `t.test()`, similar to Figure 13.4, in the bottom right panel.

FIGURE 13.4 ● Built-in help information for the function `t.test()`.

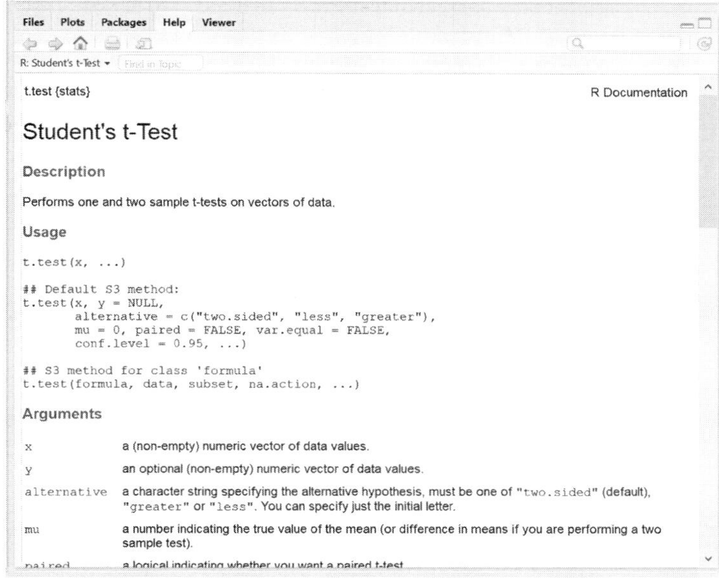

Scrolling down in the help window to the description for the argument `var.equal`, the help text tells us "a logical variable indicating whether to treat the two variances as being equal." If TRUE, then the pooled variance is used to estimate the variance; otherwise, the Welch (or Satterthwaite) approximation to the degrees of freedom is used. When we took out `var.equal = TRUE`, the function assumed variances were not equal and switched from the regular *t* test to Welch's *t* test. So what?

Well, what really changed was the number next to *df* in the output. We went from `df = 58` to `df = 47.635`. If variance is truly different between the two groups, we can't use the usual degrees of freedom and the cutoff values in Table B.2. If we don't adjust the degrees of freedom, the decision we make to reject the null could result in a Type I error. Or we could fail to reject the null and make a Type II error.

In this example, we would have made the exact same decision as we did when we assumed variances were equal, but next time, you may not be so lucky!

REAL-WORLD STATS

There's nothing like being prepared, so say Boy and Girl Scouts. But what's the best way to teach preparedness? In this study by Serkan Celik from Kirikkale University in Turkey, online versus face-to-face first aid instruction courses were compared with one another to test the effectiveness of the modes of delivery. Interestingly, with the same instructor teaching in both modes, the online form resulted in higher achievement scores at the end of the course. What did Celik do for his analysis? Independent *t* tests, of course. He found there was a difference between pre- and posttest scores.

Want to know more? Go online or to the library and find . . .

Celik, S. (2013). A media comparison study on first aid instruction. *Health Education Journal, 72,* 95–101.

Summary

The *t* test is your first introduction to performing a real statistical test between two groups and trying to understand this whole matter of significance from an applied point of view. Be sure that you understand what is in this chapter before you move on. And be sure you can do by hand the few calculations that were asked for. Next, we move on to using another form of the same test, only this time, two measures are taken from one group of participants rather than one measure taken from two separate groups.

Time to Practice

1. Using the data in the file named Chapter 13 Data Set 2 (ch13ds2.csv), test the research hypothesis at the .05 level of significance that boys raise their hand in class more often than girls. Do this practice problem by hand, using a calculator. What is your conclusion regarding the research hypothesis? Remember to first decide whether this is a one- or two-tailed test.
2. Using the same data set (Chapter 13 Data Set 2, ch13ds2.csv), test the research hypothesis at the .01 level of significance that there is a difference between boys and girls in the number of times they raise their hand in class. Do this practice problem by hand, using a calculator. What is your conclusion regarding the research hypothesis? You used the same data for this problem as for Question 1, but you have a different hypothesis (one is directional and the other is nondirectional). How do the results differ and why?
3. Time for some tedious, by-hand practice just to see if you can get the numbers right. Using the following information, calculate the *t* test statistics by hand.
   a. $X_1 = 62$ $X_2 = 60$ $n_1 = 10$ $n_2 = 10$ $s_1 = 2.45$ $s_2 = 3.16$
   b. $X_1 = 158$ $X_2 = 157.4$ $n_1 = 22$ $n_2 = 26$ $s_1 = 2.06$ $s_2 = 2.59$
   c. $X_1 = 200$ $X_2 = 198$ $n_1 = 17$ $n_2 = 17$ $s_1 = 2.45$ $s_2 = 2.35$

4. Using the results you got from Question 3 and a level of significance of .05, what are the two-tailed critical values associated with each result? Would the null hypothesis be rejected?

5. Using the following data and R, write a brief paragraph about whether the in-home treatment is equally effective as the out-of-home treatment for two separate groups. Here are the data. The outcome variable is level of anxiety after treatment on a scale from 1 to 10.

In-Home Treatment	Out-of-Home Treatment
3	7
4	6
1	7
1	8
1	7
3	6
3	5
6	6
5	4
1	2
4	5
5	4
4	3
4	6
3	7
6	5
7	4
7	3
7	8
8	7

6. Using the data in the file Chapter 13 Data Set 3 (ch13ds3.csv), test the null hypothesis that urban and rural residents have the same attitude toward gun control. Use R to complete the analysis for this problem.

7. Here's a good one to think about. A public health researcher (Dr. L) tested the hypothesis that providing new car buyers with child safety seats will also act as an incentive for parents to take

(Continued)

(Continued)

other measures to protect their children (such as driving more safely, childproofing the home, etc.). Dr. L counted all the occurrences of safe behaviors in the cars and homes of the parents who accepted the seats versus those who did not. The findings? A significant difference at the .013 level. Another researcher (Dr. R) did exactly the same study, and for our purposes, let's assume that everything was the same—same type of sample, same outcome measures, same car seats, and so on. Dr. R's results were close to significant at the .051 level. Whose results do you trust more and why?

8. Here are the results of three experiments where the means of the two groups being compared are exactly the same, but the standard deviation is quite different from experiment to experiment. Compute the effect size using Formula 13.6 and then discuss why this size changes as a function of the change in variability.

Experiment 1	Group 1 Mean	78.6	Effect Size ____________
	Group 2 Mean	73.4	
	Group 1 Standard Deviation	2.0	
	Group 2 Standard Deviation	1.8	
Experiment 2	Group 1 Mean	78.6	Effect Size ____________
	Group 2 Mean	73.4	
	Group 1 Standard Deviation	4.0	
	Group 2 Standard Deviation	5.0	
Experiment 3	Group 1 Mean	78.6	Effect Size ____________
	Group 2 Mean	73.4	
	Group 1 Standard Deviation	8.0	
	Group 2 Standard Deviation	8.0	

9. Using the data in Chapter 13 Data Set 4 (ch13ds4.csv) and R, test the null hypothesis that there is no difference in group means between the number of words spelled correctly for two groups of fourth graders. What is your conclusion?

10. For this question, you have to do two analyses. Using Chapter 13 Data Set 5 (ch13ds5.csv), compute the *t* score for the difference between two groups on the test variable (named score). Then, use Chapter 13 Data Set 6 (ch13ds6.csv) and do the same. Notice that there is a difference between the two *t* values, even though the mean scores for each group are the same. What is the source of this difference, and why—with the same sample size—did the *t* values differ?

11. Here's an interesting (and hypothetical) situation. The average score for one group on an aptitude test is 89.5 and the average score for the second group is 89.2. Both groups have sample sizes of about 1,500 and the differences between the means are significant, but the effect size is very small (let's say .1). What do you make of the fact that there can be a statistically significant difference between the two groups without there being a meaningful effect size?

Student Study Site

Get the tools you need to sharpen your study skills! Visit **edge.sagepub.com/salkindshaw** to access practice quizzes and eFlashcards, watch R tutorial videos, and download data sets!

t(EA) FOR TWO (AGAIN)

Tests Between the Means of Related Groups

Difficulty Scale ☺ ☺ ☺
(not too hard—this is the first one of this kind, but you know more than enough to master it)

WHAT YOU WILL LEARN IN THIS CHAPTER

- ✦ Understanding when the *t* test for dependent means is appropriate to use
- ✦ Computing the observed *t* value
- ✦ Interpreting the *t* value and understanding what it means
- ✦ Computing the effect size for a *t* test for dependent means

INTRODUCTION TO THE *t* TEST FOR DEPENDENT SAMPLES

With the aging of America, more research on health issues and services for people with dementia is being conducted every year. Philip Sauer, Joan Fopma-Loy, Jennifer Kinney, and Elizabeth Lokon designed a study to compare a traditional visual arts program to an art program in which the participant was paired with a student volunteer who encouraged and supported the creation of art in the person-centered program called Opening Minds through Art. All participants had a diagnosis of dementia, and consent for the study was provided by family members and primary caregivers. Ten people were observed in both types of art activities, and observers used the Greater Cincinnati Chapter Well-Being Observation Tool to rate activity participation in the areas of social interest, engagement, pleasure, disengagement, negative affect, sadness, and confusion. The researchers set a significance level of .05 for eight separate paired sample *t* tests that compared the ratings while participating in Opening Minds through Art to ratings during traditional visual arts activities, and they found observed differences in the areas of engagement ($t_{(9)} = 2.98, p = .016$); pleasure ($t_{(9)} = 2.74, p = .023$); and disengagement ($t_{(9)} = 2.50, p = .034$).

So why a test of dependent means? A *t* test for dependent means indicates that a single group of the same subjects is being studied under two conditions. In this example, the conditions are before the start of the experiment and after its conclusion. The *t* test for dependent means was used because the same people with dementia participated in both the Opening Minds through Art activities and traditional visual arts activities. As you can see from the aforementioned result, there were differences between the scores on engagement, pleasure, and disengagement. The relatively small *t* values on social interest (1.97), negative affect (1.52), sadness (−1.41), and confusion (−0.43) are not nearly extreme enough to fall outside the region where we would reject the null hypothesis. In other words, there is far too little change for us to say that this difference occurred due to something other than chance. The small differences were probably due to sampling error or variability within the groups.

Want to know more? Check out . . .

Sauer, P. E., Fopma-Loy, J., Kinney, J. M., & Lokom, E. (2016). "It makes me feel like myself": Person-centered versus traditional visual arts activities for people with dementia. *Dementia, 15*(5), 895–912.

THE PATH TO WISDOM AND KNOWLEDGE

Here's how you can use the flowchart to select the appropriate test statistic, the *t* test for dependent means. Follow along the highlighted sequence of steps in Figure 14.1.

1. The difference between the students' scores on the pretest and on the posttest is the focus.
2. Participants are being tested more than once.
3. There are two groups of scores.
4. The appropriate test statistic is the *t* test for dependent means.

There's another way that statisticians sometimes talk about dependent tests—as *repeated measures*. Dependent tests are often called "repeated measures" both because the measures are repeated across time or conditions or some factor and because they are repeated across the same cases, be each case a person, place, or thing.

FIGURE 14.1 ● Determining that a *t* test for dependent means is the correct test statistic.

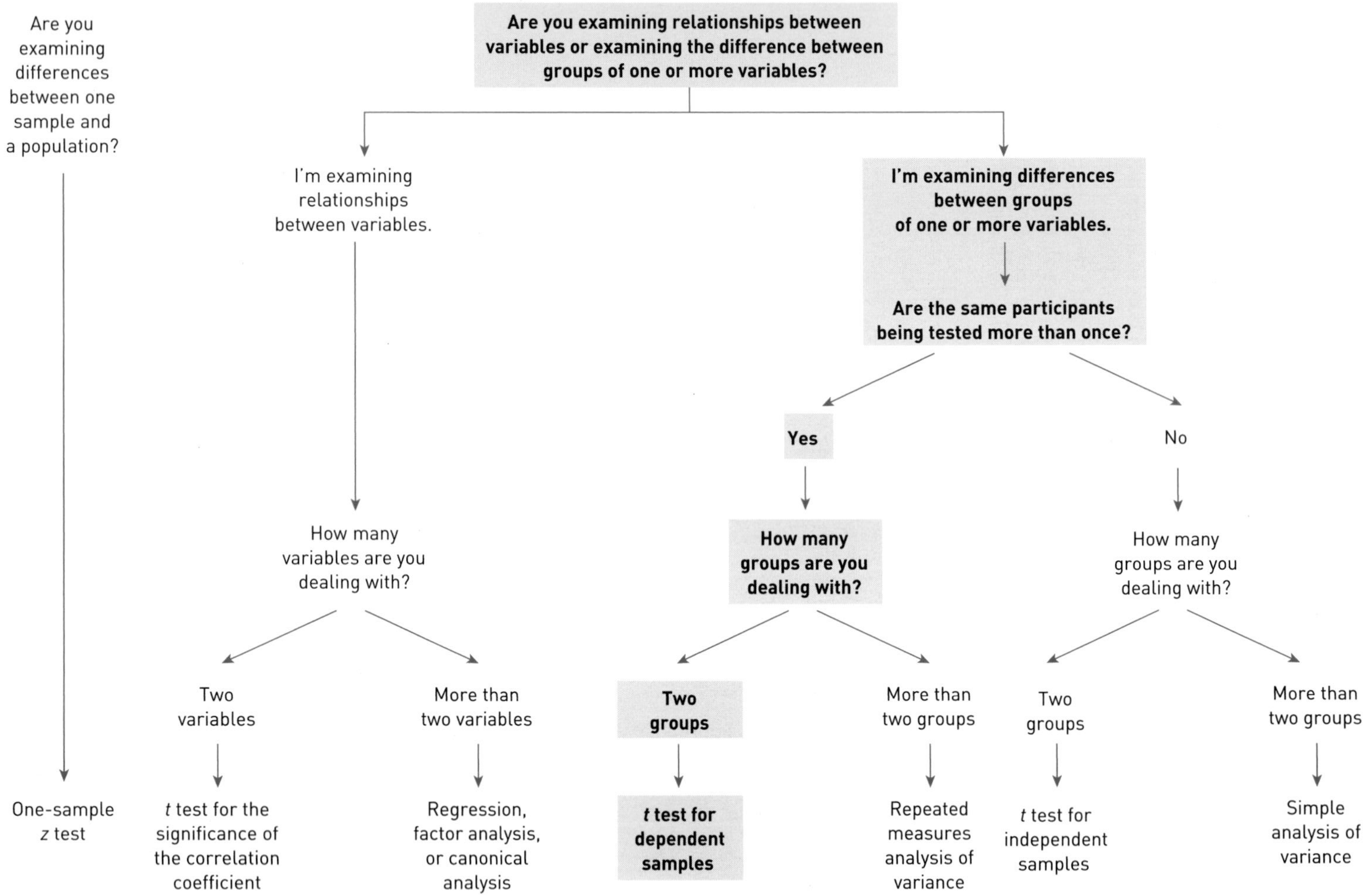

COMPUTING THE *t* TEST STATISTIC

The *t* test for dependent means involves a comparison of means from each group of scores and focuses on the differences between the scores. As you can see in Formula 14.1, the sum of the differences between the two tests forms the numerator and reflects the difference between groups of scores.

$$t = \frac{\sum D}{\sqrt{\frac{n\sum D^2 - (\sum D)^2}{n-1}}}, \tag{14.1}$$

where

- D is the difference between each individual's score from the first to the second time point,
- $\sum D$ is the sum of all the differences between groups of scores,
- $\sum D^2$ is the sum of the differences squared between groups of scores, and
- n is the number of pairs of observations.

Coming up, you'll see some data used to illustrate how the *t* value for a dependent *t* test is computed. Just as in the example discussed earlier in this chapter, there are a pretest and a posttest, and for illustration's sake, assume that these data are before-and-after scores from a reading program.

Did you notice in the formula that the numerator of the formula contains only one number, *D* for the difference? In Formulas 12.1 and 13.1 where we were testing for mean differences, we subtracted one mean from another. What isn't showing in Formula 14.1 is that the other mean value in the numerator is 0, because we want to know if the difference in scores is not 0. A variation on the formula above is Formula 14.2, and it can be helpful to explicitly include 0 to help you remember what you are testing.

$$t = \frac{\sum D - 0}{\sqrt{\frac{n\sum D^2 - (\sum D)^2}{n-1}}}. \tag{14.2}$$

Here are the famous eight steps and the computation of the *t* test statistic:

1. State the null and research hypotheses.

   The null hypothesis states that there is no difference between the means for the pretest and the posttest scores on reading achievement. The research hypothesis is one-tailed and directional because it posits that the posttest score will be higher than the pretest score.

   The null hypothesis is

$$H_0 : \mu_{posttest} = \mu_{pretest}. \tag{14.3}$$

The research hypothesis is

$$H_1 : \bar{X}_{posttest} > \bar{X}_{pretest}. \quad (14.4)$$

	Pretest	Posttest	Difference	D^2
	3	7	4	16
	5	8	3	9
	4	6	2	4
	6	7	1	1
	5	8	3	9
	5	9	4	16
	4	6	2	4
	5	6	1	1
	3	7	4	16
	6	8	2	4
	7	8	1	1
	8	7	–1	1
	7	9	2	4
	6	10	4	16
	7	9	2	4
	8	9	1	1
	8	8	0	0
	9	8	–1	1
	9	4	–5	25
	8	4	–4	16
	7	5	–2	4
	7	6	–1	1
	6	9	3	9
	7	8	1	1
	8	12	4	16
Sum	158	188	30	180
Mean	6.32	7.52	1.2	7.2
SD				

2. Set the level of risk (or the level of significance or Type I error) associated with the null hypothesis.

   The level of risk or Type I error or level of significance here is .05, but this is totally the decision of the researcher.

3. Select the appropriate test statistic.

   Using the flowchart shown in Figure 14.1, we determined that the appropriate test is a *t* test for dependent means. It is not a *t* test for independent means because the groups are not independent of each other. In fact, they're not groups of participants but groups of scores for the same participants. The groups are dependent on one another. Other names for the *t* test for dependent means are the *t* test for paired samples and the *t* test for correlated samples. You'll see in Chapter 17 that there is a very close relationship between a test of the significance of the correlation between these two sets of scores (pre- and posttest) and the *t* value we are computing here.

4. Compute the test statistic value (called the obtained value).

   Now's your chance to plug in values and do some computation. The formula for the *t* value was shown previously. When the specific values are plugged in, we get the equation shown in Formula 14.5. (We already computed the means and standard deviations for the pretest and posttest scores.)

$$t = \frac{30}{\sqrt{\frac{(25 \times 180) - 30^2}{25 - 1}}}. \tag{14.5}$$

   With the numbers plugged in, we have the following equation with a final obtained *t* value of 2.45. The mean score for pretest performance was 6.32, and the mean score for posttest performance was 7.52.

$$t = \frac{30}{\sqrt{150}} = 2.45. \tag{14.6}$$

5. Determine the value needed for rejection of the null hypothesis using the appropriate table of critical values for the particular statistic.

   Here's where we go to Appendix B and Table B.2, which lists the critical values for the test. Once again, we have a *t* test, and we'll use the same table we used in Chapter 13 to find the critical value for rejection of the null hypothesis.

   Our first task is to determine the degrees of freedom (*df*), which approximates the sample size. For this particular test statistic, the degrees of freedom is $n - 1$, where n equals the number of pairs of observations, or $25 - 1 = 24$. This is the degrees of freedom for this test statistic only and not necessarily for any other.

   Using this number (24), the level of risk you are willing to take (earlier defined as .05), and a one-tailed test (because there is a direction to the research hypothesis—the posttest score will be larger than the pretest score), the value needed for rejection of the null hypothesis is 1.711.

6. Compare the obtained value and the critical value.

   The obtained value is 2.45, larger than the critical value needed for rejection of the null hypothesis.

7. and 8. Time for a decision!

   Now comes our decision. If the obtained value is more extreme than the critical value, the null hypothesis should be rejected. If the obtained value does not exceed the critical value, the null hypothesis is the most attractive explanation. In this case, the obtained value does exceed the critical value—it is extreme enough for us to say that the difference between the pretest and the posttest occurred due to something other than chance. And if we did our experiment correctly, then what could the factor be that affected the outcome? Easy—the introduction of the daily reading program. We know the difference is due to a particular factor. The difference between the pretest and the posttest groups could not have occurred by chance but instead is due to the treatment.

So How Do I Interpret $t_{(24)} = 2.45, p < .05$?

- *t* represents the test statistic that was used.
- 24 is the number of degrees of freedom.
- 2.45 is the obtained value using the formula we showed you earlier in the chapter.
- $p < .05$ (the really important part of this little phrase) indicates that the probability is less than 5% on any one test of the null hypothesis that the average of posttest scores is greater than the average of pretest scores due to chance alone—there's something else going on. Because we defined .05 as our criterion for the research hypothesis being more attractive than the null hypothesis, our conclusion is that there is a significant difference between the two sets of scores. That's the something else.

USING R TO PERFORM A *t* TEST

Visit **edge.sagepub.com/salkindshaw** to watch an R tutorial video on this topic.

R is willing and ready to help you perform these inferential tests. Here's how to perform the one that we just did and understand the output. We are using the data set named Chapter 14 Data Set 1 (ch14ds1.csv), which was also used in the earlier example. And we are going to walk through this example in two ways. One, we will use R as a fancy calculator and manually work through the problem. Two, we will use an R function to quickly get an answer.

1. Import the data into R and name the object `ch14ds1`. Be sure that there is a separate column for pretest and posttest scores. Unlike in a *t* test for independent means, there are no groups to identify.
2. Create a vector of the difference scores.

3. Create a vector of squared difference scores.
4. Use the mean and standard deviation of the difference scores in the formula.

Starting with reading in the data and checking what we just imported:

```
> ch14ds1 <- read.csv(file.choose())
> View(ch14ds1)
>
```

Looking in the Environment pane, we see that the object contains 25 rows and two variables. Just right! Let's move on to calculating the differences between pre- and posttest scores.

```
> ch14ds1$D <- ch14ds1$Posttest - ch14ds1$Pretest
> ch14ds1$Dsq <- ch14ds1$D^2
>
```

If you view the object again, you should see four columns of numbers and a table that looks a lot like the table of numbers presented just a few pages ago. What is missing? The bottom two rows containing sum and mean values for each column. If you look at Formula 14.1, we actually only need sums for Difference and D^2. Let's calculate those first.

```
> sumD <- sum(ch14ds1$D)
> sumD
[1] 30
>
```

Checking our work against the table on page 278, we get the same answer for the sum of D ($\Sigma D = 30$), which we will use in the numerator and denominator of our formula. Now for D^2:

```
> sumDsq <- sum(ch14ds1$Dsq)
> sumDsq
[1] 180
>
```

Again, we got the value we expected, $\Sigma D^2 = 180$.

Plugging our numbers into the formula:

```
> sumD/sqrt((25*sumDsq - sumD^2)/(25 - 1))
[1] 2.44949
>
```

Like we did before, we can look for the critical value for our test in Appendix B and Table B.2. The critical value is still 1.711. Or we can ask R to give us the exact p associated with $t = 2.44949$. And R has a function for this!

```
> pt(tStat, df = 24, lower = FALSE)
[1] 0.0109915
>
```

For $t_{24} = 2.45, p = .01$ for our one-tailed test that said the intervention would increase memory scores, leading us to reject the null hypothesis that there would be no difference in pretest and posttest scores.

Now it's time for the R shortcut.

```
> t.test(ch14ds1$Posttest, ch14ds1$Pretest, paired = TRUE,
alternative = "greater")

  Paired t-test
data:  ch14ds1$Posttest and ch14ds1$Pretest
t = 2.4495, df = 24, p-value = 0.01099
alternative hypothesis: true difference in means is
greater than 0
95 percent confidence interval:
0.3618424        Inf
sample estimates:
mean of the differences
                    1.2
>
```

First, let's talk about the options we used in the `t.test` function.

- `ch14ds1$Posttest`: the vector for the posttest scores in our data. We list this first because we want the function to subtract the pretest scores from the posttest scores.
- `ch14ds1$Pretest`: the vector for the pretest scores in our data

- `paired = TRUE`: the pretest and posttest scores refer to the same person (nonindependent). This told R to use the formula for a paired *t* test.
- `alternative = "greater"`: the first vector is greater than the second vector. This option gave us one-tailed test results because we said the posttest scores would be larger than the pretest scores. If you are running a two-tailed test (scores are different but you don't know if they will be larger or smaller), you can leave this option off.

Looking at the results, R tells us which test was run (paired *t* test), the data that were used, the *t* test results with degrees of freedom, and *p*. The output even tells you the alternative hypothesis that you think the true difference is greater than 0! That is followed by the 95% confidence interval around the difference score for our one-tailed test. Finally, we are told what the mean difference is between the two scores, 1.2.

What if we had put the pretest vector first in the `t.test` function? Then we would get a negative *t* value if the average of the first variable is smaller than the average of the second variable (which, in this case, would have been a *t* value of −2.449 instead of 2.449). As long as you keep the research hypothesis foremost in mind when you interpret the results, you should be fine.

Just for fun, we're going to throw a little caveat bone in the mix here. Sometimes, and only *sometimes*, researchers will use a test of dependent means when the two measures (which are usually on the same participant) are actually collected from two different participants who are very closely matched together on all relevant characteristics (be it age, gender, social class, aggressiveness, workout speed, ice cream preference—you get the picture). Researchers also use this test to compare pairs of people, like siblings, parent-child, or romantic partners, to each other. In this case, even though they are different participants, they are considered dependent because they are matched. We're just fine-tuning the meaning of the word *dependent* and how it applies to such situations.

Believe it or not, way back in the olden days, when one of your authors and perhaps your instructor were graduate students, there were only huge mainframe computers and not a hint of such marvels as we have today on our desktops. In other words, everything that was done in our statistics class was done by hand. The great benefit of doing the calculations by hand is, first, it helps you to better understand the process. Second, should you be without a computer, you can still do the analysis. So, if the computer does not spit out everything you need, use some creativity. As long as you know the basic formula for the critical value and have the appropriate tables, you'll do fine.

THE EFFECT SIZE FOR *t*(EA) FOR TWO (AGAIN)

The formula this time differs a bit from Formulas 13.6 and 13.7 because our scores are related. In the example above, how well a person scores on a posttest is related to how well he or she did on the pretest. If we don't subtract that relatedness out, our effect size will be smaller than it should be.

$$ES = \frac{\bar{X}_{post} - \bar{X}_{pre}}{\sqrt{s_{post}^2 + s_{pre}^2 - \left(2rs_{post}s_{pre}\right)}}. \tag{14.7}$$

We need to get a few more numbers from R before we can plug all of our numbers into the formula. Specifically, we need pre- and posttest standard deviations along with the correlation between the pretest and posttest scores.

Starting with standard deviation of our pretest and posttest scores:

```
> sd(ch14ds1$Pretest)
[1] 1.725302
> sd(ch14ds1$Posttest)
[1] 1.828478
>
```

Next, we need to know the correlation between our pretest and posttest scores on reading achievement, but before we do that calculation, let's look at a scatterplot with those two variables shown in Figure 14.2.

```
> plot(ch14ds1$Pretest, ch14ds1$Posttest,
+       xlab = "Pretest", ylab = "Posttest",
+       main = "Pretest and Posttest Reading Achievement Scores")
>
```

FIGURE 14.2 ● Scatterplot of pretest and posttest.

Looking at this plot with dots very scattered, it is hard to tell if the variables are even correlated. Let's calculate the correlation.

```
> cor(ch14ds1$Pretest, ch14ds1$Posttest)
[1] 0.05071834
>
```

That result certainly explains it. The correlation between the pre- and posttest reading achievement scores is only .05. Based on Table 7.5 in Chapter 7, the relationship is weak to none. But we will still include the number in our effect size calculation.

Now let's plug in all of our numbers.

$$ES = \frac{7.52 - 6.32}{\sqrt{1.8285^2 + 1.7253^2 - (2 \times 0.05072 \times 1.8285 \times 1.7253)}} = 0.49. \quad (14.8)$$

For this analysis, the effect size (according to the guidelines proposed by Cohen and discussed in Chapter 12) is medium. Not only is the difference significant, but the bigness of the difference is for real and perhaps meaningful given the context of the research questions being asked.

REAL-WORLD STATS

You or your parents may be part of the "sandwich" generation whose adults are not only taking care of their elderly parents but also raising children. This situation (and the aging of any population such as is taking place in the United States) speaks to the importance of evaluating the elderly (however this cohort is defined) and the use of the tools we've discussed. The purpose of this study was to determine whether the life satisfaction of a sample of Thai elderly depended on their daily living practice. Matched pairs of elderly people were tested to see who perceived themselves as life satisfied or life dissatisfied, and scores of 85% and above on the life satisfaction instrument were used as a criterion to identify the elderly with life satisfaction. A two-tailed dependent t test (because the samples were matched—in effect the researchers considered the paired participants to be the same participants) was used to examine differences in mean scores both overall and for each domain of daily living practices. The life satisfaction group of elderly had significantly higher scores than their dissatisfied counterparts. One of the most interesting questions is how these results might apply to other samples of elderly participants in different cultures.

Want to know more? Go online or to the library and find . . .

Othaganont, P., Sinthuvorakan, C., & Jensupakarn, P. (2002). Daily living practice of the life-satisfied Thai elderly. *Journal of Transcultural Nursing, 13*, 24–29.

Summary

That's it for means. You've just learned how to compare data from independent (Chapter 13) and dependent (Chapter 14) groups, and now it's time to move on to another class of significance tests that deals with more than two groups (be they independent or dependent). This class of techniques, called analysis of variance, is very powerful and popular and will be a valuable tool in your war chest!

Time to Practice

1. What is the difference between a test of independent means and a test of dependent means, and when is each appropriate?
2. In the following examples, indicate whether you would perform a *t* test of independent means or dependent means.
   a. Two groups were exposed to different levels of treatment for ankle sprains. Which treatment was most effective?
   b. A researcher in nursing wanted to know if the recovery of patients was quicker when some received additional in-home care whereas others received the standard amount.
   c. A group of adolescent boys was offered interpersonal skills counseling and then tested in September and May to see if there was any impact on family harmony.
   d. One group of adult men was given instructions in reducing their high blood pressure whereas another was not given any instructions.
   e. One group of men was provided access to an exercise program and tested two times over a 6-month period for heart health.
3. For Chapter 14 Data Set 2 (ch14ds2.csv), compute the *t* value manually and write a conclusion as to whether there was a change in tons of paper used as a function of the recycling program in 25 different districts. (Hint: *Before* and *after* become the two levels of treatment.) Test the hypothesis at the .01 level.
4. Here are the data from a study in which adolescents were given counseling at the beginning of the school year to see if it had a positive impact on their tolerance for adolescents who were ethnically different from them. Assessments were made right before the treatment and then 6 months later. Did the program work? The outcome variable is scored on an attitude-toward-others test with possible scores ranging from 0 to 50; the higher the score, the higher the tolerance. Use R or some other computer application to complete this analysis.

Before Treatment	After Treatment
45	46
46	44
32	47

Before Treatment	After Treatment
34	42
33	45
21	32
23	36
41	43
27	24
38	41
41	38
47	31
41	22
32	36
22	36
34	27
36	41
19	44
23	32
22	32

5. For Chapter 14 Data Set 3 (ch14ds3.csv), compute the *t* value and write a conclusion as to whether there is a difference in families' satisfaction level, measured on a scale of 1 to 15, in their use of service centers following a social service intervention. Do this exercise using R and report the exact probability of the outcome. Also report the effect size.

6. Do this exercise the good old-fashioned way—by hand. A famous brand-name manufacturer wants to know whether people prefer Nibbles or Wribbles. Consumers get a chance to sample each type of cracker and indicate their like or dislike on a scale from 1 to 10. Which do they like the most?

Nibbles Rating	Wribbles Rating
9	4
3	7
1	6
6	8
5	7

(Continued)

(Continued)

Nibbles Rating	Wribbles Rating
7	7
8	8
3	6
10	7
3	8
5	9
2	8
9	7
6	3
2	6
5	7
8	6
1	5
6	5
3	6

7. Take a look at Chapter 14 Data Set 4 (ch14ds4.csv). Does shift matter when it comes to stress (the higher the stress score, the more stress the worker feels)?
8. Chapter 14 Data Set 5 (ch14ds5.csv) provides you with data for two groups of adults, tested in the fall and spring during a resistance weight-lifting class. The outcome variable is bone density (the higher the score, the denser the bones) on a scale from 1 to 10. Does lifting weights work? How about the effect size?

Student Study Site

Get the tools you need to sharpen your study skills! Visit **edge.sagepub.com/salkindshaw** to access practice quizzes and eFlashcards, watch R tutorial videos, and download data sets!

15 TWO GROUPS TOO MANY?

Try Analysis of Variance

Difficulty Scale ☺
(longer and harder than the others, but a very interesting and useful procedure—worth the work!)

WHAT YOU WILL LEARN IN THIS CHAPTER

- Deciding when it is appropriate to use analysis of variance
- Computing and interpreting the *F* statistic
- Using R to complete an analysis of variance
- Computing the effect size for a one-way analysis of variance

INTRODUCTION TO ANALYSIS OF VARIANCE

One of the up-and-coming fields in the area of psychology is the psychology of sports. Although the field focuses mostly on enhancing performance, it gives special attention to many aspects of sports. One area of interest is what psychological skills are necessary to be a successful athlete. With this question in mind, Marious Goudas, Yiannis Theodorakis, and Georgios Karamousalidis have tested the usefulness of the Athletic Coping Skills Inventory.

As part of their research, they used **analysis of variance** (ANOVA) to test the hypothesis that number of years of experience in sports is related to coping skill (or an athlete's score on the Athletic Coping Skills Inventory). ANOVA was used because more than two levels of the same variable were being tested, and these groups were compared on their average performance. In particular, Group 1 included athletes with 6 years of experience or fewer, Group 2 included athletes with 7 to 10 years of experience, and Group 3 included athletes with more than 10 years of experience.

The test statistic for ANOVA is the *F* test (named for R. A. Fisher, the creator of the statistic), and the results of this study on the Peaking Under Pressure subscale of the test showed that $F_{(2, 110)} = 13.08$, $p < .01$. The mean of at least one group of scores differed from the others. In other words, any difference in test score was due to number of years of experience in athletics rather than some chance occurrence of scores.

Want to know more? Go online or to the library and find . . .

Goudas, M., Theodorakis, Y., & Karamousalidis, G. (1998). Psychological skills in basketball: Preliminary study for development of a Greek form of the Athletic Coping Skills Inventory-28. *Perceptual and Motor Skills, 86,* 59–65.

THE PATH TO WISDOM AND KNOWLEDGE

Here's how you can use the flowchart shown in Figure 15.1 to select ANOVA as the appropriate test statistic. Follow along the highlighted sequence of steps.

1. We are testing for a difference between scores of different groups, in this case, the difference between the peaking scores of athletes.
2. The athletes are not being tested more than once.
3. There are three groups (6 years or fewer, 7–10 years, and more than 10 years of experience).
4. The appropriate test statistic is simple analysis of variance.

DIFFERENT FLAVORS OF ANOVA

ANOVA comes in many flavors. The simplest kind, and the focus of this chapter, is the **one-way analysis of variance**, used when one factor or one treatment variable (such as group membership) is being explored and this factor has more than two levels. The technique is called *analysis of variance* because the variance due to differences in the dependent variable is separated into (a) variance that's due to differences between individuals *between* groups and (b) variance due to differences *within* groups. Then, the two types of variance are compared with one another. The between-groups variance is due to treatment differences, while the within-group variance is due to differences between individuals within each group.

FIGURE 15.1 ● Determining that analysis of variance is the correct test statistic.

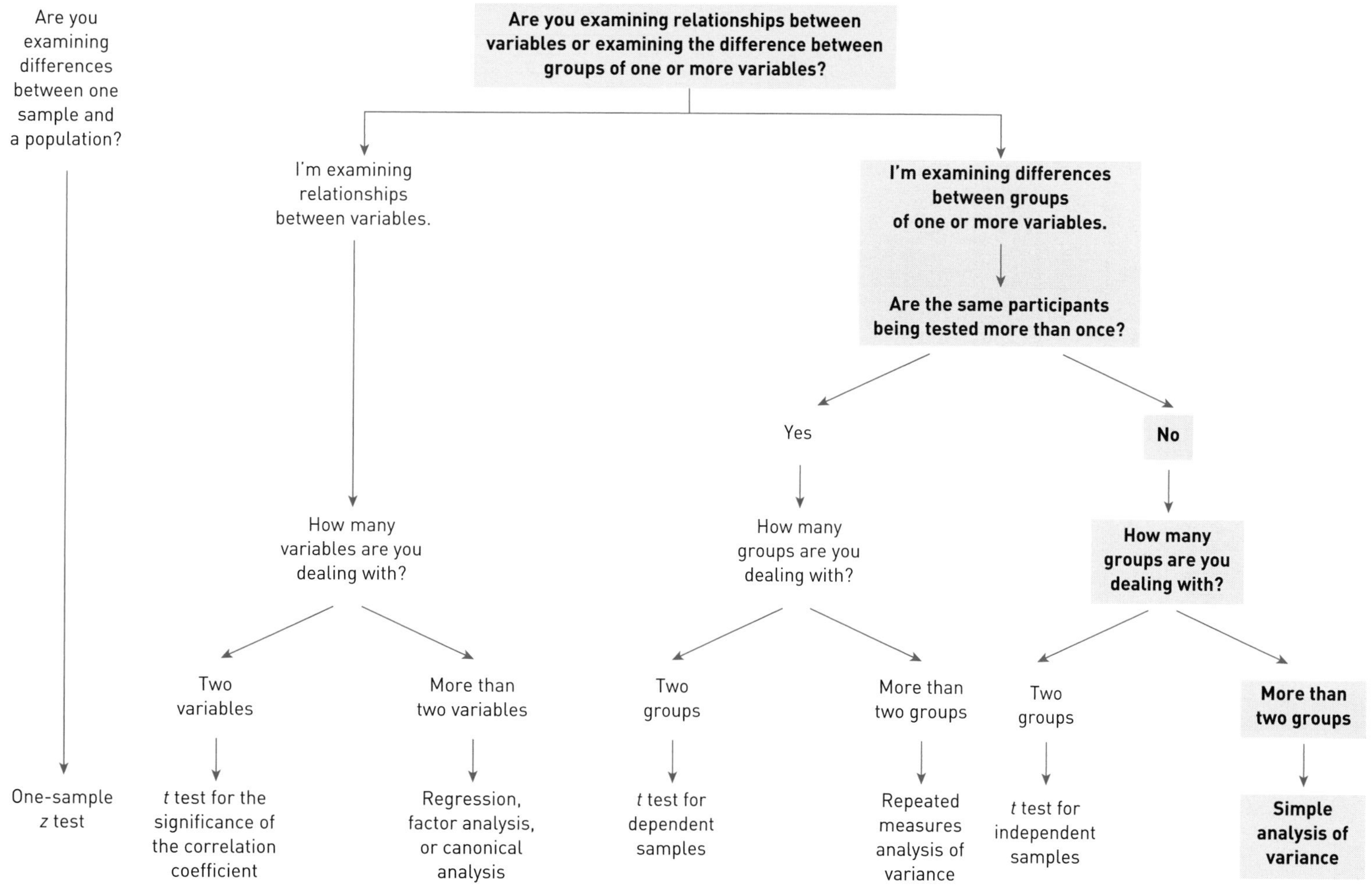

Are you examining differences between one sample and a population?

One-sample *z* test

Are you examining relationships between variables or examining the difference between groups of one or more variables?

I'm examining relationships between variables.

How many variables are you dealing with?

Two variables → t test for the significance of the correlation coefficient

More than two variables → Regression, factor analysis, or canonical analysis

I'm examining differences between groups of one or more variables.

Are the same participants being tested more than once?

Yes → How many groups are you dealing with?

Two groups → t test for dependent samples

More than two groups → Repeated measures analysis of variance

No → **How many groups are you dealing with?**

Two groups → t test for independent samples

More than two groups → **Simple analysis of variance**

In fact, ANOVA is, in many ways, similar to a t test (an ANOVA with two groups is, in effect, a t test!). In both ANOVA and t tests, differences between means are computed. But with ANOVA, there are more than two means.

For example, let's say we were investigating the effects on language development of being in preschool for 5, 10, or 20 hours per week. The group to which the children belong is the treatment variable, or the grouping or between-groups factor. Language development is the outcome measure. The experimental design will look something like this, with three levels of the one categorical variable (hours of participation). Conveniently, analysis refers to this categorical variable as a factor, as does R.

Group 1 (5 hours per week)	Group 2 (10 hours per week)	Group 3 (20 hours per week)
Language development test score	Language development test score	Language development test score

COMPUTING THE *F* TEST STATISTIC

One-way ANOVA involves testing the difference between the means of more than two groups on one factor or dimension. For example, you might want to know whether four groups of people (20, 25, 30, and 35 years of age) differ in their attitude toward public support of private schools. Or you might be interested in determining whether five groups of children from different grades (2nd, 4th, 6th, 8th, and 10th) differ in the level of parental participation in school activities.

Any analysis where

- there is only one dimension or treatment,
- there are more than two levels of the grouping factor, and
- one is looking at differences across groups in average scores

requires that one-way ANOVA be used.

The formula for the computation of the F value, which is the test statistic needed to evaluate the hypothesis that there are overall differences between groups, is shown in Formula 15.1. It is simple at this level, but it takes a bit more arithmetic to compute than some of the test statistics you have worked with in earlier chapters.

$$F = \frac{MS_{\text{between}}}{MS_{\text{within}}}, \qquad (15.1)$$

where

MS_{between} is the variance between groups, and

MS_{within} is the variance within groups.

The logic behind this ratio goes something like this. If there were absolutely no variability within each group (all the scores were the same), then any difference between groups would be meaningful, right? Probably so. The ANOVA formula (which is a ratio) compares the amount of variability between groups (which is due to the grouping factor) with the amount of variability within groups (which is due to chance). If that ratio is 1, then the amount of variability due to within-group differences is equal to the amount of variability due to between-groups differences, and any difference between groups is not significant. As the average difference between groups gets larger (and the numerator of the ratio increases in value), the *F* value increases as well. As the *F* value increases, it becomes more extreme in relation to the distribution of all *F* values and is more likely due to something other than chance. Whew!

Here are some data and some preliminary calculations to illustrate how the *F* value is computed. For our example, let's assume these are three groups of preschoolers and their language scores.

Group 1 Scores	Group 2 Scores	Group 3 Scores
87	87	89
86	85	91
76	99	96
56	85	87
78	79	89
98	81	90
77	82	89
66	78	96
75	85	96
67	91	93

Here are the famous eight steps and the computation of the *F* test statistic:

1. State the null and research hypotheses.

   The null hypothesis, shown in Formula 15.2, states that there is no difference among the means of the three different groups. ANOVA, also called the *F* test (because it produces an *F* statistic or an *F* ratio), looks for an overall difference among groups.

   Note that this test does not look at pairwise differences, such as the difference between Group 1 and Group 2. For that, we have to use another technique, which we will discuss later in the chapter.

$$H_0: \mu_1 = \mu_2 = \mu_3. \tag{15.2}$$

The research hypothesis is not as straightforward as it was with the *t* test. We now have more than two means and the research hypothesis states that not all means will be equal. We don't know whether all three means will be unique or if just $\bar{X}_1$ will be different from $\bar{X}_2$ and $\bar{X}_3$ (pick any one of the three means in this example—$\bar{X}_1$ is not special). Note that there is no direction to the hypothesized difference because all *F* tests are nondirectional.

2. Set the level of risk (or the level of significance) associated with the null hypothesis.

   The level of risk or level of significance (any other names?) is .05 here. Once again, the level of significance used is totally at the discretion of the researcher.

3. Select the appropriate test statistic.

   Using the flowchart shown in Figure 15.1, we determine that the appropriate test is a simple ANOVA.

4. Compute the test statistic value (called the obtained value).

   Now's your chance to plug in values and do some computation. There's a good deal of computation to do.

   - The *F* ratio is a ratio of the variability among groups to the variability within groups. To compute these values, we first have to compute what is called the sum of squares for each source of variability—between groups, within groups, and the total.
   - The between-groups sum of squares is equal to the sum of the differences between the mean of all scores and the mean of each group's score, which is then squared. This gives us an idea of how different each group's mean is from the overall mean.
   - The within-group sum of squares is equal to the sum of the differences between each individual score in a group and the mean of each group, which is then squared. This gives us an idea how different each score in a group is from the mean of that group.
   - The total sum of squares is equal to the sum of the between-groups and within-group sum of squares.

Okay—let's figure out these values.

> Up to now, we've talked about one- and two-tailed tests. There's no such thing when talking about ANOVA! We mentioned above that the ANOVA is nondirectional. And why is the *F* test nondirectional? Because variance can only be positive and the *F* test is a ratio of two variances that can only be positive numbers. So, talking about the specific direction does not make any sense.

Figure 15.2 shows the practice data you saw previously with all the calculations you need to compute the between-groups, within-group, and total sum of squares. First, let's look at what we have in this expanded table. We'll start with the left-hand column:

- n is the number of participants in each group (such as 10).
- $\sum X$ is the sum of the scores in each group (such as 766).
- $\bar{X}$ is the mean of each group (such as 76.60).
- $\sum(X^2)$ is the sum of each score squared (such as 59,964).
- $(\sum X)^2/n$ is the sum of the scores in each group squared and then divided by the size of the group (such as 58,675.60).

Second, let's look at the right-most column:

- N is the total number of participants (such as 30).
- $\sum\sum X$ is the sum of all the scores across groups.
- $(\sum_k\sum X)^2/n$ is the sum of all the scores across groups (k) squared and divided by n (the number of people in a single group).
- $\sum_k\sum(X^2)$ is the sum of all the sum of squared scores across all groups (k).
- $\sum_k(\sum X)^2/n$ is the sum of the sum of each group's (k) scores squared divided by n (the number of people in a single group).

That is a load of computation to carry out, but we are almost finished!

First, we compute the sum of squares for each source of variability. Here are the calculations:

$SS_{between}$	$\sum_k(\sum X)^2/n - (\sum_k\sum X)^2/n$ or 215,171.60 – 214,038.53	1,133.07
SS_{within}	$\sum_k\sum(X^2) - \sum_k(\sum X)^2/n$ or 216,910 – 215,171.6	1,738.40
SS_{total}	$\sum_k\sum(X^2) - (\sum_k\sum X)^2/n$ or 216,910 – 214,038.53	2,871.47

Second, we need to compute the mean sum of squares, which is simply an average sum of squares. These are the variance estimates that we need to eventually compute the all-important F ratio.

We do that by dividing each sum of squares by the appropriate number of degrees of freedom (df). Remember, degrees of freedom is an approximation of the sample or group size. We need two sets of degrees of freedom for ANOVA. For the between-groups estimate, it is $k - 1$, where k equals the number of groups (in this case, there are three groups and 2 degrees of freedom). For the within-group estimate, we need $N - k$, where N equals the total sample size and k is still the number of groups (which means that the number of degrees of freedom is 30 – 3, or 27). Then the F ratio is simply a ratio of the mean sum of squares due to between-groups differences to the mean sum of squares due to within-group differences, or

$$F_{(2,27)} = \frac{566.54}{64.39} = 8.799. \tag{15.3}$$

This is the obtained F value.

FIGURE 15.2 ● Computing the important values for a one-way ANOVA.

	Group	Test Score	X^2	Group	Test Score	X^2	Group	Test Score	X^2	
	1	87	7,569	2	87	7,569	3	89	7,921	
	1	86	7,396	2	85	7,225	3	91	8,281	
	1	76	5,776	2	99	9,801	3	96	9,216	
	1	56	3,136	2	85	7,225	3	87	7,569	
	1	78	6,084	2	79	6,241	3	89	7,921	
	1	98	9,604	2	81	6,561	3	90	8,100	
	1	77	5,929	2	82	6,724	3	89	7,921	
	1	66	4,356	2	78	6,084	3	96	9,216	
	1	75	5,625	2	85	7,225	3	96	9,216	
	1	67	4,489	2	91	8,281	3	93	8,649	
	10			10			10			
n		766			852			916		$N = 30.00$
$\sum X$		76.60			85.20			91.60		$\sum\sum X = 2{,}534.00$
$\bar{X}$		59,964			72,936			84,010		$(\sum\sum X)^2 / N = 214{,}038.53$
$\sum(X^2)$		58,675.60			72,590.40			83,905.60		$\sum\sum(X^2) = 216{,}910$
$(\sum X)^2/n$										$\sum(\sum X)^2/n = 215{,}171.60$

Here's a **source table** of the variance estimates used to compute the *F* ratio. This is how most *F* tables appear in professional journals and manuscripts.

Source	Sum of Squares	*df*	Mean Sum of Squares	*F*
Between groups	1,133.07	2	566.54	8.799
Within groups	1,738.40	27	64.39	
Total	2,871.47	29		

All that trouble for one little *F* ratio? Yes, but as we have said earlier, it's essential to do these procedures at least once by hand. It gives you the important appreciation of where the numbers come from and some insight into what they mean.

Because you already know about *t* tests, you might be wondering how a *t* value (which is always used for the test between the difference of the means for two groups) and an *F* value (which is always used for more than two groups) are related. Interestingly enough, an *F* value for two groups is equal to a *t* value for two groups squared, or $F = t^2$. And because they are equal, the *p*s associated with the *t* and *F* are equal! Handy trivia question, right? But also useful if you know one and need to know the other.

5. Determine the value needed for rejection of the null hypothesis using the appropriate table of critical values for the particular statistic.

   As we have done before, we have to compare the obtained and critical values. We now need to turn to the table that lists the critical values for the *F* test, Table B.3 in Appendix B, which asks for two different types of degrees of freedom and the same degrees of freedom we used in Step 4. The numerator (between-groups) degrees of freedom is $k - 1$, or $3 - 1 = 2$. The degrees of freedom for the denominator is $N - k$, or $30 - 3 = 27$. Together, they are represented as $F_{(2, 27)}$.

   The obtained value is 8.80, or $F_{(2, 27)} = 8.80$. The critical value at the .05 level with 2 degrees of freedom in the numerator (represented by columns in Table B.3) and 27 degrees of freedom in the denominator (represented by rows in Table B.3) is 3.36. So at the .05 level, with 2 and 27 degrees of freedom for an omnibus test among the means of the three groups, the value needed for rejection of the null hypothesis is 3.36.

6. Compare the obtained value and the critical value.

   The obtained value is 8.80, and the critical value for rejection of the null hypothesis at the .05 level that the three groups are different from one another (without concern for where the difference lies) is 3.36.

7. and 8. Decision time.

   Now comes our decision. If the obtained value is greater than the critical value, the null hypothesis can be rejected. If the obtained value is less than the critical value, the null hypothesis is the most attractive explanation and we fail to reject the null. In this case, the obtained value does exceed the critical value—it is extreme enough for us to say that the difference among the three groups is not due to chance. And if we did our experiment correctly, then what factor do we think affected the outcome? Easy—the number of hours of preschool. We know the difference is due to a particular factor because the difference among the groups could not have occurred by chance but instead is due to the treatment.

So How Do I Interpret $F_{(2, 27)} = 8.80$, $p < .05$?

- *F* represents the test statistic that was used.
- 2 and 27 are the numbers of degrees of freedom for the between-groups and within-group estimates, respectively.
- 8.80 is the obtained value using the formula we showed you earlier in the chapter.
- $p < .05$ (the really important part of this little phrase) indicates that the probability for $F_{(2, 27)} = 8.80$ is less than 5% on any one test of the null hypothesis that the average scores of each group's language skills differ due to chance alone rather than due to the effect of the treatment. Because we defined .05 as our criterion for the research hypothesis being more attractive than the null hypothesis, our conclusion is that there is a significant difference among the three sets of scores.

(Really Important) Tech Talk

Imagine this scenario. You're a high-powered researcher at an advertising company, and you want to see whether the use of color in advertising communications makes a difference to sales. You've decided to test this at the .05 level. So, you put together a brochure that is all black-and-white, one that is 25% color, the next 50%, then 75%, and finally 100% color—for five levels. You do an ANOVA and find out that a difference in sales exists. But because ANOVA is an omnibus test (testing all five means at the same time), you don't know where the source of the significant difference lies. So, you take two groups (or pairs) at a time (such as 25% color and 75% color) and test them against each other. In fact, you test every combination of two against each other. Kosher? No way. This is called performing multiple *t* tests, and it is actually against the law in some jurisdictions. When you do this, the Type I error rate (which you set at .05) balloons, depending on the number of tests you want to conduct. There are 10 possible comparisons (no color vs. 25%, no color vs. 50%, no color vs. 75%, etc.), and the real Type I error rate is

$$1-(1-\alpha)^k, \quad (15.4)$$

where

- α is the Type I error rate (.05 in this example), and
- k is the number of comparisons.

So, instead of .05, the actual error rate that each comparison is being tested at is

$$1 - (1 - .05)^{10} = .40 \text{ (!!!!!)}$$

This is a far cry from .05. That means you have a 40% chance of rejecting the null when you shouldn't.

USING R TO COMPUTE THE *F* RATIO

Visit **edge.sagepub.com/salkindshaw** to watch an R tutorial video on this topic.

The *F* ratio is a tedious value to compute by hand—not difficult, just time-consuming. That's all there is to it. Using the computer is much easier and more accurate because it eliminates any computational errors. That said, you should be glad you have seen the value computed manually because it's an important skill to have and helps you understand the concepts behind the process. But also be glad that there are tools such as R and the function `aov()`.

We'll use the data found in Chapter 15 Data Set 1—ch15ds1.csv (the same data used in the above preschool example).

1. Import the data and then `View`. Be sure that there is a column for Group and that you have three groups represented in that column.

   Starting with reading in and viewing our data set:

```
> ch15ds1 <- read.csv(file.choose())
> View(ch15ds1)
>
```

Following the `View(ch15ds1)` function, RStudio should show you a table like that seen in Figure 15.3. Using the scroll bar on the right, scroll down to see the groups for 10 hours and 20 hours. If you are following along, you should see something very similar on your computer.

2. Look at the descriptive statistics by Group. To do this step, we are going to use a handy function in the psych library, which we need to tell R about first. We showed you the describe function at the end of Chapter 5, but you may not have installed it, so let's start with that.

```
> install.packages("psych")
>
```

FIGURE 15.3 ● View of the first 15 rows of R object ch15ds1.

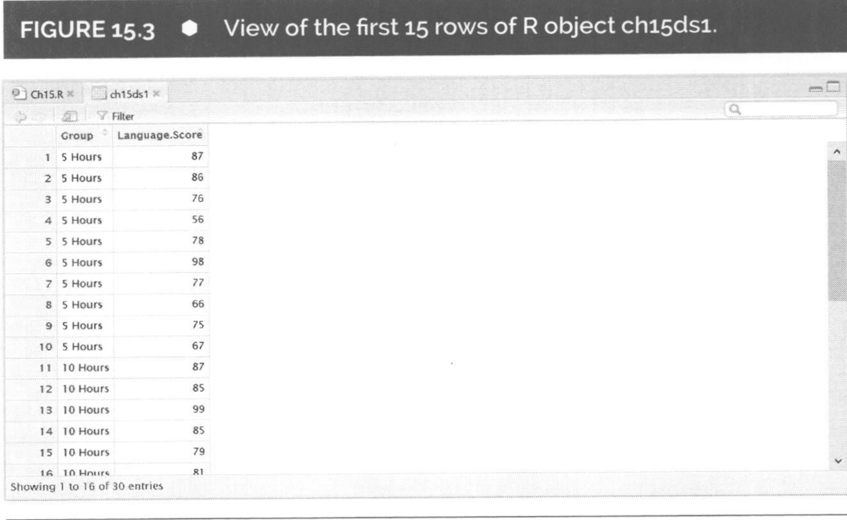

3. After installing the package, we tell R we want to use the package using the `library()` function.

```
> library(psych)
>
```

4. Now let's use `describeBy()`, which needs to know which variable to provide descriptive statistics for (mean, standard deviation, and so on), and the name of the grouping (factor) variable.

```
> describeBy(ch15ds1$Language.Score, group = ch15ds1$Group)
Descriptive statistics by group
group: 10 Hours
   vars  n  mean  sd median trimmed  mad min max range skew kurtosis   se
X1    1 10  85.2 6.2     85   84.38 5.19  78  99    21 0.89    -0.15 1.96
-----------------------------------------------------------------
group: 20 Hours
   vars  n mean   sd median trimmed  mad min max range skew kurtosis   se
X1    1 10 91.6 3.41   90.5   91.62 2.97  87  96     9 0.26    -1.72 1.08
-----------------------------------------------------------------
group: 5 Hours
   vars  n mean    sd median trimmed   mad min max range skew kurtosis   se
X1    1 10 76.6 11.96   76.5    76.5 14.08  56  98    42 0.05     -0.9 3.78
>
```

It looks like the mean for each group is different, which is what we should see if the means are not equal across all three groups. We can also see that each group has 10 observations ($n = 10$).

5. Run your ANOVA!

```
> m1 <- aov(Language.Score ~ Group, data = ch15ds1)
>
```

We started with the function `aov()`. Here is what each piece means:

- `m1`: the name of the object that stores our results
- `<-`: the assignment symbols
- `aov`: the name of the function
- `Language.Score`: the name of the dependent variable
- `~`: a symbol that means predicted by
- `Group`: the grouping variable
- `data = ch15ds1`: the name of our data object

Putting it altogether, we told R we wanted to run the `aov` on our dependent variable `Language.Score` predicted by `Group`, and those variables can be found in the object `ch15ds1`. Also, please store these results in `m1`.

To look at the results, we are going to look at a function called `summary()`.

```
> summary(m1)
            Df  Sum Sq  Mean Sq F value    Pr(>F)
Group        2    1133    566.5   8.799  0.00114 **
Residuals   27    1738     64.4
---
Signif. codes:    0 '***' 0.001 '**' 0.01 '*' 0.05 '.' 0.1 ' ' 1
>
```

Similar to the source table in the example above, R returns the degrees of freedom, sum of squares, mean sum of squares, the F value, and corresponding $p = .00114$. From this output, we could report the results of $F_{(2, 27)} = 8.80, p = .001$.

We have seen `summary()` before in Chapter 3. That time, we used it on a data frame, so R gave us summary statistics about each column of data in our data frame. This time, we are using it on the results from `aov()`. R recognizes that we are asking for summary results from a statistical computation and changes what it does accordingly. `summary()` is smart that way! In this instance, we got a table that looks like our source table along with the *p* value under `Pr(>F)` to go along with our statistic. It doesn't reproduce it exactly, but we can add the `Group` and `Residual Sum Sq` values to get our Total row.

Keep in mind that this hypothesis was tested at the .05 level. The R output provides the exact probability of the outcome, .001. This is much more accurate than the *p* value and, in this case, we know exactly how unlikely as compared to > .05.

THE EFFECT SIZE FOR ONE-WAY ANOVA

In previous chapters, you saw how we used Cohen's *d* as a measure of effect size. You can also use Cohen's *d* for ANOVA, but it will need to be calculated for each pair of groups. Here, we change directions and use a value called eta squared or η^2. This effect size applies to all groups at once. As with Cohen's *d*, η^2 has a scale of how large the effect size is:

- A small effect size is about .01.
- A medium effect size is about .06.
- A large effect size is about .14.

Now to the actual effect size.

The formula for η^2 is as follows:

$$\eta^2 = \frac{SS_{\text{between}}}{SS_{\text{total}}} = \frac{SS_{\text{between}}}{SS_{\text{between}} + SS_{\text{residual}}}, \tag{15.5}$$

and you get that information right from the source table that R (or doing it by hand) generates. Granted, R doesn't give us the total sum of squares (SS_{total}), but we can easily add the between sum of squares (SS_{between}) and residual sum of squares (SS_{residual}) to get our total. Another tricky thing is that R does not name the SS_{between} by that name. Instead, it uses the name of the grouping variable.

In the example of the three groups we used earlier, the SS_{between} equals 1,133 and the SS_{residual} equals 1,738, giving you a SS_{total} equal to 2,871. The easy computation is

$$\eta^2 = \frac{1{,}133}{1{,}133 + 1{,}738} = \frac{1{,}133}{2{,}871} = .39,$$

and according to your small–medium–large guidelines for η^2, .39 is a large effect. The effect size is a terrific tool to aid in the evaluation of *F* ratios, as indeed it is with almost any test statistic.

BUT WHERE IS THE DIFFERENCE?

Okay, so you've run an ANOVA and you know that an overall difference exists among the means of three or four or more groups. But where does that difference lie?

You already know not to perform multiple *t* tests. You need to perform what are called **post hoc**, or after-the-fact, comparisons, and you need to decide if you are going to run this test if you determine following Figure 15.1 that the ANOVA is the correct test to use. You'll compare each mean with every other mean and see where the difference lies, but what's most important is that the Type I error for each comparison is controlled at the same level as you set by planning the post hoc analysis before you even run your ANOVA. There are a bunch of ways to do these comparisons, among them being the Tukey honestly significant difference (HSD) test (how is that for a name?). Tukey's HSD compares each pair in a single test, and the results should only be examined if the *F* test on your ANOVA was statistically significant.

Before running the post hoc test, let's look at the boxplot for these three groups' scores on language. Based on what you see in Figure 15.4, what do you think the results will be from the post hoc test that will compare all pairs of mean?

FIGURE 15.4 ● Boxplot of language scores by group.

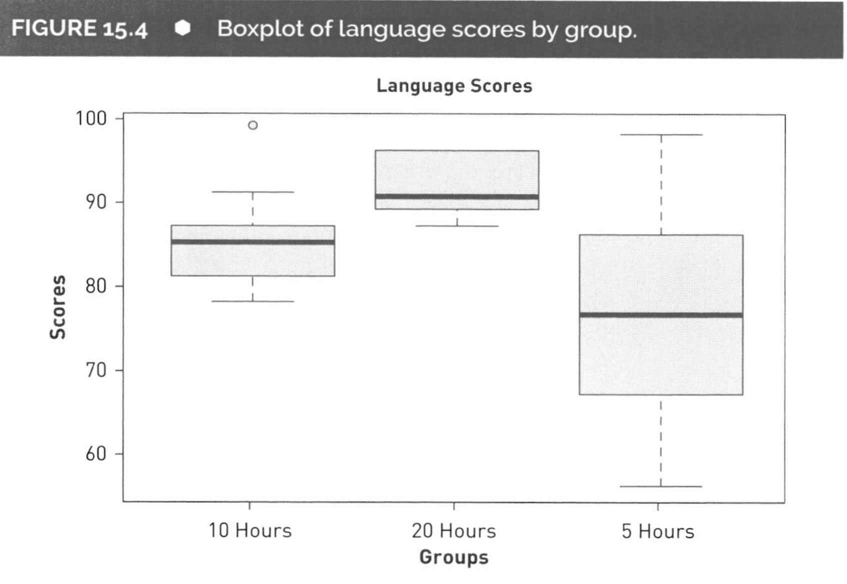

To complete this specific analysis using R, we use a function called `TukeyHSD`. The only thing the function needs is the output from running ANOVA. By default, the confidence level is 95%, which matches our *p* value of .05 for statistical significance.

```
> TukeyHSD(m1)
Tukey multiple comparisons of means
95% family-wise confidence level
Fit: aov(formula = Language.Score ~ Group, data = ch15ds1)
$`Group`
                      diff        lwr        upr     p adj
20 Hours-10 Hours      6.4  -2.497288 15.2972884 0.1941234
5 Hours-10 Hours      -8.6 -17.497288  0.2972884 0.0596448
5 Hours-20 Hours     -15.0 -23.897288 -6.1027116 0.0007780
>
```

What does this output tell us? We are first shown the name of the test, our confidence interval, and our original ANOVA command. We are then shown results about mean differences. The first row compares the 20-hours group to the 10-hours group. The difference between means for the two groups is 6.4, and the 95% confidence interval (CI) around the mean is [–2.50, 15.30] with p = .19. How do we interpret this result? For difference scores, we want to know if they are different from 0. The 95% CI contains 0, and that means the mean difference of 6.4 is not statistically different from 0. How would you report this result more formally? It would be something like this: There is no difference in language scores for children in preschool for 20 hours as compared to 10 hours, $\bar{X}_{20,10} = 6.4,\ 95\%\text{CI}\left[-2.50,\ 15.30\right], p = .19$.

Looking at the second row that compares the 5-hour group to the 10-hour group, we can draw the same conclusion that the groups are not different. But row 3 tells a different story. In this case, the difference between 5 and 20 hours is –15.0 points on average. The CI is [–23.90, –6.10] and does not contain 0. Note that p = .0007780, much smaller than .05. What can we conclude? There is a difference in language scores for children in preschool for 5 hours as compared to 20 hours, with students attending only 5 hours scoring 15.0 points less than their peers $\left(95\%\text{CI}\left[-23.90,-6.10\right],\ p<.001\right)$.

REAL-WORLD STATS

How interesting is it when researchers combine expertise from different disciplines to answer different questions? Just take a look at the journal in which this appeared: *Music and Medicine!* In this study, in which the authors examined anxiety among performing musicians, they tested five professional singers' and four flute players' arousal levels. In addition, they used a 5-point Likert-type scale to assess the subjects' nervousness. Every musician performed a relaxed and a strenuous piece with an audience (as if playing a concert) and without an audience (as though in rehearsal). Then the researchers used a one-way analysis of variance measuring heart rate (HR) and heart rate variability (HRV), which showed a significant difference across the four conditions (easy/rehearsal, strenuous/rehearsal, easy/concert, and strenuous/concert) within subjects. Moreover, there was no difference due to age, sex, or the instrument (song/flute) when those factors were examined.

Want to know more? Go online or to the library and find . . .

Harmat, L., & Theorell, T. (2010). Heart rate variability during singing and flute playing. *Music and Medicine, 2,* 10–17.

Summary

Analysis of variance (ANOVA) is the most complex of all the inferential tests you will learn in *Statistics for People Who (Think They) Hate Statistics Using R.* It takes a good deal of concentration to perform the manual calculations, and even when you use R, you have to be on your toes to understand that this is an overall test—one part will not give you information about differences between pairs of treatments. If you choose to go on and do post hoc analysis, you're only then completing all the tasks that go along with the powerful tool. We'll learn about just one more test between averages, and that's a factorial ANOVA. This, the holy grail of ANOVAs, can involve two or more factors, but we'll stick with two, and R will show us the way.

Time to Practice

1. When is analysis of variance a more appropriate statistical technique to use than a test between a pair of means?
2. If you are able to reject the null hypothesis based on the *F*, its *p* value, and your critical value, what do you know about the means of the different groups?
3. Using the following table, provide three examples of a simple one-way ANOVA, two examples of a two-factor ANOVA, and one example of a three-factor ANOVA. We show you some examples—you provide the others. Be sure to identify the grouping and the test variable as we have done here.

Design	Grouping Variable(s)	Test Variable
Simple ANOVA	Four levels of hours of training—2, 4, 6, and 8 hours	Typing accuracy
Enter your example here.	Enter your example here.	
Enter your example here.	Enter your example here.	
Enter your example here.	Enter your example here.	

(Continued)

(Continued)

4. Using the data in Chapter 15 Data Set 2 (ch15ds2.csv) and R, compute the *F* ratio for a comparison among the three levels representing the average amount of time that swimmers practice weekly (<15, 15–25, and >25 hours), with the outcome variable being their time for the 100-yard freestyle. Answer the question of whether practice time makes a difference. Don't forget to use the Options feature to get the means for the groups.
5. The data in Chapter 15 Data Set 3 (ch15ds3.csv) were collected by a researcher who wants to know whether the amount of stress is different for three groups of employees. Group 1 employees work the morning/day shift, Group 2 employees work the day/evening shift, and Group 3 employees work the night shift. The null hypothesis is that there is no difference in the amount of stress between groups. Test this in R and provide your conclusion.
6. The Noodle company wants to know what thickness of noodle consumers find most pleasing to their palate (on a scale of 1 to 5, with 1 being most pleasing), so the food manufacturer put it to the test. The data are found in Chapter 15 Data Set 4 (ch15ds4.csv). Turns out that there is a significant difference ($F_{(2, 57)} = 19.398$, $p < .001$), and thin noodles are most preferred. But what about differences among thin, medium, and thick noodles? Post hoc analysis to the rescue!
7. Why is it only appropriate to do a post hoc analysis if the *F* ratio is significant?

Student Study Site

Get the tools you need to sharpen your study skills! Visit **edge.sagepub.com/salkindshaw** to access practice quizzes and eFlashcards, watch R tutorial videos, and download data sets!

16

TWO TOO MANY FACTORS

Factorial Analysis of Variance—A Brief Introduction

Difficulty Scale ☺
(about as tough as it gets for the challenging ideas—but we're only touching on the main concepts here)

WHAT YOU WILL LEARN IN THIS CHAPTER

- Using analysis of variance with more than one factor
- Understanding main and interaction effects
- Using R to complete a factorial analysis of variance
- Computing the effect size for a factorial analysis of variance

INTRODUCTION TO FACTORIAL ANALYSIS OF VARIANCE

How people make decisions has fascinated psychologists for decades. The data resulting from their studies have been applied to such broad fields as advertising, business, planning, and even theology. Miltiades Proios and George Doganis investigated the effect of how the experience of being actively involved in the decision-making process (in a variety of settings) and age can have an impact on moral reasoning. The sample consisted of a total of 148 referees—56 who refereed soccer, 55 who refereed basketball, and 37 who refereed handball. Their ages ranged from 17 to 50 years, and gender was not considered an important variable. Within the entire sample, about 8% had not had any experience in social, political, or athletic settings where they fully participated in the decision-making process; about 53% were active but not fully participatory; and about 39% were active and did participate in the decisions made within that organization. A two-way analysis of variance showed an interaction between experience and age on moral reasoning and goal orientation of referees.

Why a two-way analysis of variance? Easy—there were two independent factors, with the first being level of experience and the second being age. This is a more complex type of ANOVA, referred to as a **factorial design**, which is used to explore more than one factor. Here, just as with any analysis of variance procedure, there are

1. a test of the main effect for age,
2. a test of the main effect for experience, and
3. a test for the interaction between experience and age (which turned out to be significant).

The very cool thing about analysis of variance when more than one factor or independent variable is tested is that the researcher can look not only at the individual effects of each factor but also at the simultaneous effects of both, through what is called an interaction. We will talk more about this later in the chapter.

Want to know more? Go online or to the library and find ...

Proios, M., & Doganis, G. (2003). Experiences from active membership and participation in decision-making processes and age in moral reasoning and goal orientation of referees. *Perceptual and Motor Skills, 96*(1), 113–126.

THE PATH TO WISDOM AND KNOWLEDGE

Here's how you can use the flowchart shown in Figure 16.1 to select ANOVA (but this time with more than one factor) as the appropriate test statistic. Follow along the highlighted sequence of steps.

1. We are testing for differences among scores of different groups, in this case, groups that differ on level of experience and age.
2. The participants are not being tested more than once.
3. We are dealing with more than two groups.
4. We are dealing with more than one factor or independent variable.
5. The appropriate test statistic is factorial analysis of variance.

As in Chapter 15, we have decided that ANOVA is the correct procedure (to examine differences among more than two groups or levels of the independent variable), but because we have more than one factor, factorial ANOVA is the right choice.

FIGURE 16.1 ● Determining that factorial analysis of variance is the correct test statistic.

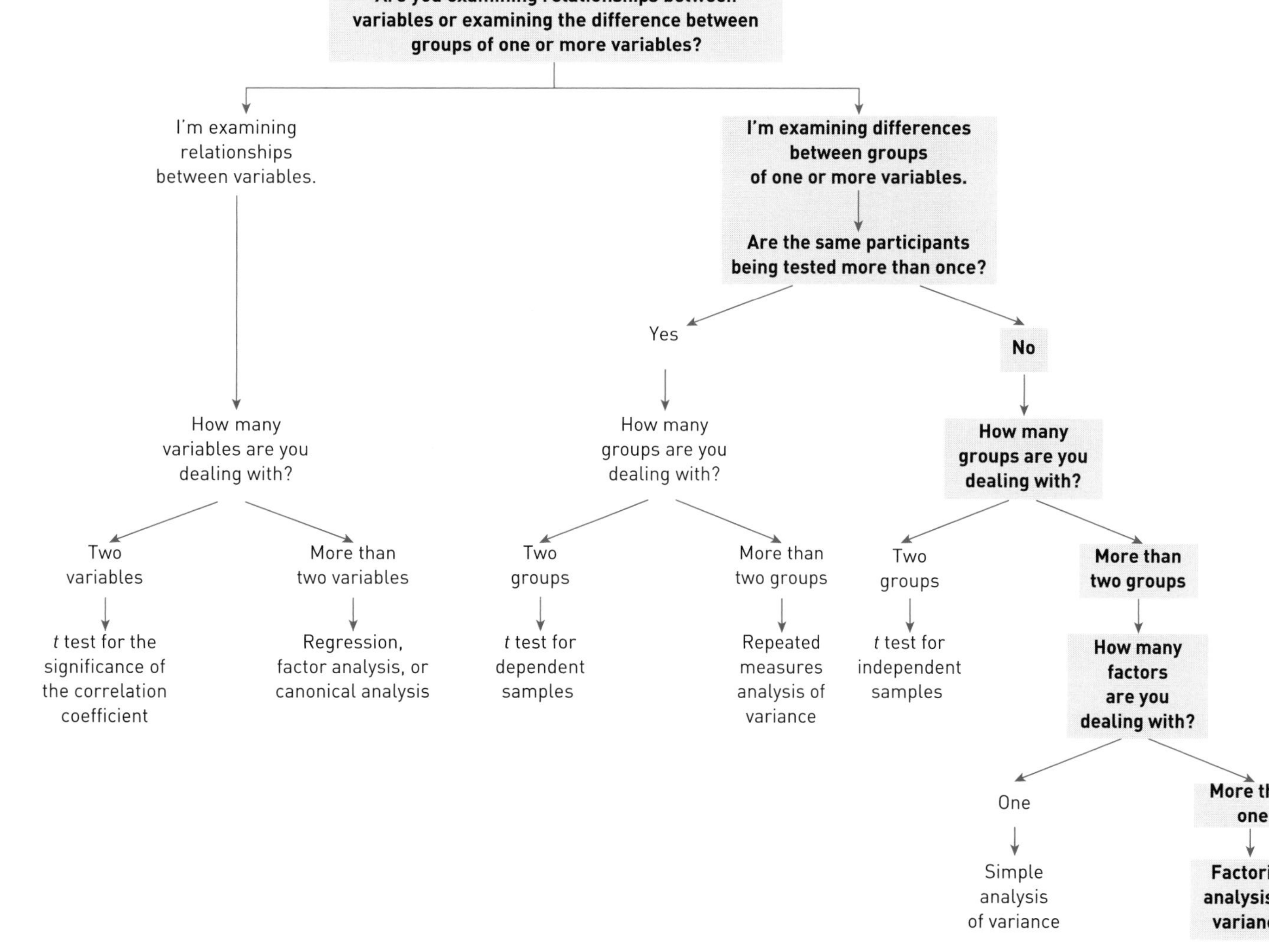

A NEW FLAVOR OF ANOVA

You already know that ANOVA comes in at least one flavor, the one-way analysis of variance we discussed in Chapter 15. With one-way analysis of variance, there is one factor or one treatment variable (such as group membership) being explored, and there are more than two groups or levels within this factor or treatment variable.

Now, we bump up the entire technique a notch so we can explore more than one factor simultaneously. This is called **factorial analysis of variance** or two-way ANOVA.

Let's look at a simple example that includes two factors, gender (male or female) and treatment (high-impact or low-impact exercise program), and the outcome (weight loss). Here's what the experimental design would look like:

		Exercise Program	
		High Impact	Low Impact
Gender	Male		
	Female		

Then, we will look at what main effects and an interaction between the factors look like. We don't see a lot of data analysis here until a bit later in the chapter—mostly now it's just look and learn. Even though the exact probabilities of the statistics are provided in the results (and we don't have to mess with statements like $p < .05$ and such), we'll use .05 as the criterion for rejection (or lack of acceptance) of the null.

There are three questions that you can ask and answer with this type of analysis:

1. Is there a difference between the effects on weight loss between two levels of exercise program, high impact and low impact?
2. Is there a difference between the effects on weight loss between two levels of gender, male and female?
3. Is the effect of being in the high- or low-impact program different for males or females?

Questions 1 and 2 deal with the presence of main effects, whereas Question 3 deals with the *interaction* between the two factors.

ALL OF THOSE EFFECTS

You might well remember that the primary task of analysis of variance is to test for the difference between two or more groups. The result associated with a single factor is referred to as the **main effect**. When we talk about the effects of both factors together, we talk about an **interaction effect**.

The Place to Start: Interaction Effects

In our example, there are 5 participants in each of the four groups, for a total of 20. And here's what the results of the analysis look like. This is a similar form of the source table we introduced in Chapter 15.

TABLE 16.1 • Tests of Between-Subjects Effects for the Dependent Variable Weight Loss.

Source	Type III Sum of Squares	*df*	Mean Square	*F*	Sig.
Intercept	86,329.8	1	86,329.8	19,845.93	**.000**
Treatment	1.8	1	1.8	0.42	**.529**
Gender	2,000.0	1	2,000.0	459.77	**.000**
Treatment × Gender	0.8	1	0.8	0.18	**.674**
Residuals	69.6	16	4.35		

Okay—let's start with the interaction, the effect of both treatment and gender (Treatment × Gender) on weight loss. The second from the last line in the table shows us that $F_{(1, 16)} = 0.18$, $p = .67$. So, treatment and gender do not interact, and we would fail to reject the null hypothesis; the groups are not different when both gender and treatment are taken into account. Now let's move on to the treatment and gender where they don't interact.

THE MAIN EVENT: MAIN EFFECTS IN FACTORIAL ANOVA

When an analysis of the data reveals a difference between the levels of any single factor, we talk about there being a main effect. In our example, there are 5 participants in each of the four groups, for a total of 20 people. And here's what the results of the analysis look like. This is a similar form of the source table we introduced in Chapter 15.

TABLE 16.2 • Tests of Between-Subjects Effects for Dependent Variable Weight Loss.

Source	Type III Sum of Squares	*df*	Mean Square	*F*	Sig.
Intercept	86,329.8	1	86,329.8	19,845.93	**.000**
Treatment	1.8	1	1.8	0.42	**.529**

(Continued)

TABLE 16.2 ● (Continued)

Source	Type III Sum of Squares	*df*	Mean Square	*F*	Sig.
Gender	2,000.0	1	2,000.0	459.77	**.000**
Treatment × Gender	0.8	1	0.8	0.18	**.674**
Residuals	69.6	16	4.35		

Pay attention to only the *Source* and the *Sig.* columns (which are bolded). The conclusion we can reach is that there is no interaction between the two main factors of treatment and gender, $F_{(1,\ 16)} = 0.8$, $p = .67$; there is a main effect for gender, $F_{(1,\ 16)} = 2{,}000.0$, $p < .001$; and there is no main effect for treatment, $F_{(1,\ 16)} = 1.8$, $p = .53$. So, as far as weight loss, there was no interaction between the treatment factor and gender. In other words, weight loss results did not differ on treatment based on gender. It didn't matter whether one was in the high- or low-impact group, but it did matter if one were male or female.

THE OTHER ROWS

The intercept refers to average weight loss before you add in the factors. The Residuals line refers to the within-subjects error variance, the part that makes up the denominator in the calculation of *F*. R will give you these two rows by default, but we are not going to interpret them.

PLOTTING THE MEANS BY GROUP

If you plotted the means of these values, you would get something that looks like Figure 16.2.

You can see a big difference in distance on the loss axis between males and females (average score is 75.7 for all males and 55.7 for all females), but for treatment (if you computed the averages), you would find there to be little difference (with the average score across all highs being 66.0 and across all lows being 65.4). Now, of course, this is an analysis of variance, and the variability in the groups does matter, but in this example, you can see the differences between groups (such as males and females) within each factor (such as gender) and how they are reflected by the results of the analysis. Another hint that Figure 16.2 provides is that the lines are parallel to each other, telling you that means change in the same way so there is no interaction.

Do you see what we did there? After checking for significance of the whole model, we look at the most complicated part first and simpler parts second. If the interaction is statistically significant, we cannot interpret the main effects because the interaction is clouding the picture. But, if the interaction is not statistically significant, we can interpret the main effects without a problem, which is what we did in this example.

FIGURE 16.2 ● Mean scores across treatments for males and females.

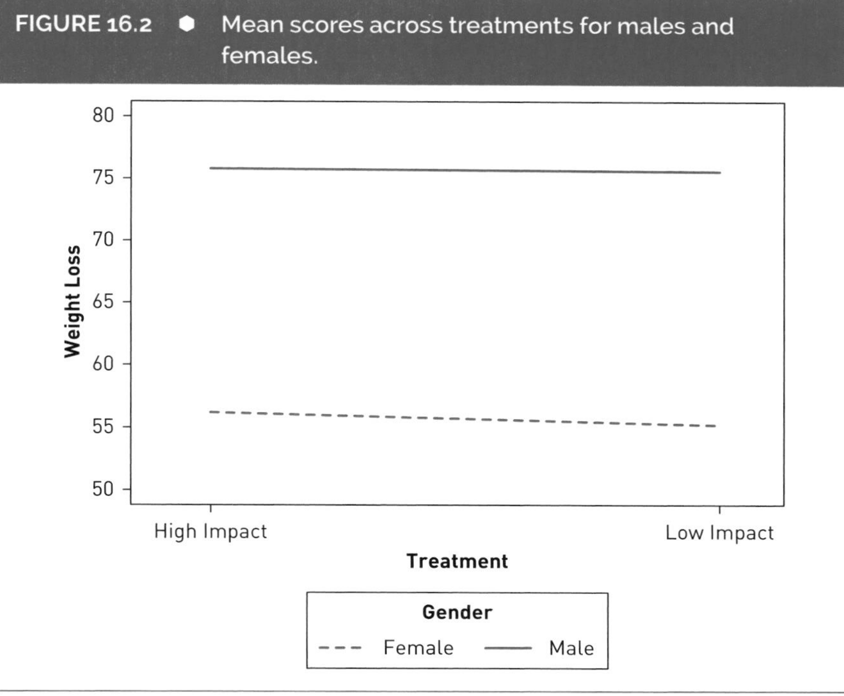

EVEN MORE INTERESTING INTERACTION EFFECTS

The results in the following table are for another study that looked at the effects of treatment and gender on weight loss. In this case, we had 10 people in each group with four groups for a total of 40 participants. Like the previous example, we also tested the interaction between treatment and gender. Here, there is an effect for the treatment-by-gender interaction, $F_{(1, 36)} = 1{,}050.63$, $p = .004$, which makes this a very interesting outcome. In effect, it does matter a whole lot if you are in both conditions simultaneously such that the treatment does have a different impact on the weight loss of males than it does on females.

TABLE 16.3 ● Tests of Between-Subjects Effects for Dependent Variable Weight Loss.

Source	Sum of Squares	*df*	Mean Square	*F*	Sig.
Intercept	218,892.025	1	218,892.025	2,017.39	**.000**
Treatment	265.225	1	265.225	2.44	**.127**
Gender	207.025	1	207.025	1.91	**.175**
Treatment × Gender	1,050.625	1	1,050.625	9.68	**.004**
Residuals	3,906.100	36	108.503		

Figure 16.3 shows what a chart of the averages for each of the four groups looks like. Unlike Figure 16.2, these lines are definitely not parallel.

FIGURE 16.3 ● Averages across treatments for males and females.

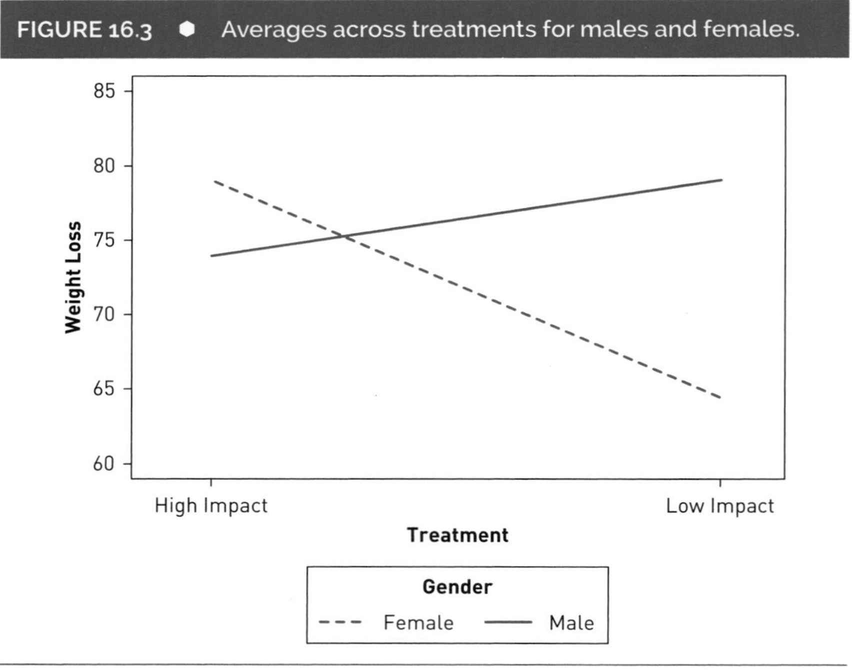

And here's what the actual means themselves look like:

	Male	Female
High impact	73.70	79.40
Low impact	78.80	64.00

What to make of this? Well, the interpretation here is pretty straightforward. Here's what we can say, and, being as smart as you are, you can recognize that these are the answers to the three questions we listed earlier:

1. There is a clear interaction between treatment and gender, which means females lose more weight than males under the high-impact treatment condition and males lose more weight than females under the low-impact condition.
2. We cannot interpret the results for the main effect of treatment.
3. We cannot interpret the results for the main effect of gender.

Indeed, one of the easiest ways to see the magnitude of an interaction (or the absence of one) is to plot the means as we did in Figure 16.3. The lines may not always cross as dramatically, and the appearance of the graph also depends on what variable the *x*-axis explores, but charting the means is often the only way to get a sense of what's going on as far as main effects and interactions.

This is all pretty remarkable stuff. If you didn't know any better (and had never read this chapter), you would think that all you have to do is a simple *t* test between the averages for males and females and then another simple *t* test for the averages between those who participated in the high-impact treatment and those who participated in the low-impact treatment—and you would have found nothing. But, using the idea of an interaction between main factors, you find out that there is a differential effect—an outcome that would have gone unnoticed otherwise. Indeed, if you can bear the cost of admission, interactions really are the most interesting outcomes in any factorial analysis of variance.

ASSUMPTIONS ABOUT VARIANCES

Back in Chapter 13 when we were looking at the *t* test results, we needed to find out if the variances were equal across the two groups. If the variances were not equal, we changed the syntax in R to ask for *Welch's t* instead. Like the *t* test, the ANOVA also assumes that the variances are equal across all groups. Luckily for us, we can use Levene's test like we did in the *t* test scenario to evaluate this for us. In the R steps below, we will check this assumption.

USING R TO COMPUTE THE *F* RATIO

Visit **edge.sagepub.com/salkindshaw** to watch an R tutorial video on this topic.

Here's a change for you. Throughout *Statistics for People Who (Think They) Hate Statistics Using R,* we have provided you with examples of how to perform particular techniques the old-fashioned way (by hand, using a calculator) as well as by using a statistical analysis package such as R. With the introduction of factorial ANOVA, we are illustrating the analysis using only R. It is not any more of an intellectual challenge to complete a factorial ANOVA using a calculator, but it certainly is more laborious. For that reason, we are not going to cover the computation by hand but go right to the computation of the important values and spend more time on the interpretation.

We'll use the data that show there is a significant interaction, as seen here, also found in Chapter 16 Data Set 1 (ch16ds1.csv).

Treatment →	High Impact	High Impact	Low Impact	Low Impact
Gender →	**Male**	**Female**	**Male**	**Female**
	76	65	88	65
	78	90	76	67
	76	65	76	67
	76	90	76	87

(Continued)

(Continued)

Treatment →	High Impact	High Impact	Low Impact	Low Impact
Gender →	Male	Female	Male	Female
	76	65	56	78
	74	90	76	56
	74	90	76	54
	76	79	98	56
	76	70	88	54
	55	90	78	56

Here are the steps and the computation of the *F* test statistic. The reason you don't see the "famous eight steps" (so okay, there are 10) is that this is the first (and only) time throughout the book that we don't do the computations by hand but use only the computer. The analysis (as we said before) is just too labor intensive for a course at this level.

1. State the null and research hypotheses.

   There are actually three null hypotheses shown here (Formulas 16.1a, 16.1b, and 16.1c) that state that there is no difference between the means for the two factors and that there is no interaction. Here we go.

   First for the treatment:

$$H_0 : \mu_{\text{high}} = \mu_{\text{low}}. \tag{16.1a}$$

   And now for gender:

$$H_0 : \mu_{\text{male}} = \mu_{\text{female}}. \tag{16.1b}$$

   And now for the interaction between treatment and gender:

$$H_0 : \mu_{\text{high.male}} = \mu_{\text{high.female}} = \mu_{\text{low.male}} = \mu_{\text{low.female}}. \tag{16.1c}$$

   The research hypotheses, shown in Formulas 16.2a and 16.2b, state that there is a difference between the means of the groups and that there is an interaction. Here they are.

   First for the treatment:

$$H_1 : \bar{X}_{\text{high}} \neq \bar{X}_{\text{low}}. \tag{16.2a}$$

   And now for gender:

$$H_1 : \bar{X}_{\text{male}} \neq \bar{X}_{\text{female}}. \tag{16.2b}$$

And now for the interaction between treatment and gender, we need to state it in a sentence because a simple formula just doesn't work: Not all four groups, created by crossing treatment and gender, have equal means.

2. Set the level of risk (or the level of significance or Type I error) associated with the null hypothesis.

   The level of risk or Type I error or level of significance is .05 here. Once again, the R analysis will provide the exact *p* value, but the level of significance used is totally at the discretion of the researcher.

3. Select the appropriate test statistic.

   Using the flowchart shown in Figure 16.1, we determined that the appropriate test is a factorial ANOVA.

4. Compute the test statistic value (called the obtained value).

   We'll use R for this, and here are the steps. We'll use the above data, which are available on the website for the book and listed in Appendix C. `Read` the data into R and `View` the file. Be sure that there is a column for each factor, including treatment, gender, and loss.

```
> ch16ds1 <- read.csv(file.choose())
> View(ch16ds1)
>
```

Let's double-check the means for each of the four groups: Female in High Impact, Female in Low Impact, Male in High Impact, and Male in Low Impact. We should get the same numbers as found in Table 16.3. For this we will use a handy function in the `psych` package called `describeBy()`.

```
> library(psych)
> describeBy(ch16ds1$Loss, group = list(ch16ds1$Treatment,
ch16ds1$Gender))
Descriptive statistics by group
: High Impact
: Female
 vars  n mean    sd median trimmed  mad min max range skew kurtosis   se
X1   1 10 79.4 11.89   84.5   79.88 8.15  65  90    25-0.23       -2 3.76
-----------------------------------------------------------------------
: Low Impact
: Female
vars  n mean    sd median trimmed  mad min  max range skew kurtosis   se
X1 1 10   64 11.23   60.5   62.38 9.64  54   87    33 0.81     -0.8 3.55
-----------------------------------------------------------------------
```

(Continued)

(Continued)

```
: High Impact
: Male
vars  n mean   sd median trimmed mad min max range skew kurtosis   se
X1 1 10 73.7 6.67     76    75.5   0  55  78    23-2.15     3.21 2.11
--------------------------------------------------------------------
: Low Impact
: Male
vars  n mean    sd median trimmed  mad min max range  skew kurtosis  se
X1 1 10 78.8 11.04     76    79.25 1.48  56  98    42 -0.25    -0.17 .49
>
```

We can see in this output that we have 10 people in each group, and the means are what we expect.

5. Use the `aov` function to calculate the source table and *F*. But before we do that, we want to tell R to change the way it is comparing the groups. There are easily half a dozen ways in which we can mathematically compare our groups. We are going to use Helmert contrast, and we only need to set it once for all ANOVAs we run during a single R session.

```
> options(contrasts = c("contr.helmert", "contr.poly"))
> options("contrasts")
$`contrasts`
[1] "contr.helmert" "contr.poly"
>
```

After we told R we wanted to use a Helmert `contrast` (`"contr.helmert"`) for categorical variables and polynomial contrasts for ordered variables (`"contr.poly"`), we can now run our ANOVA.

```
> m1 <- aov(Loss ~ Treatment + Gender +
Treatment*Gender, data = ch16ds1)
>
```

This function should look familiar. The only thing we added was another factor. Let's break it down, piece by piece:

- `m1`: the name of the R object that is storing our results
- `<-`: the characters that assign our results to `m1`

- `aov`: the function to run ANOVA
- `Loss`: our dependent variable
- ~: in shorthand, it means explained by or equal to.
- `Treatment + Gender + Treatment*Gender`: we are telling `aov` that the independent variables are Treatment, Gender, and the interaction between Treatment and Gender that we get by multiplying (*) Treatment by Gender.
- `data = ch16ds1`: use this data object.

6. Use the function `Anova()` to get Type III errors.

```
> Anova(m1, type = "III")
Anova Table (Type III tests)
Response: Loss
                 Sum Sq Df   F value      Pr(>F)
(Intercept)      218892  1 2017.3864   < 2.2e-16 ***
Treatment           265  1    2.4444    0.126693
Gender              207  1    1.9080    0.175698
Treatment:Gender   1051  1    9.6829    0.003631 **
Residuals          3906 36
---
Signif. codes: 0 '***' 0.001 '**' 0.01 '*' 0.05 '.' 0.1 ' ' 1
>
```

Now, this looks similar to the source tables we have looked at in this chapter. `Treatment:Gender` is our interaction effect and typically seen in research articles as Treatment × Gender. Recall that the Residuals row is the within-group variance. What R does not provide is the Mean Square column. The Mean Square column is easy to calculate: Sum Sq/Df.

Looking at the results, we start with the interaction of Treatment and Gender. Based on $F_{(1, 36)} = 1{,}051$, $p = .004$, we know that Treatment together with Gender matter in our sample. But can we trust our results?

7. To determine whether we can trust our results based on *F*, we need to check the assumption of equal variances across groups. The null hypothesis is that all group means are equal, and we hope to fail to reject the null. We will use .05 as our significance level.

```
> leveneTest(Loss ~ Treatment*Gender, data = ch16ds1)
Levene's Test for Homogeneity of Variance (center = median)
```

(Continued)

(Continued)

```
      Df F value Pr(>F)
group 3  2.0855 0.1193
36
>
```

Based on $F_{(3, 36)} = 2.09$, $p = .12$, which has a probability > .05, we will fail to reject the null and we can trust the results because we have met the assumption of equal variance.

8. Create an interaction plot for all four groups. For this first example of an interaction plot, we are using as many of the default options as possible. So, we just need to tell the function what variable to use for the *x*-axis (`x.factor`), what variable to use for the *y*-axis (`response`), and what variable to use for each line (`trace.factor`) along with what type of number we are plotting. By default, `interaction.plot` will plot the means of each group:

```
> interaction.plot(x.factor = ch16ds1$Treatment,
+                  trace.factor = ch16ds1$Gender,
+                  response = ch16ds1$Loss)
>
```

This syntax results in the plot you see in Figure 16.4.

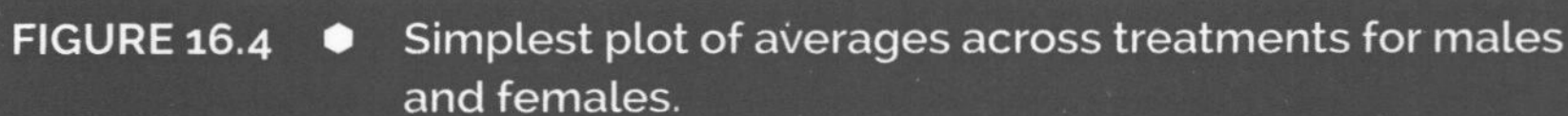

FIGURE 16.4 ● Simplest plot of averages across treatments for males and females.

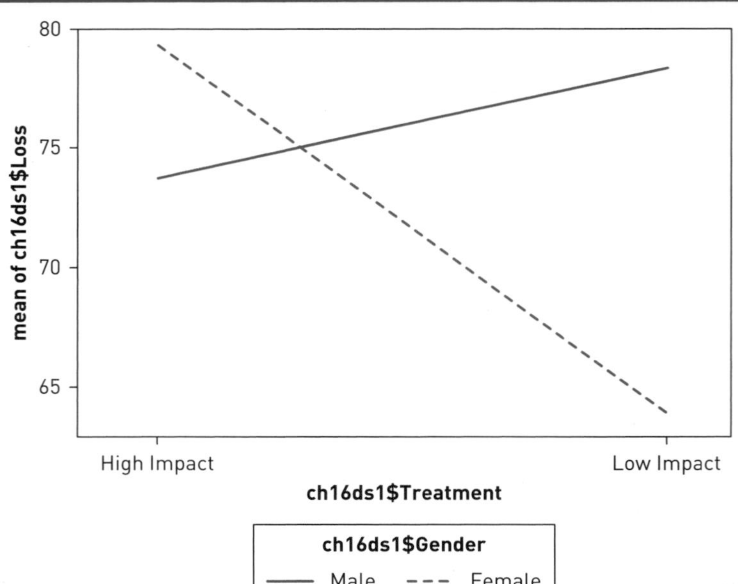

With a little bit of effort, we can produce a better-looking plot. Here is the syntax:

```
> interaction.plot(x.factor = ch16ds1$Treatment,
+                  trace.factor = ch16ds1$Gender,
+                  response = ch16ds1$Loss,
+                  fixed = TRUE,
+                  leg.bty = "b",
+                  xlab = "Treatment",
+                  ylab = "Weight Loss",
+                  trace.label = "Gender",
+                  ylim = c(60, 85))
>
```

Here is what each additional option allowed us to change in our plot, giving us a plot like Figure 16.3:

- `fixed = TRUE`: list the factors for gender in alphabetical order. In the first plot, Male was listed first because it had the highest value under "Low Impact."
- `leg.bty = "b"`: add a box around the legend
- `xlab = "Treatment"`: the label for the *x*-axis
- `ylab = "Weight Loss"`: the label for the *y*-axis
- `trace.label = "Gender"`: the label for the legend
- `ylim = c(60, 85))`: the range for the *y*-axis, from 60 to 85. In Figure 16.4, the range was just big enough to include all four means. In this example, we added extra space below the smallest mean of 64 and extra space above the largest mean of 79.4.

We're done, and we have a picture to show us what is happening with our interaction plot!

9. Finally, use the `TukeyHSD` function to compare groups. Because we now have a factorial ANOVA with two factors and interaction, `TukeyHSD` output has gotten a lot bigger.

```
> TukeyHSD(m1)
Tukey multiple comparisons of means
95% family-wise confidence level
Fit: aov(formula = Loss ~ Treatment + Gender + Treatment * Gender,
data = ch16ds1)
```

(Continued)

(Continued)

```
$`Treatment`
                          diff       lwr      upr     p adj
Low Impact-High Impact -5.15 -11.83049 1.530493 0.1266935
$Gender
             diff       lwr      upr     p adj
Male-Female 4.55 -2.130493 11.23049 0.1756979
$`Treatment:Gender`
                                       diff       lwr       upr     p adj
Low Impact:Female-High Impact:Female -15.4 -27.94609 -2.85391 0.0110583
High Impact:Male-High Impact:Female   -5.7 -18.24609  6.84609 0.6162344
Low Impact:Male-High Impact:Female    -0.6 -13.14609 11.94609 0.9992219
High Impact:Male-Low Impact:Female     9.7  -2.84609 22.24609 0.1782508
Low Impact:Male-Low Impact:Female     14.8   2.25391 27.34609 0.0154282
Low Impact:Male-High Impact:Male       5.1  -7.44609 17.64609 0.6949307
>
```

The function first gives us the group comparisons for the main effects, but we are really interested in the interaction, because that was the hypothesis we were able to reject. The one with the interaction. With four groups, we get six comparisons. If the difference is positive, then the first group that is listed had a higher mean; if the difference is negative, then the second group had a higher mean. Focusing our attention on the `p adj` column, we see that the first comparison between low-impact and high-impact females has a difference of –15.4 (95% CI [–27.95, –2.85]), and the probability that the means are the same is .01. So for females, the type of exercise matters. The only other row with probability < .05 is the second to last row. In that case, males in the low-impact group differed from females in the low-impact group with a difference of 14.8 (95% CI [2.25, 27.35], $p = .02$).

COMPUTING THE EFFECT SIZE FOR FACTORIAL ANOVA

A different formula is used to compute the effect size for a factorial ANOVA, but the idea is the same. We are still making a judgment about the magnitude of a difference that we observe.

For a factorial ANOVA, the statistic is called omega squared, represented by ω^2, and here's the formula:

$$\omega^2 = \frac{SS_{\text{between groups}} - \left(df_{\text{between groups}}\right)\left(MS_{\text{within groups}}\right)}{MS_{\text{within groups}} + SS_{\text{total}}},$$

where

- ω^2 is the value of the effect size,
- $SS_{between}$ is the sum of squares between factors,
- $df_{between}$ is the total degrees of freedom,
- MS_{within} is the mean sum of squares within treatments (SS_{within}/df_{within}), and
- SS_{total} is the total sum of squares ($SS_{between} + SS_{within}$).

Don't be thrown by this formula; the terms are ones that you have seen in Chapter 15, and the interpretation of the final ω^2 value is the same as the interpretation of the other effect sizes we discussed earlier as well. What may not be completely obvious is how to get *SS*.

For the effect size for the factor named Gender in the example in Table 16.1, we then have the following formula:

$$\omega^2 = \frac{2{,}000 - (1)(4.35)}{4.35 + (2{,}000 + 69.6)} = 0.96$$

with an effect size of .96 for gender. According to our guidelines, this effect size of .96, reflecting the strength of the association, is large.

REAL-WORLD STATS

You've seen the news: Certain disorders primarily occurring in childhood, such as autism spectrum disorders and attention-deficit/hyperactivity disorder (ADHD), have been increasing in frequency. This may be because of changing diagnostic criteria, or it may reflect an actual increase in their occurrence. In any case, certain behaviors and outcomes need to be accurately measured as a first step in considering such diagnoses. That's what this study is all about. Measures of behavioral inhibition were used to investigate the factorial validity, ecological validity, and reliability of five performance-based measures of behavioral inhibition in a sample of seventy 3-, 4-, and 5-year-old children. A 2 × 3 factorial analysis of variance using sex and age group (two factors) as independent variables showed significant main effects for sex and age and a nonsignificant interaction. Some of the measures correlated with teacher rating, and some did not, leading the researchers to conclude that some of the measures of behavioral inhibition might be useful, but others need further exploration.

Want to know more? Go online or to the library and find …

Floyd, R. G., & Kirby, E. A. (2001). Psychometric properties of measures of behavioral inhibition with preschool-age children: Implications for assessment of children at risk for ADHD. *Journal of Attention Disorders, 5,* 79–91.

Summary

Now that we are done, done, done with testing differences between means, we'll move on to examining the significance of correlations, or the relationship between two variables.

Time to Practice

1. When would you use a factorial ANOVA rather than a simple ANOVA to test the significance of the difference between the average of two or more groups?
2. Create a drawing or plan for a 2 × 3 experimental design that would lend itself to a factorial ANOVA. Be sure to identify the independent and dependent variables.
3. Using the data in Chapter 16 Data Set 2 (ch16ds2.csv) and R, complete the analysis and interpret the results for level of severity and type of treatment for pain relief. It is a 2 × 3 experiment, like the kind you created in the answer to Question 2. Hint: don't forget to set your contrasts to Helmert like in the example on page 318!
4. Use the data from Chapter 16 Data Set 3 (ch16ds3.csv) and answer the following questions about an analysis of whether level of stress and gender have an impact on caffeine consumption (measured as cups of coffee per day).
    a. Is there a difference among the levels of caffeine consumption for the high-stress, low-stress, and no-stress groups?
    b. Is there a difference between males and females, regardless of stress group?
    c. Are there any interactions?
5. This is the extra-credit question: For the data set named Chapter 16 Data Set 4 (ch16ds4.csv), are girls better (as evaluated by a test of skill ranging from 1 to 10, with 10 being best) than boys and, if so, under what conditions?

Student Study Site

Get the tools you need to sharpen your study skills! Visit **edge.sagepub.com/salkindshaw** to access practice quizzes and eFlashcards, watch R tutorial videos, and download data sets!

TESTING RELATIONSHIPS USING THE CORRELATION COEFFICIENT

Cousins or Just Good Friends?

Difficulty Scale ☺ ☺ ☺ ☺
(easy—you don't even have to figure anything out!)

WHAT YOU WILL LEARN IN THIS CHAPTER

- Testing the significance of the correlation coefficient
- Interpreting the correlation coefficient
- Distinguishing between significance and meaningfulness (again!)
- Using R to analyze correlational data and how to understand the results of the analysis

INTRODUCTION TO TESTING THE CORRELATION COEFFICIENT

In his research article on the relationship between the quality of a marriage and the quality of the relationship between the parent and the child, Daniel Shek told us that there are at least two possibilities. First, a poor marriage might enhance parent–child relationships. This is because parents who are dissatisfied with their marriage might substitute their relationship with their children for the emotional gratification lacking in their marriage. Or, according to the spillover hypothesis, a poor marriage might damage the parent–child relationship by setting the stage for increased difficulty in parenting children.

Shek examined the link between marital quality and parent–child relationships in 378 Chinese married couples over a 2-year period. He found that higher levels of marital quality were related to higher levels of quality of parent–child relationships; this was found for concurrent measures (at the present time) as well as longitudinal measures (over time). He also found that the strength of the relationship between parents and children was the same for both mothers and fathers. This is an obvious example of how the use of the correlation coefficient gives us the information we need about whether sets of variables are related to one another. Shek computed a whole bunch of different correlations across mothers and fathers as well at Time 1 and Time 2, but all with the same purpose: to see if there was a significant correlation between the variables. Remember that this does not say anything about the causal nature of the relationship, only that the variables are associated with one another.

Want to know more? Go online or to the library and find . . .

Shek, D. T. L. (1998). Linkage between marital quality and parent–child relationship: A longitudinal study in the Chinese culture. *Journal of Family Issues, 19,* 687–704.

THE PATH TO WISDOM AND KNOWLEDGE

Here's how you can use the flowchart to select the appropriate test statistic, the test for the correlation coefficient. Follow along the highlighted sequence of steps in Figure 17.1.

1. The relationship between variables, and not the difference between groups, is being examined.
2. Only two variables are being used.
3. The appropriate test statistic to use is the *t* test for the correlation coefficient.

COMPUTING THE TEST STATISTIC

Here's something you'll probably be pleased to read: The correlation coefficient can act as its own test statistic. This makes things much easier because you don't have to compute any test statistics, and examining the significance is very easy indeed.

Let's use, as an example, the following data that examine the relationship between two variables, the quality of marriage and the quality of parent–child relationships. These hypothetical (made-up) scores can range from 0 to 100, and the higher the score, the happier the marriage and the better the parenting.

Quality of Marriage	Quality of the Parent–Child Relationship
76	43
81	33
78	23
76	34
76	31
78	51
76	56
78	43
98	44
88	45
76	32
66	33
44	28
67	39
65	31
59	38
87	21
77	27
79	43
85	46
68	41
76	41
77	48
98	56
98	56
99	55
98	45
87	68
67	54
78	33

You can use Formula 7.1 from Chapter 7, which we are repeating just below this paragraph, to compute the Pearson correlation coefficient. When you do, you will find that r = .437. Now let's go through the steps of actually testing the value for significance and deciding what the value means.

$$r_{xy} = \frac{n\sum XY - \sum X \sum Y}{\sqrt{\left[n\sum X^2 - \left(\sum X\right)^2\right]\left[n\sum Y^2 - \left(\sum Y\right)^2\right]}}. \tag{7.1}$$

If you need a quick review of the basics of correlations, take a look back at Chapter 7.

Here are the famous eight steps and the computation of the t test statistic.

1. State the null and research hypotheses.

The null hypothesis states that there is no relationship between the quality of the marriage and the quality of the relationship between parents and children. The research hypothesis is a two-tailed, nondirectional research hypothesis because it posits that a relationship exists between the two variables but not the direction of that relationship. Remember that correlations can be positive (or direct) or negative (or indirect), and the most important characteristic of a correlation coefficient is its absolute value or size and not its sign (positive or negative).

The null hypothesis is shown in Formula 17.1:

$$H_0 : \rho_{xy} = 0. \tag{17.1}$$

The Greek letter ρ, or rho, represents the population estimate of the correlation coefficient.

The research hypothesis (shown in Formula 17.2) states that there is a relationship between the two values and that the relationship differs from a value of zero:

$$H_1 : r_{xy} \neq 0. \tag{17.2}$$

2. Set the level of risk (or the level of significance or Type I error) associated with the null hypothesis.

The level of risk or Type I error or level of significance is .05.

3. and 4. Select the appropriate test statistic.

Using the flowchart shown in Figure 17.1, we determined that the appropriate test is for the correlation coefficient. In this instance, we do not need to compute a test statistic because the sample r value (r_{xy} = .437) is, for our purposes, the test statistic.

FIGURE 17.1 ● Determining that a *t* test for the correlation coefficient is the correct test statistic.

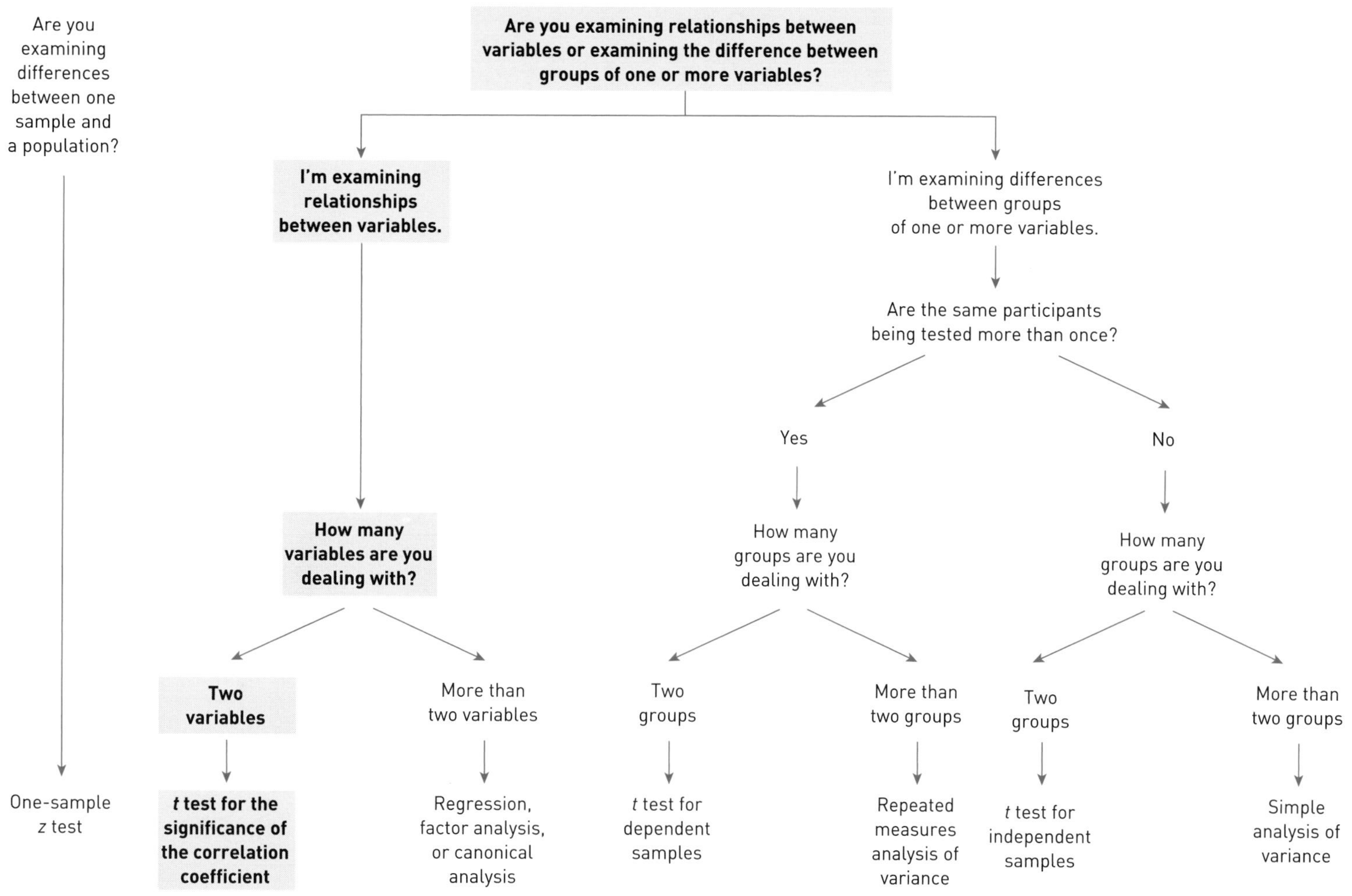

Are you examining differences between one sample and a population?

→ One-sample *z* test

Are you examining relationships between variables or examining the difference between groups of one or more variables?

- **I'm examining relationships between variables.**
  - **How many variables are you dealing with?**
    - **Two variables** → ***t* test for the significance of the correlation coefficient**
    - More than two variables → Regression, factor analysis, or canonical analysis
- I'm examining differences between groups of one or more variables.
  - Are the same participants being tested more than once?
    - Yes → How many groups are you dealing with?
      - Two groups → *t* test for dependent samples
      - More than two groups → Repeated measures analysis of variance
    - No → How many groups are you dealing with?
      - Two groups → *t* test for independent samples
      - More than two groups → Simple analysis of variance

5. Determine the value needed for rejection of the null hypothesis using the appropriate table of critical values for the particular statistic.

   Table B.4 lists the critical values for the correlation coefficient.

   Our first task is to determine the degrees of freedom (*df*), which approximates the sample size. For this particular test statistic, the degrees of freedom is $n - 2$, or $30 - 2 = 28$, where n is equal to the number of pairs used to compute the correlation coefficient. This is the degrees of freedom only for this test statistic and not necessarily for any other.

   Using this number (28), the level of risk you are willing to take (.05), and a two-tailed test (because there is no direction to the research hypothesis), the critical value is .381 (using $df = 25$ because that's more conservative than using 30). So, at the .05 level, with 28 degrees of freedom for a two-tailed test, the value needed for rejection of the null hypothesis is .381.

6. Compare the obtained value and the critical value.

   The obtained value is .437, and the critical value for rejection of the null hypothesis that the two variables are not related is .381.

7. and 8. Make a decision.

   Now comes our decision. If the obtained value (or the value of the test statistic) is more extreme than the critical value (or the tabled value), the null hypothesis can be rejected. If the obtained value does not exceed the critical value, the null hypothesis is the most attractive explanation and we fail to reject it.

   In this case, the obtained value (.437) does exceed the critical value (.381)—it is extreme enough for us to say that the relationship between the two variables (quality of marriage and quality of parent–child relationships) did occur due to something other than chance. So, we reject the null hypothesis that the correlation in the population equals 0.

One tail or two? It's pretty easy to conceptualize what a one-tailed versus a two-tailed test is when it comes to differences between means. And it may even be easy for you to understand a two-tailed test of the correlation coefficient (where any difference from zero is what's tested). But what about a one-tailed test? It's really just as easy. A directional test of the research hypothesis that there is a relationship posits that relationship as being either direct (positive) or indirect (negative). So, for example, if you think that there is a positive correlation between two variables, then the test is one-tailed. Similarly, if you hypothesize that there is a negative correlation between two variables, the test is one-tailed as well. It's only when you don't predict the direction of the relationship that the test is two-tailed. Got it?

Okay, we cheated a little. Actually, you can compute a t value (just like for the test for the difference between means) for the significance of the correlation coefficient. The formula is not any more difficult than any other you have dealt with up to now, but you won't see it here. The point is that some smart statisticians have computed the critical *r* value for different sample sizes (and, likewise, degrees of freedom) for one- and two-tailed tests at different levels of risk (.01, .05), as you see in Table B.4. But if you are reading along in an academic journal and see that a correlation was tested using a *t* value, you'll now know why.

So How Do I Interpret $r_{(28)} = .437, p < .05$?

- *r* represents the test statistic that was used.
- 28 is the number of degrees of freedom.
- .437 is the obtained value using the formula we showed you in Chapter 7.
- $p < .05$ (the really important part of this little phrase) indicates that the probability is less than 5% on any one test of the null hypothesis that the relationship between the two variables is due to chance alone. Because we defined .05 as our criterion for the research hypothesis to be more attractive than the null hypothesis, our conclusion is that a significant relationship exists between the two variables. This means that as the level of marital quality increases, so does the level of quality of the parent–child relationship. Similarly, as the level of marital quality decreases, so does the level of quality of the parent–child relationship.

CAUSES AND ASSOCIATIONS (AGAIN!)

You're probably thinking that you've heard enough of this already, but this is so important that we really can't emphasize it enough. So, we'll emphasize it again. Just because two variables are related to one another (as in the previous example), that has no bearing on whether one causes the other. In other words, having a terrific marriage of the highest quality in no way ensures that the parent–child relationship will be of a high quality as well. These two variables may be correlated because some of the same traits that might make a person a good spouse also make that person a good parent (patience, understanding, willingness to sacrifice), but it's certainly possible to see how someone could be a good husband or wife and have a terrible relationship with his or her children.

Remember the crimes and ice cream example from Chapter 7? It's the same here. Just because things are related and share something in common with one another has no bearing on whether there is a causal relationship between the two.

Correlation coefficients are used for lots of different purposes, and you're likely to read journal articles in which they've been used to estimate the reliability of a test. But you already know all this because you read Chapter 8 and mastered it! In Chapter 8, you may remember that we talked about such reliability coefficients as test–retest (the correlation of scores at two points in time), parallel forms (the correlation between scores on different forms), and internal consistency (the intercorrelation between items). Correlation coefficients also are the standard units used in more advanced statistical techniques, such as those we discuss in Chapter 20.

Significance Versus Meaningfulness (Again, Again!)

In Chapter 7, we reviewed the importance of the use of the coefficient of determination for understanding the meaningfulness of the correlation coefficient. You may remember that you square the correlation coefficient to determine the amount of variance in one variable that is accounted for by another variable. In Chapter 11, we also went over the general issue of significance versus meaningfulness.

But we should mention and discuss this topic again. Even if a correlation coefficient is significant (as was the case in the example in this chapter), it does not mean that the amount of variance accounted for is meaningful. For example, in this case, the coefficient of determination for a simple Pearson correlation value of .437 is equal to .190, indicating that 19% of the variance is accounted for and a whopping 81% of the variance is not. This leaves lots of room for doubt, doesn't it?

So, even though we know that there is a positive relationship between the quality of a marriage and the quality of a parent–child relationship and they tend to "go together," the relatively small correlation of .437 indicates that lots of other things are going on in that relationship that may be important as well. So, if ever you wanted to apply a popular saying to statistics, here goes: "What you see is not always what you get."

Visit **edge.sagepub.com/salkindshaw** to watch an R tutorial video on this topic.

USING R TO COMPUTE A CORRELATION COEFFICIENT (AGAIN)

Here, we are using Chapter 17 Data Set 1 (ch17ds1.csv), which has two measures of quality—one of marriage (time spent together in one of three categories, with the value of 1 indicating a lower quality of marriage than a value of 10) and one of parent–child relationships (strength of affection, with the higher score being more affectionate).

In Chapter 7, we used R to calculate the correlation using the function `cor()`. Let's try that again:

```
> cor(ch17ds1$Qual.Marriage, ch17ds1$Qual.PC)
[1] -0.09996305
>
```

And while we are asking for the correlation, let's look at a scatterplot of our data.

```
> plot(ch17ds1$Qual.Marriage, ch17ds1$Qual.PC,
+ xlab = "Marriage Quality", ylab = "Parent-Child
Interaction Quality",
+ main = "Scatterplot")
>
```

The lack of any clear grouping in data points shown in Figure 17.2 indicates the relationship between marriage quality and parent–child interaction quality.

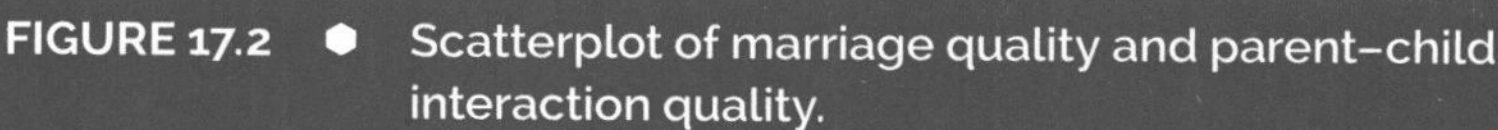

FIGURE 17.2 ● Scatterplot of marriage quality and parent–child interaction quality.

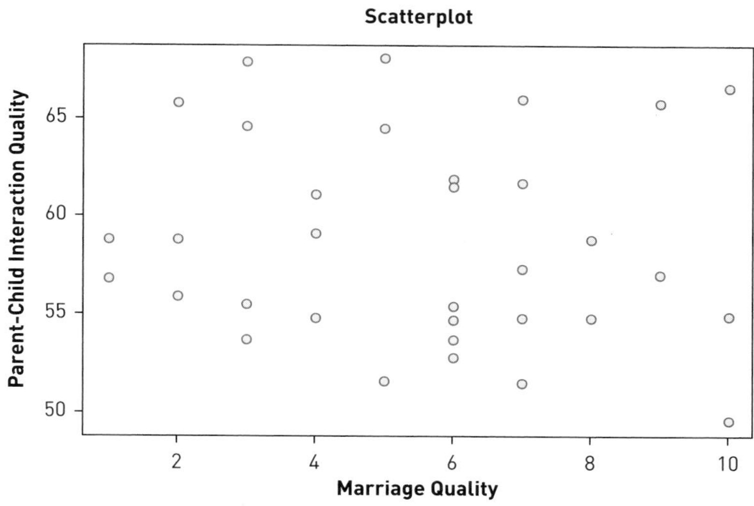

So, we asked for the correlation between `Qual.Marriage` and `Qual.PC`. R gave us the correlation, telling us that $r = -0.10$. We also saw the wide spread of data points in the scatterplot. But what about our hypothesis testing?

To get statistical significance and formally test the correlation, we need to use another function called `cor.test()`. The input to this function is the same, so we just need to change `cor` to `cor.test`:

```
> cor.test(ch17ds1$Qual.Marriage, ch17ds1$Qual.PC)
   Pearson's product-moment correlation

data: ch17ds1$Qual.Marriage and ch17ds1$Qual.PC
t = -0.58581, df = 34, p-value = 0.5619
alternative hypothesis: true correlation is not equal to
0
95 percent confidence interval:
-0.4148737 0.2363342
sample estimates:
cor
-0.09996305
>
```

The first line of the output tells us which test we ran, Pearson's product-moment correlation. This is the same test you learned about in Chapter 7. The next row tells us which two variables were used to calculate the correlation, `ch17ds1$Qual.Marriage` and `ch17ds1$Qual.PC`. This function does return the *t* statistic with correct degrees of freedom and exact *p*. If you were to report these results, you would type $t_{34} = -0.59$, $p = .56$. The alternative hypothesis is presented next for a very good reason. You can actually request a one-tailed test by adding something to our command. If you thought the relationship would be positive (greater than 0), this is how you would change the command like this:

```
> cor.test(ch17ds1$Qual.Marriage, ch17ds1$Qual.PC,+
alternative = "greater")
>
```

Below the alternative hypothesis is the 95% confidence interval around the correlation. In this case, the 95% CI = [−0.41, 0.24]. Last, but definitely not least, we see that the correlation is −0.09996305. Of course, we would shorten this to two decimal places and report $r_{34} = -0.10$, $p = .56$.

REAL-WORLD STATS

With all the attention given to social media (in the social media, of course), it's interesting to look at how researchers evaluate "social" well-being in college students who study and live outside the United States. This study investigated the relationship between the five personality domains and social well-being among 236 students enrolled at the University of Tehran. Correlations showed that some of the relationship between personality factors and dimensions of social well-being, such as neuroticism, was negatively related to social acceptance, social contribution, and social coherence. Conscientiousness was positively related to social contribution. Openness was positively related to social contribution, and social coherence and agreeableness were related to social acceptance and social contribution. Male students scored significantly higher than female students on social well-being. The researchers discussed these findings in light of cultural differences between countries and the general relationship between personality traits and well-being. Interesting stuff!

Want to know more? Go online or to the library and find …

Joshanloo, M., Rastegar, P., & Bakhshi, A. (2012). The Big Five personality domains as predictors of social wellbeing in Iranian university students. *Journal of Social and Personal Relationships, 29,* 639–660.

Summary

Correlations are powerful tools that point out the direction of a relationship and help us to understand what two different outcomes share with one another. Remember that correlations work only when you are talking about associations and never when you are talking about causal effects.

Time to Practice

1. Given the following information, use Table B.4 in Appendix B to determine whether the correlations are significant and how you would interpret the results.
   a. The correlation between speed and strength for 20 women is .567. Test these results at the .01 level using a one-tailed test.
   b. The correlation between the number correct on a math test and the time it takes to complete the test is –.45. Test whether this correlation is significant for 80 children at the .05 level of significance. Choose either a one- or a two-tailed test and justify your choice.
   c. The correlation between number of friends and grade point average (GPA) for 50 adolescents is .37. Is this significant at the .05 level for a two-tailed test?
2. Use the data in Chapter 17 Data Set 2 (ch17ds2.csv) to answer the following questions. Do the analysis manually or by using R.
   a. Compute the correlation between motivation and GPA.
   b. Test for the significance of the correlation coefficient at the .05 level using a two-tailed test.
   c. True or false? The more highly you are motivated, the more you will study. Which answer did you select and why?
3. Use the data in Chapter 17 Data Set 3 (ch17ds3.csv) to answer the following questions. Do the calculations manually or use R.
   a. Compute the correlation between income and level of education.
   b. Test for the significance of the correlation.
   c. What argument can you make to support the conclusion that "lower levels of education cause low income"?
4. Use the data in Chapter 17 Data Set 4 (ch17ds4.csv) to answer the following questions. Compute the correlation coefficient manually.
   a. Test for the significance of the correlation coefficient at the .05 level using a two-tailed test between hours of studying and grade.
   b. Interpret this correlation. What do you conclude about the relationship between the number of hours spent studying and the grade received on a test?
   c. How much variance is shared between the two variables?
   d. How do you interpret the results?

(Continued)

(Continued)

5. A study was completed that examined the relationship between coffee consumption and level of stress for a group of 50 undergraduates. The correlation was .373, and it was a two-tailed test done at the .01 level of significance. First, is the correlation significant? Second, what's wrong with the following statement: "As a result of the data collected in this study and our rigorous analyses, we have concluded that if you drink less coffee, you will experience less stress"?

6. Use the following data to answer the questions that follow. Do these calculations manually.

Age in Months	Number of Words Known
12	6
15	8
9	4
7	5
18	14
24	20
15	7
16	6
21	18
15	17

   a. Compute the correlation between age in months and number of words known.
   b. Test for the significance of the correlation at the .05 level of significance.
   c. Go way back and recall what you learned in Chapter 7 about correlation coefficients and interpret this correlation.

7. Discuss the general idea that just because two things are correlated, one does not necessarily cause the other. Provide an example (other than ice cream and crime!).

8. Chapter 17 Data Set 5 (ch17ds5.csv) contains four variables:

   Age (in years)

   Shoe_Size (small, medium, and large as 1, 2, and 3)

   Intelligence (as measured by a standardized test)

   Level_of_Education (in years)

Which variables are significantly correlated, and more important, what correlations are meaningful?

Student Study Site

Get the tools you need to sharpen your study skills! Visit **edge.sagepub.com/salkindshaw** to access practice quizzes and eFlashcards, watch R tutorial videos, and download data sets!

USING LINEAR REGRESSION

Predicting the Future

Difficulty Scale ☺
(as hard as they get!)

WHAT YOU WILL LEARN IN THIS CHAPTER

- ✦ Understanding how prediction works and how it can be used in the social and behavioral sciences
- ✦ Understanding how and why linear regression works when predicting one variable on the basis of another
- ✦ Judging the accuracy of predictions
- ✦ Understanding how multiple regression works and why it is useful

INTRODUCTION TO LINEAR REGRESSION

You've seen it all over the news—concern about obesity and how it affects work and daily life. A group of researchers in Sweden were interested in looking at how well mobility disability and/or obesity predicted job strain and whether social support at work can modify this association. The study included more than 35,000 participants, and differences in job strain mean scores were estimated using linear regression, the exact focus of what we are discussing in this chapter. The results found that level of mobile disability did predict job strain and that social support at work significantly modified the association among job strain, mobile disability, and obesity.

Here's the scoop. Not only can you compute the degree to which two variables are related to one another (by computing a correlation coefficient as we did in Chapter 7), but you can also use these correlations to predict the value of one variable based on the value of another. This is a very special case of how correlations can be used, and it is a very powerful tool for social and behavioral sciences researchers.

Want to know more? Go to the library or go online . . .

Norrback, M., De Munter, J., Tynelius, P., Ahlstrom, G., & Rasmussen, F. (2016). The association of mobility disability, weight status and job strain: A cross-sectional study. *Scandinavian Journal of Public Health, 44,* 311–319.

WHAT IS PREDICTION ALL ABOUT?

The basic idea is to use a set of previously collected data (such as data on variables *X* and *Y*), calculate how correlated these variables are with one another, and then use that correlation and the knowledge of *X* to predict *Y*. Sound difficult? It's not really, especially once you see it illustrated.

For example, a researcher collects data on total high school grade point average (GPA) and first-year college GPA for 400 students in their freshman year at the state university. He computes the correlation between the two variables. Then, he uses the techniques you'll learn about later in this chapter to take a *new* set of high school GPAs and (knowing the relationship between high school GPA and first-year college GPA from the previous set of students) predict what first-year GPA should be for a new sample of 400 students. Pretty nifty, huh?

Here's another example. A group of teachers is interested in finding out how well retention works. That is, do children who are retained in kindergarten (and not passed on to first grade) do better in first grade when they get there? Once again, these teachers know the correlation between being retained and first-grade performance from *prior* years; they can apply it to a new set of students and predict first-grade performance based on kindergarten performance.

How does regression work? Data are collected on past events (such as the existing relationship between two variables) and then applied to a future event given knowledge of only one variable. It's easier than you think.

The higher the absolute value of the correlation coefficient, regardless of whether it is direct or indirect (positive or negative), the more accurate the prediction is of one variable from the other based on that correlation. That's because the more two variables share in common, the more you know about the second variable based on your knowledge of the first variable. And you may already surmise that when the correlation is perfect (+1.0 or −1.0), the prediction is perfect as well. If $r_{xy} = -1.0$ or +1.0 and if you know the value of *X*, then you also know the exact value of *Y*. Likewise, if $r_{xy} = -1.0$ or +1.0 and you know the value of *Y*, then you also know the exact value of *X*. Either way works just fine.

What we'll do in this chapter is go through the process of using linear regression to predict a *Y* score from an *X* score. We'll begin by discussing the general logic that underlies prediction; then review some simple line-drawing skills; and, finally, discuss the prediction process using specific examples.

Why the prediction of *Y* from *X* and not the other way around? Convention. Seems like a good idea to have a consistent way to identify variables, so the *Y* variable becomes the dependent variable or the one being predicted and the *X* variable becomes the independent variable and is the variable used to predict the value of *Y*. And when predicted, the *Y* value is represented as Y' (read as **Y prime**) or $\hat{Y}$ (read as **Y-hat**)—the predicted value of *Y*.

THE LOGIC OF PREDICTION

Before we begin with the actual calculations and show you how correlations are used for prediction, let's understand the argument for why and how prediction works. We will continue with the example of predicting college GPA from high school GPA.

Prediction is the computation of future outcomes based on a knowledge of present ones. When we want to predict one variable from another, we need to first compute the correlation between the two variables. Table 18.1 shows the data we will be using in this example. Figure 18.1 shows the scatterplot (see Chapter 7) of the two variables that are being computed.

TABLE 18.1 ● Total High School GPA and First-Year College GPA.

High School GPA	First-Year College GPA
3.50	3.30
2.50	2.20
4.00	3.50
3.80	2.70
2.80	3.50
1.90	2.00
3.20	3.10
3.70	3.40
2.70	1.90
3.30	3.70

To predict college GPA from high school GPA, we have to create a **regression equation** and use that to plot what is called a **regression line**. A regression line reflects our best guess as to what score on the *Y* variable (college GPA) would be predicted by a score on the *X* variable (high school GPA). For all the data you see in Table 18.1, the regression line is drawn so that it minimizes the distance between itself and each of the points on the predicted ($\hat{Y}$) variable. You'll learn shortly how to draw that line, shown in Figure 18.2.

FIGURE 18.1 ● Scatterplot of high school GPA and college GPA.

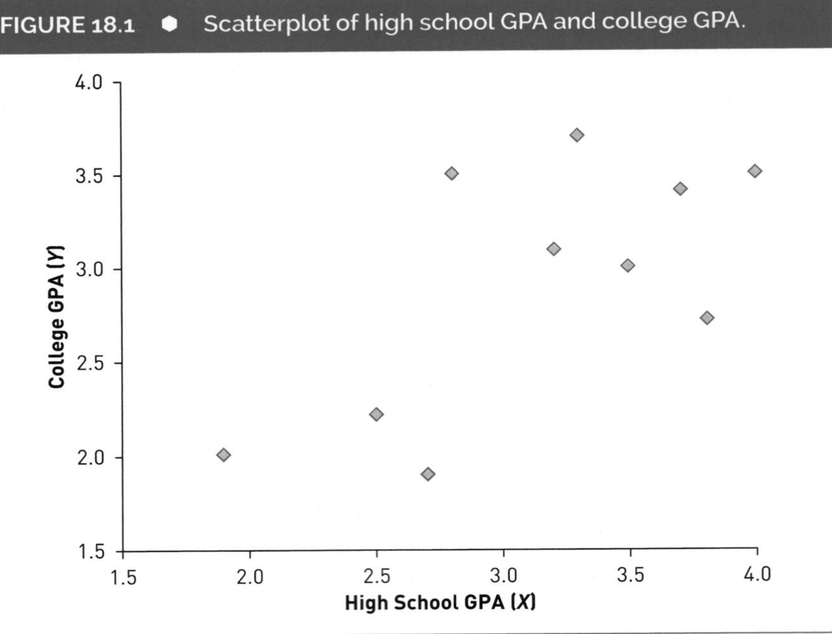

FIGURE 18.2 ● Regression line of college GPA (*Y*) on high school GPA (*X*).

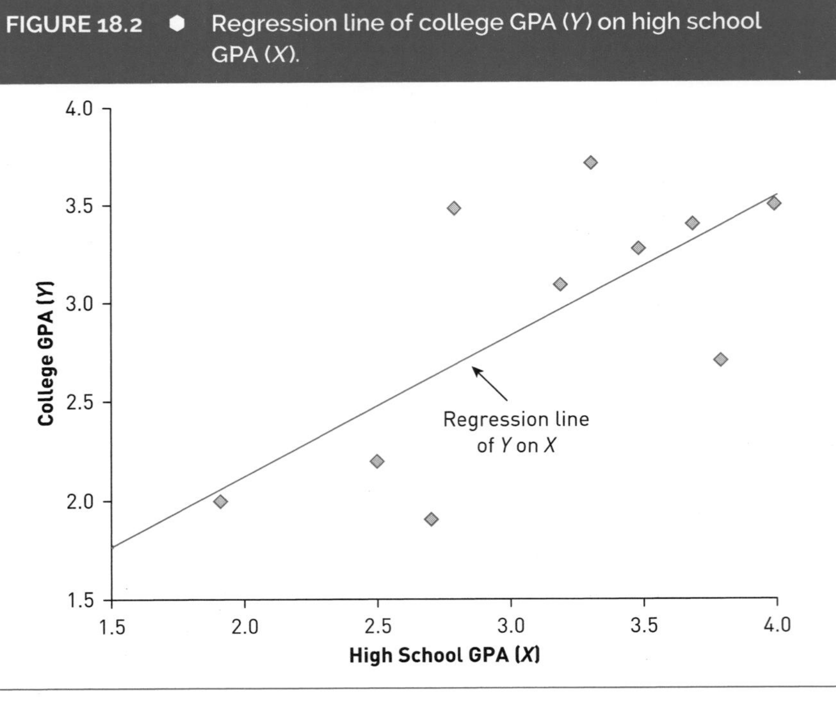

What does the regression line you see in Figure 18.2 represent?

First, it's the regression of the *Y* variable on the *X* variable. In other words, *Y* (college GPA) is being predicted from *X* (high school GPA). This regression line is also called the **line of best fit**. The line fits these data because it minimizes the squared distance between each individual point and the regression line. For example, if you take all of these points and try to find the line that best fits them all at once, the line you see in Figure 18.2 is the one you would use.

Second, it's the line that allows us our best guess (at estimating what college GPA would be, given each high school GPA). For example, if high school GPA is 3.0, then college GPA should be around (remember, this is only an eyeball prediction) 2.8. Take a look at Figure 18.3 to see how we did this. We located the predictor value (3.0) on the *x*-axis, drew a perpendicular line from the *x*-axis to the regression line, then drew a horizontal line to the *y*-axis, and finally *estimated* what the *predicted* value of *Y* would be.

FIGURE 18.3 ● Estimating college GPA given high school GPA.

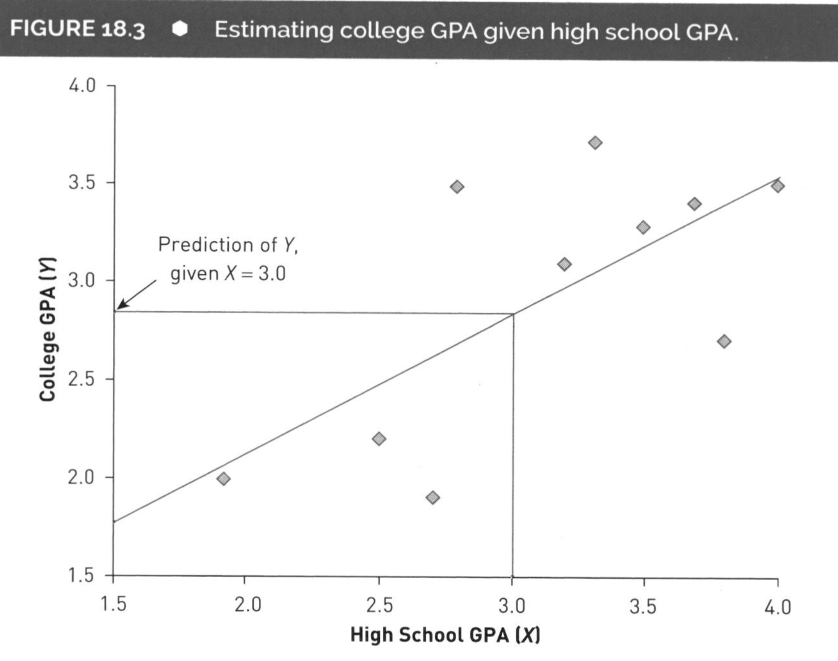

Third, the distance between each individual data point and the regression line is the **error in prediction**—a direct reflection of the correlation between the two variables. For example, if you look at data point (3.3, 3.7), marked in Figure 18.4, you can see that this (*X*, *Y*) data point is above the regression line. The distance between that point and the line is the error in prediction, as marked in Figure 18.4, because if the prediction were perfect, then all the predicted points would fall where? Right on the regression or prediction line.

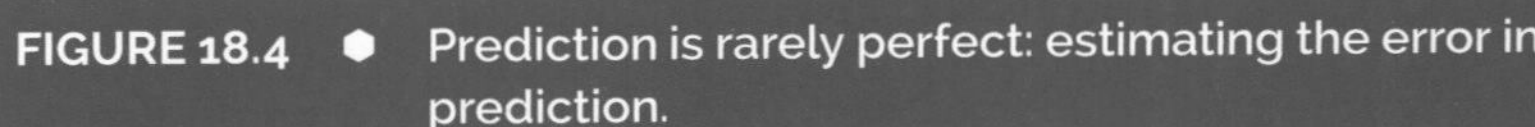
FIGURE 18.4 ● Prediction is rarely perfect: estimating the error in prediction.

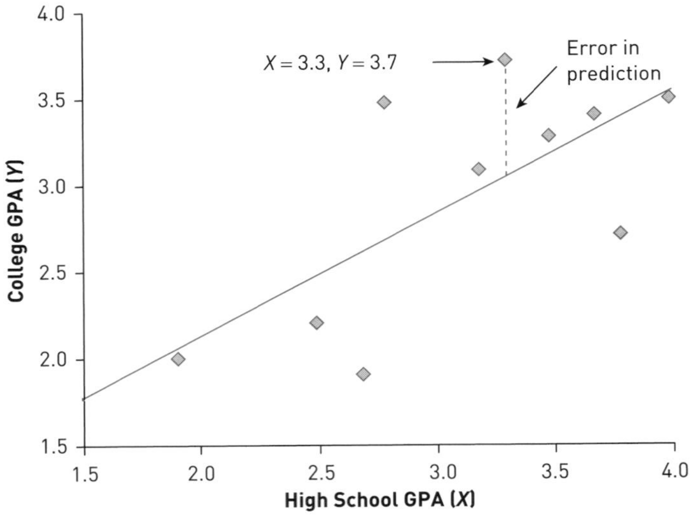

Fourth, if the correlation were perfect, all the data points would align themselves along a 45° angle, and the regression line would pass through each point (just as we said earlier in the third point).

Given the regression line, we can use it to precisely predict any future score. That's what we'll do right now—create the line and then do some prediction work.

DRAWING THE WORLD'S BEST LINE (FOR YOUR DATA)

The simplest way to think of prediction is that you are determining the score on one variable (which we'll call *Y*—the **criterion** or dependent variable) based on the value of another score (which we'll call *X*—the **predictor** or independent variable).

The way that we find out how well *X* can predict *Y* is through the creation of the regression line we mentioned earlier in this chapter. This line is created from data that have already been collected. The equations are then used to predict scores using a new value for *X*, the predictor variable.

Formula 18.1 shows the general formula for the regression line, which may look familiar because you probably used something very similar in your high school and college math courses. It's the formula for a straight line.

$$\hat{Y} = bX + a, \tag{18.1}$$

where

- $\hat{Y}$ is the predicted score of Y based on a known value of X,
- b is the slope of the line,
- X is the score being used as the predictor, and
- a is the point at which the line crosses the y-axis.

Let's use the same data shown earlier in Table 18.1, along with a few more calculations that we will need thrown in.

	X	Y	X^2	Y^2	XY
	3.5	3.3	12.25	10.89	11.55
	2.5	2.2	6.25	4.84	5.50
	4.0	3.5	16.00	12.25	14.00
	3.8	2.7	14.44	7.29	10.26
	2.8	3.5	7.84	12.25	9.80
	1.9	2.0	3.61	4.00	3.80
	3.2	3.1	10.24	9.61	9.92
	3.7	3.4	13.69	11.56	12.58
	2.7	1.9	7.29	3.61	5.13
	3.3	3.7	10.89	13.69	12.21
Total	31.4	29.3	102.50	89.99	94.75

From this table, we see that

- $\sum X$, or the sum of all the X values, is 31.4.
- $\sum Y$, or the sum of all the Y values, is 29.3.
- $\sum X^2$, or the sum of each X value squared, is 102.5.
- $\sum Y^2$, or the sum of each Y value squared, is 89.99.
- $\sum XY$, or the sum of the products of X and Y, is 94.75.

Formula 18.2 is used to compute the slope of the regression line (b in the equation for a straight line):

$$b = \frac{\sum XY - \left(\sum X \sum Y / n\right)}{\sum X^2 - \left[\left(\sum X\right)^2 / n\right]}. \tag{18.2}$$

In Formula 18.3 you can see the computed value for *b*, the slope of the line:

$$b = \frac{94.75 - \left[(31.4 \times 29.3)/10\right]}{102.5 - \left[(31.4)^2/10\right]}, \tag{18.3}$$

$$b = \frac{2.749}{3.904} = 0.704.$$

Formula 18.4 is used to compute the point at which the line crosses the *y*-axis (*a* in the equation for a straight line):

$$a = \frac{\sum Y - b\sum X}{n}. \tag{18.4}$$

In Formula 18.5, you can see the computed value for *a*, the intercept of the line:

$$a = \frac{29.3 - (0.704 \times 31.4)}{10}, \tag{18.5}$$

$$a = \frac{7.19}{10} = 0.719.$$

Now, if we go back and substitute *b* and *a* into the equation for a straight line ($\hat{Y} = bX + a$), we come up with the final regression line:

$$\hat{Y} = 0.704X + 0.719$$

Why the $\hat{Y}$ and not just a plain *Y*? Remember, we are using *X* to predict *Y*, so we use $\hat{Y}$, called *Y*-hat, to mean the predicted and not the actual value of *Y*.

So, now that we have this equation, what can we do with it? Predict *Y*, of course.

Let's start with understanding the numbers in our formula. We know from the explanation of terms in Formula 18.1 that 0.719 is the point where the line crosses the *y*-axis. In the context of our example, 0.719 is the expected college GPA if high school GPA was 0. We know, not incredibly helpful because it is a rare case in which a student has a GPA equal to 0 and would still be admitted to college, but there it is. The other number is more helpful. For every 1-unit increase in high school GPA, the college GPA will increase by 0.704.

For example, let's say that high school GPA equals 2.8 (or $X = 2.8$). If we substitute the value of 2.8 into the equation, we get the following formula:

$$\hat{Y} = 0.704(2.8) + 0.719 = 2.69.$$

So, 2.69 is the predicted value of *Y* (or $\hat{Y}$) given *X* is equal to 2.8. Now, for any *X* score, we can easily and quickly compute a predicted *Y* score.

You can use this formula and the known values to compute predicted values. That's most of what we just talked about. But you can also plot a regression line to show how well the scores (what you are trying to predict) actually fit the data from which you are predicting. Take another look at Figure 18.2, the plot of the high school–college GPA data. It includes a regression line, which is also called a **trend line**. How did we get this line? Easy. We used the same charting skills you learned in Chapter 7 to create a scatterplot; then we added a line to our plot, something you will learn how to do in a couple pages.

You can see the trend is positive (in that the line has a positive slope) and that the correlation is .6835—very positive. And you can see that the data points do not align directly on the line, but they are pretty close, which indicates that there is a relatively small amount of error.

There is a big caveat to what we just learned about the regression line and that has to do with the data used to generate the coefficients in Formula 18.1. In our example, the highest GPA for high school or college was 4.0. What if you had a student applying to college but the range for high school GPA was 0 to 5 instead of 0 to 4? Could you use the same formula to predict this applicant's college GPA? Unfortunately not. One thing we could do in this case is rescale the GPA to put it on the scale of 0 to 4 and plug the rescaled GPA into the formula.

The other assumption is whether the new student comes from the same population as the students used to get our regression line. Is that new student qualitatively different because his or her school had a larger GPA range? If yes, you might need to collect more data and get a new regression formula for students from high schools with larger GPA ranges.

HOW GOOD IS YOUR PREDICTION?

How can we measure how good a job we have done predicting one outcome from another? We know that the higher the absolute magnitude of the correlation between two variables, the better the prediction. In theory, that's great. But being practical, we can also look at the difference between the predicted value ($\hat{Y}$) and the actual value (Y) when we first compute the formula of the regression line.

For example, if the formula for the regression line is $\hat{Y} = 0.704X + 0.719$, the predicted Y (or $\hat{Y}$) for an X value of 2.8 is 0.704(2.8) + 0.719, or 2.69. We know that the actual Y value that corresponds to an X value is 3.5 (from the data set shown in Table 18.1). The difference between 3.5 and 2.69, or 0.81, is known as an error in prediction.

Another measure of error that you could use is the coefficient of determination (see Chapter 7), which is the percentage of error that is *reduced* in the relationship between variables. For example, if the correlation between two variables is .4 and the coefficient of determination is 16% or $.4^2$, the reduction in error is 16% since initially we suspect the relationship between the two variables starts at 0 or 100% error (no predictive value at all).

If we take all of these differences, we can compute the average amount that each data point differs from the predicted data point, or the **standard error of estimate.** This is a kind of standard deviation that reflects variability about the line of regression. The value tells us how much imprecision there is in our estimate. As you might expect, the higher the correlation between the two values (and the better the prediction), the lower this standard error of estimate will be. In fact, if the correlation between the two variables is perfect (either +1 or –1), then the standard error of estimate is zero. Why? Because if prediction is perfect, all of the actual data points fall on the regression line, and there's no error in estimating *Y* from *X*.

> The predicted $\hat{Y}$, or dependent variable, need not always be a continuous one, such as height, test score, or problem-solving skills. It can be a categorical variable, such as admit/don't admit, Level A/Level B, or Social Class 1/Social Class 2. But then we are talking about other types of regression. One type, logistic regression, will be briefly introduced in Chapter 20, but all other types are beyond the scope of this book. So for now, if you are thinking about how you can apply this chapter, focus on continuous, normally distributed data.

Visit **edge.sagepub.com/salkindshaw** to watch an R tutorial video on this topic.

USING R TO COMPUTE THE REGRESSION LINE

Let's use R to compute the regression line that predicts $\hat{Y}$ from *X*. The data set we are using is Chapter 18 Data Set 1 (ch18ds1.csv). We will be using the number of hours of training to predict how severe injuries will be if someone is injured playing football.

There are three variables in this data set:

Variable	Definition
Training (predictor)	Number of hours per week of strength training
Trainer (predictor)	Whether the person was working with a trainer (1) or not (0)
Injuries (outcome)	Severity of injuries on a scale from 1 to 10

Here are the steps to compute the regression line that we discussed in this chapter. Follow along and do it yourself.

1. Read in the file for Chapter 18 Data Set 1 (ch18ds1.csv) and check the data with the function `View()`.

```
> ch18ds1 <- read.csv(file.choose())
> View(ch18ds1)
>
```

You should have a data set with three columns and 30 rows. We are going to use two of the three variables in this example. The two columns are Training for our independent variable and Injuries for the dependent variable.

2. Run a linear regression model using the function `lm()`.

```
> lm(Injuries ~ Training, data = ch18ds1)
Call:
lm(formula = Injuries ~ Training, data = ch18ds1)
Coefficients:
(Intercept) Training
6.8473 -0.1251
>
```

We can tell what the function did, run a linear model with `lm()`, and the coefficients are 6.8473 and –0.1251. But, by changing this a little bit, we can find out more. Try this:

```
> sr <- lm(Injuries ~ Training, data = ch18ds1)
>
```

Let's ask for the summary of sr (short for simple regression, which is what we have—regression with one predictor), a function that is going to tell us much more about our results.

```
> summary(sr)
Call:
lm(formula = Injuries ~ Training, data = ch18ds1)
Residuals:
    Min      1Q  Median     3Q    Max
-3.8467 -1.5954 -0.3456 1.6226 4.4046
Coefficients:
            Estimate Std. Error t value  Pr(>|t|)
(Intercept) 6.84728    1.00425   6.818  2.09e-07 ***
Training   -0.12507    0.04586  -2.727    0.0109 *
---
Signif. codes: 0 '***' 0.001 '**' 0.01 '*' 0.05 '.' 0.1
' ' 1
Residual standard error: 2.182 on 28 degrees of freedom
Multiple R-squared: 0.2099,  Adjusted R-squared: 0.1816
F-statistic: 7.436 on 1 and 28 DF, p-value: 0.01091
>
```

R returned a number of rows. Let's take them one by one to see what we have learned.

a. The first two lines tell us the variables we are testing and what data object was used. In this case, we are testing `Injuries` as predicted or explained by (~) `Training`. The data object was `ch18ds1`.

b. Skip to the last line that tells us the *F* statistic for Injuries predicted by Training. For this model, $F_{(1, 28)} = 7.44$, $p = .01$ (and yes, this is the same *F* that we talked about in Chapters 15 and 16). Like the hypotheses we have tested in the other chapters where we use $p = .05$, we are using the same *p* critical value for this statistic. Our *F* statistic had $p = .01$, which is less than .05. Therefore, the result is more extreme than we expected if Training does not predict Injuries. So, we can now proceed to look at the rest of the summary output.

c. Moving back to the top, lines 3 to 5 tells us about the residuals. What are residuals? That is another word for the error in prediction we talked about on page 345. Every measurement of Injuries has its own error in prediction. These lines just tell you the minimum, maximum, and quartile values for the errors in prediction.

d. Coefficients are shown on 8 and 9. Those results can be plugged into Formula 18.1.

$$\hat{Y} = bX + a = -0.12507X + 6.84728.$$

Remember, *a* is the place where the line crosses the *y*-axis and *b* is the slope of the line. So, we know that the line crosses the *y*-axis at 6.84728 and the slope is –0.12507. For the slope, this means for every 1-unit increase in Training, the number of Injuries decreases by 0.12507. More, we are shown that the coefficients are statistically significant in their own right. The statistical test is whether the coefficient equals 0 or not with the null hypothesis being that the coefficient equals 0. The *t* statistic for the intercept, *b,* is not something we care about, so just ignore that line. We are really interested in the *b* coefficient. For Injuries, $t_{28} = -2.73$, $p = .01$. Again, using $p = .05$, our *t* statistic with $p = .01$ is more extreme than expected if Training did not predict Injuries, so we can reject that null hypothesis.

e. Skip the "Residual standard error" for the moment and move to the second to the last line. Multiple *R*-squared (R^2) is yet another effect size! $R^2 = 0.2099$ means that 21% of the variance in Injuries is explained by Training. Adjusted R^2 is a more conservative estimate of how much variance in Injuries is explained by Training. In this case, the Adjusted $R^2 = 0.18$, 18% of the variance in Injuries.

3. Draw a scatterplot. To do this, we use the plot function like we did in Chapter 7.

```
> plot(Injuries ~ Training, data = ch18ds1)
>
```

We use the same syntax in the function as we did for `lm()`. If you are following along in R, the output should look like Figure 18.5.

4. Add the regression line to the plot.

   To draw the line, we use a new function, called `abline()`, and the output of our model, `sr`.

```
> abline(sr)
>
```

The scatterplot in Figure 18.6 has the regression line drawn across it. The line starts on the left, on the y-axis, at 6.84728.

FIGURE 18.5 ● A scatterplot generated using R.

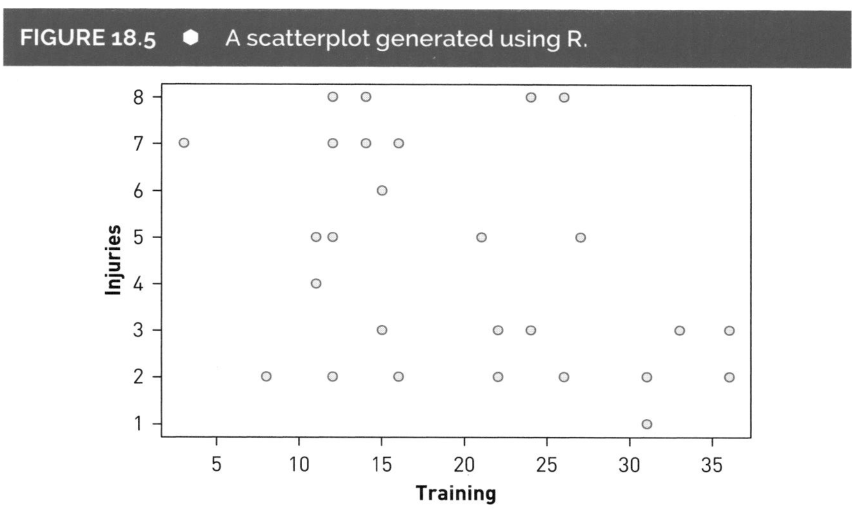

UNDERSTANDING THE R OUTPUT

The R output tells us several things.

1. The formula for the regression line is taken from the first set of output shown in Figure 18.6 as $\hat{Y} = -0.13X + 6.85$. This equation can be used to predict level of injury given the number of hours spent in strength training (provided that hours fall between 3 and 36, like our data, and you think a new person comes from the same population as the original sample).
2. As you can see in Figure 18.6, the regression line has a negative slope, reflecting a negative correlation between hours of training and severity of injuries. So it appears, given the data, that the more one trains, the fewer severe injuries occur. We can check this by calculating a correlation between our two variables.

FIGURE 18.6 ● R scatterplot with regression line.

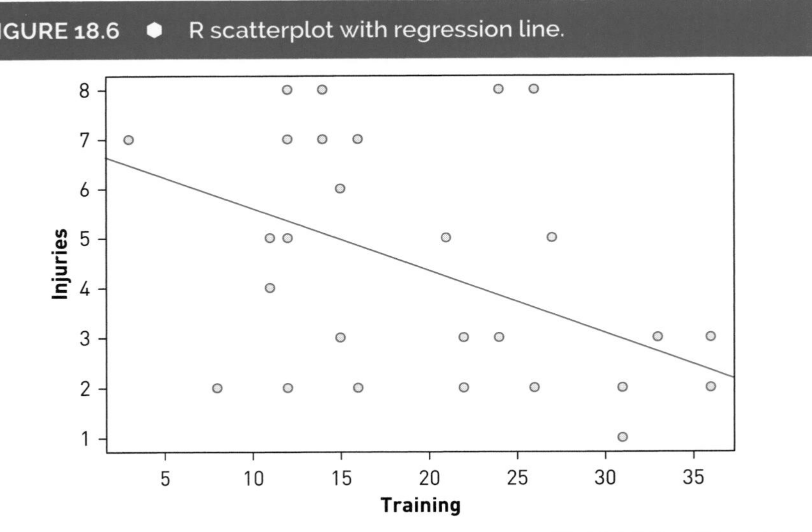

3. You can also see that the prediction is significant—in other words, predicting Y from X is based on a significant relationship between the two variables such that the test of significance for both the constant (Training) and the predicted variable (Injuries) is significantly different from zero (which it would be if there was no predictive value for X predicting Y.

So just how good is the prediction? Well, the R output also indicates that the standard error of estimate, shown as "`Residual standard error`" in the output, for Injuries (the predicted variable) is 2.182, which means that there is a 95% chance (remember it is 1 standard deviation removed from the mean) the prediction will fall between the mean of all injuries (which is 4.33) and ±2.182. So, based on the correlation coefficient, the prediction is reasonably good but not great.

THE MORE PREDICTORS THE BETTER? MAYBE

All of the examples that we have used so far in the chapter have been for one criterion or outcome measure and one predictor variable. This is referred to as **simple regression** and is the starting point for many people learning about regression. There is also the more typical case of regression where more than one predictor or independent variable is used to predict a particular outcome. If one variable can predict an outcome with some degree of accuracy, then why couldn't two do a better job? Maybe so, but there's a big caveat—read on.

Using the example above on hours of strength training predicting the severity of injury, what if you included whether the person was working with a trainer or not? So, instead of

$$\hat{Y} = bX + a,$$

FIGURE 18.7 ● Determining that regression is the correct test statistic.

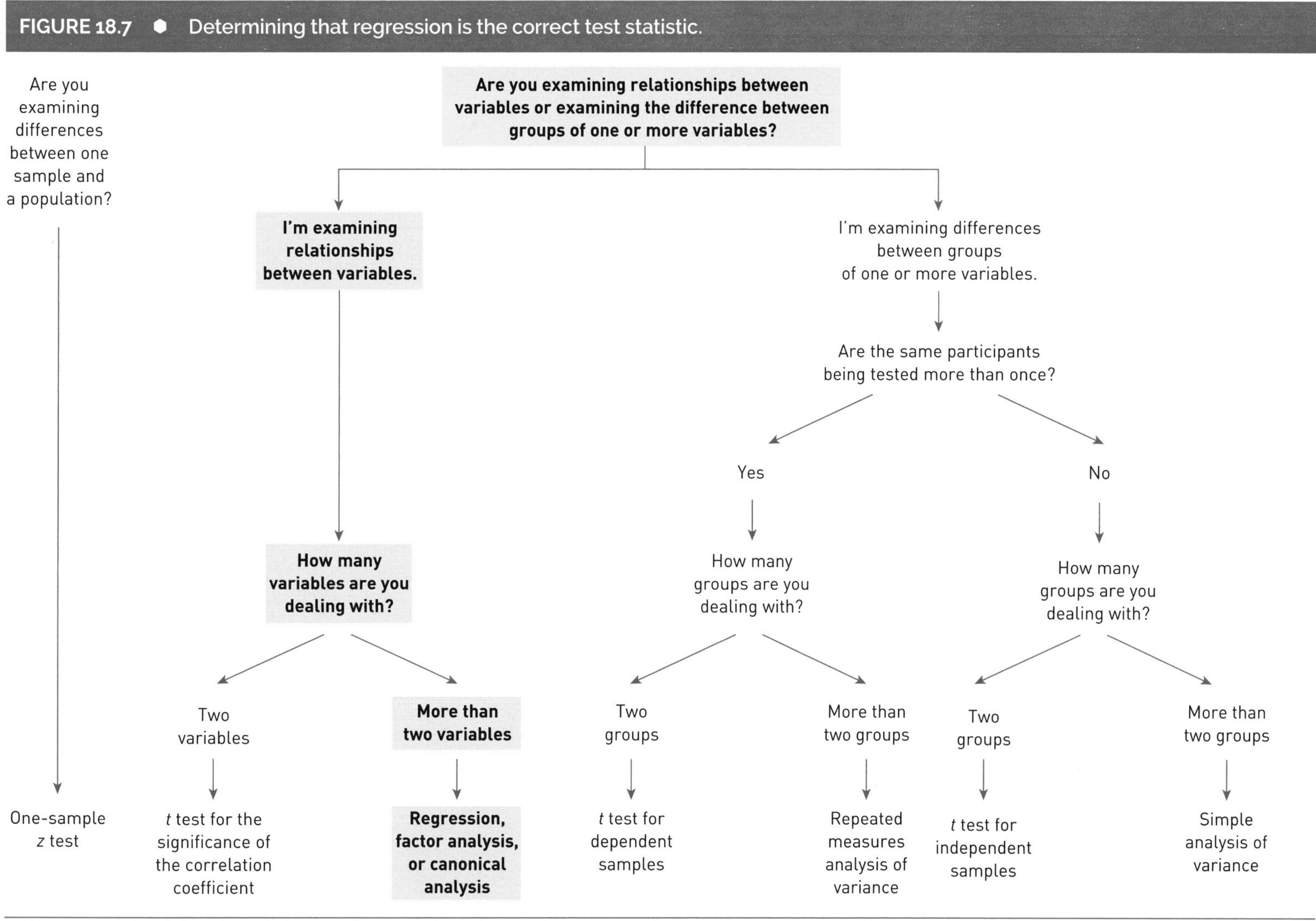

the model for the regression equation becomes

$$\hat{Y} = b_1 X_1 + b_2 X_2 + a,$$

where

- X_1 is the value of the first independent variable,
- X_2 is the value of the second independent variable,
- b_1 is the regression weight for X_1,
- b_2 is the regression weight for X_2, and
- a is the intercept of the regression line, or where the regression line crosses the y-axis.

As you may have guessed, this model is called **multiple regression** (multiple independent variables, right?). So, in theory anyway, you are predicting an outcome from two independent variables rather than one. And at this point, we return to the decision tree in Figure 18.7 that we have seen in Chapters 11 to 17.

We start at the top, where we can say we are examining relationships between variables. Moving down the left on the decision tree, we are asked how many variables we are dealing with. In this example, more than two variables. The answer is regression, factor analysis, or canonical analysis. All three methods are valid based on the decision tree, and we are going to focus on regression in this chapter. But let's talk a little bit more about whether a second variable should be added.

Any variable you add has to make a unique contribution to understanding the dependent variable. Otherwise, why use it? What do we mean by *unique?* The additional variable needs to explain differences in the predicted variable that the first predictor does not. That is, the two variables in combination should predict Y better than any one of the variables would do alone. And the additional predictor should not be too highly correlated (< 0.60) with the first predictor.

In our example, whether the person is working with a trainer or not should make a unique contribution. Take a look at the R syntax to run a regression with two predictors.

```
> mr <- lm(Injuries ~ Training + Trainer, data =
ch18ds1)
> summary(mr)
Call:
lm(formula = Injuries ~ Training + Trainer, data =
ch18ds1)
Residuals:
    Min      1Q  Median     3Q    Max
-4.0112 -1.6840 -0.2335 1.6444 4.5724
```

```
Coefficients:
             Estimate Std. Error t value Pr(>|t|)
(Intercept) 7.00759    1.08759   6.443 6.64e-07 ***
Training    -0.12454   0.04657  -2.674   0.0126 *
Trainer     -0.34188   0.80887  -0.423   0.6759
---
Signif. codes: 0 '***' 0.001 '**' 0.01 '*' 0.05 '.' 0.1
' ' 1
Residual standard error: 2.214 on 27 degrees of freedom
Multiple R-squared: 0.215,  Adjusted R-squared: 0.1569
F-statistic: 3.698 on 2 and 27 DF, p-value: 0.03805
>
```

You can see how number of hours Training is still significantly related to severity of Injuries. For every hour increase in Training, the severity of Injuries declines by 0.12. The addition of Trainer as a predictor does not appear to be useful in our model. Because our coefficient for Trainer is –0.34 with a standard error more than twice its size, we get a small *t* statistic for Trainer (–0.42) and a high *p* value (.68). Because Trainer was not a statistically significant predictor of injury severity, R^2 didn't change much at all. In the simple regression with just Training, $R^2 = 0.2099$. It is now 0.215, a difference of just 0.0051.

Let's look at one more important step. We want to run a test to see whether we should keep Trainer in our model. This test is comparing our simple regression model with just Training to our multiple regression model with Training and Trainer. We are setting our significance level at .05. If our *F* test has a p value > .05, then we keep our simple regression and fail to reject our null hypothesis that the models are not different. If our *F* test is < .05, we keep the more complex multiple regression and reject the null hypothesis that the models are not different.

R has a function for this, which is confusingly called **anova()**. The only input the function needs is the objects we stored results in. The function returns an *F* statistic.

```
> anova(sr, mr)
Analysis of Variance Table
Model 1: Injuries ~ Training
Model 2: Injuries ~ Training + Trainer
Res.Df    RSS Df Sum of Sq      F Pr(>F)
1    28 133.27
2    27 132.40  1   0.87598 0.1786 0.6759
>
```

Based on our results, we fail to reject the null, $F_{(1, 28)} = 0.18$, $p = .68$. We keep the simple regression (Model 1 in the output) with only one predictor, Training.

The Big Rule(s) When It Comes to Using Multiple Predictor Variables

If you are using more than one predictor variable, try to keep the following two important guidelines in mind:

1. When selecting an independent variable to predict an outcome, select a predictor variable (X) that is related to the predicted variable (Y). That way, the two share something in common (remember, they should be correlated).
2. When selecting more than one independent variable (such as X_1 and X_2), try to select variables that are independent or uncorrelated with one another but are both related to the outcome or predicted (Y) variable.

In effect, you want only independent or predictor variables that are related to the dependent variable and unrelated to each other. That way, each one makes as distinct a contribution as possible to predicting the dependent or predicted variable.

How many predictor variables are too many? Well, if one variable predicts some outcome, and two are even more accurate, then why not three, four, or five predictor variables? In practical terms, every time you add a variable, an expense is incurred. Someone has to go collect the data, it takes time (which is $$$ when it comes to research budgets), and so on. From a theoretical sense, there is a fixed limit on how many variables can contribute to an understanding of what we are trying to predict. Remember that it is best when the predictor or independent variables are independent or unrelated to each other. The problem is that once you get to three or four variables, fewer things can remain unrelated. Better to be accurate and conservative than to include too many variables and waste money and the power of prediction.

REAL-WORLD STATS

How children feel about what they do is often very closely related to how well they do what they do. The aim of this study was to analyze the consequences of emotion during a writing exercise. In the model this research follows, motivation and affect (the experience of emotion) play an important role during the writing process. Fourth and fifth graders were instructed to write autobiographical narratives with no emotional content, positive emotional content, and negative emotional content. The results showed no effect regarding these instructions on the proportion of spelling errors, but the results did reveal an effect on the length of narrative the children wrote. A simple regression analysis (just like the ones we did and discussed in this chapter) showed a correlation and some predictive value between working memory capacity and the number of spelling errors in the neutral condition only. Since the model on which the researchers based much of their preliminary thought about this topic states that emotions can increase the cognitive load or the amount of "work" necessary in writing, that becomes the focus of the discussion in this research article.

Want to know more? Go online or to the library and find . . .

Fartoukh, M., Chanquoy, L., & Piolat, A. (2012). Effects of emotion on writing processes in children. *Written Communication, 29,* 391–411.

Summary

Prediction is a special case of simple correlation, and it is a very powerful tool for examining complex relationships. This chapter might have been a little more difficult than others, but you'll be well served by what you have learned, especially if you can apply it to the research reports and journal articles that you have to read. We are now at the end of lots of chapters on inference, and we're about to move on in the next part of this book to using statistics when the sample size is very small or when the assumption that the scores are distributed in a normal way is violated.

Time to Practice

1. How does linear regression differ from analysis of variance?
2. Chapter 18 Data Set 2 (ch18ds2.csv) contains the data for a group of participants who took a timed test. The data are the average amount of time the participants took on each item (Time) and the number of guesses it took to get each item correct (Correct).
   a. What is the regression equation for predicting response time from number correct?
   b. What is the predicted response time if the number correct is 8?
   c. What is the difference between the predicted and the actual number correct for each of the predicted response times?
3. Betsy is interested in predicting how many 75-year-olds will develop Alzheimer's disease and is using as predictors level of education and general physical health graded on a scale from 1 to 10. But she is interested in using other predictor variables as well. Answer the following questions:
   a. What criteria should she use in the selection of other predictors? Why?
   b. Name two other predictors that you think might be related to the development of Alzheimer's disease.
   c. With the four predictor variables—level of education and general physical health and the two new ones that you named in (b)—draw out what the model of the regression equation would look like.
4. Go to the library and locate three different research studies in your area of interest that use linear regression. It's okay if the studies contain more than one predictor variable. Answer the following questions for each study:

(Continued)

(Continued)

a. What is one independent variable? What is the dependent variable?

b. If there is more than one independent variable, what argument does the researcher make that these variables are independent of one another?

c. Which of the three studies seems to present the least convincing evidence that the dependent variable is predicted by the independent variable, and why?

5. Here's where you can apply the information in one of this chapter's tips and get a chance to predict a Super Bowl winner! Joe Coach was curious to know whether the average number of games won in a year predicts Super Bowl performance (win or lose). The *X* variable was the average number of games won during the past 10 seasons. The *Y* variable was whether the team ever won the Super Bowl during the past 10 seasons. Here are the data:

Team	Average Number of Wins Over 10 Years	Bowl? (1 = yes and 0 = no)
Savannah Sharks	12	1
Pittsburgh Pelicans	11	0
Williamstown Warriors	15	0
Bennington Bruisers	12	1
Atlanta Angels	13	1
Trenton Terrors	16	0
Virginia Vipers	15	1
Charleston Crooners	9	0
Harrisburg Heathens	8	0
Eaton Energizers	12	1

a. How would you assess the usefulness of the average number of wins as a predictor of whether a team ever won a Super Bowl?

b. What's the advantage of being able to use a categorical variable (such as 1 or 0) as a dependent variable?

c. What other variables might you use to predict the dependent variable, and why would you choose them?

6. Check your calculation of the correlation coefficient of the relationship between coffee consumption and stress done in Chapter 17, Question 5. If you want to know whether coffee consumption predicts group membership:

a. What is the predictor or the independent variable?

b. What is the criterion or the dependent variable?

c. Do you have an idea what R^2 will be?

7. Time to try out multiple predictor variables. Take a look at the data shown here where the outcome is becoming a great chef. We suspect that variables such as number of years of experience cooking, level of formal culinary education, and number of different positions (sous chef, pasta station, etc.) all contribute to rankings or scores on the Great Chef Test.

By this time, you should be pretty much used to creating equations from data like these, so let's get to the real questions:

Years of Experience	Level of Education	# Positions	Score on Great Chef Test
5	1	5	88
6	2	4	78
12	3	9	56
21	3	8	88
7	2	5	97
9	1	8	90
13	2	8	79
16	2	9	85
21	2	9	60
11	1	4	89
15	2	7	88
15	3	7	76
1	3	3	78
17	2	6	98
26	2	8	91
11	2	6	88
18	3	7	90
31	3	12	98
27	2	16	88

a. Which are the best predictors of a chef's score?

b. What score can you expect from a person with 12 years of experience and a Level 2 education who has held five positions?

8. Take a look at Chapter 18 Data Set 3 (ch18ds3.csv), where number of home sales (Number_Homes_Sold) is being predicted by years in the business (Years_In_Business) and level of education in years (Level_Of_Education). Why is level of education such a poor contributor to the overall prediction (using both years in the business and level of education combined) of

(Continued)

(Continued)

number of homes sold? What's the best predictor and how do you know? (Hint: These are sort of trick questions. Before you go ahead and analyze the data, look at the raw data in the file for the characteristics you know are important for one variable to be correlated with another.)

9. For any combinations of predicted and predictor variables, what should be the nature of the relationship between them?

Student Study Site

Get the tools you need to sharpen your study skills! Visit **edge.sagepub.com/salkindshaw** to access practice quizzes and eFlashcards, watch R tutorial videos, and download data sets!

PART VI

MORE STATISTICS! MORE TOOLS! MORE FUN!

Dan shows off his data collection.

Wow—the bulk of the book (and probably the course) is behind you and you're ready to be introduced to some extra new ideas in this part of *Statistics for People Who (Think They) Hate Statistics Using R*. Our goal in Part VI of the book is to provide you with an overview of different tools that are used for a variety of purposes.

In Chapter 19, we introduce the flip side of inferential statistics—the always interesting and useful nonparametrics (in particular the chi-square statistic) used when the distribution of scores you are working with is not a normal distribution or violates some other important assumptions.

From there, Chapter 20 reviews some more advanced statistical procedures such as factor analysis and structural equation modeling. You are sure to hear about these, and others, in your studies. Although in-depth coverage is a bit beyond the level of an introductory course, we talk briefly about each technique and provide examples. This chapter will give you a peek at what some of the more advanced tools can do and how they work.

Okay, this is Part VI of six parts, and you are well on your way to being fully equipped as an expert in introductory statistics.

CHI-SQUARE AND SOME OTHER NONPARAMETRIC TESTS

What to Do When You're Not Normal

Difficulty Scale ☺ ☺ ☺ ☺ (easy)

WHAT YOU WILL LEARN IN THIS CHAPTER

- ✦ Understanding what nonparametrics are and how they are used
- ✦ Analyzing data using a chi-square test for goodness of fit
- ✦ Analyzing data using a chi-square test of independence
- ✦ When and how nonparametric statistics should be used

INTRODUCTION TO NONPARAMETRIC STATISTICS

Almost every statistical test that we've covered so far in *Statistics for People Who (Think They) Hate Statistics Using R* assumes that the data set with which you are working has certain characteristics. For example, one assumption underlying a *t* test between means (be the means independent or dependent) is that the variances of each group are homogeneous, or similar. And this assumption can be tested. Another assumption of many **parametric statistics** is that the sample is large enough to represent the population. Statisticians have found that it takes a sample size of about 30 to fulfill this assumption. Many of the statistical tests we've covered so far are also robust, or powerful, enough that even if one of these assumptions is violated, the test is still valid.

But what do you do when these assumptions may be violated? The original research questions are certainly still worth asking and answering. That's when we use **nonparametric statistics** or when we don't have continuous outcomes. These tests don't follow the same "rules" (meaning they don't require the same, possibly restrictive assumptions as the parametric tests we've reviewed), but the nonparametrics are just as valuable. The use of nonparametric tests also allows us to analyze data that come as frequencies, such as the number of children in different grades or the percentage of people receiving Social Security. And very often, these variables are measured at the nominal or categorical level. (See Chapter 4 for more information about nominal scales of measurement.)

For example, if we wanted to know whether the characteristics of people who voted for school vouchers in the most recent election were what we would expect by chance, or if there was really a pattern of preference according to one or more variables, we would then use a nonparametric technique called *chi-square.*

In this chapter, we will cover chi-square, one of the most commonly used nonparametric tests, and provide a brief review of some others just so you can become familiar with some of the tests that are available.

INTRODUCTION TO THE GOODNESS-OF-FIT (ONE-SAMPLE) CHI-SQUARE

Chi-square is an interesting nonparametric test that allows you to determine if what you observe in a distribution of frequencies is what you would expect to occur by chance. A one-sample chi-square includes only one dimension, variable, or factor, such as in the example you'll see here, and is usually referred to as a **goodness-of-fit test** (just how well do the data you collect fit the pattern you expected?). A two-sample chi-square includes two dimensions, variables, or factors and is usually referred to as a **test of independence**. For example, it might be used to test whether preference for school vouchers is *independent* of political party affiliation and gender.

We'll look at both of these types of chi-square procedures.

For a goodness-of-fit example, here are data from a sample selected at random from the 1990 U.S. Census data collected in Sonoma County, California. As you can see, the table organizes information about level of education (the only factor).

Level of Education		
No College	Some College	College Degree
25	42	17

The question of interest here is whether the number of respondents is equally distributed across all three levels of education. To answer this question, the chi-square value was computed and then tested for significance. In this example, the chi-square value is equal to 11.643, which is significant beyond the .05 level. The conclusion is that the numbers of respondents at the various levels of education for this sample are not equally distributed. In other words, the values are not what we would expect by chance.

The rationale behind the one-sample chi-square or goodness-of-fit test is that for any set of occurrences, you can easily compute what you would expect by chance. You do this by dividing the total number of occurrences by the number of classes or categories. In this example using data from the Census, the observed total number of occurrences is 84. We would expect that, by chance, 84/3 (84, which is the total of all frequencies, divided by 3, which is the total number of categories), or 28, respondents would fall into each of the three categories of level of education.

Then we look at how different what we would expect by chance is from what we observe. If there is no difference between what we expect and what we observe, the chi-square value is equal to zero.

Why "goodness of fit"? This name suggests that the statistic addresses the question of how well or "good" a set of data "fits" an existing set. The set of data is, of course, what you observe. The "fit" part suggests that there is another set of data to which the observed set can be matched, the expected values. And these expected values don't have to be set equally, like we do in the example below. Maybe you want to compare what was observed in a similar situation in another city or state. This standard is the set of expected frequencies that are calculated in the course of computing the χ^2 value. If the observed data fit, the χ^2 value is just too close to what you would expect by chance and does not differ significantly. If the observed data do not fit, then what you observed is different from what you would expect.

Let's look more closely at how the chi-square value is computed.

COMPUTING THE GOODNESS-OF-FIT CHI-SQUARE TEST STATISTIC

The one-sample goodness-of-fit chi-square test compares what is observed with what would be expected by chance. Formula 19.1 shows how to compute the chi-square value for a one-sample chi-square test.

$$\chi^2 = \sum \frac{(O - E)^2}{E}, \tag{19.1}$$

where

- χ^2 is the chi-square value,
- $\sum$ is the summation sign,
- O is the observed frequency, and
- E is the expected frequency.

Here are some sample data we'll use to compute the chi-square value for a one-dimensional analysis.

Preference for School Voucher			
For	Maybe	Against	Total
23	17	50	90

And here are the famous eight steps to test this statistic.

1. State the null and research hypotheses.

   The null hypothesis shown in Formula 19.2 states that there is no difference in the frequency or the proportion of occurrences in each category.

   $$H_0 : O = E. \tag{19.2}$$

   The O in the null hypothesis represents the observed number of occurrences in any category, and E represents the expected number in any category. This null hypothesis states that the observed count and the expected count are equal. We are using only three categories, but the number could be extended to fit the situation as long as each of the categories is *mutually exclusive,* meaning that any one observation cannot be in more than one category. For example, you can't be in both the male and female categories (the Census only lets you check one). Or you can't be both for and against the school voucher plan at the same time.

   The research hypothesis shown in Formula 19.3 states that there is a difference in the frequency of occurrences in one or more categories.

   $$H_1 : O \neq E. \tag{19.3}$$

2. Set the level of risk (or the level of significance) associated with the null hypothesis.

   The significance level is set at .05. How did we decide on this value and not some other, like .01 or .001? As we have emphasized in past chapters, we made the (somewhat) arbitrary decision to take this amount of risk.

3. Select the appropriate test statistic.

   Any test between frequencies or proportions of mutually exclusive categories (such as For, Maybe, and Against) requires the use of chi-square. The flowchart we used all along at the beginning of Chapters 12 through 18 to select the type of statistical test to use does not include nonparametric procedures.

4. Compute the test statistic value (called the obtained value).

   Let's go back to our voucher data and construct a worksheet that will help us compute the chi-square value.

Category	*O* (observed frequency)	*E* (expected frequency)	*D* (difference)	$(O - E)^2$	$(O - E)^2/E$
For	23	30	7	49	1.63
Maybe	17	30	13	169	5.63
Against	50	30	20	400	13.33
Total (Σ)	90	90			20.59

Here are the steps we took to prepare the above information.

1. Enter the categories (Category) of For, Maybe, and Against. Remember that these three categories are mutually exclusive. Any data point can be in only one category at a time.
2. Enter the observed frequency (*O*), which reflects the data that were collected.
3. Enter the expected frequency (*E*), which is the total of the observed frequencies (90) divided by the number of categories (3), or 90/3 = 30.
4. For each cell, subtract the expected frequency from the observed frequency (*D*), or vice versa. It does not matter which is subtracted from the other because these differences are squared in the next step.
5. Square the difference between the observed and expected value. You can see these values in the column named $(O - E)^2$.
6. Divide the squared difference between the observed and the expected frequencies by the expected frequency. You can see these values in the column marked $(O - E)^2/E$.
7. Sum up this last column, and you have the total chi-square value of 20.59.

5. Determine the value needed for rejection of the null hypothesis using the appropriate table of critical values for the particular statistic.

   Here's where we go to Appendix B, Table B.5 for the list of critical values for the chi-square test.

   Our first task is to determine the degrees of freedom (*df*), which approximates the number of categories in which data have been organized. For this particular test statistic, the degrees of freedom is $r - 1$, where r equals rows, or $3 - 1 = 2$.

   Using this number (2) and the level of risk you are willing to take (defined earlier as .05), you can use the chi-square table to look up the critical value. It is 5.99. So, at the .05 level, with 2 degrees of freedom, the value needed for rejection of the null hypothesis is 5.99.

6. Compare the obtained value with the critical value.

   The obtained value is 20.59, and the critical value for rejection of the null hypothesis that the frequency of occurrences in Groups 1, 2, and 3 is equal is 5.99.

7. and 8. Decision time!

   Now comes our decision. If the obtained value is more extreme than the critical value, the null hypothesis can be rejected. If the obtained value does not exceed the critical value, the null hypothesis is the most attractive explanation and we fail to reject it.

   In this case, the obtained value exceeds the critical value—it is extreme enough for us to say that the distribution of respondents across the three groups is not equal. Indeed, there is a difference in the frequency of people voting for, maybe, or against school vouchers.

So How Do I Interpret $\chi^2_{(2)} = 20.6, p < .05$?

- χ^2 represents the test statistic.
- 2 is the number of degrees of freedom.
- 20.6 is the value obtained by using the formula we showed you earlier in the chapter.
- $p < .05$ (the really important part of this little phrase) indicates that the probability is less than 5% on any one test of the null hypothesis that the frequency of votes is equally distributed across all categories by chance alone. Because we defined .05 as our criterion to deem the research hypothesis more attractive than the null hypothesis, our conclusion is that there is less than a 5% chance that the observed counts are due to chance.

INTRODUCTION TO THE TEST OF INDEPENDENCE CHI-SQUARE

We've been mostly talking about the goodness-of-fit type of chi-square test, but another one—that's just a bit more advanced—is well worth exploring: the chi-square test of independence (also called a chi-square test for association).

With this test, two different dimensions, almost always at the nominal level of measurement, are examined to see whether they are related. Take, for example, the following two-by-two table that includes men and women, those voting and those not.

		Voter Participation	
		Vote	Don't Vote
Gender	Men	50	20
	Women	40	10

What you need to keep in mind is that (1) there are two dimensions (gender and voting participation) and (2) the question asked by the chi-square test of independence is whether, in this case, gender and voting participation are independent of each other.

As with a one-dimensional chi-square, the closer the observed and expected values are to one another, the more likely the dimensions are to be independent of one another. The less similar the observed and expected values are, the less likely the two dimensions are independent of one another.

The test statistic is computed in the same manner as we did for a goodness-of-fit test (what a nice surprise); expected values are computed and used along with observed values to compute a chi-square value, which is then tested for significance. However, unlike with the one-dimensional test, the expected values for a test of independence are computed in a different fashion, which we will review below.

COMPUTING THE TEST OF INDEPENDENCE CHI-SQUARE TEST STATISTIC

Here are the steps we took to perform a test of independence given the voting–gender data you saw earlier. We followed the same steps as those you saw for the goodness-of-fit test and used the same formula. Here's our summary chart:

	Men	Women	Total
Vote	37	32	69
Don't Vote	20	31	51
Total	57	63	120

But note that while the formula is the same, the expected values are computed differently. In particular, the expected value for any cell is the product of the row total multiplied by the column total divided by the total sum of all observations.

So, for example, the expected value for Men who Vote is as follows:

$$\text{Expected} = \frac{\sum \text{Row} \times \sum \text{Column}}{\sum \text{All}} = \frac{69 \times 57}{120}. \tag{19.4}$$

1. Enter the categories (Category) of Men Vote, Men Don't Vote, Women Vote, and Women Don't Vote. Remember that all these categories are mutually exclusive; any data point can be in only one category at a time.
2. Enter the observed frequency (O), which reflects the data that were collected.
3. Enter the expected frequency (E), which is the row total times the column total divided by the total number of observations.
4. For each cell, subtract the expected frequency from the observed frequency (D), or vice versa. It does not matter which is subtracted from the other because these differences are squared in the next step.
5. Square the difference between the observed and expected value.

6. Divide the squared difference between the observed and the expected frequencies by the expected frequency. You can see these values in the section marked $(O - E)^2/E$.

7. Sum up this last column, and you have the total chi-square value of 2.441.

   Here is a summary table of the observed values (O), expected values (E), and the square of the observed minus the expected value for each cell $(O - E)^2$ calculations:

Observed (*O*)			
	Men	Women	Total
Vote	37	32	69
Don't Vote	20	31	51
Total	57	63	120
Expected (*E*)			
	Men	Women	
Vote	32.78	36.23	
Don't Vote	24.23	26.78	
(*O* – *E*)²/*E*			
	Men	Women	
Vote	0.54	0.49	
Don't Vote	0.74	0.67	

   The obtained chi-square value is .54 + .49 + .74 + .67 = 2.44.

   Here's where we go to Appendix B, Table B.5 for the list of critical values for the chi-square test.

   Our first task is to determine the degrees of freedom (*df*), which approximates the number of categories in which data have been organized. For a chi-square test of independence statistic, the degrees of freedom are $(r - 1)(c - 1)$, where r equals rows $(2 - 1 = 1)$ and c equals columns $(2 - 1 = 1)$. So $(r - 1)(c - 1)$ equals (1)(1) or 1.

   Using this number (1) and the level of risk you are willing to take (defined earlier as .05), you can use the chi-square table to look up the critical value. It is 3.84. So, at the .05 level, with 1 degree of freedom, the value needed for rejection of the null hypothesis is 3.84.

   The obtained value is 2.44, and the critical value for rejection of the null hypothesis that voting participation and gender are independent is 3.84.

8. Now comes our decision. If the obtained value is more extreme than the critical value, the null hypothesis can be rejected. If the obtained value does not exceed the critical value, the null hypothesis is the most attractive

explanation and we fail to reject the null. In this case, the obtained value does not exceed the critical value. Indeed, gender and voting participation are independent.

What if we don't expect our counts to be evenly divided across all categories? No problem! You can draw on what you know about a situation, like voting behaviors in previous years, to change your expected value. Remember, the chi-square test is all about observed and expected. There is no reason that you will always expect your proportions to be equal across all categories whether you are computing the goodness-of-fit chi-square or the independence chi-square test statistic.

USING R TO PERFORM CHI-SQUARE TESTS

Visit **edge.sagepub.com/salkindshaw** to watch an R tutorial video on this topic.

Goodness of Fit and R

Here's how to perform a simple, one-sample chi-square test using R. We are using the data set named Chapter 19 Data Set 1 (ch19ds1.csv), which was used in the school vouchers example above.

1. Read in the data set and check your data object.

```
> ch19ds1 <- read.csv(file.choose())
> View(ch19ds1)
>
```

2. Create a table of observed counts. We are calling the table gfdata for goodness-of-fit data. After we create the table, we will double-check our work by looking at gfdata.

```
> gfdata <- summary(ch19ds1$Voucher)
> gfdata
Against   For   Maybe
     50    23      17
>
```

3. Use the function `chisq.test()` to test the goodness of fit.

```
> chisq.test(gfdata, p = c(1/3, 1/3, 1/3))
  Chi-squared test for given probabilities
data: gfdata
X-squared = 20.6, df = 2, p-value = 3.363e-05
>
```

For the function, we provided the table we created and stored as gfdata. We then told R that the expected proportions were 1/3, 1/3, and 1/3 for Against, For, and Maybe, respectively. R then told us that the goodness of fit $\chi^2_2 = 20.6$, $p < .001$. The exact level of significance is so small (less than .001, for example) that R shows it as 3.363e-05, which is 3.363×10^{-5} or .00003363. A very unlikely outcome! So, it is highly likely that these three categories are not equal in frequency.

Test of Independence and R

Here's how to perform a two-dimensional chi-square test of independence using R. We are using the data set named Chapter 19 Data Set 2 (ch19ds2.csv), similar to the gender/voting participation example above. This data set has two variables, Sex and Vote. Sex has two values, Male and Female. Vote also has two values, Yes and No.

1. Read in our data set and check our data object, ch19ds2.

```
> ch19ds2 <- read.csv(file.choose())
> View(ch19ds2)
>
```

2. Create a table and check the table. We are calling our table toidata for test of independence data.

```
> toidata <- table(ch19ds2$Sex, ch19ds2$Vote)
> toidata
          No   Yes
Female    31    32
Male      20    37
>
```

3. Run the same function **chisq.test()** that we used for the goodness-of-fit test. We add one more option, correct = FALSE, because we want the results to match what we get from Formula 19.1. We would only use correct = TRUE if one of the expected cell counts was < 5. Our smallest expected value is 24.225 (see Formula 19.4) in the second row, first column, so we don't need to correct anything.

```
> chisq.test(toidata, p = c(1/4, 1/4, 1/4, 1/4), correct
= FALSE)
            Pearson's Chi-squared test
data:    toidata
X-squared = 2.441, df = 1, p-value = 0.1182
>
```

UNDERSTANDING THE R OUTPUT

The R output for the chi-square test of independence shows the following:

1. The frequencies for the various categories are listed such as Men–Yes (37), Men–No (20), Women–Yes (32), and Women–No (31).
2. The Pearson chi-square value of 2.441 and degrees of freedom (1) appear under the Chi-squared test section of the output. And the results show the same value as was computed manually earlier in the chapter.
3. The exact level of significance is .1182, and so the results are not significant at the .05 level. In other words, gender and voting participation are independent of one another.

Our interpretation? Voting participation is not a function of gender, nor is gender related to voting participation.

One nice thing about `chisq.test` is that we can skip creating the table and telling R the expected proportions. For this last example, another way to get the exact same answer is to tell R about our original two variables, Sex and Vote, and again set correct to FALSE.

```
> chisq.test(ch19ds2$Sex, ch19ds2$Vote, correct = FALSE)
        Pearson's Chi-squared test
data:   ch19ds2$Sex and ch19ds2$Vote
X-squared = 2.441, df = 1, p-value = 0.1182
>
```

A very cool chi-square value generator is available for both types of chi-square tests at http://www.quantpsy.org/chisq/chisq.htm, brought to us by Dr. Kristopher J. Preacher of Vanderbilt University. Once you do calculations by hand so you really understand how chi-square values are created, use this tool along with R to make your stats life even easier!

OTHER NONPARAMETRIC TESTS YOU SHOULD KNOW ABOUT

You may never need a nonparametric test to answer any of the research questions that you propose. On the other hand, you may very well find yourself dealing with samples that are very small (or at least fewer than 30 cases) or data that violate some of the important assumptions underlying parametric tests.

Actually, a primary reason why you may want to use nonparametric statistics is a function of the measurement level of the variable you are assessing. Most data that are categorical and are placed in categories (such as the Sharks and Jets) or that are ordinal and are ranked (first, second, and third place) call for nonparametric tests of the kind you see in Table 19.1.

If that's the case, try nonparametrics on for size. Table 19.1 provides all you need to know about some other nonparametric tests, including their name, what they are used for, and a research question that illustrates how each might be used. Keep in mind that the table represents only a few of the many different tests that are available.

TABLE 19.1 ● Nonparametric Tests to Analyze Data in Categories and by Ranks.

Test Name	When the Test Is Used	A Sample Research Question
McNemar test for significance of changes	To examine "before-and-after" changes	How effective is a phone call to undecided voters in influencing them to vote a certain way on an issue?
Fisher's exact test	To compute the exact probability of outcomes in a 2 × 2 table	What is the exact likelihood of getting six heads on a toss of six coins?
Chi-square one-sample test (the one we focused on earlier in this chapter)	To determine whether the number of occurrences across categories is random	Did brands Fruities, Whammies, and Zippies each sell an equal number of units during the recent sale?
Kolmogorov–Smirnov test	To see whether scores from a sample came from a specified population	How representative is a set of judgments about certain children at an elementary school of the entire student body of that school?
The sign test, or median test	To compare the medians from two samples	Is the median income of people who voted for Candidate A greater than the median income of people who voted for Candidate B?
Mann–Whitney *U* test	To compare two independent samples	Did the transfer of learning, measured by number correct, occur faster for Group A than for Group B?
Wilcoxon rank test	To compare the magnitude as well as the direction of differences between two groups	Is preschool twice as effective as no preschool experience for helping develop children's language skills?
Kruskal–Wallis one-way analysis of variance	To compare the overall difference between two or more independent samples	How do rankings of supervisors differ among four regional offices?

Test Name	When the Test Is Used	A Sample Research Question
Friedman two-way analysis of variance	To compare the overall difference between two or more independent samples on more than one dimension	How do rankings of supervisors differ as a function of regional office and gender?
Spearman rank correlation coefficient	To compute the correlation between ranks	What is the correlation between class rank at the end of the senior year of high school and class rank at the end of the freshman year of college?

REAL-WORLD STATS

People with strokes can lose the skills necessary to dress themselves, leaving them feeling more dependent and out of control in a basic daily activity. But what if, through work with an occupational therapist, these skills can be regained? Joanna Fletcher-Smith, Marion Walker, and Avril Drummond designed a study in which 70 cognitively impaired people who had experienced strokes were first assessed in their upper body dressing abilities. The participants were rated on two categorical variables: dressing using one or both hands and with or without assistance. Ability to complete dressing was counted as 1 and failure as 0. The patients were then reassessed 6 weeks later. The count differences in the two-by-two tables were calculated, and a chi-square test of independence was computed to determine if there was improvement over time. Fletcher-Smith and her colleagues found that individuals who could use both hands fared better than their peers who had the use of only one hand, and that those with use of one hand might improve.

Want to know more? Go online or to the library and find …

Fletcher-Smith, J., Walker, M. F., & Drummond, A. (2012). The influence of hand use on dressing outcome in cognitively impaired stroke survivors. *British Journal of Occupational Therapy, 75*(1), 2–9.

Summary

Chi-square is one of many different types of nonparametric statistics that help you answer questions based on data that violate the basic assumptions of the normal distribution or when a data set is just too small for other statistical methods to work. These nonparametric tests are a very valuable tool, and even as limited an introduction as this will help you understand their use in studies you may read and begin your own exploration of their possibilities.

Time to Practice

1. When does the obtained chi-square value equal zero? Provide an example of how this might happen.
2. Using the following data, test the question of whether an equal number of Democrats, Republicans, and Independents voted during the most recent election. Test the hypothesis at the .05 level of significance. Do your calculations by hand.

Political Affiliation		
Republican	Democrat	Independent
800	700	900

3. Using the following data, test the question of whether an equal number of boys (code = 1) and girls (code = 2) participate in soccer at the elementary level at the .01 level of significance. (The data are available as Chapter 19 Data Set 3, ch19ds3.csv.) Use R or some other statistical program to compute the exact probability of the chi-square value. What's your conclusion?

Gender	
Boys = 1	Girls = 2
45	55

4. School enrollment officials observed a change in the distribution of the number of students across grades and were not sure whether the new distribution was what they should have expected. Test the following data for goodness of fit at the .05 level.

Grade	1	2	3	4	5	6
Number of students	309	432	346	432	369	329

5. Half the marketing staff of a candy company argue that all these candy bars taste the same and are barely different from one another. The other half disagrees. Who is right? The data are ready for you to analyze as Chapter 19 Data Set 4 (ch19ds4.csv).

Candy Bar	# of People Out of 100 Who Prefer
Nuts & Grits	9
Bacon Surprise	27
Dimples	16
Froggy	17
Chocolate Delight	31

6. Here are the results of a survey that examines preference for peanut or plain M&Ms and exercise level. Are these variables related? Do the calculations by hand or using R.

M&M Preference	Exercise Level		
	High	Medium	Low
Plain	160	400	175
Peanut	150	500	250

7. In Chapter 19 Data Set 5 (ch19ds5.csv), you will find entries for two variables: age category (young, middle-aged, and old) and strength following weight training (weak, moderate, strong). Are these two factors independent of one another?

Age	Strength		
	Weak	Moderate	Strong
Young	12	18	22
Middle	20	22	20
Old	9	10	5

Student Study Site

Get the tools you need to sharpen your study skills! Visit **edge.sagepub.com/salkindshaw** to access practice quizzes and eFlashcards, watch R tutorial videos, and download data sets!

SOME OTHER (IMPORTANT) STATISTICAL PROCEDURES YOU SHOULD KNOW ABOUT

Difficulty Scale ☺ ☺ ☺ ☺ (moderately easy—just some reading and an extension of what you already know)

WHAT YOU WILL LEARN IN THIS CHAPTER

- ✦ More advanced statistical procedures and when and how they are used

In *Statistics for People Who (Think They) Hate Statistics Using R,* we have covered only a small part of the whole body of statistics. We don't have room in this textbook for everything—there's a lot of it! More important, when you are starting out, it's vital to keep things simple and direct.

However, that does not mean that in a research article you read or in a class discussion you won't come across other analytical techniques that might be important for you to know about. And if you have found you actually like statistics and intend to take more courses, you will definitely encounter one or more of the techniques mentioned in this chapter. So, for your edification, here are 10 of those techniques with descriptions of what they do and examples of studies that used the technique to answer a question. For the R packages introduced for the first time in this chapter (and all R packages introduced in this book), see the end of Appendix A for the references to find the names of the people who developed the packages and the name of the document that can tell you more.

MULTIVARIATE ANALYSIS OF VARIANCE

You won't be surprised to learn that there are many different renditions of analysis of variance (ANOVA), each one designed to fit a particular "the averages of more than two groups being compared" situation. One of these, multivariate analysis of variance (MANOVA), is used when there is more than one dependent variable. So, instead of looking at just one outcome or dependent variable, the analysis can use more than one. If the dependent or outcome variables are related to one another, it would be hard to determine clearly the effect of the treatment variable on any one outcome. Hence, MANOVA to the rescue.

For example, Erlanger Turner from the University of Houston and Jasmín Llamas from Santa Clara University examined the use of mental health services and gender on therapy fears, ethnic identity, and spirituality of college students who identify as Latino. The MANOVA analysis that they used was a 2 (mental health service use: yes and no) × 2 (gender: male and female) MANOVA. The *multivariate* part of the analysis was three different dependent variables: Thoughts About Psychotherapy Survey, Multigroup Ethnic Identity Measure–Revised, and the Spiritual Meaning Scale. Using a multivariate technique, the effects of the independent variables (service use and gender) can be estimated for each of the measures, all at once.

> *Want to know more?* Go online or to the library and find …
>
> Turner, E. A., & Llamas, J. D. (2017). The role of therapy fears, ethnic identity, and spirituality on access to mental health treatment among Latino college students. *College Counseling Services, 14,* 524–530.

MANOVA in R

There are a couple of different ways (at least!) of running a MANOVA in R. The simplest? Check out the `manova` function in the stats package that is accessible when you start R. Check out the help text and then run the example with a data set built into R.

```
> ?manova
> example(manova)
>
```

This example first sets the contrasts to Helmert for nonordered groups, creates a second outcome for the example, and then runs a MANOVA based on the npk data set.

REPEATED-MEASURES ANALYSIS OF VARIANCE

The first time we talked about repeated measures was actually in Chapter 12 with the paired *t* test. Here's another kind of analysis of variance and another kind of repeated measures. Repeated-measures analysis of variance is very similar to any other analysis of variance, in which you'll recall that the means of two or more groups are tested for differences (see Chapter 15 if you need a review). In a repeated-measures ANOVA, participants are tested on one factor more than once. That's why it's called *repeated,* because you repeat the process at more than one point in time on the same factor.

For example, Brenda Lundy, Tiffany Field, Cami McBride, Tory Field, and Shay Largie examined same-sex and opposite-sex interaction with best friends among juniors and seniors in high school. One of the researchers' main analyses was ANOVA with three factors: gender (male or female), friendship (same sex or opposite sex), and year in high school (junior or senior year). The repeated measure was year in high school, because the measurement was repeated across the same subjects.

Want to know more? Go online or to the library and find . . .

Lundy, B., Field, T., McBride, C., Field, T., & Largie, S. (1998). Same-sex and opposite-sex best friend interactions among high school juniors and seniors. *Adolescence, 33,* 279–289.

Repeated-Measures Analysis of Variance in R

One way to run a repeated-measures analysis in R is to use the `lmer` function in the lme4 package. In the example we are going to show you, the time variable is days with reaction times measured for 10 days.

```
> install.packages("lme4")
> library(lme4)
> fm1 <- lmer(Reaction ~ Days + (Days | Subject),
sleepstudy)
> summary(fm1)
```

The first line installs the package for the first time with the following line telling R we want to use functions in lme4. The third line runs the model, storing the results in an object called `fm1`. The `summary` function used in line 4 puts the results in human readable form. Many thanks to Doug Bates and his colleagues for writing the lme4 package and collecting examples to show off the work.

Bates, D., Maechler, M., Bolker, B., & Walker, S. (2015). Fitting linear mixed-effects models using lme4. *Journal of Statistical Software, 67*(1), 1–48.

ANALYSIS OF COVARIANCE

Here's our last rendition of ANOVA. Analysis of covariance (ANCOVA) is particularly interesting because it basically allows you to equalize initial differences between groups. Let's say you are sponsoring a program to increase running speed and want to compare how fast two groups of athletes can run a 100-yard dash. Because strength is often related to speed, you have to make some correction so that strength does not account for any differences in the results at the end of the program. Rather, you want to see the effects of training with strength removed. You would measure participants' strength before you started the training program and then use ANCOVA to adjust final speed based on initial strength.

Michaela Hynie, John Lydon, and Ali Taradash from McGill University used ANCOVA in their investigation of the influence of intimacy and commitment on the acceptability of premarital sex and contraceptive use. They used ANCOVA with social acceptability of sexual activity as the dependent variable (in which they were looking for group differences) and ratings of a particular scenario as the covariate. ANCOVA ensured that differences in social acceptability were corrected using ratings, so this difference was controlled.

Want to know more? Go online or to the library and find ...

Hynie, M., Lydon, J., & Taradash, A. (1997). Commitment, intimacy, and women's perceptions of premarital sex and contraceptive readiness. *Psychology of Women Quarterly, 21,* 447–464.

ANCOVA in R

In the case of ANCOVA, we can use a function that we already learned about in Chapters 15 and 16—aov. Suppose in the first data set for Chapter 17 (ch17ds1.csv), we had a variable tracking how much time a family spent per week reading to their child at home. If we controlled for how much time was spent reading in addition to preschool, we might have a better idea of how many hours are optimal for improving language in preschoolers. We didn't have the variable in our data, but if we did, the syntax would look something like this:

```
> m1 <- aov(Language.Score ~ Group + Hours.Reading, data
= ch15ds1)
```

MULTIPLE REGRESSION

You learned in Chapter 18 how the value of one variable can be used to predict the value of another, an analysis often of interest to social and behavioral sciences researchers. For example, it's fairly well established that parents' literacy behaviors (such as having books in the home) are related to how much and how well their children read. We also started to talk about the use of more than one predictor, which is more common than use of a single predictor. What we didn't talk about in the book is that many of the statistical analyses we have taught you (*t* test, ANOVA, factorial ANOVA, and correlation) could have been computed using regression. In many ways, multiple regression is one of the most flexible tools in your toolbox of statistical methods. The way it is most typically used is plain old regression with multiple predictors.

It would seem quite interesting to look at such variables as class size, percentage of class that was teacher led, instructional strategies, and behavior management strategies to see what each contributes to academic engagement. Adam Lekwa, Linda Reddy, and Elisa Shernoff did exactly that, using regression analysis to examine the contribution of classroom and teaching style on student engagement in learning. With all predictors in the model, they found that all predictors but behavior management were significant predictors on engagement.

Want to know more? Go online or to the library and find ...

Lekwa, A. J., Reddy, L. A., & Shernoff, E. S. (2019). Measuring teacher practices and student academic engagement: A convergent validity study. *School Psychology Quarterly*, *34*(1), 109–118.

Multiple Regression in R

In the case of multiple regression, we can use a function that we already learned about in Chapter 18—`lm`. Suppose in the first data set for Chapter 18 (ch18ds1.csv), we had three more variables tracking number of hours per week doing cardio, participation in a team sport (yes or no), and whether the person worked with a trainer. If so, the model would look like this example.

```
> m1 <- lm(Injuries ~ Training + Cardio + Team +
Trainer, data = ch18ds1)
```

MULTILEVEL MODELS

This particular method unfortunately goes by many names: multilevel models, hierarchical linear models, random-effects models, fixed-effects models, mixed-effects models, cross-classified, multiple membership models, and growth curve models. All this means is that if you see one of these terms, you can bet they are talking in general about multilevel models. But what are they? Multi means more than 1 and level is what you have more than 1 of. For example, suppose you wanted to study students in classrooms across your state, not just one classroom in one school. We would then have students nested in classrooms, nested in schools, and nested in school districts. In this case, we have a four-level model. We explicitly identify how the students are nested because we expect students in the same class, school, and school district to be more like each other in their learning than students in a different class, school, and school district. And because we have students in all of these different classrooms, schools, and districts, the students in a single classroom are considered nonindependent, the major assumption we would be violating if we ignored our nested structure.

Multilevel modeling then is the perfect method for looking at bullying in schools. This study included a whopping 25,896 students from 114 schools that ranged from 4th to 12th grade. After controlling for student demographics, the strongest predictor of higher cognitive engagement, better behavior, and emotional engagement was a positive school climate.

Want to know more? Go online or to the library and find …

Yang, C., Sharkey, J. D., Reed, L. A., Chen, C., & Dowdy, E. (2018). Bullying victimization and student engagement in elementary, middle, and high schools: Moderating role of school climate. *School Psychology Quarterly, 33,* 54–64.

Multilevel Models in R

There are many ways to estimate multilevel models in R. The handiest way is one we showed you under repeated-measures analysis of variance—the `lmer` function in the lme4 package (Bates et al., 2015). In that example, we had multiple observations nested in research participants. This example uses data from a data set called cake, based on a data set collected for a master's thesis in which the researcher compared three different recipes and six different temperatures for baking chocolate cake (Cook, 1938)!

```
> library(lme4)
> fm1 <- lmer(Reaction ~ recipe * temperature +
(1 | recipe:replicate),
+ data = cake, REML = FALSE)
> summary(fm1)
```

Want to know more? Go online or to the library and find …

Cook, F. E. (1938). *Chocolate cake, I. Optimum baking temperature* (Unpublished master's thesis). Iowa State College, Ames.

META-ANALYSIS

Have you ever looked up a research topic and found 20+ articles on the same basic topic? Odds are the results of each study were different from the rest. So, which one do you pay attention to? If you are into meta-analysis, the answer is "All!" With meta-analysis, researchers combine data, usually those effect sizes we kept talking about, from several studies to examine patterns and trends. Given how much data are collected today, meta-analysis is a powerful tool to help organize disparate information and guide policy decision making.

For example, this methodology is useful when it comes to studying gender differences. There are so many studies showing so many differences (and lack thereof) that a tool like meta-analysis could certainly help clarify the meaning of all those studies' outcomes. Regarding job performance, there are many different views of gender differences. Philip Roth, Kristen Purvis, and Philip Bobko suggested that males generally are evaluated higher than females across a variety of situations, which include job performance. To clarify the nature of the differences that have been found in job performance between genders, these authors conducted a meta-analysis of job performance measures from field studies. They found that while job performance ratings favored females, ratings of promotion potential were higher for males. This is pretty interesting stuff! And it's a good example of how the technique of meta-analysis gives an accurate, 30,000-foot view of findings across many different studies.

Want to know more? Go online or to the library and find . . .

Roth, P. L., Purvis, K. L., & Bobko, P. (2012). A meta-analysis of gender group differences for measures of job performance in field studies. *Journal of Management, 38,* 719–739.

Meta-Analysis in R

Meta-analysis uses many of the different statistical tests that you have learned about in this textbook, like regression. So the methods aren't that difficult and you can look back at Chapters 4, 7, and 18 to find most of what you need statistically. The most challenging part is actually finding all of the effect size information in the studies you want to include in the meta-analysis. That and a class or a good book to guide you through the process.

LOGISTIC REGRESSION

Since odds of success or failure are so often a variable of interest, logistic regression is an especially good technique to use when one wants to see what sets of variables predict success. For example, it could answer such questions as what variables differentiate those patients who succeed from those who fail. It gives us an idea of how measures and personal characteristics might distinguish one group from another.

Researchers from the University of Texas studied how exposure to advertisements about e-cigarette use predicted current use and susceptibility to e-cigarette use. For exposure, they looked at retail ads, Internet ads, TV and movie ads, and print ads such as those found in a magazine. They found that if youth were exposed to all four types of ads, the odds of ever using an e-cigarette were 1.81 over not using and 2.22 for current use over nonuse.

Want to know more? Go online or to the library and find . . .

Mantey, D. S., Cooper, M. R., Clendennen, S. L., Pasch, K. E., & Perry, C. L. (2016). E-cigarette marketing exposure is associated with e-cigarette use among US youth. *Journal of Adolescent Health, 58,* 686–690.

Logistic Regression in R

Logistic regression is easy to estimate with a function called `glm`, which stands for generalized linear model. With logistic regression, we move away from ordinary least squares, appropriate for a continuous, normal dependent variable, to maximum likelihood. Don't worry about the estimation details.

For this example, let's turn to a very cool website run by some folks at UCLA:

https://stats.idre.ucla.edu/r/dae/logit-regression/

This example predicts admission to graduate school (success or fail) based on Graduate Record Examination scores, college grade point average, and rank. The family option tells `glm` that the dependent variable is binomial (two categories).

```
> m1 <- glm(admit ~ gre + gpa + rank, data = mydata,
family = "binomial")
```

FACTOR ANALYSIS

Factor analysis is a technique based on how well various items are related to one another and form clusters or factors. Each factor represents several variables, and factors turn out to be more efficient than individual variables at representing outcomes in certain studies. In using this technique, the goal is to represent those things that are related to one another by a more general name—this is the *factor*. And the names you assign to factors are not a willy-nilly choice; the names reflect the content and the ideas underlying how the variables might be related. The other useful fact about factor analysis is that there are two main types: exploratory and confirmatory. Exploratory is used if you are testing a brand-new set of questions to see how many factors are represented in the data. Confirmatory is used if you have an idea of how the questions should be organized in factors.

For example, Rachel Freed, Benjamin Emmert-Aronson, Kevin Alschuler, and John Otis examined the factor structure of the Coping Strategies Questionnaire–Revised with veterans experiencing chronic pain. They found that the six-factor structure confirmed by authors of the measures also worked for veterans. Those factors were catastrophizing, ignoring, distracting, distancing, coping self-statements, and praying.

> *Want to know more?* Go online or to the library and find . . .
>
> Freed, R. D., Emmert-Aronson, B. O., Alschuler, K. N., & Otis, J. D. (2018). Confirmatory factor analysis of the Coping Strategies Questionnaire–Revised for veterans with pain. *Psychological Services*. Advance online publication.

Factor Analysis in R

What we didn't tell you above is that for factor analysis, all you really need are covariances, the unstandardized version of correlations. Or you can provide some functions with the mean, standard deviations, and correlations and the function will produce the covariances from that information.

There are multiple ways to conduct an exploratory factor analysis in R. We recommend using the function `fa()` in the psych package. The `summary()` will produce a couple paragraphs with the results, and `print()` will show you all of the details from the factor analysis.

```
> library(psych)
> pa <- fa(Harman74.cor$cov,4,fm="pa" ,rotate="varimax")
> summary(pa)
> print(pa, sort = TRUE)
```

PATH ANALYSIS

Here's another statistical technique that examines correlations but allows researchers to suggest direction, or causality, in the relationship between variables. Basically, path analysis examines the direction of relationships through first a postulation of some theoretical relationship between variables and then a test to see if the direction of these relationships is supported by the data.

For example, Timothy Tansey, Kanako Iwanaga, Jill Bezyak, and Nicole Ditchman examined work motivation and self-determination for people with disabilities. The final model included autonomy, competency, relatedness, outcome expectancy, and vocational rehabilitation engagement as they related to employment. Although not all of these variables related in the way the researchers expected, the final model provided some support for this new self-determined work motivation model. Cool.

Want to know more? Go online or to the library and find . . .

Tansey, T. N., Iwanaga, K., Bezyak, J., & Ditchman, N. (2017). Testing an integrated self-determined work motivation model for people with disabilities: A path analysis. *Rehabilitation Psychology, 62,* 534–544.

Path Analysis in R

Path analysis can be estimated with a package called lavaan. There are many examples on the Internet but none in the help files. RStudio supports a website called RPubs. And on RPubs is an article called "Introduction to Path Analysis in R" by Thomas Bihansky. To run just the path analysis, all you will need to install is lavaan by Yves Rosseel and you can run everything through the `summary` function. If you want to run the full example, there are six more packages you will need to install. The best thing, all of the code is provided!

Bihansky, T. (2017, August 22). Introduction to path analysis in R. Retrieved from http://www.rpubs.com/tbihansk/302732

STRUCTURAL EQUATION MODELING

Structural equation modeling (SEM) is a relatively new technique that has become increasingly popular since it was introduced in the early 1960s. Some researchers feel that it is an umbrella term for techniques such as regression, factor analysis, and path analysis. Others believe that it stands on its own as an entirely separate approach. It's based on relationships among variables (as are the previous three techniques we described).

The major difference between SEM and other advanced techniques, such as factor analysis, is that SEM is *confirmatory* rather than *exploratory*. In other words, the researcher is more likely to use SEM to confirm whether a certain model that has been proposed works (meaning the data fit that model). In contrast, exploratory techniques set out to discover a particular relationship with less (but not no) model building beforehand.

For example, Heather Gotham, Kenneth Sher, and Phillip Wood examined the relationships among young adult alcohol use disorders; preadulthood variables (gender, family history of alcoholism, childhood stressors, high school class rank, religious involvement, neuroticism, extraversion, psychoticism); and young adult developmental tasks (baccalaureate degree completion, full-time employment, marriage). Using structural equation modeling techniques, they found that preadulthood variables were stronger predictors of developmental task achievement than was a diagnosis of having a young adult alcohol use disorder.

Want to know more? Go online or to the library and find . . .

Gotham, H. J., Sher, K. J., & Wood, P. K. (2003). Alcohol involvement and developmental task completion during young adulthood. *Journal of Studies on Alcohol, 64,* 32–42.

Structural Equation Modeling in R

So technically, the examples for factor analysis and path analysis are both SEM examples. In this section, the example will combine a confirmatory factor analysis with path analysis in a simple model. What is different from path analysis is the use of factors in our regression instead of the observed variables (don't worry if this paragraph doesn't make too much sense now).

```
> install.packages("lavaan")
> library(lavaan)
> example(sem)
```

Summary

Even though you probably will not be using these more advanced procedures anytime soon, that's all the more reason to know at least something about them, because you will certainly see them mentioned in various research publications and may even hear them mentioned in another class you are taking. With a basic understanding of these combined with your grasp of the fundamentals (from all the chapters in the book up to this one), you can be confident of having mastered a good deal of important information about introductory (and even some intermediate) statistics.

Student Study Site

Get the tools you need to sharpen your study skills! Visit **edge.sagepub.com/salkindshaw** to access practice quizzes and eFlashcards, watch R tutorial videos, and download data sets!

APPENDIX A

More Fun Stuff With R and RStudio

There are many things that you can do with R that we haven't even begun to describe in this book. This appendix provides basics on installing R and RStudio on a Mac and then some extra information about cool things that you can do with R. Let this appendix serve as the starting point. Then, if you want to know even more, let curiosity be your guide and turn to the Internet and your favorite search engine.

This appendix has four sections:

- Installing R and RStudio on a Mac
- Fun functions in R
- Other cool R things
- Citations for R stuff

INSTALLING R AND RSTUDIO ON A MAC

Like the installation of R and RStudio in Chapter 2, we will first walk through the steps to install R and then RStudio. The basic steps presented here follow steps described in Chapter 2 for installing on Windows. We recommend reading these steps with the rest of Chapter 2 so that you get the full overview of R and RStudio before more practice with RStudio in Chapter 3.

INSTALLING R

Navigate to the same website shown in Figure A.1 (https://cran.r-project.org/) that we used in Chapter 2 when installing R for Windows. In this case, we will click on the link to Download R for (Mac) OS X.

FIGURE A.1 ● Main website for R.

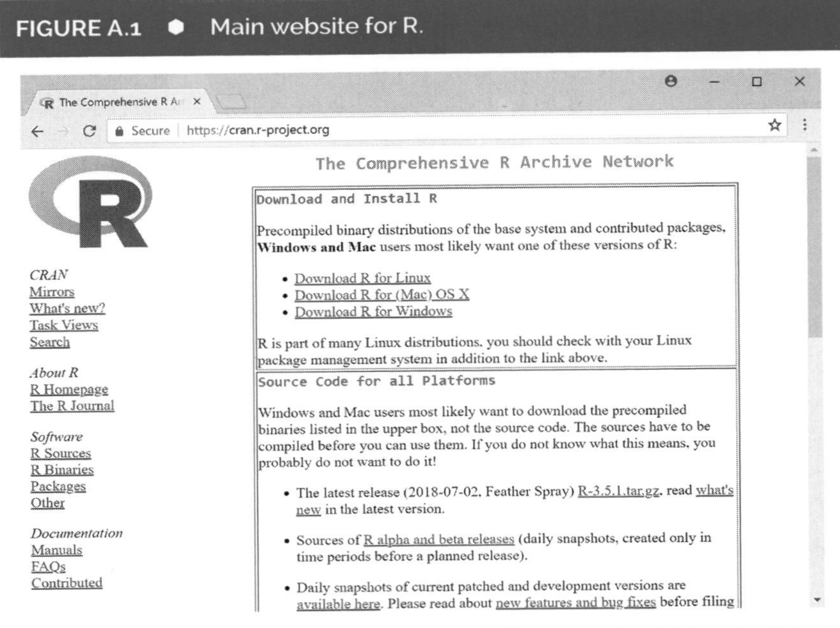

By clicking on the link to download R for Mac, we are taken to another webpage that should look very similar to Figure A.2.

FIGURE A.2 ● Webpage with R for Mac.

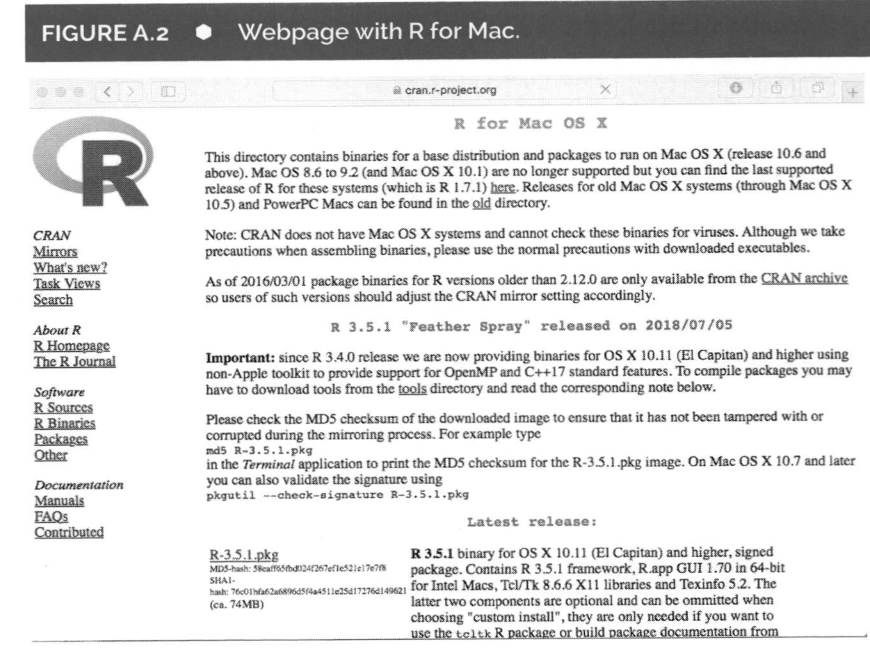

You will want to download the Latest Release. When this book was written, the Latest Release was R Version 3.5.1, so we downloaded R-3.5.1.pkg. After downloading the .pkg file, follow the steps below.

1. Open the Downloads folder and double-click on the file you just downloaded.
2. Double-click to launch the installation program.
3. Select the default settings to install R presented by the installation program until you have finished installation.
4. Open your Applications folder.
5. Scroll down to find the R icon and then double-click to open the application.

After opening R, you should see an application that looks like Figure A.3.

FIGURE A.3 ● R on a Mac.

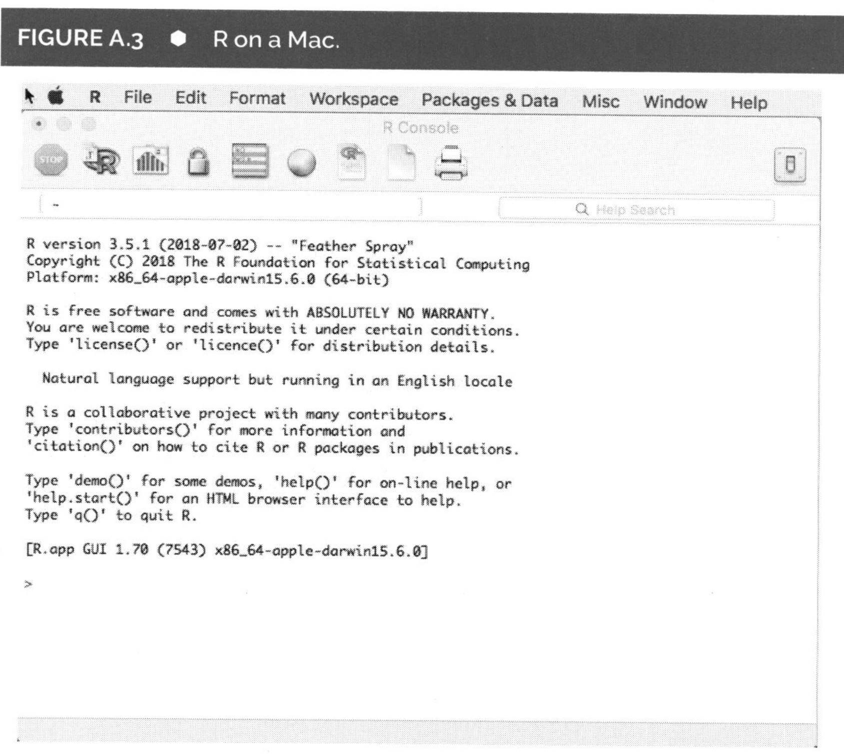

This window looks very much like Figure 2.3, which is R on Windows. Now let's test R to make sure it installed properly. To do this, we will enter some simple syntax at the > symbol.

```
> 2 + 3
```

You should get the following on the next line:

```
[1] 5
```

The [1] tells you it is showing you the first line of output and 5 is what we get from R when you add 2 + 3.

INSTALLING XQUARTZ

If you had read all of the webpage shown in Figure A.2, you may remember a section about needing to install XQuartz if you want to use the R package tcltk. We will not be using this library anywhere throughout the book, but sometimes packages in R require other packages. If you want to install XQuartz just in case it is needed, go to the webpage shown in Figure A.4 (xquartz.org) and download X11. Follow the default installation options while installing XQuartz.

FIGURE A.4 ● XQuartz for graphical functionality on a Mac.

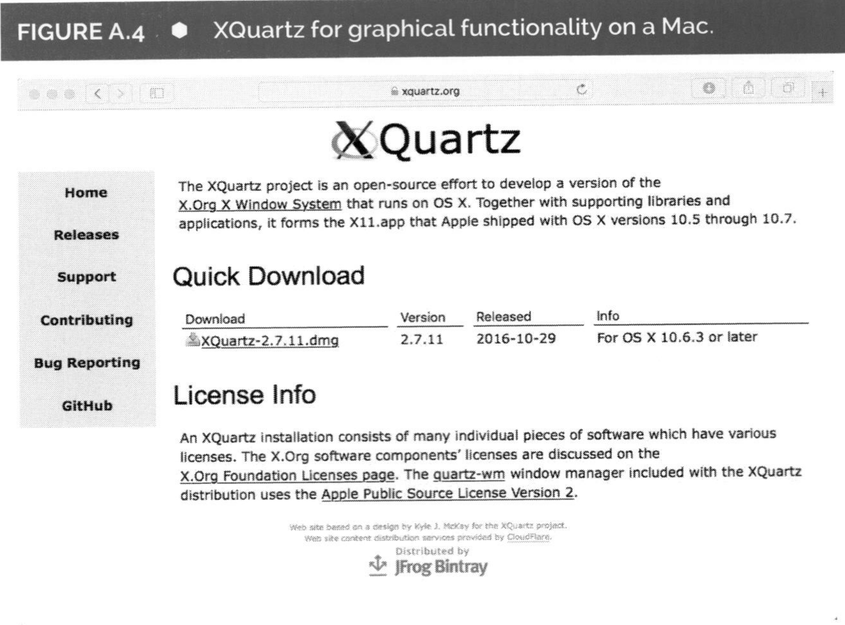

INSTALLING RSTUDIO

Now, we just need one more piece of software, RStudio. Navigate to https://www.rstudio.com/products/rstudio/download/. You should see a page like Figure A.5.

FIGURE A.5 ● Main webpage for selecting version of RStudio.

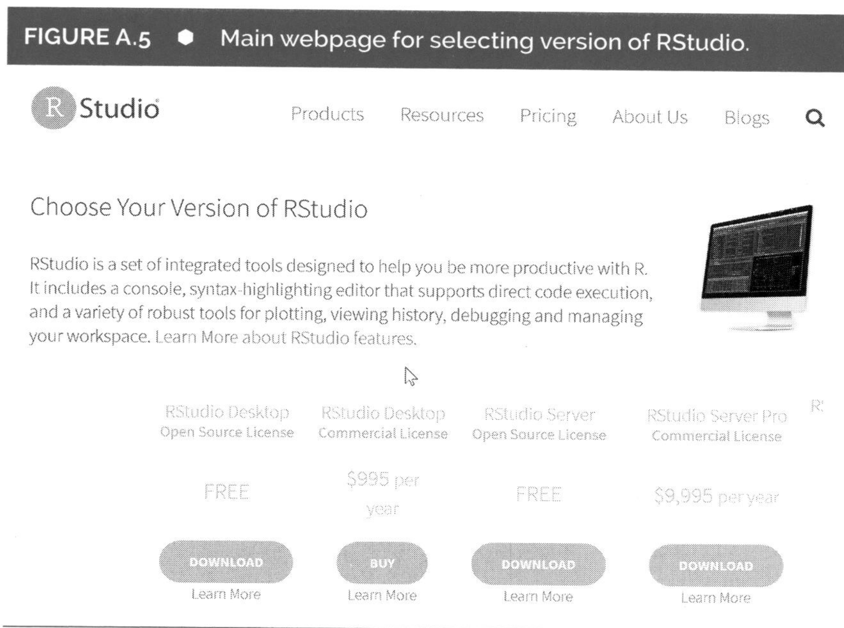

We want the page for RStudio Desktop with Open Source License. Clicking on the Download button will take you to a webpage like Figure A.6. The second link down should be for the Mac version of RStudio. The exact version will not match, but that is fine.

FIGURE A.6 ● Download links for RStudio including the version for Mac OS X.

Installers for Supported Platforms

Installers	Size	Date	MD5
RStudio 1.1.456 - Windows Vista/7/8/10	85.8 MB	2018-07-19	24ca3fe0dad8187aabd4bfbb9dc2b5ad
RStudio 1.1.456 - Mac OS X 10.6+ (64-bit)	74.5 MB	2018-07-19	4fc4f4f70845b142bf96dc1a5b1dc556
RStudio 1.1.456 - Ubuntu 12.04-15.10/Debian 8 (32-bit)	89.3 MB	2018-07-19	3493f9d5839e3a3d697f40b7bb1ce961
RStudio 1.1.456 - Ubuntu 12.04-15.10/Debian 8 (64-bit)	97.4 MB	2018-07-19	863ae806120358fa0146e4d14cd75be4
RStudio 1.1.456 - Ubuntu 16.04+/Debian 9+ (64-bit)	64.9 MB	2018-07-19	d96e63548c2add890bac633bdb883f32
RStudio 1.1.456 - Fedora 19+/RedHat 7+/openSUSE 13.1+ (32-bit)	88.1 MB	2018-07-19	1df56c7cd80e2634f8a9fdd11ca1fb2d
RStudio 1.1.456 - Fedora 19+/RedHat 7+/openSUSE 13.1+ (64-bit)	90.6 MB	2018-07-19	5e77094a88fdbddddb0d35708752462

Double-click to open the .dmg file that has been downloaded to your computer. You should see a link to your Applications folder and an RStudio icon. Drag the RStudio icon to the Applications folder. Now when you go to your Applications folder, double-click on the RStudio icon to launch RStudio. RStudio on your computer should look like Figure A.7 but matching the version of R you installed on your computer.

FIGURE A.7 ● RStudio running on a Mac.

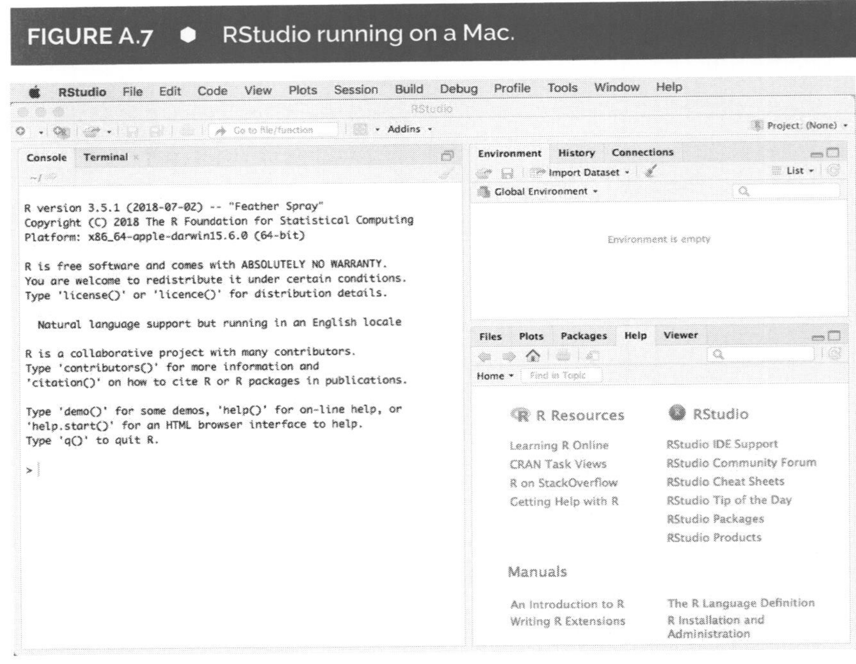

Now that you have installed R and RStudio on your Mac, you should be able to complete all of the examples and homework assignments that your instructor asks for. Good luck!

Fun Functions in R

In the early chapters, we showed you the basics. In some cases, we showed you some other functions to get the same results but packaged in a different way. With the freedom of R, there are typically many ways to accomplish a single thing. This section shows you some fun functions.

ggplot2

The package ggplot2 has some great functions for visualizing data. One is a violin plot—`geom-violin()`. Similar to a box plot, but you get to see the actual shape of the distribution—and in some cases, it kind of looks like a violin! It also has a cool function that creates a jitter in your plot. What does this mean? Sometimes when drawing a scatterplot, many points are at the same position but it just looks like 1 dot. The function `geom-jitter()` allows the dot to be placed near but not directly on its location so you can get an idea of how many points are actually in the same place.

rockchalk

This package has some useful functions for regression analysis. For looking at data like you did in Chapter 4, instead of `summary()`, this package has `summarizeFactors()` and `summarizeNumerics()` as two separate functions because we are often interested in different things when examining categorical variables versus continuous variables. If you want to combine categories in a variable like ice cream flavors, perhaps combining dark chocolate and milk chocolate into a single category of chocolate, `combineLevels()` can help with this task. Lastly, there are also some cool plotting functions like `plotPlane()` and `plotCurves()`.

stringr

Throughout this book, you have seen a lot of what R can do with numbers and with categorical data that get processed numerically. But R can do a lot with text as well. One package that is particularly user-friendly is stringr. Want to combine more than one string into a single string? Try `str_c()`. Want to put a bunch of strings in alphabetical or reverse alphabetical order? Try `str_order()`. And potentially most useful, we can use `str_sub()` to substitute one string for another.

RXKCD

This package is nothing but fun. This package will fetch a comic. You give it a number or let it choose randomly for you. We picked a number (195), and `getXKCD(195)` returned a map of Internet IP addresses. Try `getXKCD()` with any number of your choice. Note: You do need to be connected to the Internet for this function to work.

And More . . .

Everyone has their own opinion as to what is useful in R, whether it is a package or function. After you have become comfortable with the basics of R, try searching the phrase "useful functions in r" just to see what you get back. Someone else's useful function might just become your favorite!

Other Cool R Things

Creating Slide Presentations and Documents

Are you looking for another way to create slides for a presentation and want to include some cool graphics you created in R? Have you ever thought about using a markup language to create a highly polished PDF file for a paper? You can do both with RMarkdown in RStudio and more including HTML documents, Microsoft Word documents, and handouts. Check out http://rmarkdown.rstudio.com/gallery.html.

Creating Your Own Functions

Sometimes you will find yourself making copies of the same function over and over and just changing one thing, like the variable on the *x*-axis if you want to do a series of scatterplots with the same variable on the *y*-axis. Instead of copying the full syntax for a pretty scatterplot, you could create a function and then just call the function with the new *x*-axis variable. This webpage provides a nice overview on how to do this: https://www.statmethods.net/management/userfunctions.html.

Creating Your Own Packages

If R interests you enough, one day you might even create your own R package. Instead of creating a useful function here or there, you could create a whole set of functions that you would package together. Then other people could now install your package and use your functions. After all, R packages are basically a set of functions and help information on how to use those functions. Before you are ready for this step, you will probably spend a lot more time with R, but if you are curious about the basic process, check out https://hilaryparker.com/2014/04/29/writing-an-r-package-from-scratch/.

Citations for R Stuff

Although R is free, many people spend many hours to create and maintain the functions and packages you use. The least we can do is say thanks by letting the world know who we have to thank.

Package	Citation
BSDA	Kitchens, L. J. (2002). *Basic statistics and data analysis*. Boston, MA: Cengage Learning.
car	Fox, J., & Weisberg, S. (2011). *An {R} companion to applied regression* (2nd ed.). Thousand Oaks, CA: Sage. http://socserv.socsci.mcmaster.ca/jfox/Books/Companion
ggplot2	Wickham, H. (2016). *ggplot2: Elegant graphics for data analysis*. New York, NY: Springer-Verlag.
lavaan	Rosseel, Y. (2012). lavaan: An R package for structural equation modeling. *Journal of Statistical Software, 48*(2), 1–36. http://www.jstatsoft.org/v48/i02/
lme4	Bates, D., Maechler, M., Bolker, B., & Walker, S. (2015). Fitting linear mixed-effects models using lme4. *Journal of Statistical Software, 67*(1), 1–48. doi:10.18637/jss.v067.i01
ppcor	Kim, S. (2015). *ppcor: Partial and semi-partial (part) correlation*. R package version 1.1. https://CRAN.R-project.org/package=ppcor
psych	Revelle, W. (2018). *psych: Procedures for personality and psychological research*. Evanston, IL: Northwestern University. https://CRAN.R-project.org/package=psych Version = 1.8.4
R base	R Core Team. (2018). *R: A language and environment for statistical computing*. Vienna, Austria: R Foundation for Statistical Computing. https://www.R-project.org/

Package	Citation
rockchalk	Johnson, P. E. (2019). *rockchalk: Regression estimation and presentation.* R package version 1.8.140. https://CRAN.R-project.org/package=rockchalk
RXKCD	Sonego, P., & Korpela, M. (2017). *RXKCD: Get XKCD Comic from R.* R package version 1.8-2. https://CRAN.R-project.org/package=RXKCD
stringr	Wickham, H. (2019). *stringr: Simple, consistent wrappers for common string operations.* R package version 1.4.0. https://CRAN.R-project.org/package=stringr

APPENDIX B

Tables

TABLE B.1: AREAS BENEATH THE NORMAL CURVE

How to use this table:

1. Compute the z score based on the raw score and the mean of the sample.
2. Read to the right of the z score to determine the percentage of area underneath the normal curve or the area between the mean and computed z score.

TABLE B.2: *t* VALUES NEEDED FOR REJECTION OF THE NULL HYPOTHESIS

How to use this table:

1. Compute the t value test statistic.
2. Compare the obtained t value with the critical value listed in this table. Be sure you have calculated the number of degrees of freedom correctly and you have selected an appropriate level of significance.
3. If the obtained value is greater than the critical or tabled value, the null hypothesis (that the means are equal) is not the most attractive explanation for any observed differences and you reject the null hypothesis.
4. If the obtained value is less than the critical or table value, the null hypothesis is the most attractive explanation for any observed differences and you fail to reject the null hypothesis.

TABLE B.1 ● Areas Beneath the Normal Curve

z Score	Area Between the Mean and the z Score	z Score	Area Between the Mean and the z Score	z Score	Area Between the Mean and the z Score	z Score	Area Between the Mean and the z Score	z Score	Area Between the Mean and the z Score	z Score	Area Between the Mean and the z Score	z Score	Area Between the Mean and the z Score	z Score	Area Between the Mean and the z Score
0.00	0.00	0.50	19.15	1.00	34.13	1.50	43.42	2.00	47.72	2.50	49.83	3.00	49.87	3.50	49.98
0.01	0.40	0.51	19.50	1.01	34.38	1.51	43.45	2.01	47.78	2.51	49.40	3.01	49.87	3.51	49.98
0.02	0.80	0.52	19.85	1.02	34.61	1.52	43.57	2.02	47.83	2.52	49.41	3.02	49.87	3.52	49.98
0.03	1.20	0.53	20.19	1.03	34.85	1.53	43.70	2.03	47.88	2.53	49.43	3.03	49.88	3.53	49.98
0.04	1.60	0.54	20.54	1.04	35.08	1.54	43.82	2.04	47.93	2.54	49.45	3.04	49.88	3.54	49.98
0.05	1.99	0.55	20.88	1.05	35.31	1.55	43.94	2.05	47.98	2.55	49.46	3.05	49.89	3.55	49.98
0.06	2.39	0.56	21.23	1.06	35.54	1.56	44.06	2.06	48.03	2.56	49.48	3.06	49.89	3.56	49.98
0.07	2.79	0.57	21.57	1.07	35.77	1.57	44.18	2.07	48.08	2.57	49.49	3.07	49.89	3.57	49.98
0.08	3.19	0.58	21.90	1.08	35.99	1.58	44.29	2.08	48.12	2.58	49.51	3.08	49.90	3.58	49.98
0.10	3.98	0.60	22.57	1.09	36.21	1.59	44.41	2.09	48.17	2.59	49.52	3.09	49.90	3.59	49.98
0.11	4.38	0.61	22.91	1.10	36.43	1.60	44.52	2.10	48.21	2.60	49.53	3.10	49.90	3.60	49.98
0.12	4.78	0.62	23.24	1.11	36.65	1.61	44.63	2.11	48.26	2.61	49.55	3.11	49.91	3.61	49.98
0.13	5.17	0.63	23.57	1.12	36.86	1.62	44.74	2.12	48.30	2.62	49.56	3.12	49.91	3.62	49.98
0.14	5.57	0.64	23.89	1.13	37.08	1.63	44.84	2.13	48.34	2.63	49.57	3.13	49.91	3.63	49.98
0.15	5.96	0.65	24.22	1.14	37.29	1.64	44.95	2.14	48.38	2.64	49.59	3.14	49.92	3.64	49.98
0.16	6.36	0.66	24.54	1.15	37.49	1.65	45.05	2.15	48.42	2.65	49.60	3.15	49.92	3.65	49.98
0.17	6.75	0.67	24.86	1.16	37.70	1.66	45.15	2.16	48.46	2.66	49.61	3.16	49.92	3.66	49.98
0.18	7.14	0.68	25.17	1.17	37.90	1.67	45.25	2.17	48.50	2.67	49.62	3.17	49.92	3.67	49.98
0.19	7.53	0.69	25.49	1.18	38.10	1.68	45.35	2.18	48.54	2.68	49.63	3.18	49.93	3.68	49.98
0.20	7.93	0.70	25.80	1.19	38.30	1.69	45.45	2.19	48.57	2.69	49.64	3.19	49.93	3.69	49.98
0.21	8.32	0.71	26.11	1.20	38.49	1.70	45.54	2.20	48.61	2.70	49.65	3.20	49.93	3.70	49.99
0.22	8.71	0.72	26.42	1.21	38.69	1.71	45.64	2.21	48.64	2.71	49.66	3.21	49.93	3.71	49.99
0.23	9.10	0.73	26.73	1.23	39.07	1.73	45.82	2.23	48.71	2.73	49.68	3.23	49.94	3.73	49.99
0.24	9.48	0.74	27.04	1.24	39.25	1.74	45.91	2.24	48.75	2.74	49.69	3.24	49.94	3.74	49.99

(Continued)

TABLE B.1 (Continued)

z Score	Area Between the Mean and the z Score	z Score	Area Between the Mean and the z Score	z Score	Area Between the Mean and the z Score	z Score	Area Between the Mean and the z Score	z Score	Area Between the Mean and the z Score	z Score	Area Between the Mean and the z Score	z Score	Area Between the Mean and the z Score	z Score	Area Between the Mean and the z Score
0.25	9.97	0.75	27.34	1.25	39.44	1.75	45.99	2.25	48.78	2.75	49.70	3.25	49.94	3.75	49.99
0.26	10.26	0.76	27.64	1.26	39.62	1.76	46.08	2.26	48.81	2.76	49.71	3.26	49.94	3.76	49.99
0.27	10.64	0.77	27.94	1.27	39.80	1.77	46.16	2.27	48.84	2.77	49.72	3.27	49.94	3.77	49.99
0.28	11.03	0.78	28.23	1.28	39.97	1.78	46.25	2.28	48.87	2.78	49.73	3.28	49.94	3.78	49.99
0.29	11.41	0.79	28.52	1.29	40.15	1.79	46.33	2.29	48.90	2.79	49.74	3.29	49.94	3.79	49.99
0.30	11.79	0.80	28.81	1.30	40.32	1.80	46.41	2.30	48.93	2.80	49.74	3.30	49.95	3.80	49.99
0.31	12.17	0.81	29.10	1.31	40.49	1.81	46.49	2.31	48.96	2.81	49.75	3.31	49.95	3.81	49.99
0.32	12.55	0.82	29.39	1.32	40.66	1.82	46.56	2.32	48.98	2.82	49.76	3.32	49.95	3.82	49.99
0.33	12.93	0.83	29.67	1.33	40.82	1.83	46.64	2.33	49.01	2.83	49.77	3.33	49.95	3.83	49.99
0.34	13.31	0.84	29.95	1.34	40.99	1.84	46.71	2.34	49.04	2.84	49.77	3.34	49.95	3.84	49.99
0.35	13.68	0.85	30.23	1.35	41.15	1.85	46.78	2.35	49.06	2.85	49.78	3.35	49.96	3.85	49.99
0.36	14.06	0.86	30.51	1.36	41.31	1.86	46.86	2.36	49.09	2.86	49.79	3.36	49.96	3.86	49.99
0.37	14.43	0.87	30.78	1.37	41.47	1.87	46.93	2.37	49.11	2.87	49.79	3.37	49.96	3.87	49.99
0.38	14.80	0.88	31.06	1.38	41.62	1.88	46.99	2.38	49.13	2.88	49.80	3.38	49.96	3.88	49.99
0.39	15.17	0.89	31.33	1.39	41.77	1.89	47.06	2.39	49.16	2.89	49.81	3.39	49.96	3.89	49.99
0.40	15.54	0.90	31.59	1.40	41.92	1.90	47.13	2.40	49.18	2.90	49.81	3.40	49.97	3.90	49.99
0.41	15.91	0.91	31.86	1.41	42.07	1.91	47.19	2.41	49.20	2.91	49.82	3.41	49.97	3.91	49.99
0.42	16.28	0.92	32.12	1.42	42.22	1.92	47.26	2.42	49.22	2.92	49.82	3.42	49.97	3.92	49.99
0.43	16.64	0.93	32.38	1.43	42.36	1.93	47.32	2.43	49.25	2.93	49.83	3.43	49.97	3.93	49.99
0.44	17.00	0.94	32.64	1.44	42.51	1.94	47.38	2.44	49.27	2.94	49.84	3.44	49.97	3.94	49.99
0.45	17.36	0.95	32.89	1.45	42.65	1.95	47.44	2.45	49.29	2.95	49.84	3.45	49.98	3.95	49.99
0.46	17.72	0.96	33.15	1.46	42.79	1.96	47.50	2.46	49.31	2.96	49.85	3.46	49.98	3.96	49.99
0.47	18.08	0.97	33.40	1.47	42.92	1.97	47.56	2.47	49.32	2.97	49.85	3.47	49.98	3.97	49.99
0.48	18.44	0.98	33.65	1.48	43.06	1.98	47.61	2.48	49.34	2.98	49.86	3.48	49.98	3.98	49.99
0.49	18.79	0.99	33.89	1.49	43.19	1.99	47.67	2.49	49.36	2.99	49.86	3.49	49.98	3.99	49.99

TABLE B.2 ● *t* Values Needed for Rejection of the Null Hypothesis

df	One-Tailed Test 0.10	One-Tailed Test 0.05	One-Tailed Test 0.01	*df*	Two-Tailed Test 0.10	Two-Tailed Test 0.05	Two-Tailed Test 0.01
1	3.078	6.314	31.821	1	6.314	12.706	63.657
2	1.886	2.92	6.965	2	2.92	4.303	9.925
3	1.638	2.353	4.541	3	2.353	3.182	5.841
4	1.533	2.132	3.747	4	2.132	2.776	4.604
5	1.476	2.015	3.365	5	2.015	2.571	4.032
6	1.44	1.943	3.143	6	1.943	2.447	3.708
7	1.415	1.895	2.998	7	1.895	2.365	3.5
8	1.397	1.86	2.897	8	1.86	2.306	3.356
9	1.383	1.833	2.822	9	1.833	2.262	3.25
10	1.372	1.813	2.764	10	1.813	2.228	3.17
11	1.364	1.796	2.718	11	1.796	2.201	3.106
12	1.356	1.783	2.681	12	1.783	2.179	3.055
13	1.35	1.771	2.651	13	1.771	2.161	3.013
14	1.345	1.762	2.625	14	1.762	2.145	2.977
15	1.341	1.753	2.603	15	1.753	2.132	2.947
16	1.337	1.746	2.584	16	1.746	2.12	2.921
17	1.334	1.74	2.567	17	1.74	2.11	2.898
18	1.331	1.734	2.553	18	1.734	2.101	2.879
19	1.328	1.729	2.54	19	1.729	2.093	2.861
20	1.326	1.725	2.528	20	1.725	2.086	2.846
21	1.323	1.721	2.518	21	1.721	2.08	2.832
22	1.321	1.717	2.509	22	1.717	2.074	2.819
23	1.32	1.714	2.5	23	1.714	2.069	2.808
24	1.318	1.711	2.492	24	1.711	2.064	2.797
25	1.317	1.708	2.485	25	1.708	2.06	2.788
26	1.315	1.706	2.479	26	1.706	2.056	2.779
27	1.314	1.704	2.473	27	1.704	2.052	2.771
28	1.313	1.701	2.467	28	1.701	2.049	2.764
29	1.312	1.699	2.462	29	1.699	2.045	2.757

(Continued)

TABLE B.2 (Continued)

df	One-Tailed Test			df	Two-Tailed Test		
	0.10	0.05	0.01		0.10	0.05	0.01
30	1.311	1.698	2.458	30	1.698	2.043	2.75
35	1.306	1.69	2.438	35	1.69	2.03	2.724
40	1.303	1.684	2.424	40	1.684	2.021	2.705
45	1.301	1.68	2.412	45	1.68	2.014	2.69
50	1.299	1.676	2.404	50	1.676	2.009	2.678
55	1.297	1.673	2.396	55	1.673	2.004	2.668
60	1.296	1.671	2.39	60	1.671	2.001	2.661
65	1.295	1.669	2.385	65	1.669	1.997	2.654
70	1.294	1.667	2.381	70	1.667	1.995	2.648
75	1.293	1.666	2.377	75	1.666	1.992	2.643
80	1.292	1.664	2.374	80	1.664	1.99	2.639
85	1.292	1.663	2.371	85	1.663	1.989	2.635
90	1.291	1.662	2.369	90	1.662	1.987	2.632
95	1.291	1.661	2.366	95	1.661	1.986	2.629
100	1.29	1.66	2.364	100	1.66	1.984	2.626
Infinity	1.282	1.645	2.327	Infinity	1.645	1.96	2.576

TABLE B.3: CRITICAL VALUES FOR ANALYSIS OF VARIANCE OR *F* TEST

How to use this table:

1. Compute the *F* value.
2. Determine the number of degrees of freedom for the numerator ($k - 1$) and the number of degrees of freedom for the denominator ($n - k$).
3. Locate the critical value by reading across to locate the degrees of freedom in the numerator and down to locate the degrees of freedom in the denominator. The critical value is at the intersection of this column and row.
4. If the obtained value is greater than the critical or tabled value, the null hypothesis (that the means are equal to one another) is not the most attractive explanation for any observed differences and you reject the null hypothesis.
5. If the obtained value is less than the critical or tabled value, the null hypothesis is the most attractive explanation for any observed differences and you fail to reject the null hypothesis.

TABLE B.3 ● Critical Values for Analysis of Variance or *F* Test

df for the Denominator	Type I Error Rate	*df* for the Numerator					
		1	2	3	4	5	6
1	.01	4,052.00	4,999.00	5,403.00	5,625.00	5,764.00	5,859.00
	.05	162.00	200.00	216.00	225.00	230.00	234.00
	.10	39.90	49.50	53.60	55.80	57.20	58.20
2	.01	98.50	99.00	99.17	99.25	99.30	99.33
	.05	18.51	19.00	19.17	19.25	19.30	19.33
	.10	8.53	9.00	9.16	9.24	9.29	9.33
3	.01	34.12	30.82	29.46	28.71	28.24	27.91
	.05	10.13	9.55	9.28	9.12	9.01	8.94
	.10	5.54	5.46	5.39	5.34	5.31	5.28
4	.01	21.20	18.00	16.70	15.98	15.52	15.21
	.05	7.71	6.95	6.59	6.39	6.26	6.16
	.10	.55	4.33	4.19	4.11	4.05	4.01
5	.01	16.26	13.27	12.06	11.39	10.97	10.67
	.05	6.61	5.79	5.41	5.19	5.05	4.95
	.10	4.06	3.78	3.62	3.52	3.45	3.41
6	.01	13.75	10.93	9.78	9.15	8.75	8.47
	.05	5.99	5.14	4.76	4.53	4.39	4.28
	.10	3.78	3.46	3.29	3.18	3.11	3.06
7	.01	12.25	9.55	8.45	7.85	7.46	7.19
	.05	5.59	4.74	4.35	4.12	3.97	3.87
	.10	3.59	3.26	3.08	2.96	2.88	2.83
8	.01	11.26	8.65	7.59	7.01	6.63	6.37
	.05	5.32	4.46	4.07	3.84	3.69	3.58
	.10	3.46	3.11	2.92	2.81	2.73	2.67
9	.01	10.56	8.02	6.99	6.42	6.06	5.80
	.05	5.12	4.26	3.86	3.63	3.48	3.37
	.10	3.36	3.01	2.81	2.69	2.61	2.55
10	.01	10.05	7.56	6.55	6.00	5.64	5.39
	.05	4.97	4.10	3.71	3.48	3.33	3.22

(Continued)

TABLE B.3 (Continued)

df for the Denominator	Type I Error Rate	*df* for the Numerator					
		1	2	3	4	5	6
	.10	3.29	2.93	2.73	2.61	2.52	2.46
11	.01	9.65	7.21	6.22	5.67	5.32	5.07
	.05	4.85	3.98	3.59	3.36	3.20	3.10
	.10	3.23	2.86	2.66	2.54	2.45	2.39
12	.01	9.33	6.93	5.95	5.41	5.07	4.82
	.05	4.75	3.89	3.49	3.26	3.11	3.00
	.10	3.18	2.81	2.61	2.48	2.40	2.33
13	.01	9.07	6.70	5.74	5.21	4.86	4.62
	.05	4.67	3.81	3.41	3.18	3.03	2.92
	.10	3.14	2.76	2.56	2.43	2.35	2.28
14	.01	8.86	6.52	5.56	5.04	4.70	4.46
	.05	4.60	3.74	3.34	3.11	2.96	2.85
	.10	3.10	2.73	2.52	2.40	2.31	2.24
15	.01	8.68	6.36	5.42	4.89	4.56	4.32
	.05	4.54	3.68	3.29	3.06	2.90	2.79
	.10	3.07	2.70	2.49	2.36	2.27	2.21
16	.01	8.53	6.23	5.29	4.77	4.44	4.20
	.05	4.49	3.63	3.24	3.01	2.85	2.74
	.10	3.05	2.67	2.46	2.33	2.24	2.18
17	.01	8.40	6.11	5.19	4.67	4.34	4.10
	.05	4.45	3.59	3.20	2.97	2.81	2.70
	.10	3.03	2.65	2.44	2.31	2.22	2.15
18	.01	8.29	6.01	5.09	4.58	4.25	4.02
	.05	4.41	3.56	3.16	2.93	2.77	2.66
	.10	3.01	2.62	2.42	2.29	2.20	2.13
19	.01	8.19	5.93	5.01	4.50	4.17	3.94
	.05	4.38	3.52	3.13	2.90	2.74	2.63
	.10	2.99	2.61	2.40	2.27	2.18	2.11
20	.01	8.10	5.85	4.94	4.43	4.10	3.87
	.05	4.35	3.49	3.10	2.87	2.71	2.60
	.10	2.98	2.59	2.38	2.25	2.16	2.09

df for the Denominator	Type I Error Rate	*df* for the Numerator					
		1	2	3	4	5	6
21	.01	8.02	5.78	4.88	4.37	4.04	3.81
	.05	4.33	3.47	3.07	2.84	2.69	2.57
	.10	2.96	2.58	2.37	2.23	2.14	2.08
22	.01	7.95	5.72	4.82	4.31	3.99	3.76
	.05	4.30	3.44	3.05	2.82	2.66	2.55
	.10	2.95	2.56	2.35	2.22	2.13	2.06
23	.01	7.88	5.66	4.77	4.26	3.94	3.71
	.05	4.28	3.42	3.03	2.80	2.64	2.53
	.10	2.94	2.55	2.34	2.21	2.12	2.05
24	.01	7.82	5.61	4.72	4.22	3.90	3.67
	.05	4.26	3.40	3.01	2.78	2.62	2.51
	.10	2.93	2.54	2.33	2.20	2.10	2.04
25	.01	7.77	5.57	4.68	4.18	3.86	3.63
	.05	4.24	3.39	2.99	2.76	2.60	2.49
	.10	2.92	2.53	2.32	2.19	2.09	2.03
26	.01	7.72	5.53	4.64	4.14	3.82	3.59
	.05	4.23	3.37	2.98	2.74	2.59	2.48
	.10	2.91	2.52	2.31	2.18	2.08	2.01
27	.01	7.68	5.49	4.60	4.11	3.79	3.56
	.05	4.21	3.36	2.96	2.73	2.57	2.46
	.10	2.90	2.51	2.30	2.17	2.07	2.01
28	.01	7.64	5.45	4.57	4.08	3.75	3.53
	.05	4.20	3.34	2.95	2.72	2.56	2.45
	.10	2.89	2.50	2.29	2.16	2.07	2.00
29	.01	7.60	5.42	4.54	4.05	3.73	3.50
	.05	4.18	3.33	2.94	2.70	2.55	2.43
	.10	2.89	2.50	2.28	2.15	2.06	1.99
30	.01	7.56	5.39	4.51	4.02	3.70	3.47
	.05	4.17	3.32	2.92	2.69	2.53	2.42
	.10	2.88	2.49	2.28	2.14	2.05	1.98

(Continued)

TABLE B.3 (Continued)

df for the Denominator	Type I Error Rate	*df* for the Numerator					
		1	2	3	4	5	6
35	.01	7.42	5.27	4.40	3.91	3.59	3.37
	.05	4.12	3.27	2.88	2.64	2.49	2.37
	.10	2.86	2.46	2.25	2.14	2.02	1.95
40	.01	7.32	5.18	4.31	3.91	3.51	3.29
	.05	4.09	3.23	2.84	2.64	2.45	2.34
	.10	2.84	2.44	2.23	2.11	2.00	1.93
45	.01	7.23	5.11	4.25	3.83	3.46	3.23
	.05	4.06	3.21	2.81	2.61	2.42	2.31
	.10	2.82	2.43	2.21	2.09	1.98	1.91
50	.01	7.17	5.06	4.20	3.77	3.41	3.19
	.05	4.04	3.18	2.79	2.58	2.40	2.29
	.10	2.81	2.41	2.20	2.08	1.97	1.90
55	.01	7.12	5.01	4.16	3.72	3.37	3.15
	.05	4.02	3.17	2.77	2.56	2.38	2.27
	.10	2.80	2.40	2.19	2.06	1.96	1.89
60	.01	7.08	4.98	4.13	3.68	3.34	3.12
	.05	4.00	3.15	2.76	2.54	2.37	2.26
	.10	2.79	2.39	2.18	2.05	1.95	1.88
65	.01	7.04	4.95	4.10	3.65	3.31	3.09
	.05	3.99	3.14	2.75	2.53	2.36	2.24
	.10	2.79	2.39	2.17	2.04	1.94	1.87
70	.01	7.01	4.92	4.08	3.62	3.29	3.07
	.05	3.98	3.13	2.74	2.51	2.35	2.23
	.10	2.78	2.38	2.16	2.03	1.93	1.86
75	.01	6.99	4.90	4.06	3.60	3.27	3.05
	.05	3.97	3.12	2.73	2.50	2.34	2.22
	.10	2.77	2.38	2.16	2.03	1.93	1.86
80	.01	3.96	4.88	4.04	3.56	3.26	3.04
	.05	6.96	3.11	2.72	2.49	2.33	2.22
	.10	2.77	2.37	2.15	2.02	1.92	1.85

df for the Denominator	Type I Error Rate	*df* for the Numerator					
		1	2	3	4	5	6
85	.01	6.94	4.86	4.02	3.55	3.24	3.02
	.05	3.95	3.10	2.71	2.48	2.32	2.21
	.10	2.77	2.37	2.15	2.01	1.92	1.85
90	.01	6.93	4.85	4.02	3.54	3.23	3.01
	.05	3.95	3.10	2.71	2.47	2.32	2.20
	.10	2.76	2.36	2.15	2.01	1.91	1.84
95	.01	6.91	4.84	4.00	3.52	3.22	3.00
	.05	3.94	3.09	2.70	2.47	2.31	2.20
	.10	2.76	2.36	2.14	2.01	1.91	1.84
100	.01	6.90	4.82	3.98	3.51	3.21	2.99
	.05	3.94	3.09	2.70	2.46	2.31	2.19
	.10	2.76	2.36	2.14	2.00	1.91	1.83
Infinity	.01	6.64	4.61	3.78	3.32	3.02	2.80
	.05	3.84	3.00	2.61	2.37	2.22	2.10
	.10	2.71	2.30	2.08	1.95	1.85	1.78

TABLE B.4: VALUES OF THE CORRELATION COEFFICIENT NEEDED FOR REJECTION OF THE NULL HYPOTHESIS

How to use this table:

1. Compute the value of the correlation coefficient.
2. Compare the value of the correlation coefficient with the critical value listed in this table.
3. If the obtained value is greater than the critical or tabled value, the null hypothesis (that the correlation coefficient is equal to zero) is not the most attractive explanation for any observed differences and you reject the null hypothesis.
4. If the obtained value is less than the critical or tabled value, the null hypothesis is the most attractive explanation for any observed differences and you fail to reject the null hypothesis.

TABLE B.4 • Values of the Correlation Coefficient Needed for Rejection of the Null Hypothesis

One-Tailed Test			Two-Tailed Test		
df	.05	.01	*df*	.05	.01
1	.9877	.9995	1	.9969	.9999
2	.9000	.9800	2	.9500	.9900
3	.8054	.9343	3	.8783	.9587
4	.7293	.8822	4	.8114	.9172
5	.6694	.832	5	.7545	.8745
6	.6215	.7887	6	.7067	.8343
7	.5822	.7498	7	.6664	.7977
8	.5494	.7155	8	.6319	.7646
9	.5214	.6851	9	.6021	.7348
10	.4973	.6581	10	.5760	.7079
11	.4762	.6339	11	.5529	.6835
12	.4575	.6120	12	.5324	.6614
13	.4409	.5923	13	.5139	.6411
14	.4259	.5742	14	.4973	.6226
15	.412	.5577	15	.4821	.6055
16	.4000	.5425	16	.4683	.5897
17	.3887	.5285	17	.4555	.5751
18	.3783	.5155	18	.4438	.5614
19	.3687	.5034	19	.4329	.5487
20	.3598	.4921	20	.4227	.5368
25	.3233	.4451	25	.3809	.4869
30	.2960	.4093	30	.3494	.4487
35	.2746	.3810	35	.3246	.4182
40	.2573	.3578	40	.3044	.3932
45	.2428	.3384	45	.2875	.3721
50	.2306	.3218	50	.2732	.3541
60	.2108	.2948	60	.2500	.3248
70	.1954	.2737	70	.2319	.3017
80	.1829	.2565	80	.2172	.2830
90	.1726	.2422	90	.2050	.2673
100	.1638	.2301	100	.1946	.2540

TABLE B.5: CRITICAL VALUES FOR THE CHI-SQUARE TEST

How to use this table:

1. Compute the χ^2 value.
2. Determine the number of degrees of freedom for the *rows* $(R-1)$ and the number of degrees of freedom for the *columns* $(C-1)$. If your table is one-dimensional, then you have only columns.
3. Locate the critical value by locating the degrees of freedom in the *titled (df)* column. Then read across to the appropriate column for level of significance.
4. If the obtained value is greater than the critical or tabled value, the null hypothesis (that the frequencies are equal to one another) is not the most attractive explanation for any observed differences and you reject the null hypothesis.
5. If the obtained value is less than the critical or tabled value, the null hypothesis is the most attractive explanation for any observed differences and you fail to reject the null hypothesis.

TABLE B.5 ● Critical Values for the Chi-Square Test

	Level of Significance		
df	**.10**	**.05**	**.01**
1	2.71	3.84	6.64
2	4.00	5.99	9.21
3	6.25	7.82	11.34
4	7.78	9.49	13.28
5	9.24	11.07	15.09
6	10.64	12.59	16.81
7	12.02	14.07	18.48
8	13.36	15.51	20.09
9	14.68	16.92	21.67
10	16.99	18.31	23.21
11	17.28	19.68	24.72
12	18.65	21.03	26.22
13	19.81	22.36	27.69
14	21.06	23.68	29.14

(Continued)

TABLE B.5 (Continued)

	Level of Significance		
df	.10	.05	.01
15	22.31	25.00	30.58
16	23.54	26.30	32.00
17	24.77	27.60	33.41
18	25.99	28.87	34.80
19	27.20	30.14	36.19
20	28.41	31.41	37.57
21	29.62	32.67	38.93
22	30.81	33.92	40.29
23	32.01	35.17	41.64
24	33.20	36.42	42.98
25	34.38	37.65	44.81
26	35.56	38.88	45.64
27	36.74	40.11	46.96
28	37.92	41.34	48.28
29	39.09	42.56	49.59
30	40.26	43.77	50.89

APPENDIX C

Data Sets

These data files are referred to throughout *Statistics for People Who (Think They) Hate Statistics Using R*. They are available here to be entered manually, or you can download them from one of two places.

- The website hosted by SAGE at **edge.sagepub.com/salkindshaw**
- The author's website at http://onlinefilefolder.com. The username is *ancillaries*, and the password is *files*.

CHAPTER 3 SAMPLE DATA SET

Gender	Treatment	Test1	Test2
Male	Control	98	32
Female	Experiment	87	33
Female	Control	89	54
Female	Control	88	44
Male	Experiment	76	64
Male	Control	68	54
Female	Control	78	44
Female	Experiment	98	32
Female	Experiment	93	64
Male	Experiment	76	37
Female	Control	75	43
Female	Control	65	56
Male	Control	76	78
Female	Control	78	99
Female	Control	89	87

(Continued)

(Continued)

Gender	Treatment	Test1	Test2
Female	Experiment	81	56
Male	Control	78	78
Female	Control	83	56
Male	Control	88	67
Female	Control	90	88
Male	Control	93	81
Male	Experiment	89	93
Female	Experiment	86	87
Male	Control	77	80
Male	Control	89	99

CHAPTER 3 DATA SET 1

Age	Gender	Books Read by Child	Parental Interest
11	1	12	90
9	1	14	67
9	1	8	49
9	1	7	81
8	2	9	28
10	2	18	56
10	1	18	76
11	1	5	78
11	2	10	23
11	2	15	52
8	1	12	83
9	2	13	69
8	1	18	100
11	2	7	24
8	2	10	34
11	1	5	37
11	1	6	80

Age	Gender	Books Read by Child	Parental Interest
12	1	7	73
8	1	8	40
8	1	12	65
11	1	17	69
10	2	8	51
8	1	14	59
10	2	13	44
8	1	18	30
11	1	20	67
10	2	8	23
8	1	7	48
10	2	11	59
12	2	5	61
9	1	12	93
9	2	14	78
11	1	12	46
12	1	7	50
12	1	7	85
9	2	7	69
10	1	20	93
8	1	10	81
8	2	7	52
8	2	6	93
11	1	16	92
11	1	9	97
8	2	18	23
8	1	15	56
10	1	15	43
9	2	18	79
11	2	14	38
11	2	13	70
9	2	18	70
7	3	22	78

CHAPTER 4 DATA SET 1

Prejudice	Prejudice	Prejudice	Prejudice
87	87	76	81
99	77	55	82
87	89	64	99
87	99	81	93
67	96	94	94

CHAPTER 4 DATA SET 2

Score 1	Score 2	Score 3
3	34	154
7	54	167
5	17	132
4	26	145
5	34	154
6	25	145
7	14	113
8	24	156
6	25	154
5	23	123

CHAPTER 4 DATA SET 3

Beds	Infection Rate	Beds	Infection Rate
234	1.7	342	5.3
214	2.4	276	5.6
165	3.1	187	1.2
436	5.6	512	3.3
432	4.9	553	4.1

CHAPTER 4 DATA SET 4

Experience	Attitude	Experience	Attitude
Little	4	Moderate	8
Little	5	Moderate	1
Moderate	6	Little	6
Moderate	6	Little	5
Little	5	Moderate	4
Little	7	Moderate	3
Moderate	6	Lots	4
Moderate	5	Moderate	6
Lots	8	Little	7
Lots	9	Little	8

CHAPTER 5 DATA SET 1

Reaction Time	Reaction Time	Reaction Time	Reaction Time	Reaction Time
0.4	0.3	1.1	0.5	0.5
0.7	1.9	1.3	2.6	0.7
0.4	1.2	0.2	0.5	1.1
0.9	2.8	0.6	2.1	0.9
0.8	0.8	0.8	2.3	0.6
0.7	0.9	0.7	0.2	0.2

CHAPTER 5 DATA SET 2

Math Score	Reading Score	Math Score	Reading Score
78	24	72	77
67	35	98	89
89	54	88	7
97	56	74	56
67	78	58	78
56	87	98	99

(Continued)

(Continued)

Math Score	Reading Score	Math Score	Reading Score
67	65	97	83
77	69	86	69
75	98	89	89
68	78	69	73
78	85	79	60
98	69	87	96
92	93	89	59
82	100	99	89
78	98	87	87

CHAPTER 5 DATA SET 3

Height	Weight	Height	Weight
53	156	57	154
46	131	68	166
54	123	65	153
44	142	66	140
56	156	54	143
76	171	66	156
87	143	51	173
65	135	58	143
45	138	49	161
44	114	48	131

CHAPTER 5 DATA SET 4

Accuracy
12
15
11
5
3

Accuracy
8
19
16
23
19

CHAPTER 6 DATA SET 1

Reading	Reading	Reading	Reading	Reading
47	10	31	25	20
2	11	31	25	21
44	14	15	26	21
41	14	16	26	21
7	30	17	27	24
6	30	16	29	24
35	32	15	29	23
38	33	19	28	20
35	34	18	29	21
36	32	16	27	20

CHAPTER 6 DATA SET 2

Comprehension Score	Comprehension Score	Comprehension Score	Comprehension Score
12	36	49	54
15	34	45	56
11	33	45	57
16	38	47	59
21	42	43	54
25	44	31	56
21	47	12	43
8	54	14	44
6	55	15	41
2	51	16	42
22	56	22	7
26	53	29	
27	57	29	

CHAPTER 6 DATA SET 3

Monday	Tuesday	Wednesday	Thursday	Friday
12	17	10	15	20
9	11	10	4	0
6	8	9	5	10
4	0	5	4	9
9	7	8	5	11
10	5	4	4	15
13	12	7	3	10
22	16	18	15	20
1	3	6	4	2
5	8	4	6	7
7	0	3	8	2
10	4	1	8	12
4	5	8	6	9
15	12	10	9	11
3	6	4	7	10

CHAPTER 6 DATA SET 4

Pie	Pie
Cherry	Apple
Apple	Chocolate cream
Chocolate cream	Chocolate cream
Cherry	Chocolate cream
Chocolate cream	Chocolate cream
Chocolate cream	Apple
Apple	Chocolate cream
Chocolate cream	

CHAPTER 7 DATA SET 1

Income	Education	Income	Education
$36,577	11	$64,543	12
$54,365	12	$43,433	14
$33,542	10	$34,644	12
$65,654	12	$33,213	10
$45,765	11	$55,654	15
$24,354	7	$76,545	14
$43,233	12	$21,324	11
$44,321	13	$17,645	12
$23,216	9	$23,432	11
$43,454	12	$44,543	15

CHAPTER 7 DATA SET 2

Number Correct	Attitude	Number Correct	Attitude
17	94	14	85
13	73	16	66
12	59	16	79
15	80	18	77
16	93	19	91

CHAPTER 7 DATA SET 3

Speed	Strength	Speed	Strength
21.6	135	19.5	134
23.4	213	20.9	209
26.5	243	18.7	176
25.5	167	29.8	156
20.8	120	28.7	177

CHAPTER 7 DATA SET 4

Ach Inc.	Budget Inc.
0.07	0.11
0.03	0.14
0.05	0.13
0.07	0.26
0.02	0.08
0.01	0.03
0.05	0.06
0.04	0.12
0.04	0.11

CHAPTER 7 DATA SET 5

Exercise	GPA
25	3.6
30	4.0
20	3.8
60	3.0
45	3.7
90	3.9
60	3.5
0	2.8
15	3.0
10	2.5

CHAPTER 7 DATA SET 6

Age	Level	Score	Age	Level	Score
25	1	78	24	5	84
16	2	66	25	5	87

Age	Level	Score	Age	Level	Score
8	2	78	36	4	69
23	3	89	45	4	87
31	4	87	16	4	88
19	4	90	23	1	92
15	4	98	31	2	97
31	5	76	53	2	69
21	1	56	11	3	79
26	1	72	33	2	69

CHAPTER 8 DATA SET 1

ID	Item 1	Item 2	Item 3	Item 4	Item 5
1	3	5	1	4	1
2	4	4	3	5	3
3	3	4	4	4	4
4	3	3	5	2	1
5	3	4	5	4	3
6	4	5	5	3	2
7	2	5	5	3	4
8	3	4	4	2	4
9	3	5	4	4	3
10	3	3	2	3	2

CHAPTER 8 DATA SET 2

Fall	Spring	Fall	Spring
21	7	3	30
38	13	16	26
15	35	34	43
34	45	50	20
5	19	14	22

(Continued)

(Continued)

Fall	Spring	Fall	Spring
32	47	14	25
24	34	3	50
3	1	4	17
17	12	42	32
32	41	28	46
33	3	40	10
15	20	40	48
21	39	12	11
8	46	5	23

CHAPTER 8 DATA SET 3

ID	Form 1	Form 2	ID	Form 1	Form 2
1	89	78	51	73	93
2	98	75	52	91	87
3	83	70	53	81	78
4	78	97	54	97	84
5	70	91	55	97	85
6	86	82	56	91	79
7	83	97	57	71	99
8	73	88	58	82	97
9	86	81	59	95	97
10	83	80	60	70	76
11	83	95	61	70	88
12	94	75	62	96	96
13	90	96	63	70	77
14	81	87	64	71	70
15	82	93	65	87	89
16	98	82	66	97	71
17	99	84	67	81	75
18	83	78	68	89	75

ID	Form 1	Form 2	ID	Form 1	Form 2
19	72	77	69	71	73
20	86	94	70	71	82
21	80	85	71	75	81
22	80	86	72	72	97
23	93	92	73	88	78
24	100	98	74	86	77
25	84	98	75	70	92
26	89	99	76	79	88
27	87	83	77	96	81
28	82	95	78	82	88
29	95	90	79	97	74
30	99	92	80	93	72
31	82	78	81	70	82
32	94	89	82	76	84
33	97	100	83	74	88
34	71	81	84	81	81
35	91	96	85	88	86
36	83	85	86	70	90
37	95	75	87	91	73
38	72	88	88	96	94
39	98	74	89	81	99
40	89	88	90	95	86
41	83	80	91	72	100
42	100	81	92	93	90
43	72	100	93	76	78
44	97	82	94	91	90
45	71	81	95	100	78
46	74	93	96	76	92
47	79	82	97	78	87
48	91	70	98	74	88
49	81	90	99	80	92
50	87	85	100	93	96

CHAPTER 13 DATA SET 1

Group: 1 = treatment, 2 = no treatment

Group	Memory Test	Group	Memory Test	Group	Memory Test
1	7	1	5	2	3
1	3	1	7	2	2
1	3	1	1	2	5
1	2	1	9	2	4
1	3	1	2	2	4
1	8	1	5	2	6
1	8	1	2	2	7
1	5	1	12	2	7
1	8	1	15	2	5
1	5	1	4	2	6
1	5	2	5	2	4
1	4	2	4	2	3
1	6	2	4	2	2
1	10	2	5	2	7
1	10	2	5	2	6
1	5	2	7	2	2
1	1	2	8	2	8
1	1	2	8	2	9
1	4	2	9	2	7
1	3	2	8	2	6
1	1	2	8	2	8
1	1	2	8	2	9
1	4	2	9	2	7
1	3	2	8	2	6

CHAPTER 13 DATA SET 2

Gender	Hand Up	Gender	Hand Up
Boys	9	Boys	8
Girls	3	Girls	7

Gender	Hand Up	Gender	Hand Up
Girls	5	Boys	9
Girls	1	Girls	9
Boys	8	Boys	8
Boys	4	Girls	7
Girls	2	Girls	3
Girls	6	Girls	7
Boys	9	Girls	6
Boys	3	Boys	10
Girls	4	Boys	7
Boys	8	Boys	6
Girls	3	Boys	12
Boys	10	Girls	8
Girls	6	Girls	8

CHAPTER 13 DATA SET 3

Group	Attitude	Group	Attitude
Urban	6.50	Urban	4.23
Rural	7.90	Urban	6.95
Rural	4.30	Rural	6.74
Rural	6.80	Urban	5.96
Urban	9.90	Rural	5.25
Urban	6.80	Rural	2.36
Urban	4.80	Urban	9.25
Rural	6.50	Urban	6.36
Rural	3.30	Urban	8.99
Urban	4.00	Urban	5.58
Rural	13.17	Rural	4.25
Urban	5.26	Urban	6.60
Rural	9.25	Rural	1.00
Urban	8.00	Urban	5.00
Rural	1.25	Rural	3.50

CHAPTER 13 DATA SET 4

Group	Score	Group	Score
1	11	2	14
1	11	2	7
1	10	2	8
1	7	2	10
1	2	2	15
1	6	2	9
1	12	2	19
1	5	2	9
1	7	2	17
1	11	2	18
1	9	2	19
1	7	2	8
1	3	2	7
1	4	2	9
1	10	2	14

CHAPTER 13 DATA SET 5

Group	Score
1	5
2	6
1	5
2	4
1	5
2	8
1	7
2	6
1	8
2	7

CHAPTER 13 DATA SET 6

Used to compute the t score for the difference between two groups (Group 1 and Group 2) on the test variable

Group	Score
1	5
2	6
1	5
2	4
1	5
2	8
1	7
2	6
1	8
2	7
1	5
2	6
1	5
2	4
1	5
2	8
1	7
2	6
1	8
2	7

CHAPTER 14 DATA SET 1

Pretest	Posttest	Pretest	Posttest	Pretest	Posttest
3	7	6	8	9	4
5	8	7	8	8	4
4	6	8	7	7	5
6	7	7	9	7	6

(Continued)

(Continued)

Pretest	Posttest	Pretest	Posttest	Pretest	Posttest
5	8	6	10	6	9
5	9	7	9	7	8
4	6	8	9	8	12
5	6	8	8		
3	7	9	8		

CHAPTER 14 DATA SET 2

Before	After	Before	After
20	23	23	22
6	8	33	35
12	11	44	41
34	35	65	56
55	57	43	34
43	76	53	51
54	54	22	21
24	26	34	31
33	35	32	33
21	26	44	38
34	29	17	15
33	31	28	27
54	56		

CHAPTER 14 DATA SET 3

Before	After	Before	After
1.30	6.50	9.00	8.40
2.50	8.70	7.60	6.40
2.30	9.80	4.50	7.20
8.10	10.20	1.10	5.80
5.00	7.90	5.60	6.90

Before	After	Before	After
7.00	6.50	6.20	5.90
7.50	8.70	7.00	7.60
5.20	7.90	6.90	7.80
4.40	8.70	5.60	7.30
7.60	9.10	5.20	4.60

CHAPTER 14 DATA SET 4

Workers' shifts and feelings of stress

First	Second	First	Second
4	8	3	7
6	5	6	6
9	6	6	7
3	4	9	6
6	7	6	4
7	7	5	4
5	6	4	4
9	8	4	8
5	8	3	9
4	9	3	0

CHAPTER 14 DATA SET 5

Bone density in adults who participated in a weight-lifting class

Fall	Spring
2	7
7	6
6	9
5	8

(Continued)

(Continued)

Fall	Spring
8	7
7	6
8	7
9	8
8	9
9	9
4	9
6	7
5	8
2	7
5	6
4	4
3	6
6	7
7	7
6	6
5	9
4	0
3	9
5	8
4	7

CHAPTER 15 DATA SET 1

Group	Language	Group	Language
5 hours	87	10 hours	81
5 hours	86	10 hours	82

Group	Language	Group	Language
5 hours	76	10 hours	78
5 hours	56	10 hours	85
5 hours	78	10 hours	91
5 hours	98	20 hours	89
5 hours	77	20 hours	91
5 hours	66	20 hours	96
5 hours	75	20 hours	87
5 hours	67	20 hours	89
10 hours	87	20 hours	90
10 hours	85	20 hours	89
10 hours	99	20 hours	96
10 hours	85	20 hours	96
10 hours	79	20 hours	93

CHAPTER 15 DATA SET 2

Practice	Time	Practice	Time
< 15 hours	58.7	15–25 hours	54.6
< 15 hours	55.3	15–25 hours	51.5
< 15 hours	61.8	15–25 hours	54.7
< 15 hours	49.5	15–25 hours	61.4
< 15 hours	64.5	15–25 hours	56.9
< 15 hours	61.0	> 25 hours	68.0
< 15 hours	65.7	> 25 hours	65.9
< 15 hours	51.4	> 25 hours	54.7
< 15 hours	53.6	> 25 hours	53.6
< 15 hours	59.0	> 25 hours	58.7
15–25 hours	64.4	> 25 hours	58.7
15–25 hours	55.8	> 25 hours	65.7

(Continued)

(Continued)

Practice	Time	Practice	Time
15–25 hours	58.7	> 25 hours	66.5
15–25 hours	54.7	> 25 hours	56.7
15–25 hours	52.7	> 25 hours	55.4
15–25 hours	67.8	> 25 hours	51.5
15–25 hours	61.6	> 25 hours	54.8
15–25 hours	58.7	> 25 hours	57.2

CHAPTER 15 DATA SET 3

Shift	Stress	Shift	Stress
4 p.m. to midnight	7	Midnight to 8 a.m.	5
4 p.m. to midnight	7	Midnight to 8 a.m.	5
4 p.m. to midnight	6	Midnight to 8 a.m.	6
4 p.m. to midnight	9	Midnight to 8 a.m.	7
4 p.m. to midnight	8	Midnight to 8 a.m.	6
4 p.m. to midnight	7	8 a.m. to 4 p.m.	1
4 p.m. to midnight	6	8 a.m. to 4 p.m.	3
4 p.m. to midnight	7	8 a.m. to 4 p.m.	4
4 p.m. to midnight	8	8 a.m. to 4 p.m.	3
4 p.m. to midnight	9	8 a.m. to 4 p.m.	1
Midnight to 8 a.m.	5	8 a.m. to 4 p.m.	1
Midnight to 8 a.m.	6	8 a.m. to 4 p.m.	2
Midnight to 8 a.m.	3	8 a.m. to 4 p.m.	6
Midnight to 8 a.m.	5	8 a.m. to 4 p.m.	5
Midnight to 8 a.m.	4	8 a.m. to 4 p.m.	4
Midnight to 8 a.m.	6	8 a.m. to 4 p.m.	3
Midnight to 8 a.m.	5	8 a.m. to 4 p.m.	4
Midnight to 8 a.m.	4	8 a.m. to 4 p.m.	5

CHAPTER 15 DATA SET 4

Consumers' preferences for noodle thickness

Thickness	Pleasantness	Thickness	Pleasantness
Thick	1	Medium	3
Thick	3	Medium	4
Thick	2	Medium	5
Thick	3	Medium	4
Thick	4	Medium	3
Thick	4	Medium	4
Thick	5	Medium	3
Thick	4	Medium	3
Thick	3	Medium	2
Thick	4	Medium	3
Thick	3	Thin	1
Thick	2	Thin	3
Thick	2	Thin	2
Thick	3	Thin	1
Thick	3	Thin	1
Thick	4	Thin	1
Thick	5	Thin	2
Thick	4	Thin	2
Thick	3	Thin	3
Thick	2	Thin	2
Medium	3	Thin	1
Medium	4	Thin	1
Medium	3	Thin	2
Medium	2	Thin	2
Medium	3	Thin	3
Medium	4	Thin	3
Medium	4	Thin	2
Medium	4	Thin	1
Medium	3	Thin	2
Medium	3	Thin	1

CHAPTER 16 DATA SET 1

Treatment: 1 = high impact, 2 = low impact; Gender: 1 = male, 2 = female

Treatment	Gender	Loss	Treatment	Gender	Loss
High impact	Male	76	Low impact	Male	88
High impact	Male	78	Low impact	Male	76
High impact	Male	76	Low impact	Male	76
High impact	Male	76	Low impact	Male	76
High impact	Male	76	Low impact	Male	56
High impact	Male	74	Low impact	Male	76
High impact	Male	74	Low impact	Male	76
High impact	Male	76	Low impact	Male	98
High impact	Male	76	Low impact	Male	88
High impact	Male	55	Low impact	Male	78
High impact	Female	65	Low impact	Female	65
High impact	Female	90	Low impact	Female	67
High impact	Female	65	Low impact	Female	67
High impact	Female	90	Low impact	Female	87
High impact	Female	65	Low impact	Female	78
High impact	Female	90	Low impact	Female	56
High impact	Female	90	Low impact	Female	54
High impact	Female	79	Low impact	Female	56
High impact	Female	70	Low impact	Female	54
High impact	Female	90	Low impact	Female	56

CHAPTER 16 DATA SET 2

Severity	Treatment	Pain	Severity	Treatment	Pain
Severe	Drug 1	6	Mild	Drug 2	7
Severe	Drug 1	6	Mild	Drug 2	5
Severe	Drug 1	7	Mild	Drug 2	4
Severe	Drug 1	7	Mild	Drug 2	3
Severe	Drug 1	7	Mild	Drug 2	4

Severity	Treatment	Pain	Severity	Treatment	Pain
Severe	Drug 1	6	Mild	Drug 2	5
Severe	Drug 1	5	Mild	Drug 2	4
Severe	Drug 1	6	Mild	Drug 2	4
Severe	Drug 1	7	Mild	Drug 2	3
Severe	Drug 1	8	Mild	Drug 2	3
Severe	Drug 1	7	Mild	Drug 2	4
Severe	Drug 1	6	Mild	Drug 2	5
Severe	Drug 1	5	Mild	Drug 2	6
Severe	Drug 1	6	Mild	Drug 2	7
Severe	Drug 1	7	Mild	Drug 2	7
Severe	Drug 1	8	Mild	Drug 2	6
Severe	Drug 1	9	Mild	Drug 2	5
Severe	Drug 1	8	Mild	Drug 2	4
Severe	Drug 1	7	Mild	Drug 2	4
Severe	Drug 1	7	Mild	Drug 2	5
Mild	Drug 1	7	Severe	Placebo	2
Mild	Drug 1	8	Severe	Placebo	1
Mild	Drug 1	8	Severe	Placebo	3
Mild	Drug 1	9	Severe	Placebo	4
Mild	Drug 1	8	Severe	Placebo	5
Mild	Drug 1	7	Severe	Placebo	4
Mild	Drug 1	6	Severe	Placebo	3
Mild	Drug 1	6	Severe	Placebo	3
Mild	Drug 1	6	Severe	Placebo	3
Mild	Drug 1	7	Severe	Placebo	4
Mild	Drug 1	7	Severe	Placebo	5
Mild	Drug 1	6	Severe	Placebo	3
Mild	Drug 1	7	Severe	Placebo	1
Mild	Drug 1	8	Severe	Placebo	2
Mild	Drug 1	8	Severe	Placebo	4
Mild	Drug 1	8	Severe	Placebo	3
Mild	Drug 1	9	Severe	Placebo	5

(Continued)

(Continued)

Severity	Treatment	Pain	Severity	Treatment	Pain
Mild	Drug 1	0	Severe	Placebo	4
Mild	Drug 1	9	Severe	Placebo	2
Mild	Drug 1	8	Severe	Placebo	3
Severe	Drug 2	6	Mild	Placebo	4
Severe	Drug 2	5	Mild	Placebo	5
Severe	Drug 2	4	Mild	Placebo	6
Severe	Drug 2	5	Mild	Placebo	5
Severe	Drug 2	4	Mild	Placebo	4
Severe	Drug 2	3	Mild	Placebo	4
Severe	Drug 2	3	Mild	Placebo	6
Severe	Drug 2	3	Mild	Placebo	5
Severe	Drug 2	4	Mild	Placebo	4
Severe	Drug 2	5	Mild	Placebo	2
Severe	Drug 2	5	Mild	Placebo	1
Severe	Drug 2	5	Mild	Placebo	3
Severe	Drug 2	6	Mild	Placebo	2
Severe	Drug 2	6	Mild	Placebo	2
Severe	Drug 2	7	Mild	Placebo	3
Severe	Drug 2	6	Mild	Placebo	4
Severe	Drug 2	5	Mild	Placebo	3
Severe	Drug 2	7	Mild	Placebo	2
Severe	Drug 2	6	Mild	Placebo	2
Severe	Drug 2	8	Mild	Placebo	1

CHAPTER 16 DATA SET 3

Gender	CaffConsumption	Stress
Male	5	1
Male	6	3
Female	7	3
Male	7	2
Male	5	3

Gender	CaffConsumption	Stress
Male	6	3
Male	8	2
Male	8	2
Female	9	1
Female	8	1
Female	9	1
Female	7	2
Female	4	1
Female	3	1
Male	0	1
Female	4	2
Male	5	1
Female	6	2
Male	2	2
Male	4	3
Male	5	3
Female	5	3
Male	4	2
Male	3	2
Male	7	3
Female	8	2
Male	9	2
Male	11	1
Male	2	2
Male	3	1

CHAPTER 16 DATA SET 4

Gender	Training	Skill
Male	Strength emphasis	10
Male	Speed emphasis	5
Male	Strength emphasis	9
Male	Speed emphasis	3
Male	Strength emphasis	9
Male	Speed emphasis	2

(Continued)

(Continued)

Gender	Training	Skill
Male	Speed emphasis	5
Male	Strength emphasis	0
Male	Strength emphasis	0
Male	Speed emphasis	4
Male	Speed emphasis	3
Male	Speed emphasis	2
Male	Speed emphasis	2
Male	Speed emphasis	3
Male	Strength emphasis	10
Male	Speed emphasis	4
Male	Strength emphasis	3
Male	Speed emphasis	3
Male	Strength emphasis	0
Female	Speed emphasis	9
Female	Strength emphasis	3
Female	Strength emphasis	2
Female	Strength emphasis	3
Female	Speed emphasis	9
Female	Strength emphasis	1
Female	Strength emphasis	1
Female	Speed emphasis	9
Female	Speed emphasis	8
Female	Speed emphasis	7
Female	Speed emphasis	9

CHAPTER 17 DATA SET 1

Quality of marriage: 1 = low, 2 = moderate, 3 = high

MarriageQuality	ParentChildQual	MarriageQuality	ParentChildQual
1	58.7	2	54.6
1	55.3	2	51.5
1	61.8	2	54.7

MarriageQuality	ParentChildQual	MarriageQuality	ParentChildQual
1	49.5	2	61.4
1	64.5	2	56.9
1	61.0	3	68.0
1	65.7	3	65.9
1	51.4	3	54.7
1	53.6	3	53.6
1	59.0	3	58.7
2	64.4	3	58.7
2	55.8	3	65.7
2	58.7	3	66.5
2	54.7	3	56.7
2	52.7	3	55.4
2	67.8	3	51.5
2	61.6	3	54.8
2	58.7	3	57.2

CHAPTER 17 DATA SET 2

Motivation	GPA	Motivation	GPA
1	3.4	6	2.6
6	3.4	7	2.5
2	2.5	7	2.8
7	3.1	2	1.8
5	2.8	9	3.7
4	2.6	8	3.1
3	2.1	8	2.5
1	1.6	7	2.4
8	3.1	6	2.1
6	2.6	9	4.0
5	3.2	7	3.9

(Continued)

(Continued)

Motivation	GPA	Motivation	GPA
6	3.1	8	3.1
5	3.2	7	3.3
5	2.7	8	3.0
6	2.8	9	2.0

CHAPTER 17 DATA SET 3

Income	EducationLevel	Income	EducationLevel
$45,675	Low	$74,776	High
$34,214	Medium	$89,689	High
$67,765	High	$96,768	Medium
$67,654	High	$97,356	High
$56,543	Medium	$38,564	Medium
$67,865	Low	$67,375	High
$78,656	High	$78,854	High
$45,786	Medium	$78,854	High
$87,598	High	$42,757	Low
$88,656	High	$78,854	High

CHAPTER 17 DATA SET 4

StudyHours	Grade
0	80
5	93
8	97
6	100
5	75
3	83
4	98
8	100
6	90
2	78

CHAPTER 17 DATA SET 5

Age	ShoeSize	Intelligence	EducationLevel
15	Small	110	7
22	Medium	109	12
56	Large	98	15
7	Small	105	4
25	Medium	110	15
57	Large	125	8
12	Small	110	11
45	Medium	98	15
76	Large	97	12
14	Small	107	10
34	Medium	125	12
56	Large	106	12
9	Small	110	5
44	Medium	123	12
56	Large	109	18

CHAPTER 18 DATA SET 1

Training	Injuries	Training	Injuries
12	8	11	5
3	7	16	7
22	2	14	8
12	5	15	3
11	4	16	7
31	1	22	3
27	5	24	8
31	1	26	8
8	2	31	2
16	2	12	2
14	7	24	3

(Continued)

(Continued)

Training	Injuries	Training	Injuries
26	2	33	3
36	2	21	5
26	2	12	7
15	6	36	3

CHAPTER 18 DATA SET 2

Time	Record	Time	Record
14.5	5	13.9	3
13.4	7	17.3	12
12.7	6	12.5	5
16.4	2	16.7	4
21	4	22.7	3

CHAPTER 18 DATA SET 3

HomesSold	YearsInBusiness	EducationLevel
8	10	11
6	7	12
12	15	11
3	3	12
17	18	11
4	6	12
13	5	11
16	16	12
4	3	11
8	7	12
6	6	11
3	6	12
14	13	11

HomesSold	YearsInBusiness	EducationLevel
15	15	12
4	6	11
6	3	12
4	6	11
11	12	12
12	14	11
15	21	12

CHAPTER 19 DATA SET 1

Voucher	Voucher	Voucher	Voucher	Voucher
For	For	Maybe	Against	Against
For	For	Maybe	Against	Against
For	For	Maybe	Against	Against
For	For	Maybe	Against	Against
For	For	Against	Against	Against
For	Maybe	Against	Against	Against
For	Maybe	Against	Against	Against
For	Maybe	Against	Against	Against
For	Maybe	Against	Against	Against
For	Maybe	Against	Against	Against
For	Maybe	Against	Against	Against
For	Maybe	Against	Against	Against
For	Maybe	Against	Against	Against
For	Maybe	Against	Against	Against
For	Maybe	Against	Against	Against
For	Maybe	Against	Against	Against
For	Maybe	Against	Against	Against
For	Maybe	Against	Against	Against

CHAPTER 19 DATA SET 2

Sex	Vote	Sex	Vote
Male	Yes	Female	Yes
Male	Yes	Female	Yes
Male	Yes	Female	Yes
Male	Yes	Female	Yes
Male	Yes	Female	Yes
Male	Yes	Female	Yes
Male	Yes	Female	Yes
Male	Yes	Female	Yes
Male	Yes	Female	Yes
Male	Yes	Male	No
Male	Yes	Male	No
Male	Yes	Male	No
Male	Yes	Male	No
Male	Yes	Male	No
Male	Yes	Male	No
Male	Yes	Male	No
Male	Yes	Male	No
Male	Yes	Male	No
Male	Yes	Male	No
Male	Yes	Male	No
Male	Yes	Male	No
Male	Yes	Male	No
Male	Yes	Male	No
Male	Yes	Male	No
Male	Yes	Male	No
Male	Yes	Male	No
Male	Yes	Male	No
Male	Yes	Male	No
Male	Yes	Male	No
Male	Yes	Female	No

Sex	Vote	Sex	Vote
Male	Yes	Female	No
Male	Yes	Female	No
Male	Yes	Female	No
Male	Yes	Female	No
Male	Yes	Female	No
Male	Yes	Female	No
Male	Yes	Female	No
Male	Yes	Female	No
Female	Yes	Female	No
Female	Yes	Female	No
Female	Yes	Female	No
Female	Yes	Female	No
Female	Yes	Female	No
Female	Yes	Female	No
Female	Yes	Female	No
Female	Yes	Female	No
Female	Yes	Female	No
Female	Yes	Female	No
Female	Yes	Female	No
Female	Yes	Female	No
Female	Yes	Female	No
Female	Yes	Female	No
Female	Yes	Female	No
Female	Yes	Female	No
Female	Yes	Female	No
Female	Yes	Female	No
Female	Yes	Female	No
Female	Yes	Female	No
Female	Yes	Female	No
Female	Yes	Female	No
Female	Yes		

CHAPTER 19 DATA SET 3

Gender: 1 = male, 2 = female

Gender	Gender	Gender	Gender	Gender
Male	Male	Male	Female	Female
Male	Male	Male	Female	Female
Male	Male	Male	Female	Female
Male	Male	Male	Female	Female
Male	Male	Male	Female	Female
Male	Male	Female	Female	Female
Male	Male	Female	Female	Female
Male	Male	Female	Female	Female
Male	Male	Female	Female	Female
Male	Male	Female	Female	Female
Male	Male	Female	Female	Female
Male	Male	Female	Female	Female
Male	Male	Female	Female	Female
Male	Male	Female	Female	Female
Male	Male	Female	Female	Female
Male	Male	Female	Female	Female
Male	Male	Female	Female	Female
Male	Male	Female	Female	Female
Male	Male	Female	Female	Female
Male	Male	Female	Female	Female

CHAPTER 19 DATA SET 4

Preference	Preference
Nuts & Grits	Dimples
Nuts & Grits	Dimples
Nuts & Grits	Froggy
Nuts & Grits	Froggy
Nuts & Grits	Froggy
Nuts & Grits	Froggy

Preference	Preference
Nuts & Grits	Froggy
Nuts & Grits	Froggy
Nuts & Grits	Froggy
Bacon Surprise	Froggy
Bacon Surprise	Froggy
Bacon Surprise	Froggy
Bacon Surprise	Froggy
Bacon Surprise	Froggy
Bacon Surprise	Froggy
Bacon Surprise	Froggy
Bacon Surprise	Froggy
Bacon Surprise	Froggy
Bacon Surprise	Froggy
Bacon Surprise	Chocolate Delight
Bacon Surprise	Chocolate Delight
Bacon Surprise	Chocolate Delight
Bacon Surprise	Chocolate Delight
Bacon Surprise	Chocolate Delight
Bacon Surprise	Chocolate Delight
Bacon Surprise	Chocolate Delight
Bacon Surprise	Chocolate Delight
Bacon Surprise	Chocolate Delight
Bacon Surprise	Chocolate Delight
Bacon Surprise	Chocolate Delight
Bacon Surprise	Chocolate Delight
Bacon Surprise	Chocolate Delight
Bacon Surprise	Chocolate Delight
Bacon Surprise	Chocolate Delight
Bacon Surprise	Chocolate Delight
Bacon Surprise	Chocolate Delight
Dimples	Chocolate Delight
Dimples	Chocolate Delight

(Continued)

(Continued)

Preference	Preference
Dimples	Chocolate Delight
Dimples	Chocolate Delight
Dimples	Chocolate Delight
Dimples	Chocolate Delight
Dimples	Chocolate Delight
Dimples	Chocolate Delight
Dimples	Chocolate Delight
Dimples	Chocolate Delight
Dimples	Chocolate Delight
Dimples	Chocolate Delight
Dimples	Chocolate Delight
Dimples	Chocolate Delight

CHAPTER 19 DATA SET 5

Strength	Age
Strong	Young
Strong	Young
Strong	Young
Strong	Young
Strong	Young
Strong	Young
Strong	Young
Strong	Young
Strong	Young
Strong	Young
Strong	Young
Strong	Young
Strong	Young
Strong	Young
Strong	Young
Strong	Young

Strength	Age
Strong	Young
Strong	Young
Strong	Young
Strong	Young
Strong	Young
Strong	Young
Strong	Middle
Strong	Middle
Strong	Middle
Strong	Middle
Strong	Middle
Strong	Middle
Strong	Middle
Strong	Middle
Strong	Middle
Strong	Middle
Strong	Middle
Strong	Middle
Strong	Middle
Strong	Middle
Strong	Middle
Strong	Middle
Strong	Middle
Strong	Middle
Strong	Middle
Strong	Middle
Strong	Old
Strong	Old
Strong	Old
Strong	Old
Strong	Old
Moderate	Young

(Continued)

(Continued)

Strength	Age
Moderate	Young
Moderate	Young
Moderate	Young
Moderate	Young
Moderate	Young
Moderate	Young
Moderate	Young
Moderate	Young
Moderate	Young
Moderate	Young
Moderate	Young
Moderate	Young
Moderate	Young
Moderate	Young
Moderate	Young
Moderate	Young
Moderate	Young
Moderate	Middle
Moderate	Middle
Moderate	Middle
Moderate	Middle
Moderate	Middle
Moderate	Middle
Moderate	Middle
Moderate	Middle
Moderate	Middle
Moderate	Middle
Moderate	Middle
Moderate	Middle
Moderate	Middle
Moderate	Middle
Moderate	Middle

Strength	Age
Moderate	Middle
Moderate	Middle
Moderate	Middle
Moderate	Middle
Moderate	Middle
Moderate	Middle
Moderate	Middle
Moderate	Old
Moderate	Old
Moderate	Old
Moderate	Old
Moderate	Old
Moderate	Old
Moderate	Old
Moderate	Old
Moderate	Old
Moderate	Old
Weak	Young
Weak	Young
Weak	Young
Weak	Young
Weak	Young
Weak	Young
Weak	Young
Weak	Young
Weak	Young
Weak	Young
Weak	Young
Weak	Young
Weak	Middle
Weak	Middle
Weak	Middle

(Continued)

(Continued)

Strength	Age
Weak	Middle
Weak	Middle
Weak	Middle
Weak	Middle
Weak	Middle
Weak	Middle
Weak	Middle
Weak	Middle
Weak	Middle
Weak	Middle
Weak	Middle
Weak	Middle
Weak	Middle
Weak	Middle
Weak	Middle
Weak	Middle
Weak	Middle
Weak	Old
Weak	Old
Weak	Old
Weak	Old
Weak	Old
Weak	Old
Weak	Old
Weak	Old
Weak	Old

APPENDIX D

Answers to Practice Questions

CHAPTER 1

All of these questions are exploratory with no necessarily right answer. Their purpose is to get you involved in thinking about statistics as a field of study and a useful tool.

CHAPTER 2

1. R is a statistical computing language. The biggest advantage of R is that it is free. No cost! Nothing! Those people who create and maintain just ask that you give credit where credit is due in return for using R for free. The biggest minus to R is that it is very particular about its syntax—pay attention to case. There are other pluses and minuses; this is just one of each.
2. One way to get help with R is to turn to the Internet with any question. If you preface the question with "R," then the search results should return webpages pertaining to R and your question. Odds are someone has asked the exact same question as you. If you know which function you want to use, type "?*functionname*" in the R Console to get information directly.
3. Objects in R:
   a. Any type of data can be stored in a vector. You can store numbers, letters, words, TRUE and FALSE, or any combination of those things.
   b. Yes!
   c. Packages are a collection of functions. Functions perform a task for us, like providing summary information, calculating the mean, or other tasks.
4. In RStudio, run some of the functions we showed in the chapter.
   a. `library(help = "stats")`
   b. `data()`
   c. `help(help)`
   d. `library()`
5. The help text showed up in the Source pane.

6. RStudio is an integrated development environment for R. More simply, RStudio is an application that simplifies writing syntax, seeing what is in the environment, and performing many other tasks with R. R is a statistical programming language.

CHAPTER 3

1. The top left panel is the Source pane, and it is where you can write and save R syntax. The top right panel is the Environment and History pane, and here is where you can see what objects you have in your environment as well as all of the R commands you have run. The bottom left panel is the console where you can see the result of running R commands and functions. The bottom right panel is the Files, Plots, Packages, Help, and Viewer pane, with each tab showing something different. Files shows the files on your computer in the current working directory. Plots shows the charts, graphs, and plots you generate. Packages provides a list of every package installed on your local computer. Help is where the help information displays. The Viewer tab displays webpages that you create locally on your computer with R.
2. You would look at the History tab on the top right pane.
3. Enter and assign a name to the following simple data set in RStudio.
    - 513, 545, 354, 675, 873
        a. `Numbers <- c(513, 545, 354, 675, 873)`
        b. This list of objects will depend on how many objects you have created.
        c. The R syntax and result are

```
> summary(Numbers)
Min. 1st Qu. Median Mean 3rd Qu. Max.
354 513 545 592 675 873
>
```

4. The summary of Chapter 3 Data Set 1 (ch3ds1.csv).

```
> summary(ch3ds1)
      Age             Gender        Books.Read.by.Child Parental.Interest
Min.   : 7.00    Min.   :1.00    Min.   : 5.00    Min.   : 23.00
1st Qu.: 8.00    1st Qu.:1.00    1st Qu.: 7.25    1st Qu.: 46.50
Median :10.00    Median :1.00    Median :12.00    Median : 66.00
Mean   : 9.64    Mean   :1.46    Mean   :11.90    Mean   : 62.04
3rd Qu.:11.00    3rd Qu.:2.00    3rd Qu.:15.00    3rd Qu.: 78.75
Max.   :12.00    Max.   :3.00    Max.   :22.00    Max.   :100.00
>
```

CHAPTER 4

1. By hand (easy test!):

   Mean = 87.55

   Median = 88

   Mode = 94

2.

	Score 1	Score 2	Score 3
Mean	5.6	27.6	144.3
Median	5.5	25.0	149.5
Mode	5	25, 34	154

3. Here's the answer:

	Hospital Size	Infection Rate
Mean	335.10	3.7200

4. Here's what your one paragraph might look like.

   As usual, the Chicken Littles (the mode) led the way in sales. The total value of food sold was $303, for an average of $2.55 for each special.

5. There's nothing too dramatic here in terms of values that are really big or small or look weird (all reasons to use the median), so we'll just use the mean. You can see the mean for the three stores in the last column. Seems like these might be the numbers you want the new store to approximate for it to be around the average of all the stores you manage.

Average	Store 1	Store 2	Store 3	Mean
Sales (in thousands of dollars)	$323	$234	$308	$288.83
Number of items purchased	3,454	5,645	4,565	4,554.67
Number of visitors	4,534	6,765	6,654	5,984.33

6. Well, it seems like beer chicken is the winner and the fruit cup comes in last. We computed the mean since this is a rating of values across a scale that is interval (at least in its intent). Here are the data:

Snack Food	North Fans	East Fans	South Fans	West Fans	Mean Rating
Loaded Nachos	4	4	5	4	4.25
Fruit Cup	2	1	2	1	1.5
Spicy Wings	4	3	3	3	3.25
Gargantuan Overstuffed Pizza	3	4	4	5	4
Beer Chicken	5	5	5	4	4.75

7. You use the median when you have extreme scores that would disproportionately bias the mean. One situation in which the median is preferable to the mean is when income is reported. Because it varies so much, you want a measure of central tendency that is insensitive to extreme scores. As another example, say you are studying the speed with which a group of adolescents can run 100 yards when one or two individuals are exceptionally fast.
8. You would use the median because it is insensitive to extreme scores.
9. The median is the best measure of central tendency, and it is the one score that best represents the entire set of scores. Why? Because it is relatively unaffected by the (somewhat) extreme data point of $199,000. As you can see in the following table, the mean is affected (it is more than $83,000 when the highest score is included).

Before removal of highest score	Mean	$83,111
	Median	$77,153
After removal of highest score	Mean	$75,318
	Median	$76,564

10. The averages are as follows: Group 1 = 5.88, Group 2 = 5.00, and Group 3 = 7.00.
11. This should be an easy one. Any time values are expressed as categories, the only type of average that makes sense is the mode. So, who likes pie? Well, the first week, the winner is apple, and Week 2 finds apple once again the leader. For Week 3, it's Douglas County Pie, and the month is finished up in Week 4 with lots of helpings of chocolate silk.

CHAPTER 5

1. The range is the most convenient measure of dispersion, because it requires only that you subtract one number (the lowest value) from another number (the highest value). It's imprecise because it does not take into account the values that fall between the highest and the lowest values in a distribution. Use the range when you want a very gross (not very precise) estimate of the variability in a distribution.

2.

High Score	Low Score	Inclusive Range	Exclusive Range
12.1	3	10.1	9.1
92	51	42	41
42	42	1	0
7.5	6	2.5	1.5
27	26	2	24

3. For the most part, first-year students have stopped growing by that time, and the enormous variability that one sees in early childhood and adolescence has evened out. On a personality measure, however, those individual differences seem to be constant and are expressed similarly at any age.

4. As individuals score more similarly, they are closer to the mean, and the deviation about the mean is smaller. Hence, the standard deviation is smaller as well. There's strength in numbers, and the larger the data set, the more inclusive it is. That is, it includes more, rather than fewer, values that are similar to one another—hence, less variability.

5. The exclusive range is 39. The unbiased sample standard deviation equals 13.10. The biased estimate equals 12.42. The difference is due to dividing by a sample size of 9 (for the unbiased estimate) as compared with a sample size of 10 (for the biased estimate). The unbiased estimate of the variance is 171.66, and the biased estimate is 154.49.

6. The unbiased estimate is always larger than the biased estimate because the unbiased estimate actually overestimates the value of the statistic intentionally to be more conservative. And the numerator ($n - 1$) for the unbiased statistic is always less than for the biased estimate (which is n), resulting in a larger value.

7.

Test 1		Test 2		Test 3	
Mean	49.00	Mean	50.10	Mean	49.30
Median	49.00	Median	49.50	Median	48.00
Mode	49	Mode	49	Mode	45
Range	5	Range	9	Range	10
Standard deviation	1.41	Standard deviation	2.69	Standard deviation	3.94
Variance	2	Variance	7.21	Variance	15.57

Test 2 has the highest average score, and Test 1 has the smallest amount of variability. Also, there are multiple modes, and R computes and reports the smallest value.

8. The standard deviation is 12.39, and the variance is 153.53.
9. The standard deviation is the square root of the variance (which is 36), making the standard deviation 6. You can't possibly know what the range is by knowing only the standard deviation or the variance. You can't even tell whether the range is large or small, because you don't know what's being measured and you don't know the scale of the measurement (itsy-bitsy bugs or output from steam engines).
10.
   a. Range = 6, standard deviation = 2.58, variance = 6.67.
   b. Range = 0.6, standard deviation = 0.25, variance = 0.06.
   c. Range = 3.5, standard deviation = 1.58, variance = 2.49.
   d. Range = 123, standard deviation = 48.23, variance = 2,326.5.
11. Here's a chart that summarizes the results:

	Height	Weight
Standard deviation	11.44	15.65
Variance	130.78	245.00
Range	43	59

12. Okay, here's how you answer it. Compute the standard deviation for any set of 10 or so numbers by hand using the formula for the standard deviation that has $n - 1$ in the denominator (the unbiased estimate). Then compare it, using the same numbers, with the R output. As you will see, they are the same, indicating that R produces an unbiased estimate. If you got this one correct, you know what you're doing—go to the head of the class.
13. The unbiased estimate of the standard deviation is 6.49, and the biased estimate is 6.15. The unbiased estimate of the variance is 42.1, and the biased estimate is 37.89. The biased estimates are (always) smaller because they are based on a larger n and are a more conservative estimate.
14. A standard deviation of 0.94 means that on average, each score in the set of scores is a distance of 0.94 correct words from the average of all scores.

CHAPTER 6

1.
   a. Here's the frequency distribution:

Class Interval	Frequency
55–59	7
50–54	5
45–49	5
40–44	7
35–39	2
30–34	3
25–29	5
20–24	4
15–19	4
10–14	4
5–9	3
0–4	1

In Figure D.1, you can see what the histogram could look like:

FIGURE D.1 ● Histogram of data in Chapter 6 Data Set 1.

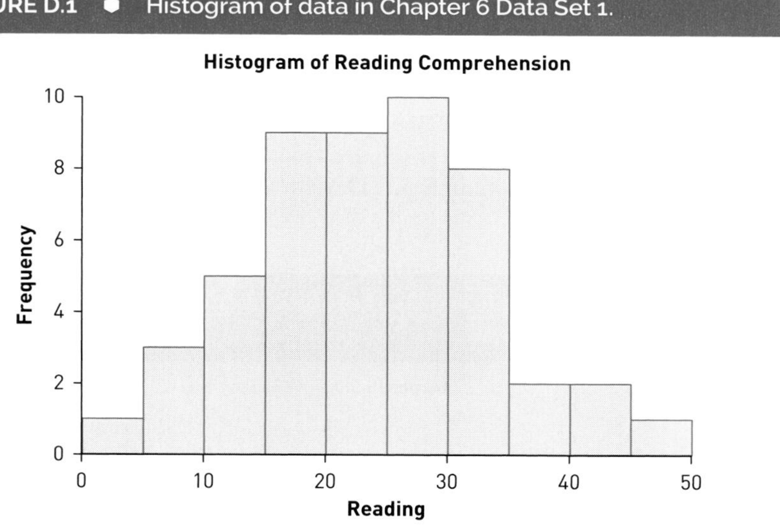

You may note that the *x*-axis in the histogram that you created is different from the one you see here. We double-clicked on it and, entering the Chart Editor, changed the number of ticks, range, and starting point for this axis. Nothing too different—it just looks a bit nicer.

b. We settled on a class interval of 5 because it allowed us to have close to 10 class intervals; it fit the criteria that we discussed in this chapter for deciding on a class interval.

c. The distribution is negatively skewed because the mean is less than the median.

2. In Figure D.2, you can see what the histogram could look like:

FIGURE D.2 ● Histogram of data in Chapter 6 Data Set 2.

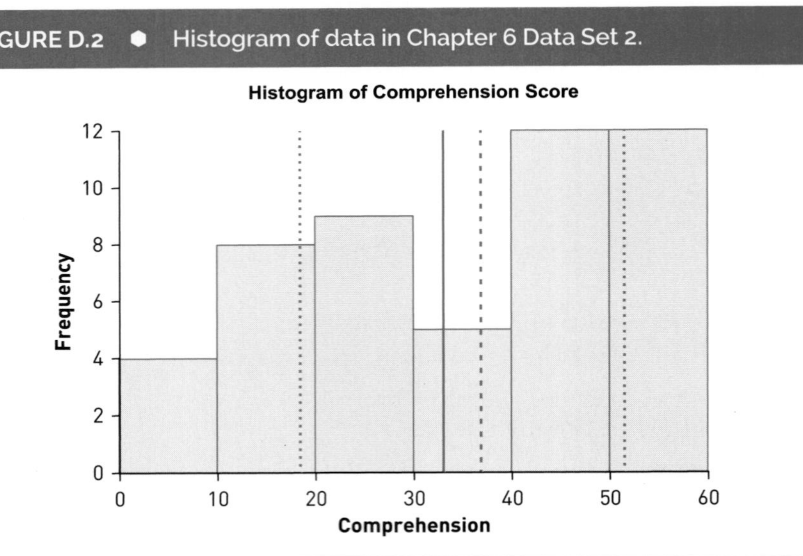

3. Your bar chart will look different depending upon the length of your *x*- and *y*-axes and other variables. The first thing you need to compute is the sum for each day, saving the results into a vector. Then use those values to create the bar chart as shown in Figure D.3.

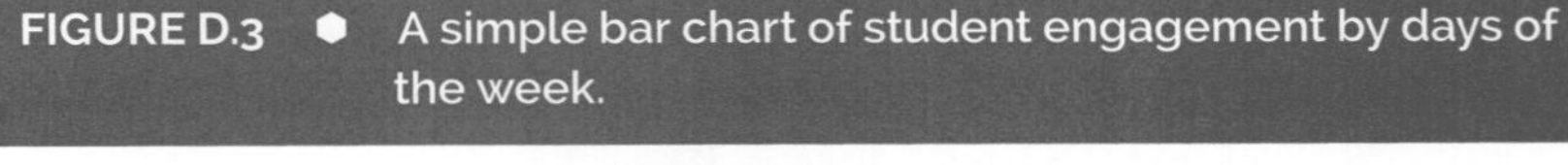
FIGURE D.3 ● A simple bar chart of student engagement by days of the week.

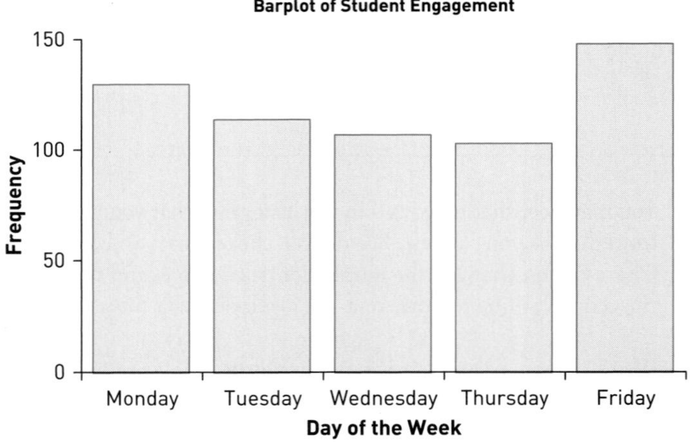

4.

   a. The line type will be dotdash.

   b. We could write `lty = 2` or `lty = "dashed"`.

5.

   a. Line because you are looking at a trend (over time).

   b. Bar because you are looking at a number of discrete categories.

   c. Bar because you are looking at a number of discrete categories.

6. You will come up with examples of your own, but here are some of ours. Draw your own examples.

   a. The number of words that a child knows as a function of ages from 12 months to 36 months

   b. The percentage of senior citizens who belong to AARP as a function of gender and ethnicity

   c. The plotting of paired scores such as height and weight for each individual. We haven't discussed this type of chart much, but you will see more like it in Chapter 7.

7. On your own!

8. We created Figure D.4, and it's as uninformative as it is ugly. Major chart junk attack.

9. A picture (a chart or graph) is worth more than 1,000 words. In other words, there are many possible answers to such a question, but in general, the purpose of a chart or a graph is to visually illustrate information in a way that is as simple as possible while communicating a central message that is clear and direct.

FIGURE D.4 ● A really, really ugly chart.

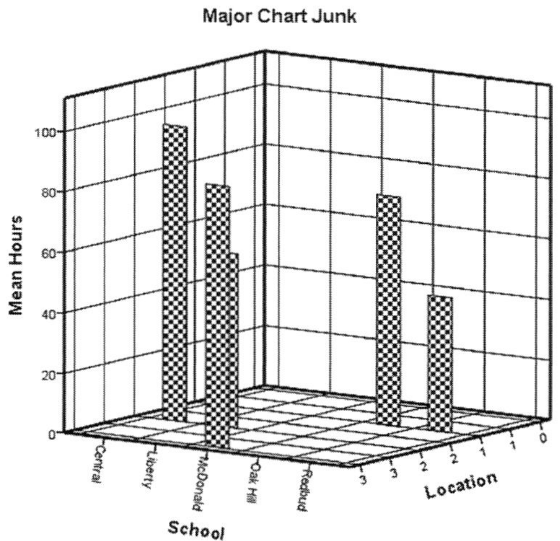

CHAPTER 7

1.

   a. r = .596.

   b. From the answer to 1a, you already know that the correlation is direct. But from the scatterplot shown in Figure D.5 (we used R, but you should do it by hand), you can predict it to be such (without actually knowing the sign of the coefficient) because the data points group themselves from the lower left corner of the graph to the upper right corner and assume a positive slope.

FIGURE D.5 ● Scatterplot of data from Chapter 7 Data Set 2.

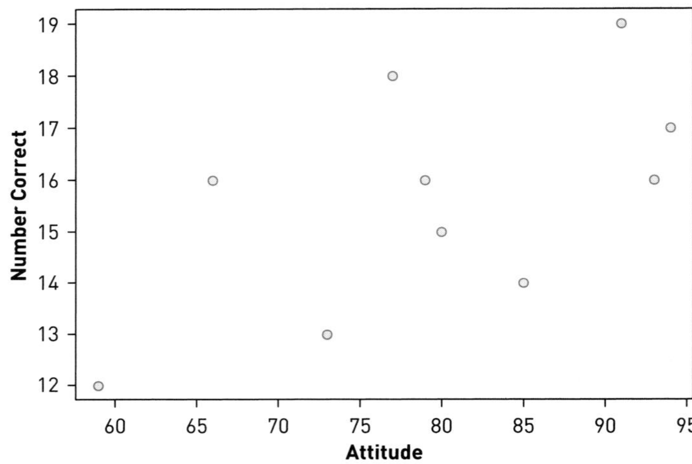

2.

   a. r = .269.

   b. According to Table 7.3, the general strength of the correlation of this magnitude is strong. The coefficient of determination is $.269^2$, so .072 or 7.2% of the variance is accounted for. The subjective analysis (strong) and the objective one (7.2% of the variance accounted for) are consistent with one another.

3. Note that the .71 and the .47 have no sign, and in that case, we always assume that (like any other number) the values are positive.

   +.36

   –.45

   +.47

   –.62

   +.71

4. The correlation is .64, meaning that increases in budget and increases in classroom achievement are positively related to one another (and note that we have to test for significance). From a descriptive perspective, a bit more than 40% of the variance is shared between the two variables.
5. The correlation between number of minutes of exercise per day and GPA is .49, showing that as exercise increases, so does GPA. And of course, as exercise decreases, so does GPA. And want to be buff and get good grades? Work out, study, read broadly (and shower often). Keep in mind that GPA has nothing to do with how good you look at the gym. That would be causality, and we're only dealing with associations here.
6. The correlation is .14 and is so low because both the hours of studying and the set of GPA scores have very little variability. When there is so little variability, there is nothing to share, and the two sets of scores have little in common—hence, the low correlation.
7.
   a. .8
   b. Very strong
   c. 1.00 – .64, or .36 (36%)
8. Here's the matrix:

	Age at Injury	Level of Treatment	12-Month Treatment Score
Age at injury	1		
Level of treatment	0.0557	1	
12-month treatment score	−0.154	0.389	1

9. To examine the relationship between sex (defined as male or female) and political affiliation, you would use the phi coefficient because both variables are nominal in nature. To examine the relationship between family configuration and high school GPA, you would use the point biserial correlation because one variable is nominal (family configuration) and the other is interval (GPA).
10. Just because two things are related does not mean that one causes the other. There are plenty of runners with average strength who can run fast and plenty of very strong people who run slowly. Strength can help people run faster—but technique is more important (and, by the way, accounts for more of the variance).
11. You will come up with your own explanations, but here are two examples.
    a. We bet you expected this one—consumption of ice cream and number of crimes

b. Amount of money spent on political ads and the number of people who vote
c. The introduction of abstinence-only programs in middle school and the number of sexually active teenagers
d. Income and job satisfaction
e. Level of education and drug use

12. An excellent question. Correlations are a reflection of how much two variables have in common, but what they have in common may have nothing to do with what causes one, or the other, variable to increase or decrease. You saw that at work regarding ice cream consumption and rate of crime (both are related to outdoor temperature, not to each other). The same could be said about the relationship between school achievement scores and parents' level of education, where many variables can be said to intervene, such as class size, family structure, and family income. So, what is shared is what's important, not what appears to be conveniently related.
13. Partial correlations are used when you want to examine the correlation between two variables with the influence of a third removed.

CHAPTER 8

1. Do this one on your own.
2. Test–retest reliability should be established when you are interested in the consistency of an assessment over time, such as pre- and posttest studies or longitudinal studies. Parallel forms reliability is important to establish to make sure those different forms of the same test are similar to one another.
3. Test–retest reliability is established through the calculation of a simple correlation coefficient for both the initial test and then the repeat. In this case, the correlation between fall and spring scores is .138. The correlation of .138 is not even close to what one might need (at least .85) to conclude that the test is reliable over time.
4. In general, a test that is reliable but not valid does what it does over and over, but it does not do what it is supposed to. And, oops! A test cannot be valid without being reliable, because if it does not do anything consistently, then it certainly cannot do one thing consistently.
5. The reliability coefficient for these parallel forms of the same test is –.09. You did a great job as far as calculating the coefficient, but as for the reliability of the test? Not so great.
6. It's simple. A test must first be able to do what it does over and over again (reliability) before one can conclude that it does what it should (validity). If a test is inconsistent (or unreliable), then it can't possibly be valid. For example, although a test consisting of items like this one

$$15 \times 3 = ?$$

is surely reliable, if the 15 items on the test were labeled "Spelling Test," the test surely would not be valid.

7. You need to use both a reliable and a valid test because if you get a null result, you will never be sure whether the instrument is not measuring what it is supposed to or the hypothesis is actually faulty.

8. Content validity looks at a test to see whether, "on the face of it," it samples from an entire universe of possible items. For example, does a high school history test on the American Revolution contain items that reflect that subject area of American history?

   Predictive validity examines how well a test predicts a particular outcome. For example, how well does a test of spatial skills predict success as a mechanical engineer?

   Construct validity is present when a testing instrument assesses an underlying construct. For example, how well does an observation tool assess one dimension of bipolar disorder in young adolescents?

9. This is a tough one. Let's assume (as you would need to) that you have a strong theoretical basis for "out-of-the-box thinking" that can form the basis of test items. You would locate an independent group of "out-of-the-box experts," have them "take" the test, and have scorers observe and score the behaviors on the items you created. In theory, if your construct holds up and if the test works, then those people who have been independently verified as being out-of-the-box thinkers would score differently from those verified independently as not thinking in unique ways. Those items that differentiate between the two groups become the set of test items. This can be approached in many ways, and what we just presented is only one.

CHAPTER 9

1. On your own!
2. On your own again!
3.
   a. *Null:* Children with short attention spans, as measured by the Attention Span Observation Scale, have the same frequency of out-of-seat behavior as those with long attention spans.
      Directional: Children with short attention spans, as measured by the Attention Span Observation Scale, have a higher frequency of out-of-seat behavior than those with long attention spans.
      Nondirectional: Children with short attention spans, as measured by the Attention Span Observation Scale, differ in their frequency of out-of-seat behavior from those with long attention spans.
   b. *Null:* There is no relationship between the overall quality of a marriage and spouses' relationships with their siblings.
      Directional: There is a positive relationship between the overall quality of a marriage and spouses' relationships with their siblings.

Nondirectional: There is a relationship between the overall quality of a marriage and spouses' relationships with their siblings.

c. *Null:* Pharmacological treatment combined with traditional psychotherapy has the same effect in treating anorexia nervosa as does traditional psychotherapy alone.

Directional: Pharmacological treatment combined with traditional psychotherapy is more effective in treating anorexia nervosa than is traditional psychotherapy alone.

Nondirectional: Pharmacological treatment combined with traditional psychotherapy has a different effect than does treating anorexia nervosa with traditional psychotherapy alone.

4. On your own!
5. The most significant problem is that the test of the research hypothesis will probably be inconclusive. Regardless of the outcome, poor language leads to misleading conclusions. In addition, the study may be impossible to replicate and the findings to be generalized—all in all, a questionable effort.
6. The null (which literally means "void") represents the lack of any observed difference between groups of outcomes. It is *the* starting point in any research endeavor and differs from the research hypothesis is many ways, but primarily it is a statement of equality while the research hypothesis is a statement of inequality.
7. If you're at the beginning of exploring a question (which then becomes a hypothesis) and you have little knowledge about the outcome (which is why you are asking the question and performing the test), then the null is the perfect starting point. It is a statement of equality that basically says, "Given no other information about the relationships that we are studying, I should start at the beginning, where I know very little." The null is the perfect, unbiased, and objective starting point because it is the place where everything is thought to be equal unless proven otherwise.
8. As you already know, the null hypothesis states that there is no relationship between variables. Why? Simply, that's the best place to start given no other information. For example, if you are investigating the role of early events in the development of linguistic skills, then it is best to assume that they have no role whatsoever unless you prove otherwise. That's why we set out to *test* null hypotheses and not *prove* them. We want to be as unbiased as possible.

CHAPTER 10

1. In a normal curve, the mean, median, and mode are equal to one another; the curve is symmetrical about the mean; and the tails are asymptotic. Height and weight are examples, as are intelligence and problem-solving skills.
2. The raw score, the mean, and the standard deviation
3. Because they all use the same metric—the standard deviation—and we can compare scores in units of standard deviations

4. A z score is a standard score (comparable to others of the same type of score) because it is based on the degree of variability within its respective distribution of scores. A z score is always a measure of the distance between the mean and some point on the x-axis (regardless of the mean and standard deviation differences from one distribution to the next). Because the same units are used (units of standard deviation), the z scores can be compared with one another. That's the magic—comparability.

5. The z score for a raw score of 55, where the mean is 50 and the standard deviation is 2.5, is 2. So, the amount of variability in the set of scores is half as much, and the corresponding z score is twice as large (it went from 1 to 2). This indicates that as variability increases, and all other things are held constant, the same raw score becomes more extreme. The lower the difference between scores (and the lower the variability), the less extreme the same score will be.

6.

Raw Score	*z* Score
68.0	−0.61
58.16	−1.60
82.0	0.79
92.09	1.80
69.0	−0.51
69.14	−0.50
85.0	1.09
91.10	−0.50
72.0	−0.21

7.

18	−1.01
19	−0.88
15	−1.41
20	−0.75
25	−0.10
31	0.69
17	−1.14
35	1.21
27	0.17

(Continued)

(Continued)

18	-1.01
22	-0.49
34	1.08
29	0.43
40	1.87
33	0.95
21	-0.62

8.

a. The probability of a score falling between a raw score of 70 and a raw score of 80 is .5646. A *z* score for a raw score of 70 is –0.78, and a *z* score for a raw score of 80 is 0.78. The area between the mean and a *z* score of 0.78 is 28.23%. The area between the two scores is 28.23 times 2, or 56.46%.

b. The probability of a score falling above a raw score of 80 is .2177. A *z* score for a raw score of 80 is 0.78. The area between the mean and a *z* score of 0.78 is 28.23%. The area below a *z* score of 0.78 is .50 + .2823, or .7823. The difference between 1 (the total area under the curve) and .7823 is .2177, or 21.77%.

c. The probability of a score falling between a raw score of 81 and a raw score of 83 is .068. A *z* score for a raw score of 81 is 0.94, and a *z* score for a raw score of 83 is 1.25. The area between the mean and a *z* score of 0.94 is 32.64%. The area between the mean and a *z* score of 1.25 is 39.44%. The difference between the two is .3944 – .3264 = .068, or 6.8%.

d. The probability of a score falling below a raw score of 63 is .03. A *z* score for a raw score of 63 is –1.88. The area between the mean and a *z* score of –1.88 is 46.99%. The area below a *z* score of 1.88 is 1 – (.50 + .4699) = .03, or 3%.

9.

a. This is negatively skewed because the majority of athletes scored in the upper range.

b. This is not skewed at all. In fact, the distribution is like a rectangle because everyone scored exactly the same.

c. This distribution is positively skewed, because most of the spellers scored very low.

10. A little magic lets us solve for the raw score using the same formulas for computing the *z* score that you've seen throughout this chapter. Here's the transformed formula:

$$X = (s \times z) + \bar{X}.$$

And taking this one step further, all we really need to know is the *z* score of 90% (or 40% in Table B.1), which is 1.29.

So we have the following formula:

$$X = (s \times z) + \bar{X}.$$

or

$$X = 78 + (5.5 \times 1.29) = 85.095.$$

Jake is home free if he gets that score and, along with it, his certificate.

11. It doesn't make sense to just compute the average of the five scores because the program average is going to differ for each test along with the variance. We convert the original test scores to *z* scores to put all of the scores on the same scale and then average them.

12. Here's the info with the unknown values in bold.

	Math		
Class mean	81		
Class standard deviation	2		
	Reading		
Class mean	87		
Class standard deviation	10		
	Raw Scores		
	Math Score	**Reading Score**	**Average**
Noah	85	88	86.5
Talya	87	81	84.0
	***z* Scores**		
	Math Score	**Reading Score**	**Average**
Noah	**2**	**0.1**	**1.05**
Talya	**3**	**−0.6**	**1.2**

Noah has the higher average raw score (86.5 vs. 84 for Talya), but Talya has the higher average *z* score (1.2 vs. 1.05 for Noah). Remember that we asked who was the better student relative to the rest, which requires the use of a standard score (we used *z* scores). But why is Talya the better student relative to Noah? It's because on the tests with the lowest variability (Math with an $SD = 2$), Talya really stands out with a *z* score of 3. That put her ahead to stay.

13. The fact that the tails do not touch the *x*-axis indicates that there is always a chance—even though it may be very, very small—that extreme scores (all the way far out in either direction on the *x*-axis) are possible. If the tails did touch the *x*-axis, it would mean there is a limit to how improbable an outcome can be. In other words, no matter what the outcome, there's always a chance it will occur.

CHAPTER 11

1. The concept of significance is crucial to the study and use of inferential statistics because significance (reflected in the idea of a significance level) sets the criterion for being confident that the outcomes we observe are "truthful." It further determines to what extent these outcomes can be generalized to the larger population from which the sample was selected.
2. Statistical significance is the idea that certain outcomes are due not to chance but to factors that have been identified and tested by the researcher. These outcomes can be assigned a value that represents the probability that they are due to chance or some other factor or set of factors. The statistical significance of these outcomes is the value of that probability.
3. The critical value represents the minimum value at which the null hypothesis is no longer the accepted explanation for any differences that are observed. It is the cut point: Obtained values that are more extreme indicate that there is no equality but instead a difference (and the nature of that difference depends on the question being asked). Do remember that this cut point is set by the researcher (even if .01 and .05 are conventional and often used cut points).
4.
    a. Reject the null hypothesis. Because the level of significance is less than 5%, there is a relationship between a person's choice of music and his or her crime rate.
    b. Fail to reject the null hypothesis. The probability is greater than .05, meaning there is no relationship between the amount of coffee consumed and GPA.
    c. Nope—no relationship with a probability that high.
5.
    a. *Level of significance* refers only to a single, independent test of the null hypothesis and not to multiple tests.
    b. It is impossible to set the error rate to zero because it is not possible that we might not reject a null hypothesis when it is actually true. There's always a chance that we would.
    c. The level of risk that you are willing to take to reject the null hypothesis when it is true has nothing to do with the meaningfulness of the outcomes of your research. You can have a highly significant

outcome that is meaningless, or you can have a relatively high Type I error rate (.10) and a very meaningful finding.

6. At the .01 level, less room is left for errors or mistakes because the test is more rigorous. In other words, it is "harder" to find an outcome that is sufficiently removed from what you would expect by chance (the null hypothesis) when the probability associated with that income is smaller (such as .01) rather than larger (such as .05).

7. Here's a fine point but one that people get pretty excited about. We can't "reject" the null because we never directly test it. Remember, nulls reflect population characteristics, and the whole point is that we cannot directly test populations, only samples. If we can't test it, how can we reject it?

8. *Significance* is a statistical term that simply defines an area at which the probability associated with the null hypothesis is too small for us to conclude anything other than "The research hypothesis is the most attractive explanation." Meaningfulness has to do with the application of the findings and whether, within the broad context of the question being asked, the findings have relevance or importance.

9. You can come up with the substance of these yourself, but how about the following examples?

   a. A significant difference between two groups of readers was found, with the group that received intensive comprehension training outperforming the group that got no training (but the same amount of attention) on a test of reading comprehension.

   b. Examining a huge sample (which is why the finding was significant), a researcher found a very strong positive correlation between shoe size and calories eaten on a daily basis. Silly, but true. . . .

10. Chance is reflected in the degree of risk (Type I error) that we are willing to take in the possible rejection of a true null hypothesis. It is, first and foremost, always a plausible explanation for any difference that we might observe, and it is the most attractive explanation given no other information.

11.

   a. The striped area represents values that are extreme enough that none of them reflects a finding that supports the null hypothesis.

   b. A larger number of values reflects a higher likelihood of a Type I error.

CHAPTER 12

1. The one-sample z test is used when you want to compare a sample mean with a population parameter. Actually, think of it as a test to see whether one number (which is a mean) belongs to a huge set of numbers.

2. The (BIG) Z is similar to the small z for one very good reason: It is a standard score. The z score has the sample standard deviation

as the denominator, whereas the z test value has the standard error of the mean (or a measure of the variability of all the means from the population) as the denominator. In other words, they both use a standard measure that allows us to use the normal curve table (in Appendix B) to understand how far the values are from what we would expect by chance alone.

3.

   a. The weight loss of Bob's group on the chocolate-only diet is not representative of weight loss in a large population of middle-aged men who are on a chocolate-only diet.

   b. The rate of flu infections per 1,000 citizens for this past flu season is not comparable to the rate of infection over the past 50 seasons.

   c. Blair's costs for this month are not different from his average monthly costs over the past 20 years.

4. The z test results in a value of −1.48. This is not nearly extreme enough (we would need a value of ±1.96) to conclude that the average number of cases (15) is any different from that of the state (which is 16).

5. The z test results in a value of 0.31, which is not as extreme as would be needed to say that the group of stockers in the sample specialty stores (at 500 products stocked) does better (or even differently) than the larger group of stockers (at 496 products) who work in the chain.

6. What's missing here is the significance level at which the hypothesis is being tested. If the level is .01, then the critical z value for rejecting the null and concluding that the sample is different from the population is 1.96. If the level at which the hypothesis is being tested is .05, then the critical z value is 1.65. This presents the most interesting of questions regarding the trade-off between making a Type I error (1% or 5% of true nulls being rejected) versus stating statistical significance. You should be able to justify your answer as to which level of significance you chose.

7. If you plug in the data according to Formula 10.1, you get a z test score of 12.22, which is way, way off the charts (at the extended end of the curve). But, remember, the lower the golf score, the better, so Millman's group is in no way similar in membership to the pros. Too bad for Millman.

8. The value of 31,456 lies well within ($t = -1.681$, $p = .121$) the general range of values of last year's months of unit sales. Nope, not different.

CHAPTER 13

1. The mean for boys equals 7.93, and the mean for girls equals 5.31. The obtained t value is 3.006, and the critical t value at the .05 level for rejection of the null hypothesis for a one-tailed test (boys *more* than girls, remember?) is 1.701. Conclusion? Boys raise their hands significantly more!

2. Now this is very interesting. We have the same exact data, of course, but a different hypothesis. Here, the hypothesis is that the number of times is *different* (not just more or less), necessitating a two-tailed test. So, using Table B.2 and at the .01 level for a two-tailed test, the critical value is 2.764. The obtained value of 3.006 (same results as when you did the analysis for Question 1 in this chapter) does exceed what we would expect by chance, and given this hypothesis, there is a difference. So, in comparison with one another, a one-tailed finding (see Question 1) need not be as extreme as a two-tailed finding, given the same data, to support the same conclusion (that the research hypothesis is supported).

3.
   a. $t(18) = 1.58$.
   b. $t(46) = 0.88$.
   c. $t(32) = 2.43$.

4.
   a. $t_{crit}(18) = 2.101$. Because the observed t value exceeds the critical t value, we do not reject the null hypothesis.
   b. $t_{crit}(46) = 2.009$ (using the value for 50 degrees of freedom). Because the observed t value does not exceed the critical t value, we fail to reject the null hypothesis.
   c. $t_{crit}(32) = 2.03$ (using the value for 35 degrees of freedom). Because the observed t value exceeds the critical t value, we reject the null hypothesis.

5. First, here's the output for the t test between independent samples that was conducted using R.

					95% Confidence Interval of the Difference	
t	*df*	*p* Value	Group 1 Mean	Group 2 Mean	Lower	Upper
-2.15	38	.038	4.15	5.50	-2.62	-0.08

And here's one summary paragraph:

There was a significant difference between the mean performance for the group that received treatment in the home versus the group that received treatment out of the home. The mean for the In Home group was 4.15, and the mean for the Out of Home group was 5.50. The probability associated with this difference was .038, meaning that there is a less than 4% chance that the observed difference is due to chance. It is much more likely that the Out of Home program was more effective.

6. There is no significant difference ($t_{28} = -1.168$, $p = .253$) between urban and rural dwellers in their attitude toward gun control.

7. This certainly is a good one to think about, as it has many different "correct" answers and raises a bunch of issues. If all you are concerned about is the level of Type I error, then we suppose that Dr. L's findings are more trustworthy because these results imply that one is less likely to make a Type I error. However, both of these findings are significant, even if one of them is marginally so. Thus, if your personal system of evaluating these kinds of outcomes says, "I believe that significant is significant—that's what's important," then both should be considered equally valid and equally trustworthy. However, do remember to keep in mind that the meaningfulness of outcomes is critical as well (and you should get extra points if you bring this into the discussion). It seems to us that regardless of the level of Type I error, the results from both studies are highly meaningful because the program will probably result in safer children.

8. Here are the data plus the answers:

Experiment	Effect Size
1	2.73
2	1.15
3	0.65

As you can see, as the standard deviation doubles, the effect size is half as much. Why? If you remember, effect size gives you another indication of how meaningful the differences between groups are. If there is very little variability, there is not much difference between individuals, and any mean differences become more interesting (and probably more meaningful). When the standard deviation is 2 in the first experiment, then the effect size is 2.73. But when the variability increases to 8 (the third experiment), interestingly, the effect size is reduced to 0.65. It's tough to talk about how meaningful differences between groups might be when there is less and less similarity among members of those groups.

9. And the answer? As you can see, Group 2 scored a higher mean of 12.20 (compared with a mean for Group 1 of 7.67), and based on the results $t = -3.16$, $df = 28$, $p = .004$. If we set our null hypothesis to reject if $p < .05$ and the difference is significant at the .004 level, which is less than .05, then our conclusion is that we can reject the statement that the two groups spelled the same number of correct words.

10. For Chapter 13 Data Set 5 (ch13ds5.csv), the *t* value is –.218. For Chapter 13 Data Set 6 (ch13ds6.csv), the *t* value is –.327. And in both cases, the means are 6.00 (for Group 1) and 6.2 (for Group 2). Also, the variability of the larger set is slightly less. The reason why the second set of data has a larger (or more extreme) *t* score is that it is based on a sample size that is twice as large (20 vs. 10). The *t* test takes this into account, producing a more extreme score (and one headed in the direction of "significance"), because the large sample more closely approximates the population size. One might make the argument that with the same mean and less variability, the score would not only be more extreme but also be related to the effect of sample size.

11. This question actually has an easier answer than you might initially think. Specifically, the difference between two groups is somewhat (if not entirely) independent of the effect size. In this example, the statistically significant difference is probably due to the very large sample size, yet the effect is not very pronounced. This result is entirely possible and feasible and adds a new dimension to understanding the dual importance of significance and effect size.

CHAPTER 14

1. A *t* test for independent means tests two distinct groups of participants, and each group is tested once. A *t* test for dependent means tests one group of participants, and each participant is tested twice.
2.
   a. Independent
   b. Independent
   c. Dependent
   d. Independent
   e. Dependent
3. The mean before the recycling program was 34.44, and the mean afterward was 34.84. There is an increase in recycling. Is the difference across the 25 districts significant? The obtained *t* value is 0.262, and with 24 degrees of freedom, the difference is not significant at the .01 level—the level at which the research hypothesis is being tested. Conclusion: The recycling program does not result in an increase in paper recycled.
4. Here's the output for this *t* test between dependent or paired means.

Paired Samples Test

	Mean Difference	95% Confidence Interval of the Difference		*t*	*df*	Sig. (2-tailed)
		Lower	Upper			
Pair 1 Before_ Treatment After_Treatment	−4.10	−9.06	0.86	−1.73	19	.100

The conclusion? The before-treatment mean was lower (showing less tolerance) than the after-treatment mean. However, the difference between the two means is not significant, so the direction of the difference is irrelevant.

5. There was an increase in level of satisfaction, from 5.480 to 7.595, resulting in a t value of –3.893. This difference has an associated probability level of .001. It's very likely that the social service intervention worked. The effect size is 0.92.
6. The average score for Nibbles preference was 5.1, and the average score for Wribbles preference was 6.5. With 19 degrees of freedom, the t value for this test of dependent means was –1.965, with a critical value for rejecting the null of 2.093. Because the obtained t value of –1.965 does not exceed the critical value, the marketing consultant's conclusion is that both crackers are preferred about the same.
7. Nope. The means are not that different (5.35 for the first shift and 6.15 for the second), and the t value of –1.303 (so there is a bit less stress) is not significant. It doesn't matter what shift one works: The level of stress is the same.
8. Absolutely. The scores increased from 5.52 to 7.04, and the difference between the two sets is significant at the .005 level. And, as a bonus, the effect size is .61—large.

CHAPTER 15

1. Although both of these techniques look at differences between means, ANOVA is appropriate when more than two means are being compared. It can be used for a simple test between means, but it assumes that the groups are independent of one another.
2. A one-way ANOVA only examines differences across different levels of one variable, while a factorial ANOVA looks at differences across two or more levels when more than one variable is involved.
3.

Grouping Variable(s)	Test Variable
Four levels of hours of training—2, 4, 6, and 8 hours	Typing accuracy
Three age groups—20-, 25-, and 30-year-olds	Strength
Six levels of job types	Job performance

4. The means for the three groups are 58.05 seconds, 57.96 seconds, and 59.03 seconds, and the probability of this F value, $F_{(2, 33)} = 0.160$, occurring by chance is .853, far above what we would expect due to the treatment. Our conclusion? The number of hours of practice makes no difference in how fast you swim!
5. The F value is 28.773, which is significant at the .000 (!) level, indicating that the amount of stress differs across the three groups. As you can see, the least stressed is the 8:00 a.m. to 4:00 p.m. group.

6. For this problem, post hoc analysis (and we use the Bonferroni procedure) is required. As you can see by the R output, thin noodles were rated differently from both medium and thick noodles. And the difference for each comparison was negative, indicating thick was rated less pleasant than medium, and thin was rated less pleasant than both medium and thick.

7. Remember that the *F* test in ANOVA is a robust or overall test of the difference between means and does not specify where that difference lies. So, if the overall *F* ratio is not significant, comparing individual groups through a post hoc procedure does not make sense because there is no difference to investigate!

CHAPTER 16

1. Easy. Factorial ANOVA is used only when you have more than one factor or independent variable! And actually, this is not so easy an answer to get (but if you get it, you really understand the material) when you hypothesize an interaction.

2. Here's one of many different possible examples. There are three levels of one treatment (or factor) and two levels of severity of illness.

		Treatment		
		Drug 1	Drug 2	Placebo
Severity of Illness	Severe			
	Mild			

3. And the source table looks like this:

   Tests of Between-Subjects Effects

   Dependent Variable: PAIN_SCO

Source	Type III Sum of Squares	*df*	Mean Square	*F*	Sig.
Intercept	3,070.408	1	3,070.408	1,509.711	.000
Severity	.075	1	.075	.037	.848
Treatment	263.517	2	131.758	64.785	.000
Severity * Treatment	3.150	2	1.575	.774	.463
Residuals	231.850	114	2.034		

As far as our interpretation, in this data set, there is no interaction between the two main factors, no main effect for severity, and there is a main effect for treatment.

4.

a. No. The F value for the ANOVA test is nonsignificant ($F = 0.004$, $p = .996$).

b. No. The F value for the ANOVA test is nonsignificant ($F = 0.899$, $p = .352$).

c. There are no significant interactions.

5. Indeed, once you use R to do the analysis, you can see that there is no main effect for gender, but there is one for training and also a significant interaction. But then, when you plot the means and actually create a visual image of the interaction, you can see that the skill levels of males are higher under strength-training conditions and those levels for females are higher under speed-training conditions. When evaluating interactions, it is very important to look carefully at these visual plots.

CHAPTER 17

1.

a. With 18 degrees of freedom ($df = n - 2$) at the .01 level, the critical value for rejection of the null hypothesis is 0.516. There is a significant correlation between speed and strength, and the correlation accounts for 32.15% of the variance.

b. With 78 degrees of freedom at the .05 level, the critical value for rejection of the null hypothesis is 0.183 for a one-tailed test. There is a significant correlation between number correct and time. A one-tailed test was used because the research hypothesis was that the relationship was indirect or negative, and approximately 20% of the variance is accounted for.

c. With 48 degrees of freedom at the .05 level, the critical value for rejection of the null hypothesis is 0.273 for a two-tailed test. There is a significant correlation between number of friends a child might have and GPA, and the correlation accounts for 13.69% of the variance.

2.

Correlations

		Motivation	GPA
Motivation	Pearson correlation	1	.434[a]
	Sig. (2-tailed)		.017
	N	30	30

		Motivation	GPA
GPA	Pearson correlation	.434[a]	1
	Sig. (2-tailed)	.017	
	N	30	30

[a]Correlation is significant at the .05 level (two-tailed).

a. and b. We used R to compute the correlation as .434, which is significant at the .017 level using a two-tailed test.

c. True. The more motivated you are, the more you will study, and the more you study, the more you are motivated. But (and this is a big "but") studying more does not cause you to be more highly motivated, nor does being more highly motivated cause you to study more.

3.

		Income	Level_Education
Income	Pearson correlation	1	.629[a]
	Sig. (2-tailed)		.003
	N	20	20
Level_ Education	Pearson correlation	.629[a]	1
	Sig. (2-tailed)	.003	
	N	20	20

[a]Correlation is significant at the .05 level (2-tailed).

a. The correlation between income and education is .629, as you can see by examining the R output.

b. The correlation is significant at the .003 level.

c. The only argument you can make is that these two variables share something in common (and the more they share, the higher the correlation) and that neither one can cause the other.

4.

a. $r_{(8)}$ = .69.

b. $t_{crit}(8)$ = 0.6319. The observed correlation of .69 exceeds the critical value using 8 degrees of freedom. Therefore, our observed correlation coefficient is statistically significant at the .05 level.

c. The shared variance equals 47% ($r^2_{\text{hours.grade}}$ = .47).

d. There is a strong positive relationship between the number of hours spent studying and the grade earned on a test, and this relationship is statistically significant. The more hours a student studies, the higher his or her test grade, or the fewer hours spent studying, the lower the test grade!

5. The correlation is significant at the .01 level, and what's wrong with the statement is that an association between two variables does not imply that one causes the other. These two are correlated, which may be for many other reasons, but regardless of how much coffee one drinks, we cannot say it results in a change in stress levels as a function of cause and effect.

6.

   a. The correlation is .671.

   b. With 8 degrees of freedom, and at the .05 level, the critical value for rejection of the null hypothesis that the correlation equals zero is 0.5494 (see Table B.4). The obtained value of .671 is greater than the critical value (or what you would expect by chance), and our conclusion is that the correlation is significant and the two variables are related.

   c. If you recall, the best way to interpret any Pearson product-moment correlation is by squaring it, which gives us a coefficient of determination of .58, meaning that 58% of the variance in age is accounted for by the variance in number of words known. That's not huge, but as correlations between variables in human behavior go, it's pretty substantial.

7. The example here is the number of hours you study and your performance on your first test in statistics. These variables are not causally related. For example, you will have classmates who studied for hours and did poorly because they never understood the material and classmates who did very well without any studying at all because they had some of the same material in another class. Just imagine if we forced someone to stay at his or her desk and study for 10 hours each of four nights before the exam. Would that ensure that he or she got a good grade? Of course not. Just because the variables are related does not mean that one causes the other.

8. It's really up to you and the way that you interpret these correlations how you decide which significant correlations are meaningful. For example, shoe size and age are, of course, significantly correlated ($r = .938$), because as one gets older, the size of his or her feet increases. But meaningful? We think not. On the other hand, for example, intelligence is unrelated to all three other variables. And you may expect such, given that the test is standardized for age, so that at all ages, 100 is average. In other words, for this test, you don't get smarter as you get older (despite what parents tell children).

CHAPTER 18

1. The major difference is that linear regression is used to explore whether one variable predicts another. Analysis of variance examines differences between group means but does not have predictive capabilities.

2.

a. The regression equation is $\hat{Y} = -0.214$ (number correct) + 17.202.

b. $\hat{Y} = -0.214(8) + 17.202 = 15.49$.

c.

Time (Y)	# Correct (X)	$\hat{Y}$	$Y - \hat{Y}$
14.5	5	16.13	−1.6
13.4	7	15.70	−2.3
12.7	6	15.92	−3.2
16.4	2	16.77	−0.4
21.0	4	16.35	4.7
13.9	3	16.56	−2.7
17.3	12	14.63	2.7
12.5	5	16.13	−3.6
16.7	4	16.35	0.4
22.7	3	16.56	6.1

3.

a. The other predictor variables should not be related to any other predictor variable. Only when they are independent of one another can they each contribute unique information to predicting the outcome or dependent variable.

b. Examples are living arrangements (single or in a group) and access to health care (high, medium, or low).

c. Presence of Alzheimer's = (level of education)X_{IV1} + (general physical health)X_{IV2} + (living arrangements)X_{IV3} + (access to health care)X_{IV4} + a.

4. This one you do on your own, being sure to focus on your major area or some question that you are really interested in.

5.

a. You could compute the correlation between the two variables, which is .204. According to the information in Chapter 7, the magnitude of such a correlation is quite low. You could reach the conclusion that the number of wins is not a very good predictor of whether a team ever won a Super Bowl.

b. Many variables are categorical by nature (gender, race, social class, and political party) and cannot be easily measured on a scale from 1 to 100, for example. Using categorical variables allows us more flexibility.

c. Some other variables might be number of All-American players, win–loss record of coaches, and home game attendance.

6.

a. Caffeine consumption

b. Stress group

c. The correlation coefficient calculated from Chapter 17 is .373, which you would square to get .139, or R^2. Pretty nifty!

7.

a. The best predictor of the three is years of experience, but because none is significant (.102), one could say that the three are equally good (or bad)!

b. And here's the regression equation:

$$\hat{Y} = 0.959(X_1) - 5.786(X_2) - 1.839(X_3) + 96.377.$$

If we substitute the values for X_1, X_2, and X_3, we get the following:

$$\hat{Y} = 0.959(12) - 5.786(2) - 1.839(5) + 96.377.$$

And the chef's predicted score is 64.062.

	Unstandardized Coefficients	Standardized Coefficients	Sig.		
	B	Standard Error	Beta	*t*	
(Constant)	97.237	7.293		13.334	.000
Years_Ex	1.662	0.566	1.163	2.937	.102
Level_Ed	-7.017	2.521	-0.722	-2.783	.162
Num_Pos	-2.555	1.263	-0.679	-2.022	.212

Note also that years of experience and level of education were significant predictors.

8. The reason why level of education is such a poor predictor is that it has low variability, which means it has a very small correlation with number of homes sold (–.074, contributing nothing) and, for that matter, little correlation with any other variable. Therefore, it has no predictive value. The best predictor? Years in business, which is significant way beyond the .001 level. When you do the multiple regression analysis, you find that, as a predictor, level of education (as you would expect given the simple correlation) contributes nothing as well to our understanding of why these real estate agents (and others, if we want to infer such) differ in the number of homes sold.

9. To maximize the value of the predictors, they should all be related to the predicted or outcome variable but not have anything in common with the other predictors (if at all possible).

CHAPTER 19

1. This occurs when the expected and the observed values are identical. One example would be when you expected an unequal number of first-year and second-year students to show up and they really did!

2. Here's the worksheet for computing the chi-square value:

Category	*O* (observed frequency)	*E* (expected frequency)	*D* (difference)	$(O - E)^2$	$(O - E)^2/E$
Republican	800	800	0	0	0.00
Democrat	700	800	100	10,000	12.50
Independent	900	800	100	10,000	12.50

With 2 degrees of freedom at the .05 level, the critical value needed for rejection of the null hypothesis is 5.99. The obtained value of 25.00 allows us to reject the null and conclude that there is a significant difference in the numbers of people who voted as a function of political party.

3. Here's the worksheet for computing the chi-square value:

Category	*O* (observed frequency)	*E* (expected frequency)	*D* (difference)	$(O - E)^2$	$(O - E)^2/E$
Boys	45	50	5	25	0.50
Girls	55	50	5	25	0.50

With 1 degree of freedom at the .01 level of significance, the critical value needed for rejection of the null hypothesis is 6.64. The obtained value of 1.00 means that the null cannot be rejected, and there is no difference between the number of boys and girls who play soccer.

4. Some fun facts first. The total number of students enrolled in all six grades is 2,217, and the expected frequency value of each cell is 2,217/6 or 369.50.

   The obtained chi-square value is 36.98. With 5 degrees of freedom at the .05 level, the value needed for rejection of the null hypothesis is 11.07. Because the obtained value of 36.98 exceeds the critical value, the conclusion is that the enrollment numbers are not those expected, and indeed, significantly different proportions are enrolled in each grade.

5. Okay, gang, here's the deal. The chi-square value is 15.8, significant at the .003 level, meaning that there certainly is a preference among candy bar tasters.

6. The chi-square value for this test of independence is 8.1, and with 2 degrees of freedom, it is more than large enough (actually $p = .0174$) to conclude that the null hypothesis of independence cannot be accepted and indeed preference for plain or peanut is dependent upon exercise level.

7. As you can see in the output, the chi-square value of 3.969 with 4 degrees of freedom (2 × 2) is significant at the .41 level—not significant and not extreme enough for us to conclude that these two variables are dependent upon one another or related.

APPENDIX E

Math: Just the Basics

If you're reading this, then you know you may need a bit of help with your basic math skills. Lots of people need such help, especially after coming back to school after a break. There's nothing wrong with taking this little side trip before you continue working in *Statistics for People Who (Think They) Hate Statistics Using R*.

Most of the skills you need to work the examples in this book and to complete the practice exercises at the end of the chapters you already know. For example, you can add, subtract, multiply, and divide. You also probably know how to use a calculator to compute the square root of a number.

The confusion begins when we start dealing with equations and the various operations that can take place within parentheses, like these → ( ), and brackets, like these → [ ].

That's where we will spend most of our time, and we'll show you examples so you better understand how to work through what appear to be complex operations. Rest assured, once they are reduced to their individual parts, completing them is a cinch.

THE BIG RULES: SAY HELLO TO " PRETTY PLEASE MY DEAR AUNT SALLY"

Maybe you don't have an Aunt Sally, but this sentence can help you remember what arithmetic to do first.

It is simply an acronym that indicates the order in which operations take place in an expression or an equation.

PPMDAS goes like this . . .

P is for parentheses, such as ( ), or sometimes brackets, like this [ ], both of which are sometimes present in an expression or equation.

P is for power or order, as in raise 4 to the power of 2 or 4^2.

M is multiplication, as in 6×3.

D is division, as in 6/3.

A is addition, as in $2 + 3$.

S is subtraction, as in $5 - 1$.

You perform these operations in the above order. For example, the first thing you do is work within parentheses (or brackets), then take numbers to a power (such as squaring), then multiply, then divide, and so on. If there's nothing to square, skip the *Pretty* step, and if there's nothing to add, skip the *Aunt* step. If both brackets and parentheses are present, do the math inside the innermost set of parentheses or brackets.

For example, take a look at this simple expression:

$$(3 + 2) \times 2 = ?$$

Using the PPMDAS acronym, we know that

1. The first thing we do is any operation within parentheses. So, 3 + 2 = 5.
2. Moving on, the next available step is multiplying 5 times 2 for a total of 10, and 10 is the answer.

Here's another:

$$(4/2 \times 5) + 7 = ?$$

And here's what we do:

1. First is the division of 4 by 2, which equals 2, and that 2 is multiplied by 5 for a value of 10.
2. Then, 10 is added to 7 for a final sum of 17.

Let's get a bit fancier and use some squaring of numbers.

$$(10^2 \times 3)/150 = ?$$

Here's what we do:

1. Look within the parentheses (as always for the first step).
2. Square 10 to equal 100, and then multiply it by 3 for a value of 300.
3. Divide 300 by 150 for a value of 2.

Let's add another layer of complexity—sometimes we have more than one set of brackets or parentheses. All you need to remember is that we always begin with the innermost brackets first and work our way out as we work through the acronym.

Here we go:

$$[(15 \times 2) - (5 + 7)]/6 = ?$$

1. 15 times 2 is 30.
2. 5 plus 7 is 12.
3. 30 – 12 is 18.
4. 18 divided by 6 is 3.

The Little Rules

Just a few more. There are negative and positive numbers used throughout the book, and you need to know how they act when combined in different ways.

When multiplying negative and positive numbers, the following is true:

1. A negative number multiplied by a positive number (or a positive number multiplied by a negative number) always, always, always equals a negative number. For example:

$$-3 \times 2 = -6$$

or

$$4 \times -5 = -20$$

2. A negative number multiplied by another negative number results in a positive number. For example:

$$-4 \times -3 = 12$$

or

$$-2.5 \times -3 = 7.5$$

And a negative number divided by a positive number results in a negative number. For example:

$$-10/2 = -5$$

or

$$25/-5 = -5$$

And finally, a negative number divided by a negative number results in a positive number. For example:

$$-10/-5 = 2$$

Practice makes perfect, so here are 10 problems with the answers following. If you can't get the right answer, review the order of operations above and also ask someone in your study group to review where you might have gone wrong.

Here we go:

1. 75 + 10
2. 104 – 50

3. 50 – 104
4. 42 × –2
5. –50 × –60
6. 25/5 – 6/3
7. 6,392 – (–700)
8. (510 – 500)/–10
9. $[(40^2 - 207) - (80^2 - 400)]/35 \times 24$
10. ([(502 – 300) – 25] – [(242 – 100) – 50])/20 × 30

ANSWERS

1. 85
2. 54
3. –54
4. –84
5. 3,000
6. 3
7. 7,092
8. –1
9. –5.48
10. 0.141

Want some more help and more practice? Take a look at these sites:

http://www.webmath.com/index.html

http://www.math.com/homeworkhelp/BasicMath.html

There's nothing worse than starting a course and being so anxious that any meaningful learning just can't take place. Thousands of students less well prepared than you have succeeded, and you can as well. Reread the tips in Chapter 1 on how to approach the material in this course—and good luck!

APPENDIX F

The 10 (or More) Best (and Most Fun) Internet Sites for Statistics Stuff

Of course you use (and love) the Internet. It's probably your first stop when you want to find out about something new. Well, just like recipes, music-sharing apps, and the latest NCAA basketball scores, a ton of material on statistics is available for those who are new to (and those who are not so new to) its study and application. If you're not yet using the Internet as a specific tool in your learning and research activities, you are missing out on an extraordinary resource.

What's available on the Internet will not make up for a lack of studying or motivation—nothing will do that—but you can certainly find a great deal of information that will enhance your whole college experience. And this doesn't even begin to include all the fun you can have!

So, now that you're a certified novice statistician, here are some Internet sites that you might find very useful should you want to learn more about statistics.

Although the locations of websites on the Internet are more stable than ever, they still can change frequently. The URL (the uniform resource locator—what we all call the "web address") that worked today might not work tomorrow. If you don't get to where you want to go, use Google or some other search engine and search on the name of the website—perhaps there's a new URL or another web address that works.

WHERE DO I GO FOR R HELP?!!!??!???

As you might have guessed, YouTube can be a great resource to find answers to all types of questions about R. For example, we searched on the string "installing rstudio on mac" (https://www.youtube.com/results?search_query=installing+rstudio+on+mac), and YouTube returned 40 videos.

What if you want to write an actual question? This FAQ page from RStudio (https://community.rstudio.com/faq) provides some guides on how to write the questions to get the answers you are seeking. There are also some guidelines for participating in their discussion forum so that it remains a friendly resource on the web.

Last but definitely not least is UCLA's Institute for Digital Research and Education (https://stats.idre.ucla.edu/r/faq/). They have pages organized by statistical software first and then by types of data analysis. This link will take you to a page with a list of 43 different examples.

WHO'S WHO AND WHAT'S HAPPENED?

The History of Statistics page located at https://www.york.ac.uk/depts/maths/histstat/ contains portraits and bibliographies of famous statisticians and a timeline of important contributions to the field of statistics. Do names like Bernoulli, Galton, Fisher, and Spearman pique your curiosity? How about the development of the first test between two averages during the early 20th century? It might seem a bit boring until you have a chance to read about the people who make up this field and their ideas—in sum, pretty cool ideas and pretty cool people.

And of course, Wikipedia at http://en.wikipedia.org/wiki/History_of_statistics does a great job of introducing the history of this topic, as does eMathZone at http://www.emathzone.com/tutorials/basic-statistics/history-of-statistics.html.

IT'S ALL HERE

SurfStat Australia (https://surfstat.anu.edu.au/surfstat-home/contents.html) is the online component of a basic stats course taught at the University of Newcastle, Australia, but it has grown far beyond just the notes originally written by Annette Dobson in 1987 and updated over several years' use by Anne Young, Bob Gibberd, and others. Among other things, SurfStat contains a complete interactive statistics text. Besides the text, there are exercises, a list of other statistics sites on the Internet, and a collection of Java applets (cool little programs you can use to work with different statistical procedures).

HYPERSTAT

This online tutorial with 18 lessons, at http://davidmlane.com/hyperstat/, offers nicely designed and user-friendly coverage of the important basic topics. What we really like about the site is the glossary, which uses hypertext to connect different concepts to one another. On the webpage, you can see topics that are hyperlinked (the live underlined words) to others. Click on any of those and zap! You're there (or at least on your way).

DATA? YOU WANT DATA?

There are data all over the place, ripe for the picking. Here are just a few. What to do with these? Download them to be used as examples in your work or as examples of analysis that you might want to do. You can use these as models:

- Statistical Reference Datasets at http://itl.nist.gov/div898/strd/

- United States Census Bureau (a huge collection and a gold mine of data courtesy of American FactFinder) at http://factfinder.census.gov/faces/nav/jsf/pages/index.xhtml
- The Data and Story Library, with great annotations of the data, at https://dasl.datadescription.com/ (look for the "stories" link)
- Tons of economic data sets provided by Growth Data Sets at http://www.bris.ac.uk/Depts/Economics/Growth/datasets.htm

Even more data sets are available through the federal government (besides the Census Bureau and others highlighted above). Your tax money supports these resources, so why not use them? For example, there's FedStats (at https://nces.ed.gov/partners/fedstat.asp), where more than 70 agencies in the U.S. government publish statistics of interest to the public. The Federal Interagency Council on Statistical Policy maintains this site to provide easy access to the full range of statistics and information produced by these agencies for public use. Here you can find country profiles contributed by the CIA; public school student, staff, and faculty data (from the National Center for Education Statistics); and the Atlas of United States Mortality (from the National Center for Health Statistics). What a ton of data!

And most states have their data available for the clicking. Check out https://www.data.gov/.

MORE AND MORE RESOURCES

The University of Michigan's Research Guides site (https://guides.lib.umich.edu/?b=s) has hundreds and hundreds of resource links, including to information on banking; book publishing; the elderly; and, for those of you with allergies, pollen count. Browse to see what you find or search for exactly what you need—either way, you are guaranteed to find something interesting.

ONLINE STATISTICAL TEACHING MATERIALS

You're so good at this statistics stuff that you might as well start helping your neighbor and colleague in class. If that's the case, turn to Teaching Statistics (http://www.statisticsteacher.org/), brought to us by the American Statistical Association. You can also find more about teaching statistics from Vanderbilt University, https://cft.vanderbilt.edu/2013/06/new-teaching-guide-for-statistics-instructors/.

AND, OF COURSE, YOUTUBE . . .

Yes, you can now find stats stuff on YouTube in the form of Statz Rappers (http://www.youtube.com/watch?v=JS9GmU5hr5w), a group of talented young men and women who seem to be having a great time making just a bit of fun of their stats course—a very fitting stop on this path of what the Internet holds for those interested in exploring statistics. But there's also much more serious information. See, for example, http://www.youtube.com/watch?v=HvDqbzu0i0E from KhanAcademy .org—another cool place that is full of thousands—yes, thousands—of video tutorials on everything from algebra to economics to investing to, of course (you guessed it), statistics!

AND, FINALLY . . .

At http://animatedsoftware.com/statglos/statglos.htm#index, you'll find the mother and father lode of definitions of statistics terms, brought to us by Dr. Howard S. Hoffman. Informative and very much fun.

APPENDIX G

The 10 Commandments of Data Collection

Now that you know how to analyze data, you would be well served to read something about collecting them. The data collection process can be long and rigorous. Even if it involves only a simple, one-page questionnaire given to a group of students, parents, patients, or voters, data collection may very well be the most time-consuming part of your project. But as many researchers realize, good data collection is essential to good research outcomes.

Here they are: the 10 commandments for making sure your data get collected in such a way that they are usable. Unlike the original Ten Commandments, these should not be carved in stone (because they can certainly change), but if you follow them, you can avoid lots of aggravation.

> *Commandment 1.* As you begin thinking about a research question, also begin thinking about the type of data you will have to collect to answer that question. Interview? Questionnaire? Paper and pencil? Computer? Find out how other people have done it in the past by reading the relevant journals in your area of interest. Then consider doing what they did. At least one of the lessons here is to not repeat others' mistakes. If something didn't work for them, it's most likely not going to work for you.
>
> *Commandment 2.* As you think about the type of data you will be collecting, think about where you will be getting the data. If you are using the library for historical data or accessing files of data that have already been collected, such as census data (available through the U.S. Census Bureau at http://www.census.gov and other locations online), you will have few logistical problems. But what if you want to assess the interaction between newborns and their parents? The attitude of teachers toward unionizing? The age at which people over 50 think they are old? All of these questions require people to provide the answers, and finding people can be tough. Start now.
>
> *Commandment 3.* Make sure that the data collection forms you use are clear and easy to use. Practice on a set of pilot data so you can make sure it is easy to transfer data from the original scoring sheets or the data collection form to a digital format. And then have some colleagues complete the form to make sure it works.

Commandment 4. Always make a duplicate copy of the data file and the data collection sheets and keep them in a separate location. Keep in mind that there are two types of people: those who have lost their data and those who will. In fact, make two backups of your electronic data! These days, you can use online data backup services such as Carbonite (https://www.carbonite.com), Mozy (https://www.mozy.com), or CrashPlan (https://www.code42.com/crashplan/) in addition to your own physical backup. If you are going to use a USB drive, invest in quality so you can have a better chance at accessing your files in the future.

Commandment 5. Do not rely on other people to collect or transfer your data unless you have personally trained them and are confident that they understand the data collection process as well as you do. It is great to have people help you, and it helps keep morale up during those long data collection sessions. But unless your helpers are competent beyond question, you could easily sabotage all your hard work and planning.

Commandment 6. Plan a detailed schedule of when and where you will be collecting your data. If you need to visit three schools and each of 50 children needs to be tested for a total of 10 minutes at each school, that is 25 hours of testing. That does not mean you can allot a mere 25 hours from your schedule for this activity. What about travel from one school to another? What about the child who is in the bathroom when it is his turn and you have to wait 10 minutes until he comes back to the classroom? What about the day you show up and Cowboy Bob is the featured guest . . . and on and on. Be prepared for anything, and allocate 25% to 50% more time in your schedule for unforeseen events.

Commandment 7. As soon as possible, cultivate possible sources for your subject pool. Because you already have some knowledge in your own discipline, you probably also know of people who work with the population you are interested in or who might be able to help you gain access to these samples. If you are in a university community, it is likely that hundreds of other people are competing for the same subject sample that you need. Instead of competing, why not try a more out-of-the-way (maybe 30 minutes away) school district or social group or civic organization or hospital, where you might be able to obtain a sample with less competition?

Commandment 8. Try to follow up on subjects who missed their testing session or interview. Call them back and try to reschedule. Once you get in the habit of skipping possible participants, it becomes too easy to cut the sample down to too small a size. And you can never tell—the people who drop out might be dropping out for reasons related to what you are studying. This can mean that your final sample of people is qualitatively different from the sample with which you started.

Commandment 9. Never discard the original data, such as the test booklets, interview notes, and so forth. Other researchers might want to use the same data, or you may have to return to the original materials to glean further information from them.

And Commandment 10? Follow the previous nine commandments. No kidding!

APPENDIX H

Glossary

Analysis of variance: A test for the difference between two or more means. A one-way analysis of variance (or ANOVA) has only one independent variable, whereas a factorial analysis of variance tests the means of more than one independent variable. One-way analysis of variance looks for differences between the means of more than two groups.

Argument: Information that a function acts upon.

Arithmetic mean: A measure of central tendency calculated by summing all the scores and dividing by the number of scores. *See* Mean.

Asymptotic: The quality of the normal curve such that the tails never touch the horizontal axis.

Average: The most representative score in a set of scores.

Bell-shaped curve: A distribution of scores that is symmetrical about the mean, median, and mode and has asymptotic tails. Often called the *normal curve*.

Class interval: A fixed range of values, used in the creation of a frequency distribution.

Coefficient of alienation: The amount of variance in one variable that is not accounted for by the variance in another variable.

Coefficient of determination: The amount of variance in one variable that is accounted for by the variance in another variable.

Coefficient of nondetermination: *See* Coefficient of alienation.

Concurrent criterion validity: How well a test outcome is consistent with a criterion that exists in the present.

Confidence interval: The best estimate of the range of a population value given the sample value.

Construct validity: How well a test reflects an underlying idea, such as intelligence or aggression.

Content validity: A type of validity that examines how well a test samples a universe of items.

Correlation coefficient: A numerical index that reflects the relationship between two variables, specifically how the value of one variable changes when the value of the other variable changes.

Correlation matrix: A table showing correlation coefficients among more than two variables.

Criterion: *See* Dependent variable.

Criterion validity: A type of validity that examines how well a test reflects some criterion that exists in either the present (*concurrent*) or the future (*predictive*).

Critical value: The value resulting from application of a statistical test that is necessary for rejection (or nonacceptance) of the null hypothesis.

Cumulative frequency distribution: A frequency distribution that shows frequencies for class intervals along with the cumulative frequency at each.

Data: A record of an observation or an event such as a test score, a grade in math class, or response time.

Data frame: A collection of information (vectors) that is arranged in rows and columns (and can just be a single row or a single column) and can contain different types of variables such as you see (both text and numeric).

Data point: An observation.

Data set: A set of data points.

Degrees of freedom: A value, which is different for different statistical tests, that approximates the sample size of the number of individual cells in an experimental design.

Dependent variable: The outcome variable or the predicted variable in a regression equation.

Descriptive statistics: Values that organize and describe the characteristics of a collection of data, sometimes called a *data set*.

Direct correlation: A positive correlation where the values of both variables change in the same direction.

Directional research hypothesis: A research hypothesis that posits a difference between groups in one direction. *See* Nondirectional research hypothesis.

Effect size: A measure of the magnitude of difference between two groups, usually calculated as Cohen's *d*.

Error in prediction: The difference between the observed score (Y) and the predicted score ($\hat{Y}$).

Error score: The part of a test score that is random and contributes to the unreliability of a test.

Factorial analysis of variance: An analysis of variance with more than one factor or independent variable.

Factorial design: A research design used to explore more than one treatment variable.

Frequency distribution: A method for illustrating how often scores occur in groups called class intervals.

Frequency polygon: A graphical representation of a frequency distribution that uses a continuous line to show the number of values that fall within a *class interval*.

Function: A collection of commands used to accomplish a task.

Goodness-of-fit test: A chi-square test on one dimension, which examines whether the distribution of frequencies is different from what one would expect by chance.

Histogram: A graphical representation of a frequency distribution that uses bars of different heights to show the number of values that fall within each *class interval*.

Hypothesis: An if–then statement of conjecture that relates variables to one another and is used to reflect the general problem statement or question that is the motivation for asking a research question.

Independent variable: The treatment variable that is manipulated or the predictor variable in a regression equation.

Indirect correlation: A negative correlation where the values of variables move in opposite directions.

Inferential statistics: Tools that are used to infer characteristics of a population based on data from a sample of that population.

Interaction effect: The outcome where the effect of one factor is differentiated across another factor.

Internal consistency reliability: A type of reliability that examines whether items on a test measure only one dimension, construct, or area of interest.

Interrater reliability: A type of reliability that examines whether observers are consistent with one another.

Interval level of measurement: A level of measurement that places a variable's values into categories that are equidistant from each other, as when points are evenly spaced along a scale.

Kurtosis: The quality of a distribution that defines how flat or peaked it is.

Leptokurtic: The quality of a normal curve that is relatively peaked compared with a normal distribution.

Line of best fit: The regression line that best fits the observed scores and minimizes the error in prediction.

Linear correlation: A correlation that is best expressed visually as a straight line.

List: An object that contains many different types of objects within it.

Main effect: In analysis of variance, when a factor or an independent variable has a significant effect upon the outcome variable.

Mean: A type of average calculated by summing values and dividing that sum by the number of values.

Mean deviation: The average deviation for all scores from the mean of a distribution, calculated as the sum of the absolute value of the scores' deviations from the mean divided by the number of scores.

Measures of central tendency: The mean, the median, and the mode.

Median: The midpoint in a set of values, such that 50% of the cases in a distribution fall below the median and 50% fall above it.

Midpoint: The central point in a class interval.

Mode: The most frequently occurring score in a distribution.

Multiple regression: A statistical technique whereby several variables are used to predict one.

Negative correlation: *See* Indirect correlation.

Nominal level of measurement: The most gross level of measurement by which a variable's value can be placed in one and only one category.

Nondirectional research hypothesis: A research hypothesis that posits a difference between groups but not in either direction. *See* Directional research hypothesis.

Nonparametric statistics: Distribution-free statistics that do not require the same assumptions as do parametric statistics.

Normal curve: *See* Bell-shaped curve.

Null hypothesis: A statement of equality between sets of variables. *See* Research hypothesis.

Object: Anything created in R.

Observed score: The score that is recorded or observed. *See* True score.

Obtained value: The value that results from the application of a statistical test.

Ogive: A visual representation of a cumulative frequency distribution.

One-sample *z* test: Used to compare a sample mean to a population mean.

One-tailed test: A directional test, reflecting a directional hypothesis.

One-way analysis of variance: *See* Analysis of variance.

Ordinal level of measurement: A level of measurement that places a variable's value into a category and assigns that category an order with respect to other categories.

Packages: A collection of functions.

Parallel forms reliability: A type of reliability that examines consistency across different forms of the same test.

Parametric statistics: Statistics used for the inference from a sample to a population that assume the variances of each group are similar and that the sample is large enough to represent the population. *See* Nonparametric statistics.

Partial correlation: A numerical index that reflects the relationship between two variables with the removal of the influence of a third variable (called a mediating or confounding variable).

Pearson product-moment correlation: *See* Correlation coefficient.

Percentile point: The percentage of cases equal to and below a particular score in a distribution or set of scores.

Platykurtic: The quality of a normal curve that is relatively flat compared with a normal distribution.

Population: All the possible subjects or cases of interest. *See* Sample.

Positive correlation: *See* Direct correlation.

Post hoc: After the fact, referring to tests done to determine the true source of a difference among three or more groups.

Predictive validity: How consistent a test outcome is with a criterion that occurs in the future.

Predictor: *See* Independent variable.

R: A statistical computing language.

Range: The positive difference between the highest and lowest score in a distribution. It is a gross measure of variability. Exclusive range is the highest score minus the lowest score. Inclusive range is the highest score minus the lowest score plus 1.

Ratio level of measurement: A level of measurement defined as having an absolute zero.

R base: The R packages that are part of R when it is first installed.

R Console: The window used to enter R commands and see results if the function provides output.

Regression equation: The equation that defines the points and the line that are closest to the observed scores.

Regression line: The line drawn based on values in a regression equation. Also known as a *trend line*.

Reliability: The consistency of a test.

Research hypothesis: A statement of inequality between two variables. *See* Null hypothesis.

RStudio: An integrated development environment for working in R.

Sample: A subset of a population. *See* Population.

Sampling error: The difference between sample and population values.

Scales of measurement: Different ways of categorizing measurement outcomes: nominal, ordinal, interval, and ratio.

Scattergram or scatterplot: A plot of paired data points on an *x*- and a *y*-axis, used to visually represent a correlation.

Significance level: The risk set by the researcher for rejecting a null hypothesis when it is true.

Simple regression: Regression in which only one predictor is used to predict *Y*.

Skew or skewness: The quality of a distribution that defines the disproportionate frequency of certain scores. A longer right tail than left corresponds to a smaller number of occurrences at the high end of the distribution; this is a *positively skewed distribution*. A shorter right tail than left corresponds to a larger number of occurrences at the high end of the distribution; this is a *negatively skewed distribution*.

Source table: An analysis of variance summary table that lists sources of variance.

Standard deviation: The average amount of variability in a set of scores or the scores' average deviation from the mean.

Standard error of estimate: A measure of accuracy in prediction that reflects variability about the regression line. *See* Error in prediction.

Standard score: *See z* score.

Statistical significance: *See* Significance level.

Statistics: A set of tools and techniques used to describe, organize, and interpret information or data.

Test of independence: A chi-square test of two dimensions or more that examines whether the distribution of frequencies on a variable is independent of other variables.

Test–retest reliability: A type of reliability that examines a test's consistency over time.

Test statistic value: *See* Obtained value.

Trend line: *See* Regression line.

True score: The score that, if it could be observed, would reflect the actual ability or behavior being measured. *See* Observed score.

Two-tailed test: A nondirectional test, reflecting a nondirectional hypothesis.

Type I error: The probability of rejecting a null hypothesis when it is true.

Type II error: The probability of accepting a null hypothesis when it is false.

Unbiased estimate: A conservative estimate of a population parameter.

Validity: How well a test measures what it says it does.

Variability: How much scores differ from one another or, put another way, the amount of spread or dispersion in a set of scores.

Variance: The square of the standard deviation and another measure of a distribution's spread or dispersion.

Vector: A collection of data that are all of the same type.

$\hat{Y}$ or Y-hat: The predicted *Y* value in a regression equation.

Y′ or Y prime: The predicted *Y* value in a regression equation.

***z* score:** A raw score that is adjusted for the mean and standard deviation of the distribution from which the raw score comes.

APPENDIX I

The Reward

The Brownie Recipe

What the heck is a brownie recipe doing in an introductory statistics book? Good question.

In all seriousness, you have probably worked hard on this material, whether for a course, as a review, or just for your own edification. And, because of all your effort, you deserve a reward. Here it is. The recipe is based on several different recipes and some tweaking, and it's all Neil's and he is happy to share it with you. There, the secret is out.

Right out of the pan, not even cooled, these brownies are terrific with ice cream. Once they've aged a bit, they get very nice and chewy and are great from the fridge. If you freeze them, note that it takes more calories to defrost them in your mouth than are contained in the brownies themselves, so there is a net loss. Eat as many frozen as you want. ☺

1 stick (8 tablespoons) butter

4 ounces unsweetened chocolate (or more)

½ tablespoon salt

2 eggs

1 cup flour

2 cups sugar

1 tablespoon vanilla

2 tablespoons mayonnaise (I know)

6 ounces chocolate chips (or more)

1 cup whole walnuts (optional)

How to do it:

1. Preheat oven to 325°F.
2. Melt unsweetened chocolate and butter in a saucepan.

3. Mix flour and salt together in a bowl.
4. Add sugar, vanilla, nuts, mayonnaise, and eggs to melted chocolate-butter stuff and mix well.
5. Add all of Step 4 to flour mixture and mix well.
6. Add chocolate chips.
7. Pour into an 8″ × 8″ greased baking dish.
8. Bake for about 35 to 40 minutes or until tester comes out clean.

NOTES

- I know about the mayonnaise thing. If you think it sounds weird, then don't put it in. These brownies are not delicious for nothing, though, so leave out this ingredient at your own risk.
- Use good chocolate—the higher the fat content, the better. And you can use up to 6 ounces of unsweetened chocolate and even more of the chocolate chips.

INDEX